The Autobiography of William Butler Yeats

The
Autobiography of
William Butler Yeats

CONSISTING OF

Reveries over Childhood and Youth

The Trembling of the Veil

AND

Dramatis Personae

COLLIER BOOKS

A Division of Macmillan Publishing Co., Inc.

NEW YORK

SIXTH PRINTING 1978

The index for this edition was prepared by Sandra
Berwind, Bryn Mawr College.

THE PHOTOGRAPH ON THE COVER OF THIS EDITION WAS
MADE IN 1932 BY PIRIE MACDONALD, HON. F.R.P.S., AND
IS USED BY PERMISSION.

COVER DESIGN BY CARL SMITH

Macmillan Publishing Co., Inc.
866 Third Avenue, New York, N.Y. 10022

Printed in the United States of America

CONTENTS

Reveries over Childhood and Youth

To those few people
mainly personal friends
who have read
all that I have written

PREFACE

Sometimes when I remember a relative that I have been fond of, or a strange incident of the past, I wander here and there till I have somebody to talk to. Presently I notice that my listener is bored; but now that I have written it out, I may even begin to forget it all. In any case, because one can always close a book, my friend need not be bored.

I have changed nothing to my knowledge; and yet it must be that I have changed many things without my knowledge; for I am writing after many years and have consulted neither friend, nor letter, nor old newspaper, and describe what comes oftenest into my memory.

I say this fearing that some surviving friend of my youth may remember something in a different shape and be offended with my book.

Christmas Day, 1914.

The Autobiography of William Butler Yeats

I

My first memories are fragmentary and isolated and contemporaneous, as though one remembered some first moments of the Seven Days. It seems as if time had not yet been created, for all thoughts connected with emotion and place are without sequence.

I remember sitting upon somebody's knee, looking out of an Irish window at a wall covered with cracked and falling plaster, but what wall I do not remember, and being told that some relation once lived there. I am looking out of a window in London. It is at Fitzroy Road. Some boys are playing in the road and among them a boy in uniform, a telegraph boy perhaps. When I ask who the boy is, a servant tells me that he is going to blow the town up, and I go to sleep in terror.

After that come memories of Sligo, where I live with my grandparents. I am sitting on the ground looking at a mastless toy boat with the paint rubbed and scratched, and I say to myself in great melancholy, "It is further away than it used to be," and while I am saying it I am looking at a long scratch in the stern, for it is especially the scratch which is further away. Then one day at dinner my great-uncle William Middleton says, "We should not make light of the troubles of children. They are worse than ours, because we can see the end of our trouble and they can never see any end," and I feel grateful for I know that I am very unhappy and have often said to myself, "When you grow up, never talk as grown-up people do of the happiness of childhood." I may have already had the night of misery when, having prayed for several days that I might die, I began to be afraid that I was dying and prayed that I might live. There was no reason for my unhappiness. Nobody was unkind, and my grandmother has still after so many years my gratitude and my reverence. The house was so big that there was always a room to hide in, and I had a red pony and a garden where I could wander, and there were two dogs to follow at my heels, one white with some black spots on his head and the other with long black hair all over him. I used to think about God and fancy that I was very wicked, and one day when I threw a stone and hit a duck in the yard by mischance and broke its wing, I was full of wonder when I was told that the duck would be cooked for dinner and that I should not be punished.

Some of my misery was loneliness and some of it fear of old William Pollexfen my grandfather. He was never unkind, and I cannot remember that he ever spoke harshly to me, but it was the custom to fear and admire him. He had won the freedom of some Spanish city, for saving life perhaps, but was so silent that his wife never knew it till he was near eighty, and then from the chance visit of some old sailor. She asked him if it was true and he said it was true, but she knew him too well to question and his old shipmate had left the town. She too had the habit of fear. We knew that he had been in many parts of the world, for there was a great scar on his hand made by a whaling-hook, and in the dining-room was a cabinet with bits of coral in it and a jar of water from the Jordan for the baptizing of his children and Chinese pictures upon rice-paper and an ivory walking-stick from India that came to me after his death. He had great physical strength and had the reputation of never ordering a man to do anything he would not do himself. He owned many sailing ships and once, when a captain just come to anchor at Rosses Point reported something wrong with the rudder, had sent a messenger to say "Send a man down to find out what's wrong." "The crew all refuse" was the answer, and to that my grandfather answered, "Go down yourself," and not being obeyed, he dived from the main deck, all the neighbourhood lined along the pebbles of the shore. He came up with his skin torn but well informed about the rudder. He had a violent temper and kept a hatchet at his bedside for burglars and would knock a man down instead of going to law, and I once saw him hunt a party of men with a horsewhip. He had no relation for he was an only child and, being solitary and silent, he had few friends. He corresponded with Campbell of Islay who had befriended him and his crew after a shipwreck, and Captain Webb, the first man who had swum the Channel and who was drowned swimming the Niagara Rapids, had been a mate in his employ and a close friend. That is all the friends I can remember and yet he was so looked up to and admired that when he returned from taking the waters at Bath his men would light bonfires along the railway line for miles; while his partner William Middleton whose father after the great famine had attended the sick for weeks, and taken cholera from a man he carried in his arms into his own house and died of it, and was himself civil to everybody and a cleverer man than my grandfather, came and went without notice. I think I confused my grandfather with God, for I remember in one of my attacks of melancholy praying that he might punish me for my sins, and I was shocked and astonished when a daring little girl—a cousin I think—having waited under a group of trees in the avenue, where she knew he would pass near four o'clock on the way to his dinner, said to him, "If I were you and you were a little girl, I would give you a doll."

Yet for all my admiration and alarm, neither I nor any one else thought it wrong to outwit his violence or his rigour; and his lack of suspicion and something helpless about him made that easy while it stirred our affection. When I must have been still a very little boy, seven or eight years old perhaps, an uncle called me out of bed one night, to ride the five or six miles to Rosses Point to borrow a railway-pass from a cousin. My grandfather had one, but thought it dishonest to let another use it, but the cousin was not so particular. I was let out through a gate that opened upon a little lane beside the garden away from earshot of the house, and rode delighted through the moonlight, and awoke my cousin in the small hours by tapping on his window with a whip. I was home again by two or three in the morning and found the coachman waiting in the little lane. My grandfather would not have thought such an adventure possible, for every night at eight he believed that the stable-yard was locked, and he knew that he was brought the key. Some servant had once got into trouble at night and so he had arranged that they should all be locked in. He never knew, what everybody else in the house knew, that for all the ceremonious bringing of the key the gate was never locked.

Even to-day when I read *King Lear* his image is always before me and I often wonder if the delight in passionate men in my plays and in my poetry is more than his memory. He must have been ignorant, though I could not judge him in my childhood, for he had run away to sea when a boy, "gone to sea through the hawsehole" as he phrased it, and I can but remember him with two books—his Bible and Falconer's *Shipwreck*, a little green-covered book that lay always upon his table; he belonged to some younger branch of an old Cornish family. His father had been in the Army, had retired to become an owner of sailing ships, and an engraving of some old family place my grandfather thought should have been his hung next a painted coat of arms in the little back parlour. His mother had been a Wexford woman, and there was a tradition that his family had been linked with Ireland for generations and once had their share in the old Spanish trade with Galway. He had a good deal of pride and disliked his neighbours, whereas his wife, a Middleton, was gentle and patient and did many charities in the little back parlour among frieze coats and shawled heads, and every night when she saw him asleep went the round of the house alone with a candle to make certain there was no burglar in danger of the hatchet. She was a true lover of her garden, and before the care of her house had grown upon her, would choose some favourite among her flowers and copy it upon rice-paper. I saw some of her handiwork the other day and I wondered at the delicacy of form and colour and at a handling that may have needed a magnifying glass it was so minute. I can remember no other pictures but the Chinese paintings, and some coloured prints of battles in the Crimea upon the wall of a passage, and the painting of a ship at the passage end darkened by time.

My grown-up uncles and aunts, my grandfather's many sons and daughters, came and went, and almost all they said or did has faded from my memory, except a few harsh words that convince me by a vividness out of proportion to their harshness that all were habitually kind and considerate. The youngest of my uncles was stout and humorous and had a tongue of leather over the keyhole of his door to keep the draught out, and another whose bedroom was at the end of a long stone passage had a model turret ship in a glass case. He was a clever man and had designed the Sligo quays, but was now going mad and inventing a vessel of war that could not be sunk, his pamphlet explained, because of a hull of solid wood. Only six months ago my sister awoke dreaming that she held a wingless sea bird in her arms and presently she heard that he had died in his mad-house, for a sea bird is the omen that announces the death or danger of a Pollexfen. An uncle, George Pollexfen, afterwards astrologer and mystic, and my dear friend, came but seldom from Ballina, once to a race meeting with two postillions dressed in green; and there was that younger uncle who had sent me for the railway-pass. He was my grandmother's favourite, and had, the servants told me, been sent away from school for taking a crowbar to a bully.

I can only remember my grandmother punishing me once. I was playing in the kitchen and a servant in horseplay pulled my shirt out of my trousers in front just as my grandmother came in and I, accused of I knew not what childish indecency, was given my dinner in a room by myself. But I was always afraid of my uncles and aunts, and once the uncle who had taken the crowbar to the bully found me eating lunch which my grandmother had given me and reproved me for it and made me ashamed. We breakfasted at nine and dined at four and it was considered self-indulgent to eat anything between meals; and once an aunt told me that I had reined in my pony and struck it at the same moment that I might show it off as I rode through the town, and I, because I had been accused of what I thought a very dark crime, had a night of misery. Indeed I remember little of childhood but its pain. I have grown happier with every year of life as though gradually conquering something in myself, for certainly my miseries were not made by others but were a part of my own mind.

2

One day some one spoke to me of the voice of the conscience, and as I brooded over the phrase I came to think that my soul,

because I did not hear an articulate voice, was lost. I had some
wretched days until being alone with one of my aunts I heard
a whisper in my ear, "What a tease you are!" At first I thought
my aunt must have spoken, but when I found she had not, I
concluded it was the voice of my conscience and was happy
again. From that day the voice has come to me at moments of
crisis, but now it is a voice in my head that is sudden and star-
tling. It does not tell me what to do, but often reproves me. It
will say perhaps, "That is unjust" of some thought; and once
when I complained that a prayer had not been heard, it said,
"You have been helped." I had a little flagstaff in front of the
house and a red flag with the Union Jack in the corner. Every
night I pulled my flag down and folded it up and laid it on a
shelf in my bedroom, and one morning before breakfast I found
it, though I knew I had folded it up the night before, knotted
round the bottom of the flagstaff so that it was touching the grass.
I must have heard the servants talking of the faeries for I concluded at once that a faery had tied those four knots and from
that on believed that one had whispered in my ear. I have been
told, though I do not remember it myself, that I saw, whether
once or many times I do not know, a supernatural bird in the
corner of the room. Once too I was driving with my grandmother
a little after dark close to the Channel that runs for some five
miles from Sligo to the sea, and my grandmother showed me the
red light of an outward-bound steamer and told me that my
grandfather was on board, and that night in my sleep I screamed
out and described the steamer's wreck. The next morning my
grandfather arrived on a blind horse found for him by grateful
passengers. He had, as I remember the story, been asleep when
the captain aroused him to say they were going on the rocks.
He said, "Have you tried sail on her?" and judging from some
answer that the captain was demoralised took over the command
and, when the ship could not be saved, got the crew and passengers into the boats. His own boat was upset and he saved himself and some others by swimming; some women had drifted
ashore, buoyed up by their crinolines. "I was not so much afraid
of the sea as of that terrible man with his oar," was the comment
of a schoolmaster who was among the survivors. Eight men were,
however, drowned and my grandfather suffered from that mem-

ory at intervals all his life, and if asked to read family prayers
never read anything but the shipwreck of St. Paul.

I remember the dogs more clearly than any one except my
grandfather and grandmother. The black hairy one had no tail
because it had been sliced off, if I was told the truth, by a railway train. I think I followed at their heels more than they did
at mine, and that their journeys ended at a rabbit-warren behind
the garden; and sometimes they had savage fights, the black hairy
dog, being well protected by its hair, suffering least. I can remember one so savage that the white dog would not take his
teeth out of the black dog's hair till the coachman hung them
over the side of a water-butt, one outside and one in the water.
My grandmother once told the coachman to cut the hair like a
lion's hair and, after a long consultation with the stable-boy, he
cut it all over the head and shoulders and left it on the lower
part of the body. The dog disappeared for a few days, and I did
not doubt that its heart was broken.

There was a large garden behind the house full of apple trees,
with flower-beds and grass-plots in the centre, and two figure-
heads of ships, one among the strawberry plants under a wall
covered with fruit trees and one among the flowers. The one
among the flowers was a white lady in flowing robes, while the
other, a stalwart man in uniform, had been taken from a three-
masted ship of my grandfather's called *The Russia*, and there
was a belief among the servants that the stalwart man represented
the Tsar and had been presented by the Tsar himself. The avenue, or as they say in England the drive, that went from the hall
door through a clump of big trees to an insignificant gate and a
road bordered by broken and dirty cottages, was but two or three
hundred yards, and I often thought it should have been made to
wind more, for I judged people's social importance mainly by
the length of their avenues. This idea may have come from the
stable-boy, for he was my principal friend. He had a book of
Orange rhymes, and the days when we read them together in
the hay-loft gave me the pleasure of rhyme for the first time.
Later on I can remember being told, when there was a rumour
of a Fenian rising, that rifles had been served out to the Orange-
men; and presently, when I had begun to dream of my future
life, I thought I would like to die fighting the Fenians. I was to

build a very fast and beautiful ship and to have under my command a company of young men who were always to be in training like athletes and so become as brave and handsome as the young men in the story-books, and there was to be a big battle on the seashore near Rosses and I was to be killed. I collected little pieces of wood and piled them up in a corner of the yard, and there was an old rotten log in a distant field I often went to look at because I thought it would go a long way in the making of the ship. All my dreams were of ships; and one day a sea captain who had come to dine with my grandfather put a hand on each side of my head and lifted me up to show me Africa, and another day a sea captain pointed to the smoke from the pern mill on the quays rising up beyond the trees of the lawn, as though it came from the mountain, and asked me if Ben Bulben was a burning mountain.

Once every few months I used to go to Rosses Point or Ballisodare to see another little boy, who had a piebald pony that had once been in a circus and sometimes forgot where it was and went round and round. He was George Middleton, son of my great-uncle William Middleton. Old Middleton had bought land, then believed a safe investment, at Ballisodare and at Rosses, and spent the winter at Ballisodare and the summer at Rosses. The Middleton and Pollexfen flour mills were at Ballisodare, and a great salmon weir, rapids and a waterfall, but it was more often at Rosses that I saw my cousin. We rowed in the rivermouth or were taken sailing in a heavy slow schooner yacht or in a big ship's boat that had been rigged and decked. There were great cellars under the house, for it had been a smuggler's house a hundred years before, and sometimes three loud raps would come upon the drawing-room window at sun-down, setting all the dogs barking: some dead smuggler giving his accustomed signal. One night I heard them very distinctly and my cousins often heard them, and later on my sister. A pilot had told me that, after dreaming three times of a treasure buried in my uncle's garden, he had climbed the wall in the middle of the night and begun to dig but grew disheartened "because there was so much earth." I told somebody what he had said and was told that it was well he did not find it for it was guarded by a spirit that looked like a flat iron. At Ballisodare there was a cleft among the rocks that I passed with terror because I believed that a murderous monster lived there that made a buzzing sound like a bee.

It was through the Middletons perhaps that I got my interest in country stories, and certainly the first faery stories that I heard were in the cottages about their houses. The Middletons took the nearest for friends and were always in and out of the cottages of pilots and of tenants. They were practical, always doing something with their hands, making boats, feeding chickens, and without ambition. One of them had designed a steamer many years before my birth and, long after I had grown to manhood, one could hear it—it had some sort of obsolete engine—many miles off wheezing in the Channel like an asthmatic person. It had been built on the lake and dragged through the town by many horses, stopping before the windows where my mother was learning her lessons, and plunging the whole school into candlelight for five days, and was still patched and repatched mainly because it was believed to be a bringer of good luck. It had been called after the betrothed of its builder *Janet*, long corrupted into the more familiar *Jennet*, and the betrothed died in my youth having passed her eightieth year and been her husband's plague because of the violence of her temper. Another Middleton who was but a year or two older than myself used to shock me by running after hens to know by their feel if they were on the point of dropping an egg. They let their houses decay and the glass fall from the windows of their greenhouses, but one among them at any rate had the second sight. They were liked but had not the pride and reserve, the sense of decorum and order, the instinctive playing before themselves that belongs to those who strike the popular imagination.

Sometimes my grandmother would bring me to see some old Sligo gentlewoman whose garden ran down to the river, ending there in a low wall full of wallflowers, and I would sit up upon my chair, very bored, while my elders ate their seed-cake and drank their sherry. My walks with the servants were more interesting; sometimes we would pass a little fat girl and a servant persuaded me to write her a love letter, and the next time she passed she put her tongue out. But it was the servants' stories that interested me. At such and such a corner a man had got a shilling from a drill sergeant by standing in a barrel and had then rolled out of it and shown his crippled legs. And in such and such a house an old woman had hid herself under the bed of her guests, an officer and his wife, and on hearing them abuse her beaten them with a broomstick. All the well-known families had their grotesque or tragic or romantic legends, and I often said to myself how terrible it would be to go away and die where nobody would know my story. Years afterwards, when I was ten or twelve years old and in London, I would remember Sligo with tears, and when I began to write, it was there I hoped to find my audience. Next to Merville where I lived, was another tree-surrounded house where I sometimes went to see a little boy who stayed there occasionally with his grandmother, whose name I forget and who seemed to me kind and friendly, though when I went to see her in my thirteenth or fourteenth year I discovered that she only cared for very little boys. When the visitors called I hid in the hay-loft and lay hidden behind the great heap of hay while a servant was calling my name in the yard.

I do not know how old I was (for all these events seem at the same distance) when I was made drunk. I had been out yachting with an uncle and my cousins and it had come on very rough. I had lain on deck between the mast and the bowsprit and a wave had burst over me and I had seen green water over my head. I was very proud and very wet. When we got into Rosses again, I was dressed up in an older boy's clothes so that the trousers came down below my boots and a pilot gave me a little raw whiskey. I drove home on an outside car and was so pleased with the strange state in which I found myself that for all my uncle could do, I cried to every passer-by that I was drunk, and went on crying it through the town and everywhere until I was put to bed by my grandmother and given something to drink that tasted of black currants and so fell asleep.

3

Some six miles off towards Ben Bulben and beyond the Channel, as we call the tidal river between Sligo and the Rosses, and on top of a hill there was a little square two-storied house covered with creepers and looking out upon a garden where the box borders were larger than any I had ever seen, and where I saw for the first time the crimson streak of the gladiolus and awaited its blossom with excitement. Under one gable a dark thicket of small trees made a shut-in mysterious place, where one played and believed that something was going to happen. My great-aunt Micky lived there. Micky was not her right name for she was Mary Yeats and her father had been my great-grandfather, John Yeats, who had been Rector of Drumcliffe, a few miles further off, and died in 1847. She was a spare, high-coloured, elderly woman and had the oldest-looking cat I had ever seen, for its hair had grown into matted locks of yellowy white. She farmed and had one old man-servant, but could not have farmed at all, had not neighbouring farmers helped to gather in the crops, in return for the loan of her farm implements and "out of respect for the family," for as Johnny MacGurk, the Sligo barber said to me, "The Yeats's were always very respectable." She was full of family history; all her dinner-knives were pointed like daggers through much cleaning, and there was a little James the First cream-jug with the Yeats motto and crest, and on her dining-room mantelpiece a beautiful silver cup that had belonged to my great-great-grandfather, who had married a certain Mary Butler. It had upon it the Butler crest and had been already old at the date 1534, when the initials of some bride and bridegroom were engraved under the lip. All its history for generations was rolled up inside it upon a piece of paper yellow with age, until some caller took the paper to light his pipe.

Another family of Yeats, a widow and her two children on whom I called sometimes with my grandmother, lived near in a long low cottage, and owned a very fierce turkey-cock that did battle with their visitors; and some miles away lived the secretary to the Grand Jury and Land Agent, my great-uncle Mat Yeats and his big family of boys and girls; but I think it was only in later years that I came to know them well. I do not think any of these liked the Pollexfens, who were well off and seemed to them purse-proud, whereas they themselves had come down in the world. I remember them as very well-bred and very religious in the Evangelical way and thinking a good deal of Aunt Micky's old histories. There had been among our ancestors a King's County soldier, one of Marlborough's generals, and when his nephew came to dine he gave him boiled pork, and when the nephew said he disliked boiled pork he had asked him to dine again and promised him something he would like better. However, he gave him boiled pork again and the nephew took the hint in silence. The other day as I was coming home from America, I met one of his descendants whose family has not another discoverable link with ours, and he too knew the boiled pork story and nothing else. We have the General's portrait, and he looks very fine in his armour and his long curly wig, and underneath it, after his name, are many honours that have left no tradition among us. Were we country people, we could have summarised his life in a legend. Other ancestors or great-uncles bore a part in Irish history; one saved the life of Sarsfield at the battle of Sedgmoor; another, taken prisoner by King James's army, owed his to Sarsfield's gratitude; another, a century later, roused the gentlemen of Meath against some local Jacquère, and was shot dead upon a county road, and yet another "chased the United Irishmen for a fortnight, fell into their hands and was hanged." The notorious Major Sirr, who arrested Lord Edward Fitzgerald and gave him the bullet wound he died of in the jail, was godfather to several of my great-great-grandfather's children; while to make a balance, my great-grandfather had been Robert Emmett's friend and was suspected and imprisoned though but for a few hours. One great-uncle fell at New Orleans in 1813, while another, who became Governor of Penang, led the forlorn hope at the taking of Rangoon, and even in the last generation of all there had been lives of some power and pleasure. An old man who had entertained many famous people, in his eighteenth-century house, where battlement and tower showed the influence of Horace Walpole, had but lately, after losing all his money, drowned himself, first taking off his rings and chain and watch as became a collector of many beautiful things; and once to remind us of more passionate life, a gunboat put into Rosses, commanded by the illegitimate son of some great-uncle or other. Now that I can look at their miniatures, turning them over to find the name of soldier, or lawyer, or Castle official, and wondering if they cared for good books or good music, I am delighted with all that joins my life to those who had power in Ireland or with those anywhere that were good servants and poor bargainers, but I cared nothing as a child for Micky's tales. I could see my grandfather's ships come up the bay or the river, and his sailors treated me with deference, and a ship's carpenter made and mended my toy boats and I thought that nobody could be so important as my grandfather. Perhaps, too, it is only now that I can value those more gentle natures so unlike his passion and violence. An old Sligo priest has told me how my great-grandfather John Yeats always went into his kitchen rattling the keys, so much did he fear finding some one doing wrong, and of a speech of his when the agent of the great landowner of his parish brought him from cottage to cottage to bid the women send their children to the Protestant school. All promised till they came to one who cried, "Child of mine will never darken your door." "Thank you, my woman," he said, "you are the first honest woman I have met to-day." My uncle, Mat Yeats, the Land Agent, had once waited up every night for a week to catch some boys who stole his apples and when he caught them had given them sixpence and told them not to do it again. Perhaps it is only fancy or the softening touch of the miniaturist that makes me discover in their faces some courtesy and much gentleness. Two eighteenth-century faces interest me the most, one that of a great-great-grandfather, for both have under their powdered curling wigs a half-feminine charm, and as I look at them I discover a something clumsy and heavy in myself. Yet it was a Yeats who spoke the only eulogy that turns my head: "We have ideas and no passions, but by marriage with a Pollexfen we have given a tongue to the sea cliffs."

Among the miniatures there is a larger picture, an admirable drawing by I know not what master, that is too harsh and merry for its company. He was a connection and close friend of my great-grandmother Corbet, and though we spoke of him as "Uncle Beattie" in our childhood, no blood relation. My great-grandmother who died at ninety-three had many memories of him. He was the friend of Goldsmith and was accustomed to boast, clergyman though he was, that he belonged to a hunt-club of which every member but himself had been hanged or transported for treason, and that it was not possible to ask him a question he could not reply to with a perfectly appropriate blasphemy or indecency.

4

Because I had found it hard to attend to anything less interesting than my thoughts, I was difficult to teach. Several of my uncles and aunts had tried to teach me to read, and because they could not, and because I was much older than children who read easily, had come to think, as I have learnt since, that I had not all my faculties. But for an accident they might have thought it for a long time. My father was staying in the house and never went to church, and that gave me the courage to refuse to set out one Sunday morning. I was often devout, my eyes filling with tears at the thought of God and for my own sins, but I hated church. My grandmother tried to teach me to put my toes first to the ground because I suppose I stumped on my heels and that took my pleasure out of the way there. Later on when I had learnt to read I took pleasure in the words of the hymn, but never understood why the choir took three times as long as I did in getting to the end; and the part of the service I liked, the sermon and passages of the Apocalypse and Ecclesiastes, were no compensation for all the repetitions and for the fatigue of so much standing. My father said if I would not go to church he would teach me to read. I think now that he wanted to make me go for my grandmother's sake and could think of no other way. He was an angry and impatient teacher and flung the reading-book at my head, and next Sunday I decided to go to church. My father had, however, got interested in teaching me, and only shifted the lesson to a weekday till he had conquered my wandering mind. My first clear image of him was fixed on my imagination, I believe, but a few days before the first lesson. He had just arrived from London and was walking up and down the nursery floor. He had a very black beard and hair, and one cheek bulged out with a fig that was there to draw the pain out of a bad tooth. One of the nurses (a nurse had come from London with my brothers and sisters) said to the other that a live frog, she had heard, was best of all. Then I was sent to a dame school kept by an old woman who stood us in rows and had a long stick like a billiard cue to get at the back rows. My father was still at Sligo when I came back from my first lesson and asked me what I had been taught. I said I had been taught to sing, and he said, "Sing then" and I sang

> Little drops of water,
> Little grains of sand,
> Make the mighty ocean,
> And the pleasant land

high up in my head. So my father wrote to the old woman that I was never to be taught to sing again, and afterwards other teachers were told the same thing. Presently my eldest sister came on a long visit and she and I went to a little two-storied house in a poor street where an old gentlewoman taught us spelling and grammar. When we had learned our lesson well, we were allowed to look at a sword presented to her father who had led troops in India or China and to spell out a long complimentary inscription on the silver scabbard. As we walked to her house or home again we held a large umbrella before us, both gripping the handle and guiding ourselves by looking out of a round hole gnawed in the cover by a mouse. When I had got beyond books of one syllable, I began to spend my time in a room called the Library, though there were no books in it that I can remember except some old novels I never opened and a many-volumed encyclopaedia published towards the end of the eighteenth century. I read this encyclopaedia a great deal and can remember a long passage considering whether fossil wood despite its appearance might not be only a curiously shaped stone.

My father's unbelief had set me thinking about the evidences of religion and I weighed the matter perpetually with great anxiety, for I did not think I could live without religion. All my religious emotions were, I think, connected with clouds and cloudy glimpses of luminous sky, perhaps because of some Bible picture of God's speaking to Abraham or the like. At least I can remember the sight moving me to tears. One day I got a decisive argument for belief. A cow was about to calve, and I went to the field where the cow was with some farm hands who carried a lantern, and next day I heard that the cow had calved in the early morning. I asked everybody how calves were born, and because nobody would tell me, made up my mind that nobody knew. They were the gift of God, that much was certain, but it was plain that nobody had ever dared to see them come, and children must come in the same way. I made up my mind that when I was a man, I would wait up till calf or child had come. I was certain there would be a cloud and a burst of light and God would bring the calf in the cloud out of the light. That thought made me content until a boy of twelve or thirteen who had come on a visit for the day, sat beside me in a hay-loft and explained all the mechanism of sex. He had learnt all about it from an elder boy whose pathic he was (to use a term he would not have understood) and his description, given as I can see now, as if he were telling of any other fact of physical life, made me miserable for weeks. After the first impression wore off, I began to doubt if he had spoken truth, but one day I discovered a passage in the encyclopaedia, that though I only partly understood its long words, confirmed what he had said. I did not know enough to be shocked at his relation to the elder boy, but it was the first breaking of the dream of childhood.

My realisation of death came when my father and mother and my two brothers and my two sisters were on a visit. I was in the Library when I heard feet running past and heard somebody say in the passage that my younger brother, Robert, had died. He had been ill for some days. A little later my sister and I sat at the table, very happy, drawing ships with their flags half-mast high. We must have heard or seen that the ships in the harbour had their flags at half-mast. Next day at breakfast I heard people telling how my mother and the servant had heard the banshee crying the night before he died. It must have been after this that I told my grandmother I did not want to go with her when she went to see old bedridden people because they would soon die.

5

At length when I was eight or nine an aunt said to me, "You are going to London. Here you are somebody. There you will be nobody at all." I knew at the time that her words were a blow at my father not at me, but it was some years before I knew her reason. She thought so able a man as my father could have found out some way of painting more popular pictures if he had set his mind to it and that it was wrong of him "to spend every evening at his club." She had mistaken, for what she would have considered a place of wantonness Heatherley's Art School.

My mother and brother and sister were at Sligo perhaps when I was sent to England, for my father and I and a group of landscape painters lodged at Burnham Beeches with an old Mr. and Mrs. Earle. My father was painting the first big pond you come to if you have driven from Slough through Farnham Royal. He began it in spring and painted all through the year, the picture changing with the seasons, and gave it up unfinished when he had painted the snow upon the heath-covered banks. He is never satisfied and can never make himself say that any picture is finished. In the evening he heard me my lessons or read me some novel of Fenimore Cooper's. I found delightful adventures in the woods—one day a blind worm and an adder fighting in a green hollow, and sometimes Mrs. Earle would be afraid to tidy the room because I had put a bottle full of newts on the mantelpiece. Now and then a boy from a farm on the other side of the road threw a pebble at my window at daybreak, and he and I went fishing in the big second pond. Now and then another farmer's boy and I shot sparrows with an old pepper-box revolver and the boy would roast them on a string. There was an old horse one of the painters called the scaffolding, and sometimes a son of old Earle's drove with me to Slough and once to Windsor, and at Windsor we made our lunch of cold sausages bought from a public-house. I did not know what it was to be alone, for I could wander in pleasant alarm through the enclosed parts of the Beeches, then very large, or round some pond imagining ships going in and out among the reeds and thinking of Sligo or of strange sea-faring adventures in the fine ship I should launch when I grew up. I had always a lesson to learn before night and that was a continual misery, for I could very rarely, with so much to remember, set my thoughts upon it and then only in fear. One day my father told me that a painter had said I was very thick-skinned and did not mind what was said to me, and I could not understand how anybody could be so unjust. It made me wretched to be idle but one could not help it. I was once surprised and shocked. All but my father and myself had been to London, and Kennedy and Farrar and Page, I remember the names vaguely, arrived laughing and talking. One of them had carried off a card of texts from the waiting-room of the station and hung it up on the wall. I thought "he had stolen it," but my father and all made it a theme of merry conversation.

Then I returned to Sligo for a few weeks as I was to do once or twice in every year for years, and after that we settled in London. Perhaps my mother and the other children had been there all the time, for I remember my father now and again going to London. The first house we lived in was close to Burne Jones's house at North End, but we moved after a year or two to Bedford Park. At North End we had a pear tree in the garden and plenty of pears, but the pears used to be full of maggots, and almost opposite lived a schoolmaster called O'Neill, and when a little boy told me that the schoolmaster's great-grandfather had been a king I did not doubt it. I was sitting against the hedge and iron railing of some villa-garden there, when I heard one boy say to another it was something wrong with my liver that gave me such a dark complexion and that I could not live more than a year. I said to myself a year is a very long time, one can do such a lot of things in a year, and put it out of my head. When my father gave me a holiday and later when I had a holiday from school I took my schooner boat to the round pond sailing it very commonly against the two cutter yachts of an old naval officer. He would sometimes look at the ducks and say, "I would like to take that fellow home for my dinner," and he sang me a sailor's song about a "coffin ship" which left Sligo after the great famine, that made me feel very important. The servants at Sligo had told me the story. When she was moved from the berth she had lain in, an unknown dead man's body had floated up, a very evil omen; and my grandfather, who was Lloyd's agent, had condemned her, but she slipped out in the night. The pond had its own legends; and a boy who had seen a certain model steamer "burned to the water's edge" was greatly valued as a friend. There was a little boy I was kind to because I knew his father had done something disgraceful though I did not know what. It was years before I discovered that his father was but the maker of certain popular statues, many of which are now in public places. I had heard my father's friends speak of him. Sometimes my sister came with me, and we would look into all the sweet shops and toy shops on our way home, especially into one opposite Holland House because there was a cutter yacht made of sugar in the window, and we drank at all the fountains. Once a stranger spoke to us and bought us sweets and came with us almost to our door. We asked him to come in and told him our father's name. He would not come in, but laughed and said, "Oh, that is the painter who scrapes out every day what he painted the day before." A poignant memory came upon me the other day while I was passing the drinking-fountain near Holland Park, for there I and my sister had spoken together of our longing for Sligo and our hatred of London. I know we were both very close to tears and remember with wonder, for I had never known any one that cared for such mementoes, that I longed for a sod of earth from some field I knew, something of Sligo to hold in my hand. It was some old race instinct like that of a savage, for we had been brought up to laugh at all display of emotion. Yet it was our mother, who would have thought its display a vulgarity, who kept alive that love. She would spend hours listening to stories or telling stories of the pilots and fishing people of Rosses Point, or of her own Sligo girlhood, and it was always assumed between her and us that Sligo was more beautiful than other places. I can see now that she had great depth of feeling, that she was her father's daughter. My memory of what she was like in those days has grown very dim, but I think her sense of personality, her desire of any life of her own, had disappeared in her care for us and in much anxiety about money. I always see her sewing or knitting in spectacles and wearing some plain dress. Yet ten years ago when I was in San Francisco, an old cripple came to see me who had left Sligo before her marriage; he came to tell me, he said, that my mother "had been the most beautiful girl in Sligo."

The only lessons I had ever learned were those my father taught me, for he terrified me by descriptions of my moral degradation and he humiliated me by my likeness to disagreeable people; but presently I was sent to school at Hammersmith. It was a Gothic building of yellow brick: a large hall full of desks, some small class-rooms and a separate house for boarders, all built perhaps in 1860 or 1870. I thought it an ancient building and that it had belonged to the founder of the school, Lord Godolphin, who was romantic to me because there was a novel about him. I never read the novel, but I thought only romantic people were put in books. On one side, there was a piano factory of yellow brick, upon two sides half-finished rows of little shops and villas all yellow brick, and on the fourth side, outside the wall of our playing field, a brick-field of cinders and piles of half-burned yellow bricks. All the names and faces of my school-fellows have faded from me except one name without a face and the face and name of one friend, mainly no doubt because it was all so long ago, but partly because I only seem to remember things dramatic in themselves or that are somehow associated with unforgettable places.

For some days as I walked homeward along the Hammersmith Road, I told myself that whatever I most cared for had been taken away. I had found a small, green-covered book given to my father by a Dublin man of science; it gave an account of the strange sea creatures the man of science had discovered among the rocks at Howth or dredged out of Dublin Bay. It had long been my favourite book; and when I read it I believed that I was growing very wise, but now I should have no time for it nor for my own thoughts. Every moment would be taken up learning or saying lessons, or in walking between school and home four times a day for I came home in the middle of the day for dinner. But presently I forgot my trouble, absorbed in two things I had never known, companionship and enmity. After my first day's lesson, a circle of boys had got around me in a playing field and asked me questions, "Who's your father?" "What does he do?" "How much money has he?" Presently a boy said something insulting. I had never struck anybody or been struck, and now all in a minute, without any intention upon my side, but as if I had been a doll moved by a string, I was hitting at the boys within reach and being hit. After that I was called names for being Irish, and had many fights and never, for years, got the better in any one of them; for I was delicate and had no muscles. Sometimes, however, I found means of retaliation, even of aggression. There was a boy with a big stride, much feared by little boys, and finding him alone in the playing field, I went up to him and said, "Rise upon Sugaun and sink upon Gad." "What does that mean?" he said. "Rise upon hay-leg and sink upon straw," I answered and told him that in Ireland the sergeant tied straw and hay to the ankles of a stupid recruit to show him the difference between his legs. My ears were boxed, and when I complained to my friends, they said I had brought it upon myself, and that I deserved all I got. I probably dared myself to other feats of a like sort, for I did not think English people intelligent or well-behaved unless they were artists. Every one I knew well in Sligo despised Nationalists and Catholics, but all disliked England with a prejudice that had come down perhaps from the days of the Irish Parliament. I knew stories to the discredit of England, and took them all seriously. My mother had met some English woman who did not like Dublin because the legs of the men were too straight, and at Sligo, as everybody knew, an Englishman had once said to a car-driver, "If you people were not so lazy, you would pull down the mountain and spread it out over the sand and that would give you acres of good fields." At Sligo there is a wide river mouth and at ebb tide most of it is dry sand, but all Sligo knew that in some way I cannot remember it was the spreading of the tide over the sand that left the narrow channel fit for shipping. At any rate the carman had gone chuckling all over Sligo with his tale. People would tell it to prove that Englishmen were always grumbling. "They grumble about their dinners and everything—there was an Englishman who wanted to pull down Knocknarea" and so on. My mother had shown them to me kissing at railway stations, and taught me to feel disgust at their lack of reserve, and my father told how my grandfather, William Yeats, who had died before I was born, when he came home to his Rectory in County Down from an English visit, spoke of some man he had met on a coach road who "Englishman-like" told him all his affairs. My father explained that an Englishman generally believed that his private affairs did him credit, while an Irishman, being poor and probably in debt, had no such confidence. I, however, did not believe in this explanation. My Sligo nurses, who had in all likelihood the Irish Catholic political hatred, had never spoken well of any Englishman. Once when walking in the town of Sligo I had turned to look after an English man and woman whose clothes attracted me. The man I remember had grey clothes and knee-breeches and the woman a grey dress, and my nurse had said contemptuously, "Tow-rows"—perhaps before my time, there had been some English song with the burden "tow row row"—and everybody had told me that English people ate skates and even dog-fish, and I myself had only just arrived in England when I saw an old man put marmalade in his porridge.

I was divided from all those boys, not merely by the anecdotes that are everywhere perhaps a chief expression of the distrust of races, but because our mental images were different. I read their boys' books and they excited me, but if I read of some English victory, I did not believe that I read of my own people. They thought of Cressy and Agincourt and the Union Jack and were all very patriotic, and I, without those memories of Limerick and the Yellow Ford that would have strengthened an Irish Catholic, thought of mountain and lake, of my grandfather and of ships. Anti-Irish feeling was running high, for the Land League had been founded and landlords had been shot, and I, who had no politics, was yet full of pride, for it is romantic to live in a dangerous country.

I daresay I thought the rough manners of a cheap school, as my grandfather Yeats had those of a chance companion, typical of all England. At any rate I had a harassed life and got many a black eye and had many outbursts of grief and rage. Once a boy, the son of a great Bohemian glass-maker, who was older than the rest of us, and had been sent out of his country because of a love affair, beat a boy for me because we were "both foreigners." And a boy, who grew to be the school athlete and my chief friend, beat a great many. His are the face and name that I remember— his name was of Huguenot origin and his face like his gaunt and lithe body had something of the American Indian in colour and lineament.

I was very much afraid of the other boys, and that made me doubt myself for the first time. When I had gathered pieces of wood in the corner for my great ship, I was confident that I could keep calm among the storms and die fighting when the great battle came. But now I was ashamed of my lack of courage; for I wanted to be like my grandfather who thought so little of danger that he had jumped overboard in the Bay of Biscay after an old hat. I was very much afraid of physical pain, and one day when I had made some noise in class, my friend the athlete was accused and I allowed him to get two strokes of the cane before I gave myself up. He had held out his hands without flinching and had not rubbed them on his sides afterwards. I was not caned, but was made to stand up for the rest of the lesson. I suffered very much afterwards when the thought came to me, but he did not reproach me.

I had been some years at school before I had my last fight. My friend, the athlete, had given me many months of peace, but at last refused to beat any more and said I must learn to box, and not go near the other boys till I knew how. I went home with him every day and boxed in his room, and the bouts had always the same ending. My excitability gave me an advantage at first and I would drive him across the room, and then he would drive me across and it would end very commonly with my nose bleeding. One day his father, an elderly banker, brought us out into the garden and tried to make us box in a cold-blooded, courteous way, but it was no use. At last he said I might go near the boys again and I was no sooner inside the gate of the playing field than a boy flung a handful of mud and cried out, "Mad Irishman." I hit him several times on the face without being hit, till the boys round said we should make friends. I held out my hand in fear; for I knew if we went on I should be beaten, and he took it sullenly. I had so poor a reputation as a fighter that it was a great disgrace to him, and even the masters made fun of his swollen face; and though some little boys came in a deputation to ask me to lick a boy they named, I had never another fight with a school-fellow. We had a great many fights with the street boys and the boys of a neighbouring charity school. We had always the better because we were not allowed to fling stones, and that compelled us to close or do our best to close. The monitors had been told to report any boy who fought in the street, but they only reported those who flung stones. I always ran at the athlete's heels, but I never hit any one. My father considered these fights absurd, and even that they were an English absurdity, and so I could not get angry enough to like hitting and being hit; and then too my friend drove the enemy before him. He had no doubts or speculations to lighten his fist upon an enemy, that, being of low behaviour, should be beaten as often as possible, and there were real wrongs to avenge: one of our boys had been killed by the blow of a stone hid in a snowball. Sometimes we on our side got into trouble with the parents of boys. There was a quarrel between the athlete and an old German who had a barber's shop we passed every day on our way home, and one day he spat through the window and hit the German on his bald head—the monitors had not forbidden spitting. The German ran after us, but when the athlete squared up he went away. Now, though I knew it was not right to spit at people, my admiration for my friend arose to a great height. I spread his fame over the school, and next day there was a fine stir when somebody saw the old German going up the gravel walk to the head-master's room. Presently there was such a noise in the passage that even the master had to listen. It was the head-master's red-haired brother turning the old German out and shouting to the man-servant, "See that he doesn't steal the topcoats." We heard afterwards that he had asked the names of the two boys who passed his window every day and had been told the names of the two head boys who passed also but were notoriously gentlemanly in their manners. Yet my friend was timid also and that restored my confidence in myself. He would often ask me to buy the sweets or the ginger-beer because he was afraid sometimes when speaking to a stranger.

I had one reputation that I valued. At first when I went to the Hammersmith swimming-baths with the other boys, I was afraid to plunge in until I had gone so far down the ladder that the water came up to my thighs; but one day when I was alone I fell from the spring-board which was five or six feet above the water. After that I would dive from a greater height than the others and I practised swimming under water and pretending not to be out of breath when I came up. And then if I ran a race, I took care not to pant or show any sign of strain. And in this I had an advantage even over the athlete, for though he could run faster and was harder to tire than anybody else he grew very pale; and I was often paid compliments. I used to run with my friend when he was training to keep him in company. He would give me a long start and soon overtake me.

I followed the career of a certain professional runner for months, buying papers that would tell me if he had won or lost. I had seen him described as "the bright particular star of Ameri-can athletics", and the wonderful phrase had thrown enchant-ment over him. Had he been called the particular bright star, I should have cared nothing for him. I did not understand the symptom for years after. I was nursing my own dream, my form of the common schoolboy dream, though I was no longer gathering the little pieces of broken and rotting wood. Often instead of learning my lesson, I covered the white squares of the chessboard on my little table with pen and ink pictures of myself, doing all kinds of courageous things. One day my father said, "There was a man in Nelson's ship at the battle of Trafalgar, a ship's purser, whose hair turned white; what a sensitive temperament; that man should have achieved something!" I was vexed and bewildered, and am still bewildered and still vexed, finding it a poor and crazy thing that we who have imagined so many noble persons cannot bring our flesh to heel.

6

The head-master was a clergyman, a good-humoured, easy-going man, as temperate, one had no doubt in his religious life as in all else, and if he ever lost sleep on our account, it was from a very proper anxiety as to our gentility. I was in disgrace once because I went to school in some brilliant blue homespun serge my mother had bought in Devonshire, and I was told I must never wear it again. He had tried several times, though he must have known it was hopeless, to persuade our parents to put us into Eton clothes, and on certain days we were compelled to wear gloves. After my first year, we were forbidden to play marbles because it was a form of gambling and was played by nasty little boys, and a few months later told not to cross our legs in class. It was a school for the sons of professional men who had failed or were at the outset of their career, and the boys held an indignation meeting when they discovered that a new boy was an apothecary's son (I think at first I was his only friend), and we all pretended that our parents were richer than they were. I told a little boy who had often seen my mother knitting or mending my clothes that she only mended or knitted because she liked it, though I knew it was necessity.

It was like, I suppose, most schools of its type, an obscene, bullying place, where a big boy would hit a small boy in the wind to see him double up, and where certain boys, too young for any emotion of sex, would sing the dirty songs of the street, but I daresay it suited me better than a better school. I have heard the head-master say, "How has so-and-so done in his Greek?" and the class-master reply, "Very badly, but he is doing well in his cricket," and the head-master reply to that, "Oh, leave him alone." I was unfitted for school work, and though I would often work well for weeks together, I had to give the whole evening to one lesson if I was to know it. My thoughts were a great excitement, but when I tried to do anything with them, it was like trying to pack a balloon into a shed in a high wind. I was always near the bottom of my class, and always making excuses that but added to my timidity; but no master was rough with me. I was known to collect moths and butterflies and to get into no worse mischief than hiding now and again an old tailless white rat in my coat-pocket or my desk.

There was but one interruption of our quiet habits, the brief engagement of an Irish master, a fine Greek scholar and vehement teacher, but of fantastic speech. He would open the class by saying, "There he goes, there he goes," or some like words as the head-master passed by at the end of the hall. "Of course this school is no good. How could it be with a clergyman for head-master?" And then perhaps his eye would light on me, and he would make me stand up and tell me it was a scandal I was so idle when all the world knew that any Irish boy was cleverer than a whole class-room of English boys, a description I had to pay for afterwards. Sometimes he would call up a little boy who had a girl's face and kiss him upon both cheeks and talk of taking him to Greece in the holidays, and presently we heard he had written to the boy's parents about it, but long before the holidays he was dismissed.

7

Two pictures come into my memory. I have climbed to the top of a tree by the edge of the playing field, and am looking at my school-fellows and am as proud of myself as a March cock when it crows to its first sunrise. I am saying to myself, "If when I grow up I am as clever among grown-up men as I am among these boys, I shall be a famous man." I remind myself how they think all the same things and cover the school walls at election times with

the opinions their fathers find in the newspapers. I remind myself that I am an artist's son and must take some work as the
whole end of life and not think as the others do of becoming
well off and living pleasantly. The other picture is of a hotel
sitting-room in the Strand, where a man is hunched up over the
fire. He is a cousin who has speculated with another cousin's
money and has fled from Ireland in danger of arrest. My father
has brought us to spend the evening with him, to distract him
from the remorse that he must be suffering.

8

For years Bedford Park was a romantic excitement. At North
End my father had announced at breakfast that our glass chan-
delier was absurd and was to be taken down, and a little later he
described the village Norman Shaw was building. I had thought
he said, "There is to be a wall round and no newspapers to be
allowed in." And when I had told him how put out I was at finding neither wall nor gate, he explained that he had merely described what ought to be. We were to see De Morgan tiles,
peacock-blue doors and the pomegranate pattern and the tulip
pattern of Morris, and to discover that we had always hated doors
painted with imitation grain, the roses of mid-Victoria, and tiles
covered with geometrical patterns that seemed to have been
shaken out of a muddy kaleidoscope. We went to live in a house
like those we had seen in pictures and even met people dressed
like people in the story-books. The streets were not straight and
dull as at North End, but wound about where there was a big
tree or for the mere pleasure of winding, and there were wood
palings instead of iron railings. The newness of everything, the
empty houses where we played at hide-and-seek, and the strangeness of it all, made us feel that we were living among toys. We
could imagine people living happy lives as we thought people did
long ago when the poor were picturesque and the master of a
house could tell of strange adventures over the sea. Only the
better houses had been built. The commercial builder had not
begun to copy and to cheapen, and besides we only knew the
most beautiful houses, the houses of artists. My two sisters and
my brother and myself had dancing lessons in a low, red-brick

and tiled house that drove away dreams, long cherished, of some day living in a house made exactly like a ship's cabin. The dining-room table, where Sinbad the sailor might have sat, was painted peacock-blue, and the woodwork was all peacock-blue and upstairs a window niche was so big and high up that there was a flight of steps to go up and down by and a table in the niche. The two sisters of the master of the house, a well-known pre-Raphaelite painter, were our teachers, and they and their old mother were dressed in peacock-blue and in dresses so simply cut that they seemed a part of every story. Once when I had been looking with delight at the old woman, my father who had begun to be influenced by French art, muttered, "Imagine dressing up your old mother like that."

My father's friends were painters who had been influenced by the pre-Raphaelite movement but had lost their confidence. Wilson, Page, Nettleship, Potter are the names I remember, and at North End, I remember them most clearly. I often heard one and another say that Rossetti had never mastered his materials, and though Nettleship had already turned lion-painter, my father talked constantly of the designs of his youth, especially of "God creating Evil," which Rossetti praised in a letter my father had seen "as the most sublime conception in ancient or modern Art." In those early days, that he might not be tempted from his work by society, he had made a rent in the tail of his coat; and I have heard my mother tell how she had once sewn it up, but before he came again he had pulled out all the stitches. Potter's exquisite "Dormouse," now in the Tate Gallery, hung in our house for years. His dearest friend was a pretty model who was, when my memory begins, working for some position in a board-school. I can remember her sitting at the side of the throne in the North End studio, a book in her hand and my father hearing her say a Latin lesson. Her face was the typical mild, oval face of the painting of that time, and may indeed have helped in the moulding of an ideal of beauty. I found it the other day drawn in pencil on a blank leaf of a volume of *The Earthly Paradise*. It was at Bedford Park a few years later that I was to hear Farrar, whom I had first known at Burnham Beeches, tell of Potter's death and burial. Potter had been very poor and had died from the effects of semi-starvation. He had lived so long on bread and tea that his stomach withered—I am sure that was the word used—and when his relations found out and gave him good food, it was too late. Farrar had been at the funeral and had stood behind some well-to-do people who were close about the grave and saw one point to the model, who had followed the hearse on foot and was now crying at a distance, and say, "That is the woman who had all his money." She had often begged him to allow her to pay his debts, but he would not have it. Probably his rich friends blamed his poor friends, and they the rich, and I daresay, nobody had known enough to help him. Besides, he had a strange form of dissipation, I have heard some one say; he was devoted to children, and would become interested in some child—his "Dormouse" is a portrait of a child—and spend his money on its education. My sister remembers seeing him paint with a dark glove on his right hand, and his saying that he had used so much varnish the reflection of the hand would have teased him but for the glove. "I will soon have to paint my face some dark colour," he added. I have no memory, however, but of noticing that he sat at the easel, whereas my father always stands and walks up and down, and that there was dark blue, a colour that always affects me, in the background of his picture. There is a public gallery of Wilson's work in his native Aberdeen and my sisters have a number of his landscapes—wood-scenes for the most part—painted with phlegm and melancholy, the romantic movement drawing to its latest phase.

9

My father read out poetry, for the first time, when I was eight or nine years old. Between Sligo and Rosses Point, there is a tongue of land covered with coarse grass that runs out into the sea or the mud according to the state of the tide. It is the place where dead horses are buried. Sitting there, my father read me *The Lays of Ancient Rome*. It was the first poetry that had moved me after the stable-boy's *Orange Rhymes*. Later on he read me *Ivanhoe* and *The Lay of the Last Minstrel*, and they are still vivid in the memory. I re-read *Ivanhoe* the other day, but it has all vanished except Gurth, the swineherd, at the outset and Friar Tuck and his venison pasty, the two scenes that laid hold of me in childhood. *The Lay of the Last Minstrel* gave me a wish to turn magician that competed for years with the dream of being killed upon the seashore. When I first went to school, he tried to keep me from reading boys' papers, because a paper, by its very nature, as he explained to me, had to be made for the average boy or man and so could not but thwart one's growth. He took away my paper and I had not courage to say that I was but reading and delighting in a prose retelling of the *Iliad.* But after a few months, my father said he had been too anxious and became less urgent about my lessons and less violent if I had learnt them badly, and he ceased to notice what I read. From that on I shared the excitement which ran through all my fellows on Wednesday afternoons when the boys' papers were published, and I read endless stories I have forgotten as I have forgotten *Grimm's Fairy Tales* that I read at Sligo, and all of Hans Andersen except the "Ugly Duckling" which my mother had read to me and to my sisters. I remember vaguely that I liked Hans Andersen better than Grimm because he was less homely, but even he never gave me the knights and dragons and beautiful ladies that I longed for. I have remembered nothing that I read, but only those things that I heard or saw. When I was ten or twelve my father took me to see Irving play *Hamlet,* and did not understand why I preferred Irving to Ellen Terry, who was, I can now see, the idol of himself and his friends. I could not think of her, as I could of Irving's *Hamlet,* as but myself, and I was not old enough to care for feminine charm and beauty. For many years Hamlet was an image of heroic self-possession for the poses of youth and childhood to copy, a combatant of the battle within myself. My father had read me the story of the little boy murdered by the Jews in Chaucer and the tale of Sir Topaz, explaining the hard words, and though both excited me, I had liked Sir Topaz best and been disappointed that it left off in the middle. As I grew older, he would tell me plots of Balzac's novels, using incident or character as an illustration for some profound criticism of life. Now that I have read all the *Comédie Humaine,* certain pages have an unnatural emphasis, straining and overbalancing the outline, and I remember how in some suburban street, he told me of Lucien de Rubempré's duel after the betrayal of his master, and how the wounded Lucien hearing some one say that he was not dead had muttered "So much the worse."

I now can but share with a friend my thoughts and my emotions, and there is a continual discovery of difference, but in those days, before I had found myself, we could share adventures. When friends plan and do together, their minds become one mind and the last secret disappears. I was useless at games. I cannot remember that I ever kicked a goal or made a run, but I was a mine of knowledge when I and the athlete and those two notoriously gentlemanly boys—theirs was the name that I remember without a face—set out for Richmond Park, for Coomb Wood or Twyford Abbey to look for butterflies and moths and beetles. Sometimes to-day I meet people at lunch or dinner whose address sounds familiar and I remember of a sudden that a gamekeeper chased me from the plantation behind their house, or that I turned over the cow-dung in their paddock in search for some rare beetle believed to haunt the spot. The athlete was our watchman and our safety. He would suggest, should we meet a carriage on the drive, that we take off our hats and walk on as though about to pay a call. And once when we were sighted by a gamekeeper at Coomb Wood, he persuaded the eldest of the brothers to pretend to be a schoolmaster taking his boys for a walk, and the keeper, instead of swearing and threatening the law, was sad and argumentative. No matter how charming the place (and there is a little stream in a hollow where Wimbledon Common flows into Coomb Wood that is pleasant in the memory), I knew that those other boys saw something I did not see. I was a stranger there. There was something in their way of saying the names of places that made me feel this.

10

When I arrived at the Clarence Basin, Liverpool (the dock Clarence Mangan had his first name from), on my way to Sligo for my holidays I was among Sligo people. When I was a little boy, an old woman who had come to Liverpool with crates of fowl made me miserable by throwing her arms around me, the moment I had alighted from my cab, and telling the sailor who carried my luggage that she had held me in her arms when I was a baby. The sailor may have known me almost as well, for I was often at Sligo quay to sail my boat; and I came and went once or twice in every year upon the s.s. *Sligo* or the s.s. *Liverpool* which belonged to a company that had for directors my grandfather and his partner William Middleton. I was always pleased if it was the *Liverpool*, for she had been built to run the blockade during the war of North and South.

I waited for this voyage always with excitement and boasted to other boys about it, and when I was a little boy had walked with my feet apart as I had seen sailors walk. I used to be sea-sick, but I must have hidden this from the other boys and partly even from myself; for, as I look back, I remember very little about it, while I remember stories I was told by the captain or by his first mate, and the look of the great cliffs of Donegal, and Tory Island men coming alongside with lobsters, talking Irish and, if it was night, blowing on a burning sod to draw our attention. The captain, an old man with square shoulders and a fringe of grey hair round his face, would tell his first mate, a very admiring man, of fights he had had on shore at Liverpool; and perhaps it was of him I was thinking when I was very small and asked my grandmother if God was as strong as sailors. Once, at any rate, he had been nearly wrecked; the *Liverpool* had been all but blown upon the Mull of Galloway with her shaft broken, and the captain had said to his mate, "Mind and jump when she strikes, for we don't want to be killed by the falling spars"; and when the mate answered, "My God, I cannot swim," he had said, "Who could keep afloat for five minutes in a sea like that?" He would often say his mate was the most timid of men and that "a girl along the quays could laugh him out of anything." My grandfather had more than once given him a ship of his own, but he had always thrown up his berth to sail with his old captain where he felt safe. Once he had been put in charge of a ship in a dry dock in Liverpool, but a boy was drowned in Sligo, and before the news could have reached him he wired to his wife, "Ghost, come at once, or I will throw up berth." He had been wrecked a number of times, and maybe that had broken his nerve or maybe he had a sensitiveness that would in another class have given him taste and culture. I once forgot a copy of *Count Robert of Paris* on a deck-seat, and when I found it again, it was all covered with the prints of his dirty thumb. He had once seen the coach-a-baur or death coach. It came along the road, he said, till it was hidden by a cottage and it never came out on the other side of the cottage.

Once I smelled new-mown hay when we were quite a long way from land, and once when I was watching the sea-parrots (as the sailors call the puffin), I noticed they had different ways of tucking their heads under their wings, or I fancied it, and said to the captain, "They have different characters." Sometimes my father came too, and the sailors when they saw him coming would say, "There is John Yeats and we shall have a storm," for he was considered unlucky.

I no longer cared for little shut-in places, for a coppice against the stable-yard at Merville where my grandfather lived or against the gable at Seaview where Aunt Micky lived, and I began to climb the mountains, sometimes with the stable-boy for companion, and to look up their stories in the county history. I fished for trout with a worm in the mountain streams and went out herring-fishing at night; and because my grandfather had said the English were in the right to eat skates, I carried a large skate all the six miles or so from Rosses Point, but my grandfather did not eat it.

One night just as the equinoctial gales were coming, when I was sailing home in the coastguard's boat, a boy told me a beetle of solid gold, strayed maybe from Poe's "gold bug," had been seen by somebody in Scotland and I do not think that either of us doubted his news. Indeed, so many stories did I hear from sailors along the wharf, or round the fo'castle fire of the little steamer that ran between Sligo and Rosses, or from boys out fishing that the world seemed full of monsters and marvels. The foreign sailors wearing earrings did not tell me stories, but like the fishing boys, I gazed at them in wonder and admiration.

When I look at my brother's picture, "Memory Harbour"— houses and anchored ship and distant lighthouse all set close together as in some old map—I recognise in the blue-coated man with the mass of white shirt the pilot I went fishing with, and I am full of disquiet and of excitement, and I am melancholy because I have not made more and better verses. I have walked on Sinbad's yellow shore and never shall another's hit my fancy.

I had still my red pony, and once my father came with me

riding too, and was very exacting. He was indignant and threatening because he did not think I rode well. "You must do everything well," he said, "that the Pollexfens respect, though you must do other things also." He used to say the same about my lessons, and tell me to be good at mathematics. I can see now that he had a sense of inferiority among those energetic, successful people. He himself, some Pollexfen told me, though he rode very badly, would go hunting upon anything and take any ditch. His father, the County Down Rector, though a courtly man and a scholar, had been so dandified a horseman that I had heard of his splitting three riding breeches before he had settled into his saddle for a day's hunting, and of his first rector exclaiming, "I had hoped for a curate but they have sent me a jockey."

Left to myself, I rode without ambition, though getting many falls, and more often to Rathbroughan where my great-uncle Mat lived, than to any place else. His children and I used to sail our toy-boats in the river before his house, arming them with toy-cannon, touch-paper at all the touch-holes, always hoping but always in vain that they would not twist about in the eddies but fire their cannon at one another. I must have gone to Sligo sometimes in the Christmas holidays, for I can remember riding my red pony to a hunt. He balked at the first jump, to my relief, and when a crowd of boys began to beat him, I would not allow it. They all jeered at me for being afraid. I found a gap and when alone tried another ditch, but the pony would not jump that either; so I tied him to a tree and lay down among the ferns and looked up into the sky. On my way home I met the hunt again and noticed that everybody avoided the dogs, and to find out why they did so rode to where the dogs had gathered in the middle of the lane and stood my pony amongst them, and everybody began to shout at me.

Sometimes I would ride to Castle Dargan, where lived a brawling squireen, married to one of my Middleton cousins, and once I went thither on a visit with my cousin George Middleton. It was, I daresay, the last household where I could have found the reckless Ireland of a hundred years ago in final degradation. But I liked the place for the romance of its two ruined castles facing one another across a little lake, Castle Dargan and Castle Fury. The squireen lived in a small house his family had moved to from their castle some time in the eighteenth century, and two old Miss Furys, who let lodgings in Sligo, were the last remnants of the breed of the other ruin. Once in every year he drove to Sligo for the two old women, that they might look upon the ancestral stones and remember their gentility, and he would put his wildest horses into the shafts to enjoy their terror.

He himself, with a reeling imagination, knew not where to find a spur for the heavy hours. The first day I came there he gave my cousin a revolver (we were upon the high road), and to show it off, or his own shooting, he shot a passing chicken; and half an hour later, at the lake's edge under his castle, now but the broken corner of a tower with a winding stair, he fired at or over an old countryman walking on the far edge of the lake. The next day I heard him settling the matter with the old countryman over a bottle of whiskey, and both were in good humour. Once he had asked a timid aunt of mine if she would like to see his last new pet, and thereupon had marched a racehorse in through the hall door and round the dining-room table. And once she came down to a bare table because he had thought it a good joke to open the window and let his harriers eat the breakfast. There was a current story, too, of his shooting, in the pride of his marksmanship, at his own door with a Martini-Henry rifle till he had shot the knocker off. At last he quarrelled with my great-uncle William Middleton, and to avenge himself gathered a rabble of wild country lads, mounted them and himself upon the most broken-down rascally horses he could lay hands on and marched them through Sligo under a land-league banner. After that, having now neither friends nor money, he made off to Australia or to Canada.

I fished for pike at Castle Dargan and shot at birds with a muzzle-loading pistol until somebody shot a rabbit and I heard it squeal. From that on I would kill nothing but the dumb fish.

II

We left Bedford Park for a long thatched house at Howth, Co., Dublin. The land war was now at its height and our Kildare land, that had been in the family for many generations, was slipping from us. Rents had fallen more and more, we had to sell to pay some charge or mortgage, but my father and his tenants parted without ill-will. During the worst times an old tenant had under his roof my father's shooting-dog and gave it better care than the annual payment earned. He had set apart for its comfort the best place at the fire; and if some man were in the place when the dog walked into the house, the man must needs make room for the dog. And a good while after the sale, I can remember my father being called upon to settle some dispute between this old man and his sons.

I was now fifteen; and as he did not want to leave his painting my father told me to go to Harcourt Street and put myself to school. I found a bleak eighteenth-century house, a small playing-field full of mud and pebbles, fenced by an iron railing, and opposite a long hoarding and a squalid, ornamental railway station. Here, as I soon found, nobody gave a thought to decorum. We worked in a din of voices. We began the morning with prayers, but when class began the head-master, if he was in the humour, would laugh at Church and Clergy. "Let them say what they like," he would say, "but the earth does go round the sun." On the other hand there was no bullying and I had not thought it possible that boys could work so hard. Cricket and football, the collection of moths and butterflies, though not forbidden, were discouraged. They were for idle boys. I did not know, as I used to, the mass of my school-fellows; for we had little life in common outside the class-rooms. I had begun to think of my school work as an interruption of my natural history studies, but even had I never opened a book not in the school course, I could not have learned a quarter of my night's work. I had always done Euclid easily, making the problems out while the other boys were blundering at the blackboard, and it had often carried me from the bottom to the top of my class; but these boys had the same natural gift and instead of being in the fourth or fifth book were in the modern books at the end of the primer; and in place of a dozen lines of Virgil with a dictionary, I was expected to learn with the help of a crib a hundred and fifty lines. The other boys were able to learn the translation off, and to remember what words of Latin and English corresponded with one another, but I, who it may be had tried to find out what happened in the parts we had not read, made ridiculous mistakes; and what could

I, who never worked when I was not interested, do with a history lesson that was but a column of seventy dates? I was worst of all at literature, for we read Shakespeare for his grammar exclusively.

One day I had a lucky thought. A great many lessons were run through in the last hour of the day, things we had learnt or should have learnt by heart overnight, and not having known one of them for weeks, I cut off that hour without anybody's leave. I asked the mathematical master to give me a sum to work and nobody said a word. My father often interfered, and always with disaster, to teach me my Latin lesson. "But I have also my geography," I would say. "Geography," he would reply, "should never be taught. It is not a training for the mind. You will pick up all that you need, in your general reading." And if it was a history lesson, he would say just the same, and "Euclid," he would say, "is too easy. It comes naturally to the literary imagination. The old idea, that it is a good training for the mind, was long ago refuted." I would know my Latin lesson so that it was a nine days' wonder, and for weeks after would be told it was scandalous to be so clever and so idle. No one knew that I had learnt it in the terror that alone could check my wandering mind. I must have told on him at some time or other for I remember the head-master saying, "I am going to give you an imposition because I cannot get at your father to give him one." Sometimes we had essays to write; and though I never got a prize, for the essays were judged by handwriting and spelling, I caused a measure of scandal. I would be called up before some master and asked if I really believed such things, and that would make me angry for I had written what I had believed all my life, what my father had told me, or a memory of the conversation of his friends. I was asked to write an essay on "Men may rise on stepping-stones of their dead selves to higher things." My father read the subject to my mother who had no interest in such matters. "That is the way," he said, "boys are made insincere and false to themselves. Ideals make the blood thin, and take the human nature out of people." He walked up and down the room in eloquent indignation, and told me not to write on such a subject at all, but upon Shakespeare's lines, "To thine own self be true, and it must follow as the night the day thou canst not then be false to any man." At another time, he would denounce the idea of duty; "Imagine," he would say, "how the right sort of woman would despise a dutiful husband"; and he would tell us how much my mother would scorn such a thing. Maybe there were people among whom such ideas were natural, but they were the people with whom one does not dine. All he said was, I now believe right, but he should have taken me away from school. He would have taught me nothing but Greek and Latin, and I would now be a properly educated man, and would not have to look in useless longings at books that have been, through the poor mechanism of translation, the builders of my soul, nor face authority with the timidity born of excuse and evasion. Evasion and excuse were in the event as wise as the house-building instinct of the beaver.

12

My London school-fellow, the athlete, spent a summer with us, but the friendship of boyhood, founded upon action and adventure, was drawing to an end. He was still my superior in all physical activity and climbed to places among the rocks that even now are uncomfortable memories, but I had begun to criticise him. One morning I proposed a journey to Lambay Island, and was contemptuous because he said we should miss our mid-day meal. We hoisted a sail on our small boat and ran quickly over the nine miles and saw on the shore a tame sea-gull, while a couple of boys, the sons of a coastguard, ran into the water in their clothes to pull us to land, as we had read of savage people doing. We spent an hour upon the sunny shore and I said, "I would like to live here always, and perhaps some day I will." I was always discovering places where I would like to spend my whole life. We started to row home, and when dinner-time had passed for about an hour, the athlete lay down on the bottom of the boat doubled up with the gripes. I mocked at him and at his fellow-countrymen whose stomachs struck the hour as if they were clocks.

Our natural history, too, began to pull us apart. I planned some day to write a book about the changes through a twelvemonth among the creatures of some hole in the rock, and had some theory of my own, which I cannot remember, as to the colour of sea-anemones: and after much hesitation, trouble and bewilderment, was hot for argument in refutation of Adam and Noah and the Seven Days. I had read Darwin and Wallace, Huxley and Haeckel, and would spend hours on a holiday plaguing a pious geologist, who, when not at some job in Guinness's brewery, came with a hammer to look for fossils in the Howth Cliffs. "You know," I would say, "that such and such human remains cannot be less, because of the strata they were found in, than fifty thousand years old." "Oh!" he would answer, "they are an isolated instance." And once when I pressed hard my case against Ussher's chronology, he begged me not to speak of the subject again. "If I believed what you do," he said, "I could not live a moral life." But I could not even argue with the athlete who still collected his butterflies for the adventure's sake, and with no curiosity but for their names. I began to judge his intelligence, and to tell him that his natural history had as little to do with science as his collection of postage stamps. Even during my schooldays in London, influenced perhaps by my father, I had looked down upon the postage stamps.

13

Our house for the first year or so was on the top of a cliff, so that in stormy weather the spray would soak my bed at night, for I had taken the glass out of the window, sash and all. A literary passion for the open air was to last me for a few years. Then for another year or two, we had a house overlooking the harbour where the one great sight was the going and coming of the fishing fleet. We had one regular servant, a fisherman's wife, and the occasional help of a big, red-faced girl who ate a whole pot of jam while my mother was at church and accused me of it. Some such arrangement lasted until long after the time I write of, and until my father going into the kitchen by chance found a girl, engaged during a passing need, in tears at the thought of leaving our other servant, and promised that they should never be parted. I have no doubt that we lived at the harbour for my mother's sake. She had, when we were children, refused to take us to a seaside place because she heard it possessed a bathing box, but she loved the activities of a fishing village. When I think of her,

I almost always see her talking over a cup of tea in the kitchen with our servant, the fisherman's wife, on the only themes outside our house that seemed of interest—the fishing people of Howth, or the pilots and fishing people of Rosses Point. She read no books, but she and the fisherman's wife would tell each other stories that Homer might have told, pleased with any moment of sudden intensity and laughing together over any point of satire. There is an essay called "Village Ghosts" in my *Celtic Twilight* which is but a record of one such afternoon, and many a fine tale has been lost because it had not occurred to me soon enough to keep notes. My father was always praising her to my sisters and to me, because she pretended to nothing she did not feel. She would write him letters, telling of her delight in the tumbling clouds, but she did not care for pictures, and never went to an exhibition even to see a picture of his, nor to his studio to see the day's work, neither now nor when they were first married. I remember all this very clearly and little after it until her mind had gone in a stroke of paralysis and she had found, liberated at last from financial worry, perfect happiness feeding the birds at a London window. She had always, my father would say, intensity, and that was his chief word of praise; and once he added to the praise, "No spendthrift ever had a poet for a son, though a miser might."

14

The great event of a boy's life is the awakening of sex. He will bathe many times a day, or get up at dawn and having stripped leap to and fro over a stick laid upon two chairs and hardly know, and never admit, that he had begun to take pleasure in his own nakedness, nor will he understand the change until some dream discovers it. He may never understand at all the greater change in his mind.

It all came upon me when I was close upon seventeen like the bursting of a shell. Somnambulistic country girls, when it is upon them, throw plates about or pull them with long hairs in simulation of the polter-geist, or become mediums for some genuine spirit-mischief, surrendering to their desire of the marvellous. As I look backward, I seem to discover that my passions, my loves and my despairs, instead of being my enemies, a disturbance and an attack, became so beautiful that I had to be constantly alone to give them my whole attention. I notice that now, for the first time, what I saw when alone is more vivid in my memory than what I did or saw in company.

A herd had shown me a cave some hundred and fifty feet below the cliff path and a couple of hundred above the sea, and told me that an evicted tenant called Macrom, dead some fifteen years, had lived there many years, and shown me a rusty nail in the rock which had served perhaps to hold up some wooden protection from wind and weather. Here I stored a tin of cocoa and some biscuits, and instead of going to my bed, would slip out on warm nights and sleep in the cave on the excuse of catching moths. One had to pass over a rocky ledge, safe enough for any one with a fair head, yet seeming, if looked at from above, narrow and sloping; and a remonstrance from a stranger who had seen me climbing along it doubled my delight in the adventure. When, however, upon a bank holiday, I found lovers in my cave, I was not content with it again till I heard that the ghost of Macrom had been seen a little before the dawn, stooping over his fire in the cave-mouth. I had been trying to cook eggs, as I had read in some book, by burying them in the earth under a fire of sticks.

At other times, I would sleep among the rhododendrons and rocks in the wilder part of the grounds of Howth Castle. After a while my father said I must stay indoors half the night, meaning that I should get some sleep in my bed; but I, knowing that I would be too sleepy and comfortable to get up again, used to sit over the kitchen fire till half the night was gone. Exaggerated accounts spread through the school, and sometimes when I did not know a lesson some master would banter me about the way my nights were spent. My interest in science began to fade, and presently I said to myself, "It has all been a misunderstanding." I remembered how soon I tired of my specimens, and how little I knew after all my years of collecting, and I came to believe that I had gone through so much labour because of a text, heard for the first time in St. John's Church in Sligo, and copied Solomon, who had knowledge of hyssop and of tree that I might be certain of my own wisdom. I still carried my green net but I began to play at being a sage, a magician or a poet. I had many idols, and as I climbed along the narrow ledge I was now Manfred on his glacier, and now Prince Athanase with his solitary lamp, but I soon chose Alastor for my chief of men and longed to share his melancholy, and maybe at last to disappear from everybody's sight as he disappeared drifting in a boat along some slow-moving river between great trees. When I thought of women they were modelled on those in my favourite poets and loved in brief tragedy, or like the girl in *The Revolt of Islam,* accompanied their lovers through all manner of wild places, lawless women without homes and without children.

15

My father's influence upon my thoughts was at its height. We went to Dublin by train every morning, breakfasting in his studio. He had taken a large room with a beautiful eighteenth-century mantelpiece in a York Street tenement house, and at breakfast he read passages from the poets, and always from the play or poem at its most passionate moment. He never read me a passage because of its speculative interest, and indeed did not care at all for poetry where there was generalisation or abstraction however impassioned. He would read out the first speeches of the *Prometheus Unbound,* but never the ecstatic lyricism of that famous fourth act; and another day the scene where Coriolanus comes to the house of Aufidius and tells the impudent servants that his home is under the canopy. I have seen *Coriolanus* played a number of times since then, and read it more than once, but that scene is more vivid than the rest, and it is my father's voice that I hear and not Irving's or Benson's. He did not care even for a fine lyric passage unless he felt some actual man behind its elaboration of beauty, and he was always looking for the lineaments of some desirable, familiar life. When the spirits sang their scorn of Manfred, and Manfred answered, "O sweet and melancholy voices," I was told that they could not, even in anger, put off their spiritual sweetness. He thought Keats a greater poet than Shelley, because less abstract, but did not read him, caring little, I think, for any of that most beautiful poetry which has come in modern times from the influence of painting. All must be an idealisation

of speech, and at some moment of passionate action or somnambulistic reverie. I remember his saying that all contemplative men
were in a conspiracy to overrate their state of life, and that all
writers were of them, excepting the great poets. Looking back-
wards, it seems to me that I saw his mind in fragments, which
had always hidden connections I only now begin to discover.
He disliked the Victorian poetry of ideas, and Wordsworth but
for certain passages or whole poems. He said one morning over
his breakfast that he had discovered in the shape of the head of a
Wordsworthian scholar, an old and greatly respected clergyman
whose portrait he was painting, all the animal instincts of a prize-
fighter. He despised the formal beauty of Raphael, that calm
which is not an ordered passion but an hypocrisy, and attacked
Raphael's life for its love of pleasure and its self-indulgence. In
literature he was always pre-Raphaelite, and carried into literature
principles that, while the Academy was still unbroken, had made
the first attack upon academic form.

He no longer read me anything for its story, and all our discussion was of style.

16

I began to make blunders when I paid calls or visits, and a
woman I had known and liked as a child told me I had changed
for the worse. I wanted to be wise and eloquent, an essay on the
younger Ampère had helped me to this ambition, and when I was
alone I exaggerated my blunders and was miserable. I had begun
to write poetry in imitation of Shelley and of Edmund Spenser,
play after play—for my father exalted dramatic poetry above all
other kinds—and I invented fantastic and incoherent plots. My
lines but seldom scanned, for I could not understand the prosody
in the books, although there were many lines that taken by themselves had music. I spoke them slowly as I wrote and only discovered when I read them to somebody else that there was no
common music, no prosody. There were, however, moments of
observation; for, even when I caught moths no longer, I still noticed all that passed; how the little moths came out at sunset, and
how after that there were only a few big moths till dawn brought

little moths again; and what birds cried out at night as if in their
sleep.

17

At Sligo, where I still went for my holidays, I stayed with my
uncle, George Pollexfen, who had come from Ballina to fill the
place of my grandfather, who had retired. My grandfather had no
longer his big house, his partner William Middleton was dead,
and there had been legal trouble. He was no longer the rich man
he had been, and his sons and daughters were married and scat-
tered. He had a tall, bare house overlooking the harbour, and
had nothing to do but work himself into a rage if he saw a mud-
lighter mismanaged or judged from the smoke of a steamer that
she was burning cheap coal, and to superintend the making of
his tomb. There was a Middleton tomb and a long list of Middletons on the wall, and an almost empty place for Pollexfen names,
but he had said, because there was a Middleton there he did not
like, "I am not going to lie with those old bones"; and already
one saw his name in large gilt letters on the stone fence of the
new tomb. He ended his walk at St. John's churchyard almost
daily, for he liked everything neat and compendious as upon
shipboard, and if he had not looked after the tomb himself the
builder might have added some useless ornament. He had, however, all his old skill and nerve. I was going to Rosses Point on
the little trading steamer and saw him take the wheel from the
helmsman and steer her through a gap in the channel wall, and
across the sand, an unheard-of course, and at the journey's end
bring her alongside her wharf at Rosses without the accustomed
zigzagging or pulling on a rope but in a single movement. He
took snuff when he had a cold, but had never smoked nor taken
alcohol; and when in his eightieth year his doctor advised a stimulant, he replied, "No, no, I am not going to form a bad habit."

My brother had partly taken my place in my grandmother's
affections. He had lived permanently in her house for some years
now, and went to a Sligo school where he was always bottom of
his class. My grandmother did not mind that, for she said, "He is
too kindhearted to pass the other boys." He spent his free hours
going here and there with crowds of little boys, sons of pilots and

sailors, as their well-liked leader, arranging donkey races or driving donkeys tandem, an occupation which requires all one's intellect because of their obstinacy. Besides he had begun to amuse everybody with his drawings; and in half the pictures he paints to-day I recognise faces that I have met at Rosses or the Sligo quays. It is long since he has lived there, but his memory seems as accurate as the sight of the eye.

George Pollexfen was as patient as his father was impetuous, and did all by habit. A well-to-do, elderly man, he lived with no more comfort than when he had set out as a young man. He had a little house and one old general servant and a man to look after his horse, and every year he gave up some activity and found that there was one more food that disagreed with him. A hypochondriac, he passed from winter to summer through a series of woolens that had always to be weighed; for in April or May or, whatever the date was, he had to be sure he carried the exact number of ounces he had carried upon that date since boyhood. He lived in despondency, finding in the most cheerful news reasons of discouragement, and sighing every twenty-second of June over the shortening of the days. Once in later years, when I met him in Dublin sweating in a midsummer noon, I brought him into the hall of the Kildare Street Library, a cool and shady place, without lightening his spirits; for he but said in a melancholy voice, "How very cold this place must be in wintertime." Sometimes when I had pitted my cheerfulness against his gloom over the breakfast table, maintaining that neither his talent nor his memory nor his health were running to the dregs, he would rout me with the sentence, "How very old I shall be in twenty years." Yet this inactive man, in whom the sap of life seemed to be dried away, had a mind full of pictures. Nothing had ever happened to him except a love affair, not I think very passionate, that had gone wrong, and a voyage when a young man. My grandfather had sent him in a schooner to a port in Spain where the shipping agents were two Spaniards called O'Neill, descendants of Hugh O'Neill, Earl of Tyrone, who had fled from Ireland in the reign of James I; and their Irish trade was a last remnant of the Spanish trade that had once made Galway wealthy. For some years he and they had corresponded for they cherished the memory of their origin. In some Connaught burying-ground, he had chanced upon the funeral of a child with but one mourner, a distinguished foreign-looking man. It was an Austrian count burying the last of an Irish family, long nobles of Austria, who were always carried to that half-ruined burying-ground.

My uncle had almost given up hunting and was soon to give it up altogether, and he had once ridden steeplechases and been, his horse-trainer said, the best rider in Connaught. He had certainly great knowledge of horses, for I have been told, several counties away, that at Ballina he cured horses by conjuring. He had, however, merely great skill in diagnosis, for the day was still far off when he was to give his nights to astrology and ceremonial magic. His servant, Mary Battle, who had been with him since he was a young man, had the second sight and that, may be, inclined him to strange studies. One morning she was about to bring him a clean shirt, but stopped saying there was blood on the shirt-front and that she must bring him another. On his way to his office he fell, crossing over a little wall, and cut himself and bled on the linen where she had seen the blood. In the evening, she told him that the shirt she had thought bloody was quite clean. She could neither read nor write and her mind, which answered his gloom with its merriment, was rammed with every sort of old history and strange belief. Much of my *Celtic Twilight* is but her daily speech.

My uncle had the respect of the common people as few Sligo men have had it; he would have thought a stronger emotion an intrusion on his privacy. He gave to all men the respect due to their station or their worth with an added measure of ceremony, and kept among his workmen a discipline that had about it something of a regiment or a ship, knowing nothing of any but personal authority. If a carter, let us say, was in fault, he would not dismiss him, but send for him and take his whip away and hang it upon the wall; and having reduced the offender, as it were, to the ranks for certain months, would restore him to his post and his whip. This man of diligence and of method, who had no enterprise but in contemplation, and claimed that his wealth, considerable for Ireland, came from a brother's or partner's talent, was the confidant of my boyish freaks and reveries. When I said to him, echoing some book I had read, that one

never knew a countryside till one knew it at night he was pleased
('though nothing would have kept him from his bed a moment
beyond the hour); for he loved natural things and had learnt
two cries of the lapwing, one that drew them to where he stood
and one that made them fly away. And he approved, and arranged
my meals conveniently, when I told him I was going to walk
round Lough Gill and sleep in a wood. I did not tell him all my
object, for I was nursing a new ambition. My father had read
to me some passage out of *Walden*, and I planned to live some
day in a cottage on a little island called Innisfree, and Innisfree
was opposite Slish Wood where I meant to sleep.

I thought that having conquered bodily desire and the inclina-
tion of my mind towards women and love, I should live, as Thoreau lived, seeking wisdom. There was a story in the county
history of a tree that had once grown upon that island guarded
by some terrible monster and borne the food of the gods. A young
girl pined for the fruit and told her lover to kill the monster and
carry the fruit away. He did as he had been told, but tasted the
fruit; and when he reached the mainland where she had waited
for him, he was dying of its powerful virtue. And from sorrow
and from remorse she too ate of it and died. I do not remember
whether I chose the island because of its beauty or for the story's
sake, but I was twenty-two or three before I gave up the dream.

I set out from Sligo about six in the evening, walking slowly,
for it was an evening of great beauty; but though I was well into
Slish Wood by bed-time, I could not sleep, not from the discomfort of the dry rock I had chosen for my bed, but from my fear
of the wood-ranger. Somebody had told me, though I do not
think it could have been true, that he went his round at some
unknown hour. I kept going over what I should say if found
and could not think of anything he would believe. However, I
could watch my island in the early dawn and notice the order
of the cries of the birds.

I came home next day unimaginably tired and sleepy, having
walked some thirty miles partly over rough and boggy ground.
For months afterwards, if I alluded to my walk, my uncle's general servant (not Mary Battle, who was slowly recovering from
an illness and would not have taken the liberty) would go into
fits of laughter. She believed I had spent the night in a different

fashion and had invented the excuse to deceive my uncle, and would say to my great embarrassment, for I was as prudish as an old maid, "And you had good right to be fatigued."

Once when staying with my uncle at Rosses Point where he went for certain months of the year, I called upon a cousin towards midnight and asked him to get his yacht out, for I wanted to find what sea birds began to stir before dawn. He was indignant and refused; but his elder sister had overheard me and came to the head of the stairs and forbade him to stir, and that so vexed him that he shouted to the kitchen for his sea boots. He came with me in great gloom for he had people's respect, he declared, and nobody so far said that he was mad as they said I was, and we got a very sleepy boy out of his bed in the village and set up sail. We put a trawl out, as he thought it would restore his character if he caught some fish, but the wind fell and we were becalmed. I rolled myself in the mainsail and went to sleep for I could sleep anywhere in those days. I was awakened towards dawn to see my cousin and the boy turning out their pockets for money and had to rummage in my own pockets. A boat was rowing in from Roughley with fish and they wanted to buy some and pretend they had caught it, but all our pockets were empty. I had wanted the birds' cries for the poem that became fifteen years afterwards "The Shadowy Waters," and it had been full of observation had I been able to write it when I first planned it. I had found again the windy light that moved me when a child. I persuaded myself that I had a passion for the dawn, and this passion, though mainly histrionic like a child's play, an ambitious game, had moments of sincerity. Years afterwards when I had finished *The Wanderings of Oisin*, dissatisfied with its yellow and its dull green, with all that overcharged colour inherited from the romantic movement, I deliberately reshaped my style, deliberately sought out an impression as of cold light and tumbling clouds. I cast off traditional metaphors and loosened my rhythm, and recognising that all the criticism of life known to me was alien and English, became as emotional as possible but with an emotion which I described to myself as cold. It is a natural conviction for a painter's son to believe that there may be a landscape that is symbolical of some spiritual condition and awakens a hunger such as cats feel for valerian.

18

I was writing a long play on a fable suggested by one of my father's early designs. A king's daughter loves a god seen in the luminous sky above her garden in childhood, and to be worthy of him and put away mortality, becomes without pity and commits crimes, and at last, having made her way to the throne by murder, awaits his coming among her courtiers. One by one they become chilly and drop dead, for unseen by all but her, her god is in the hall. At last he is at her throne's foot and she, her mind in the garden once again, dies babbling like a child.

19

Once when I was sailing with my cousin, the boy who was our crew talked of a music-hall at a neighbouring seaport, and how the girls there gave themselves to men, and his language was as extravagant as though he praised that courtesan after whom they named a city or the queen of Sheba herself. Another day he wanted my cousin to sail some fifty miles along the coast and put in near some cottages where he had heard there were girls "and we would have a great welcome before us." He pleaded with excitement (I imagine that his eyes shone) but hardly hoped to persuade us, and perhaps but played with fabulous images of life and of sex. A young jockey and horse-trainer, who had trained some horses for my uncle, once talked to me of wicked England while we cooked a turkey for our Christmas dinner making it twist about on a string in front of his harness-room fire. He had met two lords in England where he had gone racing, who "always exchanged wives when they went to the Continent for a holiday." He himself had once been led into temptation and was going home with a woman, but having touched his scapular by chance, saw in a moment an angel waving white wings in the air. Presently I was to meet him no more and my uncle said he had done something disgraceful about a horse.

20

I was climbing up a hill at Howth when I heard wheels behind me and a pony-carriage drew up beside me. A pretty girl was
driving alone and without a hat. She told me her name and said
we had friends in common and asked me to ride beside her. After
that I saw a great deal of her and was soon in love. I did not tell
her I was in love, however, because she was engaged. She had
chosen me for her confidant and I learned all about her quarrels
with her lover. Several times he broke the engagement off, and
she fell ill, and friends had to make peace. Sometimes she would
write to him three times a day, but she could not do without a
confidant. She was a wild creature, a fine mimic and given to
bursts of religion. I had known her to weep at a sermon, call
herself a sinful woman, and mimic it after. I wrote her some bad
poems and had more than one sleepless night through anger with
her betrothed.

21

At Ballisodare an event happened that brought me back to
the superstitions of my childhood. I do not know when it was,
for the events of this period have as little sequence as those of
childhood. I was staying with cousins at Avena house, a young
man a few years older, and a girl of my own age and perhaps
her sister who was a good deal older. My girl cousin had often
told me of strange sights she had seen at Ballisodare or Rosses.
An old woman three or four feet in height and leaning on a
stick had once come to the window and looked in at her, and
sometimes she would meet people on the road who would say,
"How is so-and-so," naming some member of her family, and
she would know, though she could not explain how, that they
were not people of this world. Once she had lost her way in a
familiar field, and when she found it again the silver mounting
on a walking-stick belonging to her brother which she carried
had vanished. An old woman in the village said afterwards, "You
have good friends amongst them, and the silver was taken instead of you."

Though it was all years ago what I am going to tell now must be accurate, for no great while ago she wrote out her unprompted memory of it all and it was the same as mine. She was sitting under an old-fashioned mirror reading and I was reading in another part of the room. Suddenly I heard a sound as if somebody was throwing a shower of peas at the mirror. I got her to go into the next room and rap with her knuckles on the other side of the wall to see if the sound could come from there, and while I was alone a great thump came close to my head upon the wainscot and on a different wall of the room. Later in the day a servant heard a heavy footstep going through the empty house, and that night, when I and my two cousins went for a walk, she saw the ground under some trees all in a blaze of light. I saw nothing, but presently we crossed the river and went along its edge where, they say, there was a village destroyed, I think in the wars of the seventeenth century, and near an old graveyard. Suddenly we all saw a light moving over the river where there is a great rush of waters. It was like a very brilliant torch. A moment later the girl saw a man coming towards us who disappeared in the water. I kept asking myself if I could be deceived. Perhaps after all, though it seemed impossible, somebody was walking in the water with a torch. But we could see a small light low down on Knocknarea seven miles off, and it began to move upward over the mountain slope. I timed it on my watch and in five minutes it reached the summit, and I, who had often climbed the mountain, knew that no human footstep was so speedy.

From that on I wandered about raths and faery hills and questioned old women and old men and, when I was tired out or unhappy, began to long for some such end as True Thomas found. I did not believe with my intellect that you could be carried away body and soul, but I believed with my emotions and the belief of the country people made that easy. Once when I had crawled into the stone passage in some rath of the third Rosses, the pilot who had come with me called down the passage: "Are you all right, sir?"

And one night as I came near the village of Rosses on the road from Sligo, a fire blazed up on a green bank at my right side seven or eight feet above me, and another fire suddenly answered from Knocknarea. I hurried on doubting, and yet hardly doubting in my heart that I saw again the fires that I had seen by the river at Ballisodare. I began occasionally telling people that one should believe whatever had been believed in all countries and periods, and only reject any part of it after much evidence, instead of starting all over afresh and only believing what one could prove. But I was always ready to deny or turn into a joke what was for all that my secret fanaticism. When I had read Darwin and Huxley and believed as they did, I had wanted, because an established authority was upon my side, to argue with everybody.

22

I no longer went to the Harcourt Street school and we had moved from Howth to Rathgar. I was at the Art School in Kildare Street, but my father, who came to the school now and then, was my teacher. The masters left me alone, for they liked a very smooth surface and a very neat outline, and indeed understood nothing but neatness and smoothness. A drawing of the Discobolus, after my father had touched it, making the shoulder stand out with swift and broken lines, had no meaning for them; and for the most part I exaggerated all that my father did. Sometimes indeed, out of rivalry to some student near, I too would try to be smooth and neat. One day I helped the student next me, who certainly had no artistic gifts, to make a drawing of some plaster fruit. In his gratitude he told me his history. "I don't care for art," he said. "I am a good billiard player, one of the best in Dublin; but my guardian said I must take a profession, so I asked my friends to tell me what I could do without passing an examination, and here I am." It may be that I myself was there for no better reason. My father had wanted me to go to Trinity College and, when I would not, had said, "My father, and grandfather and great-grandfather have been there." I did not tell him that neither my classics nor my mathematics were good enough for any examination.

I had for fellow-student an unhappy "village genius" sent to Dublin by some charitable Connaught landlord. He painted religious pictures upon sheets nailed to the wall of his bedroom, a

"Last Judgment" among the rest. Then there was a wild young man who would come to school of a morning with a daisy-chain hung round his neck; and George Russell, "A. E.," the poet and mystic. He did not paint the model as we tried to, for some other image rose always before his eyes (a St. John in the Desert I remember), and already he spoke to us of his visions. One day he announced that he was leaving the Art School because his will was weak and the arts or any other emotional pursuit could but weaken it further.

Presently I went to the modelling class to be with certain elder students who had authority among us. Among these were John Hughes and Oliver Sheppard, well known now as Irish sculptors. The day I first went into the studio where they worked, I stood still upon the threshold in amazement. A pretty, gentle-looking girl was modelling in the middle of the room, and all the men were swearing at her for getting in their light with the most violent and fantastic oaths, and calling her every sort of name, and through it all she worked in undisturbed diligence. Presently the man nearest me saw my face and called out, "She is stone deaf, so we always swear at her and call her names when she gets in our light." In reality I soon found that every one was kind to her, carrying her drawing-boards and the like, and putting her into the tram at the day's end.

We had no scholarship, no critical knowledge of the history of painting, and no settled standards. A student would show his fellows some French illustrated paper that we might all admire now some statue by Rodin or Dalou and now some declamatory Parisian monument, and if I did not happen to have discussed the matter with my father I would admire with no more discrimination than the rest. That pretentious monument to Gambetta made a great stir among us. No influence touched us but that of France, where one or two of the older students had been already and all hoped to go. Of England I alone knew anything. Our ablest student had learnt Italian to read Dante, but had never heard of Tennyson or Browning, and it was I who carried into the school some knowledge of English poetry, especially of Browning who had begun to move me by his air of wisdom. I do not believe that I worked well, for I wrote a great deal and that tired me, and the work I was set to bored me. When alone and uninfluenced, I longed for pattern, for pre-Raphaelitism, for an art allied to poetry, and returned again and again to our National Gallery to gaze at Turner's "Golden Bough." Yet I was too timid, had I known how, to break away from my father's style and the style of those about me. I was always hoping that my father would return to the style of his youth, and make pictures out of certain designs now lost, that one could still find in his portfolios. There was one of an old hunchback in vague medieval dress, going through some underground place where there are beds with people in the beds: a girl half rising from one has seized his hand and is kissing it. I have forgotten its story, but the strange old man and the intensity in the girl's figure are vivid as in my childhood.[1] There is some passage, I believe in the Bible, about a man who saved a city and went away and was never heard of again, and here he was in another design, an old ragged beggar in the market-place laughing at his own statue. But my father would say: "I must paint what I see in front of me. Of course I shall really paint something different because my nature will come in unconsciously." Sometimes I would try to argue with him, for I had come to think the philosophy of his fellow-artists and himself a misunderstanding created by Victorian science, and science I had grown to hate with a monkish hate; but no good came of it, and in a moment I would unsay what I had said and pretend that I did not really believe it. My father was painting many fine portraits, Dublin leaders of the bar, college notabilities, or chance comers whom he would paint for nothing if he liked their heads; but all displeased me. In my heart I thought that only beautiful things should be painted, and that only ancient things and the stuff of dreams were beautiful. And I almost quarrelled with my father when he made a large water-colour, one of his finest pictures and now lost, of a consumptive beggar girl. And a picture at the Hibernian Academy of cocottes with yellow faces sitting before a café by some follower of Manet's made me miserable for days, but I was happy when partly through my father's planning some Whistlers were brought over and exhibited, and did not agree when my father said: "Imagine making your old mother an arrangement in grey!"

[1] This little picture has been found and hangs in my house. 1926.

I did not care for mere reality and believed that creation should be deliberate, and yet I could only imitate my father. I could not compose anything but a portrait and even to-day I constantly see people, as a portrait painter, posing them in the mind's eye before such and such a background. Meanwhile I was still very much of a child, sometimes drawing with an elaborate frenzy, simulating what I believed of inspiration, and sometimes walking with an artificial stride in memory of Hamlet and stopping at shop windows to look at my tie gathered into a loose sailor-knot and to regret that it could not be always blown out by the wind like Byron's tie in the picture. I had as many ideas as I have now, only I did not know how to choose from among them those that belonged to my life.

23

We lived in a villa where the red bricks were made pretentious and vulgar with streaks of slate colour, and there seemed to be enemies everywhere. At one side indeed there was a friendly architect, but on the other some stupid stout woman and her family. I had a study with a window opposite some window of hers, and one night when I was writing I heard voices full of derision and saw the stout woman and her family standing in the window. I have a way of acting what I write and speaking it aloud without knowing what I am doing. Perhaps I was on my hands and knees, or looking down over the back of a chair talking into what I imagined an abyss. Another day a woman asked me to direct her on her way and while I was hesitating, being so suddenly called out of my thought, a woman from some neighbouring house came by. She said I was a poet and my questioner turned away contemptuously. Upon the other hand, the policeman and tramway conductor thought my absence of mind sufficiently explained when our servant told them I was a poet. "Oh well," said the policeman, who had been asking why I went indifferently through clean and muddy places, "if it is only the poetry that is working in his head!" I imagine I looked gaunt and emaciated, for the little boys at the neighbouring cross-road used to say when I passed by: "Oh, here is King Death again." One morning when my father was on the way to his studio, he met his landlord and they had this conversation: "Do you think now that Tennyson should have been given that peerage?" "One's only doubt is if he should have accepted it: it was a finer thing to be Alfred Tennyson." There was a silence, and then: "Well, all the people I know think he should not have got it." Then, spitefully: "What's the good of poetry?" "Oh, it gives our minds a great deal of pleasure." "But wouldn't it have given your mind more pleasure if he had written an improving book?" "Oh, in that case I should not have read it." My father returned in the evening delighted with his story, but I could not understand how he could take such opinions lightly and not have seriously argued with the man.

None of these people had ever seen any poet but an old white-haired man who had written volumes of easy, too-honied verse, and run through his money and gone clean out of his mind. He was a common figure in the streets and lived in some shabby neighbourhood of tenement houses where there were hens and chickens among the cobble stones. Every morning he carried home a loaf and gave half of it to the hens and chickens, the birds, or to some dog or starving cat. He was known to live in one room with a nail in the middle of the ceiling from which innumerable cords were stretched to other nails in the walls. In this way he kept up the illusion that he was living under canvas in some Arabian desert. I could not escape like this old man from house and neighbourhood, but hated both, hearing every whisper, noticing every passing glance.

When my grandfather came for a few days to see a doctor, I was shocked to see him in our house. My father read out to him in the evening Clark Russell's *Wreck of the "Grosvenor"*; but the doctor forbade it, for my grandfather got up in the middle of the night and acted through the mutiny, as I acted my verse, saying the while, "Yes, yes, that is the way it would all happen."

24

From our first arrival in Dublin, my father had brought me from time to time to see Edward Dowden. He and my father had been college friends and were trying, perhaps, to take up again their old friendship. Sometimes we were asked to breakfast, and afterwards my father would tell me to read out one of my poems. Dowden was wise in his encouragement, never overpraising and never unsympathetic, and he would sometimes lend me books. The orderly, prosperous house where all was in good taste, where poetry was rightly valued, made Dublin tolerable for a while, and for perhaps a couple of years he was an image of romance. My father would not share my enthusiasm and soon, I noticed, grew impatient at these meetings. He would sometimes say that he had wanted Dowden when they were young to give himself to creative art, and would talk of what he considered Dowden's failure in life. I know now that he was finding in his friend what he himself had been saved from by the conversation of the pre-Raphaelites. "He will not trust his nature," he would say, or "He is too much influenced by his inferiors," or he would praise "Renunciants," one of Dowden's poems, to prove what Dowden might have written. I was not influenced for I had imagined a past worthy of that dark, romantic face. I took literally his verses, touched here and there with Swinburnian rhetoric, and believed that he had loved, unhappily and illicitly; and when through the practice of my art I discovered that certain images about the love of woman were the properties of a school, I but changed my fancy and thought of him as very wise.

I was constantly troubled about philosophic questions. I would say to my fellow-students at the Art School, "Poetry and sculpture exist to keep our passions alive"; and somebody would say, "We would be much better without our passions." Or I would have a week's anxiety over the problem: do the arts make us happier, or more sensitive and therefore more unhappy. And I would say to Hughes or Sheppard, "If I cannot be certain they make us happier I will never write again." If I spoke of these things to Dowden he would put the question away with good-humoured irony: he seemed to condescend to everybody and everything and was now my sage. I was about to learn that if a man is to write lyric poetry he must be shaped by nature and art to some one out of half a dozen traditional poses, and be lover or saint, sage or sensualist, or mere mocker of all life; and that none but that stroke of luckless luck can open before him the accumulated expression of the world. And this thought before it could be knowledge was an instinct.

I was vexed when my father called Dowden's irony timidity, but after many years his impression has not changed for he wrote to me but a few months ago, "It was like talking to a priest. One had to be careful not to remind him of his sacrifice." Once after breakfast Dowden read us some chapters of the unpublished *Life of Shelley,* and I who had made the *Prometheus Unbound* my sacred book was delighted with all he read. I was chilled, however, when he explained that he had lost his liking for Shelley and would not have written it but for an old promise to the Shelley family. When it was published, Matthew Arnold made sport of certain conventionalities and extravagances that were, my father and I had come to see, the violence or clumsiness of a conscientious man hiding from himself a lack of sympathy.

Though my faith was shaken, it was only when he urged me to read George Eliot that I became angry and disillusioned and worked myself into a quarrel or half-quarrel. I had read all Victor Hugo's romances and a couple of Balzac's and was in no mind to like her. She seemed to have a distrust or a distaste for all in life that gives one a springing foot. Then too she knew so well how to enforce her distaste by the authority of her mid-Victorian science or by some habit of mind of its breeding, that I, who had not escaped the fascination of what I loathed, doubted while the book lay open whatsoever my instinct knew of splendour. She disturbed me and alarmed me, but when I spoke of her to my father, he threw her aside with a phrase, "Oh, she was an ugly woman who hated handsome men and handsome women"; and he began to praise *Wuthering Heights.*

Only the other day, when I got a volume of Dowden's letters, did I discover that the friendship between Dowden and my father had long been an antagonism. My father had written from Fitzroy Road in the sixties that the brotherhood, by which he meant the poet Edwin Ellis, Nettleship and himself, "abhorred Wordsworth"; and Dowden, not remembering that another week would bring a different mood and abhorrence, had written a pained and solemn letter. My father had answered that Dowden believed too much in the intellect, that all valuable education was but a stirring up of the emotions and that this did not mean excitability. "In the completely emotional man," he wrote, "the least awakening of feeling is a harmony in which every chord of every feeling vibrates. Excitement is the feature of an insufficiently emotional nature, the harsh vibrating discourse of but one or two chords." Living in a free world accustomed to the gay exaggeration of the talk of equals, of men who talk and write to discover truth and not for popular instruction, he had already, when both men were in their twenties, decided it is plain that Dowden was a Provincial.

25

It was only when I began to study psychical research and mystical philosophy that I broke away from my father's influence. He had been a follower of John Stuart Mill and so had never shared Rossetti's conviction that it mattered to nobody whether the sun went round the earth or the earth round the sun. But through this new research, this reaction from popular science, I had begun to feel that I had allies for my secret thought.

Once when I was in Dowden's drawing-room a servant announced my late head-master. I must have got pale or red, for Dowden with some ironical, friendly remark, brought me into another room and there I stayed until the visitor was gone. A few months later, when I met the head-master again I had more courage. We chanced upon one another in the street and he said, "I want you to use your influence with so-and-so, for he is giving all his time to some sort of mysticism and he will fail in his examination." I was in great alarm, but I managed to say something about the children of this world being wiser than the children of light. He went off with a brusque "Good morning." I do not think that even at that age I would have been so grandiloquent but for my alarm. He had, however, aroused all my indignation. My new allies and my old had alike sustained me. "Intermediate examinations," which I had always refused, meant money for pupil and for teacher, and that alone. My father had brought me up never when at school to think of the future or of any practical result. I have even known him to say, "When I was young, the definition of a gentleman was a man not wholly occupied in getting on." And yet this master wanted to withdraw my friend from the pursuit of the most important of all the truths. My friend, now in his last year at school, was a "show boy," and had beaten all Ireland again and again, but now he and I were reading Baron Reichenbach on Odic Force and manuals published by the Theosophical Society. We spent a good deal of time in the Kildare Street Museum passing our hands over the glass cases, feeling or believing we felt the Odic Force flowing from the big crystals. We also found pins blindfolded and read papers on our discoveries to the Hermetic Society that met near the roof in York Street. I had, when we first made our society, proposed for our consideration that whatever the great poets had affirmed in their finest moments was the nearest we could come to an authoritative religion, and that their mythology, their spirits of water and wind were but literal truth. I had read *Prometheus Unbound* with this thought in mind and wanted help to carry my study through all literature. I was soon to vex my father by defining truth as "the dramatically appropriate utterance of the highest man." And if I had been asked to define the "highest man," I would have said perhaps, "We can but find him as Homer found Odysseus when he was looking for a theme."

My friend had written to some missionary society to send him to the South Seas, when I offered him Renan's *Life of Christ* and a copy of *Esoteric Buddhism*. He refused both, but a few days later while reading for an examination in Kildare Street Library, he asked in an idle moment for *Esoteric Buddhism* and came out an esoteric Buddhist. He wrote to the missionaries withdrawing his letter and offered himself to the Theosophical Society as a *chela*. He was vexed now at my lack of zeal, for I had stayed somewhere between the books, held there perhaps by my father's scepticism. I said, and he thought it was a great joke though I was serious, that even if I were certain in my own mind, I did not know "a single person with a talent for conviction." For a time he made me ashamed of my world and its lack of zeal, and I wondered if his world (his father was a notorious Orange leader) where everything was a matter of belief was not better than mine. He himself proposed the immediate conversion of the other "show boy," a clever little fellow, now a Dublin mathematician and still under five feet. I found him a day later in much depression. I said, "Did he refuse to listen to you?" "Not at all," was the answer, "for I had only been talking for a quarter of an hour when he said he believed." Certainly those minds, parched by many examinations, were thirsty.

Sometimes a professor of Oriental Languages at Trinity College, a Persian, came to our Society and talked of the magicians of the East. When he was a little boy, he had seen a vision in a pool of ink, a multitude of spirits singing in Arabic, "Woe unto those that do not believe in us." And we persuaded a Brahmin philosopher to come from London and stay for a few days with the only one among us who had rooms of his own. It was my first meeting with a philosophy that confirmed my vague speculations and seemed at once logical and boundless. Consciousness, he taught, does not merely spread out its surface but has, in vision and in contemplation, another motion and can change in height and in depth. A handsome young man with the typical face of Christ, he chaffed me good-humouredly because he said I came at breakfast and began some question that was interrupted by the first caller, waited in silence till ten or eleven at night when the last caller had gone, and finished my question.

26

I thought a great deal about the system of education from which I had suffered, and believing that everybody had a philosophical defence for all that he did, I desired greatly to meet some schoolmaster that I might question him. For a moment it seemed as if I should have my desire. I had been invited to read out a poem called *The Island of Statues,* an arcadian play in imitation of Edmund Spenser, to a gathering of critics who were to decide whether it was worthy of publication in the College magazine. The magazine had already published a lyric of mine, the first ever printed, and people began to know my name. We met in the rooms of Mr. C. H. Oldham, now professor of Political Economy at our new University; and though Professor Bury, then a very young man, was to be the deciding voice, Mr. Oldham had asked quite a large audience. When the reading was over and the poem had been approved I was left alone, why I cannot remember, with a young man who was, I had been told, a schoolmaster. I was silent, gathering my courage, and he also was silent; and presently I said without anything to lead up to it, "I know you will defend the ordinary system of education by saying that it strengthens the will, but I am convinced that it only seems to do so because it weakens the impulses." Then I stopped, overtaken by shyness. He made no answer but smiled and looked surprised as though I had said, "You will say they are Persian attire; but let them be changed."

27

I had begun to frequent a club founded by Mr. Oldham, and not from natural liking, but from a secret ambition. I wished to become self-possessed, to be able to play with hostile minds as Hamlet played, to look in the lion's face, as it were, with un-quivering eyelash. In Ireland harsh argument which had gone out of fashion in England was still the manner of our conversation, and at this club Unionist and Nationalist could interrupt one another and insult one another without the formal and tradi-tional restraint of public speech. Sometimes they would change the subject and discuss Socialism, or a philosophical question, merely to discover their old passions under a new shape. I spoke easily and I thought well till some one was rude and then I would become silent or exaggerate my opinion to absurdity, or hesitate and grow confused, or be carried away myself by some party passion. I would spend hours afterwards going over my words and putting the wrong ones right. Discovering that I was only self-possessed with people I knew intimately, I would often go to a strange house where I knew I would spend a wretched hour for schooling sake. I did not discover that Hamlet had his self-possession from no schooling but from indifference and passion-conquering sweetness, and that less heroic minds can but hope it from old age.

28

I had very little money and one day the toll-taker at the metal bridge over the Liffey and a gossip of his laughed when I re-fused the halfpenny and said, "No, I will go round by O'Connell

Bridge." When I called for the first time at a house in Leinster Road several middle-aged women were playing cards and suggested my taking a hand and gave me a glass of sherry. The sherry went to my head and I was impoverished for days by the loss of sixpence. My hostess was Ellen O'Leary, who kept house for her brother John O'Leary the Fenian, the handsomest old man I had ever seen. He had been condemned to twenty years' penal servitude but had been set free after five on condition that he did not return to Ireland for fifteen years. He had said to the Government, "I will not return if Germany makes war on you, but I will return if France does." He and his old sister lived exactly opposite the Orange leader for whom he had a great respect. His sister stirred my affection at first for no better reason than her likeness of face and figure to the matron of my London school, a friendly person, but when I came to know her I found sister and brother alike were of Plutarch's people. She told me of her brother's life, of the foundation of the Fenian movement, and of the arrests that followed (I believe that her own sweetheart had somehow fallen among the wreckage), of sentences of death pronounced upon false evidence amid a public panic, and told it all without bitterness. No fanaticism could thrive amid such gentleness. She never found it hard to believe that an opponent had as high a motive as her own and needed upon her difficult road no spur of hate.

Her brother seemed very unlike on a first hearing for he had some violent oaths, "Good God in Heaven" being one of them; and if he disliked anything one said or did, he spoke all his thought, but in a little one heard his justice match her charity. "Never has there been a cause so bad," he would say, "that it has not been defended by good men for good reasons." Nor would he overvalue any man because they shared opinions; and when he lent me the poems of Davis and the Young Irelanders, of whom I had known nothing, he did not, although the poems of Davis had made him a patriot, claim that they were very good poetry.

He had the moral genius that moves all young people and moves them the more if they are repelled by those who have strict opinions and yet have lived commonplace lives. I had begun, as would any other of my training, to say violent and paradoxical things to shock provincial sobriety, and Dowden's ironical calm had come to seem but a professional pose. But here was something as spontaneous as the life of an artist. Sometimes he would say things that would have sounded well in some heroic Elizabethan play. It became my delight to rouse him to these outbursts for I was the poet in the presence of his theme. Once when I was defending an Irish politician who had made a great outcry because he was treated as a common felon, by showing that he did it for the cause's sake, he said, "There are things that a man must not do to save a nation." He would speak a sentence like that in ignorance of its passionate value, and would forget it the moment after.

I met at his house friends of later life, Katharine Tynan who still lived upon her father's farm, and Dr. Hyde, still a college student who took snuff like those Mayo county people, whose stories and songs he was writing down. One constant caller looked at me with much hostility—jealous of my favour in O'Leary's eyes perhaps, though later on he found solider reason for hostility—John F. Taylor, an obscure great orator. The other day in Dublin I overheard a man murmuring to another one of his speeches as I might some Elizabethan lyric that is in my very bones. It was delivered at some Dublin debate, some College society perhaps. The Lord Chancellor had spoken with balanced unemotional sentences, now self-complacent, now derisive. Taylor began, hesitating and stopping for words, but after speaking very badly for a little, straightened his figure and spoke as out of a dream: "I am carried to another age, a nobler society, and another Lord Chancellor is speaking. I am at the court of the first Pharaoh." Thereupon he put into the mouth of that Egyptian all his audience had listened to, but now it was spoken to the children of Israel. "If you have any spirituality as you boast, why not use our great empire to spread it through the world, why still cling to that beggarly nationality of yours? what are its history and its works weighed with those of Egypt?" Then his voice changed and sank: "I see a man at the edge of the crowd; he is standing listening there, but he will not obey"; and then with his voice rising to a cry, "had he obeyed he would never have come down the mountain carrying in his arms the Tables of the Law in the language of the outlaw."

I braved Taylor again and again as one might a savage animal as a test of courage, but always found him worse than my expectation. I would say, quoting Mill, "Oratory is heard, poetry is overheard." And he would answer, his voice full of contempt, that there was always an audience; and yet, in his moments of lofty speech, he himself was alone no matter what the crowd.

At other times his science or his Catholic orthodoxy, I never could discover which, would become enraged with my supernaturalism. I can but once remember escaping him unabashed and unconquered. I said with deliberate exaggeration at some evening party at O'Leary's, "Five out of every six people have seen a ghost"; and Taylor fell into my net with, "Well, I will ask everybody here." I managed that the first answer should come from a man who had heard a voice he believed to be that of his dead brother, and the second from a doctor's wife who had lived in a haunted house and met a man with his throat cut, whose throat as he drifted along the garden-walk "had opened and closed like the mouth of a fish." Taylor threw up his head like an angry horse, but asked no further question, and did not return to the subject that evening. If he had gone on he would have heard from everybody some like story though not all at first hand, and Miss O'Leary would have told him what happened at the death of one of the MacManus brothers, well known in the politics of Young Ireland. One brother was watching by the bed where the other lay dying and saw a strange hawk-like bird fly through the open window and alight upon the breast of the dying man. He did not dare to drive it away and it remained there, as it seemed, looking into his brother's eyes until death came, and then it flew out of the window. I think, though I am not sure, that she had the story from the watcher himself.

With O'Leary, Taylor was always, even when they differed, as they often did, gentle and deferential, but once only, and that was years afterwards, did I think that he was about to include me among his friends. We met by chance in a London street and he stopped me with an abrupt movement: "Yeats," he said, "I have been thinking. If you and . . . (naming another aversion), were born in a small Italian principality in the Middle Ages, he would have friends at court and you would be in exile with a price on your head." He went off without another word, and the next time we met he was no less offensive than before. He, imprisoned in himself, and not the always unperturbed O'Leary comes before me as the tragic figure of my youth. The same passion for all moral and physical splendour that drew him to O'Leary would make him beg leave to wear, for some few days, a friend's ring or pin, and gave him a heart that every pretty woman set on fire. I doubt if he was happy in his loves; for those his powerful intellect had fascinated were, I believe, repelled by his coarse red hair, his gaunt ungainly body, his stiff movements as of a Dutch doll, his badly rolled, shabby umbrella. And yet with women, as with O'Leary, he was gentle, deferential, almost diffident.

A young Ireland Society met in the lecture hall of a workman's club in York Street with O'Leary for president, and there four or five university students and myself and occasionally Taylor spoke on Irish history or literature. When Taylor spoke, it was a great event, and his delivery in the course of a speech or lecture of some political verse by Thomas Davis gave me a conviction of how great might be the effect of verse, spoken by a man almost rhythm-drunk, at some moment of intensity, the apex of long mounting thought. Verses that seemed when one saw them upon the page flat and empty caught from that voice, whose beauty was half in its harsh strangeness, nobility and style. My father had always read verse with an equal intensity and a greater subtlety, but this art was public and his private, and it is Taylor's voice that has rung in my ears and awakens my longing when I have heard some player speak lines, "so naturally," as a famous player said to me, "that nobody can find out that it is verse at all." I made a good many speeches, more I believe as a training for self-possession than from desire of speech.

Once our debates roused a passion that came to the newspapers and the streets. There was an excitable man who had fought for the Pope against the Italian patriots and who always rode a white horse in our Nationalist processions. He got on badly with O'Leary who had told him that "attempting to oppress others was a poor preparation for liberating your own country." O'Leary had written some letter to the press condemning the "Irish-American Dynamite Party" as it was called, and defining the limits of "honourable warfare." At the next meeting, the papal soldier rose in the middle of the discussion on some other matter and moved a vote of censure on O'Leary. "I myself," he said, "do not approve of bombs, but I do not think that any Irishman should be discouraged." O'Leary ruled him out of order. He refused to obey and remained standing. Those round him began to threaten. He swung the chair he had been sitting on round his head and defied everybody. However he was seized from all sides and thrown out, and a special meeting called to expel him. He wrote letters to the papers and addressed a crowd somewhere. "No Young Ireland Society," he protested, "could expel a man whose grandfather had been hanged in 1798." When the night of the special meeting came his expulsion was moved, but before the vote could be taken an excited man announced that there was a crowd in the street, that the papal soldier was making a speech, that in a moment we should be attacked. Three or four of us ran and put our backs to the door while others carried on the debate. It was an inner door with narrow glass windows at each side and through these we could see the street-door and the crowd in the street. Presently a man asked us through the crack in the door if we would as a favour "leave the crowd to the workman's club upstairs." In a couple of minutes there was a great noise of sticks and broken glass, and after that our landlord came to find out who was to pay for the hall-lamp.

29

From these debates, from O'Leary's conversation, and from the Irish books he lent or gave me has come all I have set my hand to since. I had begun to know a great deal about the Irish poets who had written in English. I read with excitement books I should find unreadable to-day, and found romance in lives that had neither wit nor adventure. I did not deceive myself, I knew how often they wrote a cold and abstract language, and yet I who had never wanted to see the houses where Keats and Shelley lived would ask everybody what sort of place Inchedony was, because Callanan had named after it a bad poem in the manner of *Childe Harold*. Walking home from a debate, I remember saying to some college student, "Ireland cannot put from her the habits learned from her old military civilisation and from a church that prays in Latin. Those popular poets have not touched her heart, her poetry when it comes will be distinguished and lonely." O'Leary had once said to me, "Neither Ireland nor England knows the good from the bad in any art, but Ireland unlike England does not hate the good when it is pointed out to her." I began to plot and scheme how one might seal with the right image the soft wax before it began to harden. I had noticed that Irish Catholics among whom had been born so many political martyrs had not the good taste, the household courtesy and decency of the Protestant Ireland I had known, yet Protestant Ireland seemed to think of nothing but getting on in the world. I thought we might bring the halves together if we had a national literature that made Ireland beautiful in the memory, and yet had been freed from provincialism by an exacting criticism, an European pose.

30

Some one at the Young Ireland Society gave me a newspaper that I might read some article or letter. I began idly reading verses describing the shore of Ireland as seen by a returning, dying emigrant. My eyes filled with tears and yet I knew the verses were badly written—vague, abstract words such as one finds in a newspaper. I looked at the end and saw the name of some political exile who had died but a few days after his return to Ireland. They had moved me because they contained the actual thoughts of a man at a passionate moment of life, and when I met my father I was full of the discovery. We should write out our own thoughts in as nearly as possible the language we thought them in, as though in a letter to an intimate friend. We should not disguise them in any way; for our lives give them force as the lives of people in plays give force to their words. Personal utterance, which had almost ceased in English literature, could be as fine an escape from rhetoric and abstraction as drama itself. But my father would hear of nothing but drama; personal utterance was only egotism. I knew it was not, but as yet did not know how to explain the difference. I tried from that on to write out of my emotions exactly as they came to me in life, not changing them to make them more beautiful. "If I can be sincere and make my language natural, and without becoming discursive, like a novelist, and so indiscreet and prosaic," I said to myself, "I shall, if good luck or bad luck make my life interesting, be a great poet; for it will be no longer a matter of literature at all." Yet when I re-read those early poems which gave me so much trouble, I find little but romantic convention, unconscious drama. It is so many years before one can believe enough in what one feels even to know what the feeling is.

31

Perhaps a year before we returned to London, a Catholic friend brought me to a spiritualistic séance at the house of a young man lately arrested under a suspicion of Fenianism, but released for lack of evidence. He and his friends had been sitting weekly about a table in the hope of spiritual manifestation and one had developed mediumship. A drawer full of books had leaped out of the table when no one was touching it, a picture had moved upon the wall. There were some half-dozen of us, and our host began by making passes until the medium fell asleep sitting upright in his chair. Then the lights were turned out, and we sat waiting in the dim light of a fire. Presently my shoulders began to twitch and my hands. I could easily have stopped them, but I had never heard of such a thing and I was curious. After a few minutes the movement became violent and I stopped it. I sat motionless for a while and then my whole body moved like a suddenly unrolled watch-spring, and I was thrown backward on the wall. I again stilled the movement and sat at the table. Everybody began to say I was a medium, and that if I would not resist some wonderful thing would happen. I remembered that Balzac had once desired to take opium for the experience' sake, but would not because he dreaded the surrender of his will. We were now holding each other's hands and presently my right hand banged the knuckles of the woman next to me upon the table. She laughed, and the medium, speaking for the first time, and with difficulty, out of his mesmeric sleep, said, "Tell her there is great danger." He stood up and began walking round me making movements with his hands as though he were pushing something away. I was now struggling vainly with this force which compelled me to movements I had not willed, and my movements became so violent that the table was broken. I tried to pray, and because I could not remember a prayer, repeated in a loud voice—

> "Of Man's first disobedience and the fruit
> Of that forbidden tree whose mortal taste
> Brought death into the world and all our woe . . .
> Sing heavenly muse."

My Catholic friend had left the table and was saying a Pater Noster and Ave Maria in the corner. Presently all became still and so dark that I could not see anybody. I described it to somebody next day as like going out of a noisy political meeting on to a quiet country road. I said to myself, "I am now in a trance but I no longer have any desire to resist." But when I turned my eyes to the fireplace I could see a faint gleam of light, so I thought, "No, I am not in a trance." Then I saw shapes faintly appearing in the darkness and thought, "They are spirits"; but they were only the spiritualists and my friend at her prayers. The medium said in a faint voice, "We are through the bad spirits." I said, "Will they ever come again do you think?" and he said, "No, never again I think," and in my boyish vanity I thought it was I who had banished them.

For years afterwards I would not go to a séance or turn a table and would often ask myself what was that violent impulse that had run through my nerves? was it a part of myself—something always to be a danger perhaps; or had it come from without, as it seemed?

32

I had published my first book of poems by subscription, O'Leary finding many subscribers, and a book of stories, when I heard that my grandmother was dead and went to Sligo for the funeral. She had asked to see me but by some mistake I was not sent for. She had heard that I was much about with a beautiful, admired woman and feared that I did not speak of marriage because I was poor, and wanted to say to me, "Women care nothing about money." My grandfather was dying also and only survived her a few weeks. I went to see him and wondered at his handsome face now sickness had refined it, and noticed that he foretold the changes in the weather by indications of the light and of the temperature that would have meant nothing to another. As I sat there my old childish fear returned and I was glad to get away. I stayed with my uncle whose house was opposite where my grandfather lived, and walking home one day we met the doctor. The doctor said there was no hope and that my grandfather should be told, but my uncle would not allow it. He said, "It would make a man mad to know he was dying." In vain the doctor pleaded that he had never known a man not made calmer by the knowledge. I listened sad and angry, but my uncle always took a low view of human nature, his very tolerance which was exceedingly great came from his hoping nothing of anybody. Before he had given way my grandfather lifted up his arms and cried out, "There she is," and fell backward dead. Before he was dead, old servants of that house where there had never been noise or disorder began their small pilferings, and after his death there was a quarrel over the disposition of certain mantelpiece ornaments of no value.

33

For some months now I have lived with my own youth and childhood, not always writing indeed but thinking of it almost every day, and I am sorrowful and disturbed. It is not that I have accomplished too few of my plans, for I am not ambitious; but when I think of all the books I have read, and of the wise words I have heard spoken, and of the anxiety I have given to parents and grandparents, and of the hopes that I have had, all life weighed in the scales of my own life seems to me a preparation for something that never happens.

The Trembling
of the Veil

To John Quinn
my friend and helper
and friend and helper of certain people
mentioned in this book

PREFACE

I have found in an old diary a saying from Stephane Mallarmé, that his epoch was troubled by the trembling of the veil of the Temple. As those words were still true, during the years of my life described in this book, I have chosen The Trembling of the Veil for its title.

Except in one or two trivial details, where I have the warrant of old friendship, I have not, without permission, quoted conversation or described occurrence from the private life of named or recognisable living persons. I have not felt my freedom abated, for most of the friends of my youth are dead and over the dead I have an historian's rights. They were artists and writers and certain among them men of genius, and the life of a man of genius, because of his greater sincerity, is often an experiment that needs analysis and record. At least my generation so valued personality that it thought so. I have said all the good I know and all the evil: I have kept nothing back necessary to understanding.

W. B. YEATS.

Thoor Ballylee.
May 1922.

BOOK I

Four Years: 1887–1891

I

At the end of the 'Eighties my father and mother, my brother and sisters and myself, all newly arrived from Dublin, were settled in Bedford Park in a red-brick house with several mantelpieces of wood, copied from marble mantelpieces designed by the brothers Adam, a balcony and a little garden shadowed by a great horse-chestnut tree. Years before we had lived there, when the crooked ostentatiously picturesque streets with great trees casting great shadows had been a new enthusiasm: the pre-Raphaelite movement at last affecting life. But now exaggerated criticism had taken the place of enthusiasm, the tiled roofs, the first in modern London, were said to leak, which they did not, and the drains to be bad, though that was no longer true; and I imagine that houses were cheap. I remember feeling disappointed because the co-operative stores, with their little seventeenth-century panes, had lost the romance I saw there when I passed them still unfinished on my way to school; and because the public-house, called The Tabard after Chaucer's Inn, was so plainly a common public-house; and because the great sign of a trumpeter designed by Rooke, the pre-Raphaelite artist, had been freshened by some inferior hand. The big red-brick church had never pleased me, and I was accustomed, when I saw the wooden balustrade that ran along the slanting edge of the roof where nobody ever walked or could walk, to remember the opinion of some architect friend of my father's, that it had been put there to keep the birds from falling off. Still, however, it had some village characters and helped us to feel not wholly lost in the metropolis. I no longer went to church as a regular habit, but go I sometimes did, for one Sunday morning I saw these words painted on a board in the porch: "The congregation are requested to kneel during prayers; the kneelers are afterwards to be hung upon pegs provided for the purpose." In front of every seat hung a little cushion and these cushions were called "kneelers." Presently the joke ran through the community, where there were many artists who considered religion at best an unimportant accessory to good architecture and who disliked that particular church.

2

I could not understand where the charm had gone that I had felt, when as a schoolboy of twelve or thirteen I had played among the unfinished houses, once leaving the marks of my two hands, blacked by a fall among some paint, upon a white balustrade. Yet I was in all things pre-Raphaelite. When I was fifteen or sixteen my father had told me about Rossetti and Blake and given me their poetry to read; and once at Liverpool on my way to Sligo I had seen Dante's *Dream* in the gallery there, a picture painted when Rossetti had lost his dramatic power and to-day not very pleasing to me, and its colour, its people, its romantic architecture had blotted all other pictures away. It was a perpetual bewilderment that when my father, moved perhaps by some memory of his youth, chose some theme from poetic tradition, he would soon weary and leave it unfinished. I had seen the change coming bit by bit and its defence elaborated by young men fresh from the Paris art schools. "We must paint what is in front of us," or "A man must be of his own time," they would say, and if I spoke of Blake or Rossetti they would point out his bad drawing and tell me to admire Carolus Duran and Bastien-Lepage. Then, too, they were very ignorant men; they read nothing, for nothing mattered but "knowing how to paint," being in reaction against a generation that seemed to have wasted its time upon so many things. I thought myself alone in hating these young men, their contempt for the past, their monopoly of the future, but in a few months I was to discover others of my own age, who thought as I did, for it is not true that youth looks before it with the mechanical gaze of a well-drilled soldier. Its quarrel is not with the past, but with the present, where its elders are so obviously powerful and no cause seems lost if it seem to threaten that power. Does cultivated youth ever really love the future, where the eye can discover no persecuted Royalty hidden among oak leaves, though from it certainly does come so much proletarian rhetoric?

I was unlike others of my generation in one thing only. I am very religious, and deprived by Huxley and Tyndall, whom I detested, of the simple-minded religion of my childhood, I had made a new religion, almost an infallible church of poetic tradition, of a fardel of stories, and of personages, and of emotions, inseparable from their first expression, passed on from generation to generation by poets and painters with some help from philosophers and theologians. I wished for a world, where I could discover this tradition perpetually, and not in pictures and in poems only, but in tiles round the chimney-piece and in the hangings that kept out the draft. I had even created a dogma: "Because those imaginary people are created out of the deepest instinct of man, to be his measure and his norm, whatever I can imagine those mouths speaking may be the nearest I can go to truth." When I listened they seemed always to speak of one thing only: they, their loves, every incident of their lives, were steeped in the supernatural. Could even Titian's "Ariosto" that I loved beyond other portraits have its grave look, as if waiting for some perfect final event, if the painters before Titian had not learned portraiture, while painting into the corner of compositions full of saints and Madonnas, their kneeling patrons? At seventeen years old I was already an old-fashioned brass cannon full of shot, and nothing had kept me from going off but a doubt as to my capacity to shoot straight.

3

I was not an industrious student and knew only what I had found by accident and I found nothing I cared for after Titian, and Titian I knew from an imitation of his *Supper of Emmaus* in Dublin, till Blake and the pre-Raphaelites; and among my father's friends were no pre-Raphaelites. Some indeed had come to Bedford Park in the enthusiasm of the first building and others to be near those that had. There was Todhunter, a well-off man who had bought my father's pictures while my father was still pre-Raphaelite; once a Dublin doctor he was now a poet and a writer of poetical plays; a tall, sallow, lank, melancholy man, a good scholar and a good intellect; and with him my father carried on a warm exasperated friendship, fed I think by old memories and wasted by quarrels over matters of opinion. Of all the survivors he was the most dejected and the least estranged, and I remember encouraging him, with a sense of worship shared, to buy a very expensive carpet designed by Morris. He displayed it without strong liking and would have agreed had there been any to find fault. If he had liked anything strongly he might have been a famous man, for a few years later he was to write, under some casual patriotic impulse, certain excellent verses now in all Irish anthologies; but with him every book was a new planting, and not a new bud on an old bough. He had I think no peace in himself. But my father's chief friend was York Powell, a famous Oxford Professor of history, a broad-built, broad-headed, brown-bearded man clothed in heavy blue cloth and looking, but for his glasses and the dim sight of a student, like some captain in the merchant service. One often passed with pleasure from Todhunter's company to that of one who was almost ostentatiously at peace. He cared nothing for philosophy, nothing for economics, nothing for the policy of nations; for history, as he saw it, was a memory of men who were amusing or exciting to think about. He impressed all who met him, seemed to some a man of genius, but had not enough ambition to shape his thought, nor enough conviction to give rhythm to his style and remained always a poor writer. I was too full of unfinished speculations and premature convictions to value rightly his conversation, informed by a vast erudition, which would give itself to every casual association of speech and company, precisely because he had neither cause nor design. My father, however, found Powell's concrete narrative manner in talk a necessary completion of his own, and when I asked him in a letter many years later where he got his philosophy replied "From York Powell" and thereon added, no doubt remembering that Powell was without ideas, "by looking at him." Then there was a good listener, a painter in whose hall hung a big picture painted in his student days of Ulysses sailing home from the Phaeacian court, an orange and a skin of wine at his side, blue mountains towering behind; but who lived by drawing domestic scenes and lovers' meetings for a weekly magazine that had an immense circulation among the imperfectly educated. To escape the boredom of work, which he never turned to but under pressure of necessity and usually late at night, with the publisher's messenger in the hall, he had half-filled his studio with mechanical toys of his own invention, and perpetually increased their number. A model railway train at intervals puffed its way along the walls, passing several railway stations and signal-boxes; and on the floor lay a camp with attacking and defending soldiers and a fortification that blew up when the attackers fired a pea through a certain window; while a large model of a Thames barge hung from the ceiling. Opposite our house lived an old artist who worked also for the illustrated papers for a living, but painted landscapes for his pleasure, and of him I remember nothing except that he had outlived ambition, was a good listener, and that my father explained his gaunt appearance by his descent from Pocahontas. If all these men were a little like becalmed ships, there was certainly one man whose sails were full. Three or four doors off on our side of the road lived a decorative artist in all the naïve confidence of popular ideals and the public approval. He was our daily comedy. "I myself and Sir Frederick Leighton are the greatest decorative artists of the age," was among his sayings, and to show that he at any rate knew nothing of discouragement a great Lychgate, bought from some country churchyard, reared its thatched roof, meant to shelter bearers and coffin, above the entrance to his front garden. In this fairly numerous company—there were others though no other face rises before me—my father and York Powell found listeners for a conversation that had no special loyalties, or antagonisms; while I could only talk upon set topics, being in the heat of my youth, and the topics that filled me with excitement were never spoken of.

4

Bedford Park had a red-brick clubhouse with a little theatre that began to stir my imagination. I persuaded Todhunter to write a pastoral play and have it performed there.

A couple of years before, while we were still in Dublin, he had given at Hengler's Circus, remodelled as a Greek Theatre, a most expensive performance of his *Helena of Troas*, an oratorical Swinburnian play which I had thought as unactable as it was unreadable. Since I was seventeen I had constantly tested my own ambition with Keats's praise of him who "left great verses to a little clan," so it was but natural that I should persuade him for the moment that we had nothing to do with the great public, that it should be a point of honour to be content with our own little public, that he should write of shepherds and shepherdesses because people would expect them to talk poetry and move without melodrama. He wrote his *Sicilian Idyll*, which I have not looked at for thirty years, and never rated very high as poetry, and had the one unmistakable success of his life. The little theatre was full for twice the number of performances intended, for artists, men of letters and students had come from all over London.

I made through these performances a close friend and a discovery that was to influence my life. Todhunter had engaged several professional actors with a little reputation, but had given the chief woman's part to Florence Farr, who had qualities no contemporary professional practice could have increased, the chief man's part to an amateur, Heron Allen, solicitor, fiddler and popular writer on palmistry. Heron Allen and Florence Farr read poetry for their pleasure. While they were upon the stage no one else could hold an eye or an ear. Their speech was music, the poetry acquired a nobility, a passionate austerity that made it akin for certain moments to the great poetry of the world. Heron Allen, who had never spoken in public before except to lecture upon the violin, had the wisdom to reduce his acting to a series of poses, to be the stately shepherd with not more gesture than was needed to "twitch his mantle blue" and to let his grace be foil to Florence Farr's more impassioned delivery. When they closed their mouths, and some other player opened his, breaking up the verse to make it conversational, jerking his body or his arms that he might seem no austere poetical image but very man, I listened in raging hatred. I kept my seat with difficulty, I searched my memory for insulting phrases, I even muttered them to myself that the people about might hear. I had discovered for the first time that in the performance of all drama that depends for its effect upon beauty of language, poetical culture may be more important than professional experience.

Florence Farr lived in lodgings some twenty minutes' walk away at Brook Green, and I was soon a constant caller, talking over plays that I would some day write her. She had three great gifts, a tranquil beauty like that of Demeter's image near the British Museum reading-room door, and an incomparable sense of rhythm and a beautiful voice, the seeming natural expression of the image. And yet there was scarce another gift that she did not value above those three. We all have our simplifying image, our genius, and such hard burden does it lay upon us that, but for the praise of others, we would deride it and hunt it away. She could only express hers through an unfashionable art, an art that has scarce existed since the seventeenth century, and so could only earn unimportant occasional praise. She would dress without care or calculation as if to hide her beauty and seem contemptuous of its power. If a man fell in love with her she would notice that she had seen just that movement upon the stage or had heard just that intonation and all seemed unreal. If she read out some poem in English or in French all was passion, all a traditional splendour, but she spoke of actual things with a cold wit or under the strain of paradox. Wit and paradox alike sought to pull down whatever had tradition or passion and she was soon to spend her days in the British Museum reading-room and become erudite in many heterogeneous studies moved by an insatiable, destroying curiosity. I formed with her an enduring friendship that was an enduring exasperation—"why do you play the part with a bent back and a squeak in the voice? How can you be a character actor, you who hate all our life, you who belong to a life that is a vision?" But argument was no use, and some Nurse in Euripides must be played with all an old woman's infirmities and not as I would have it, with all a Sybil's majesty, because "it is no use doing what nobody wants," or because she would show that she "could do what the others did."

I used in my rage to compare her thoughts, when her worst mood was upon her, to a game called Spillikens which I had seen played in my childhood with little pieces of bone that you had to draw out with a hook from a bundle of like pieces. A bundle of bones instead of Demeter's golden sheaf! Her sitting-room at the Brook Green lodging-house was soon a reflection of her mind, the walls covered with musical instruments, pieces of oriental drapery, and Egyptian gods and goddesses painted by herself in the British Museum.

5

Presently a hansom drove up to our door at Bedford Park with Miss Maud Gonne, who brought an introduction to my father from old John O'Leary, the Fenian leader. She vexed my father by praise of war, war for its own sake, not as the creator of certain virtues but as if there were some virtue in excitement itself. I supported her against my father, which vexed him the more, though he might have understood that, apart from the fact that Carolus Duran and Bastien-Lepage were somehow involved, a man young as I could not have differed from a woman so beautiful and so young. To-day, with her great height and the unchangeable lineaments of her form, she looks the Sybil I would have had played by Florence Farr, but in that day she seemed a classical impersonation of the Spring, the Virgilian commendation "She walks like a goddess" made for her alone. Her complexion was luminous, like that of apple blossoms through which the light falls, and I remember her standing that first day by a great heap of such blossoms in the window. In the next few years I saw her always when she passed to and fro between Dublin and Paris, surrounded, no matter how rapid her journey and how brief her stay at either end of it, by cages full of birds, canaries, finches of all kinds, dogs, a parrot, and once a full-grown hawk from Donegal. Once when I saw her to her railway carriage I noticed how the cages obstructed wraps and cushions and wondered what her fellow-travellers would say but the carriage remained empty. It was years before I could see into the mind that lay hidden under so much beauty and so much energy.

6

Some quarter of an hour's walk from Bedford Park, out on the high road to Richmond, lived W. E. Henley, and I, like many others, began under him my education. His portrait, a lithograph by Rothenstein, hangs over my mantelpiece among portraits of other friends. He is drawn standing, but doubtless because of his crippled legs he leans forward, resting his elbows upon some slightly suggested object—a table or a window-sill. His heavy figure and powerful head, the disordered hair standing upright, his short irregular beard and moustache, his lined and wrinkled face, his eyes steadily fixed upon some object, in complete confidence and self-possession, and yet as in half-broken reverie, all are there exactly as I remember him. I have seen other portraits and they too show him exactly as I remember him, as though he had but one appearance and that seen fully at the first glance and by all alike. He was most human—human I used to say like one of Shakespeare's characters—and yet pressed and pummelled, as it were, into a single attitude, almost into a gesture and a speech as by some overwhelming situation. I disagreed with him about everything, but I admired him beyond words. With the exception of some early poems founded upon old French models I disliked his poetry, mainly because he wrote in *vers libre,* which I associated with Tyndall and Huxley, and Bastien-Lepage's clownish peasant staring with vacant eyes at her great boots; and filled it with unimpassioned description of an hospital ward where his leg had been amputated. I wanted the strongest passions, passions that had nothing to do with observation, and metrical forms that seemed old enough to have been sung by men half-asleep or riding upon a journey. Furthermore, pre-Raphaelism affected him as some people are affected by a cat in the room, and though he professed himself at our first meeting without political interests or convictions, he soon grew into a violent unionist and imperialist. I used to say when I spoke of his poems: "He is like a great actor with a bad part; yet who would look at Hamlet in the grave scene if Salvini played the grave-digger?" and I might so have explained much that he said and did. I meant that he was like a great actor of passion—character-acting meant nothing to me for many years—and an actor of passion will display some one quality of soul, personified again and again, just as a great poetical painter, Titian, Botticelli, Rossetti, may depend for his greatness upon a type of beauty which presently we call by his name. Irving, the last of the sort on the

English stage, and in modern England and France it is the rarest sort, never moved me but in the expression of intellectual pride and though I saw Salvini but once I am convinced that his genius was a kind of animal nobility. Henley, half inarticulate—"I am very costive," he would say—beset with personal quarrels, built up an image of power and magnanimity till it became, at moments, when seen as it were by lightning, his true self. Half his opinions were the contrivance of a subconsciousness that sought always to bring life to the dramatic crisis and expression to that point of artifice where the true self could find its tongue. Without opponents there had been no drama, and in his youth Ruskinism and pre-Raphaelitism, for he was of my father's generation, were the only possible opponents. How could one resent his prejudice when, that he himself might play a worthy part, he must find beyond the common rout, whom he derided and flouted daily, opponents he could imagine moulded like himself? Once he said to me in the height of his imperial propaganda, "Tell those young men in Ireland that this great thing must go on. They say Ireland is not fit for self-government, but that is nonsense. It is as fit as any other European country, but we cannot grant it." And then he spoke of his desire to found and edit a Dublin newspaper. It would have expounded the Gaelic propaganda then beginning, though Dr. Hyde had, as yet, no league, our old stories, our modern literature—everything that did not demand any shred or patch of government. He dreamed of a tyranny, but it was that of Cosimo de' Medici.

7

We gathered on Sunday evenings in two rooms, with folding doors between, and hung, I think, with photographs from Dutch masters, and in one room there was always, I think, a table with cold meat. I can recall but one elderly man—Dunn his name was—rather silent and full of good sense, an old friend of Henley's. We were young men, none as yet established in his own, or in the world's opinion, and Henley was our leader and our confidant. One evening, I found him alone amused and exasperated: "Young A——," he cried, "has just been round to ask my advice. Would I think it a wise thing if he bolted with Mrs.

B——? 'Have you quite determined to do it?' I asked him. 'Quite.'
'Well,' I said, 'in that case I refuse to give you any advice.'"
Mrs. B—— was a beautiful talented woman, who, as the Welsh
Triad said of Guinevere, "was much given to being carried off."
I think we listened to him, and often obeyed him, partly because
he was quite plainly not upon the side of our parents. We might
have a different ground of quarrel, but the result seemed more
important than the ground, and his confident manner and speech
made us believe, perhaps for the first time, in victory. And besides, if he did denounce, and in my case he certainly did, what
we held in secret reverence, he never failed to associate it with
things or persons that did not move us to reverence. Once I found
him just returned from some art congress in Liverpool or in Man-
chester. "The salvation armyism of art," he called it, and gave a
grotesque description of some city councillor he had found admiring Turner. He, who hated all that Ruskin praised, thereupon had derided Turner, and finding the city councillor the
next day on the other side of the gallery, admiring some pre-
Raphaelite there, derided that pre-Raphaelite. The third day
Henley discovered the poor man on a chair in the middle of the
room staring disconsolately upon the floor. He terrified us also
and certainly I did not dare, and I think none of us dared, to
speak our admiration for book or picture he condemned, but he
made us feel always our importance, and no man among us
could do good work, or show the promise of it, and lack his
praise. I can remember meeting of a Sunday night Charles
Whibley, Kenneth Grahame, author of *The Golden Age,* Barry
Pain, now a well-known novelist, R. A. M. Stevenson, art critic
and a famous talker, George Wyndham, later on a cabinet minister and Irish chief secretary, and now or later Oscar Wilde,
who was some ten years older than the rest of us. But faces and
names are vague to me and while faces that I met but once may
rise clearly before me, a face met on many a Sunday has perhaps vanished. Kipling came sometimes, I think, but I never met
him; and Stepniak, the Nihilist, whom I knew well elsewhere
but not there, said—"I cannot go more than once a year, it is
too exhausting." Henley got the best out of us all, because he
had made us accept him as our judge and we knew that his judgment could neither sleep, nor be softened, nor changed, nor

turned aside. When I think of him, the antithesis that is the foundation of human nature being ever in my sight, I see his crippled legs as though he were some Vulcan perpetually forging swords for other men to use; and certainly I always thought of C——, a fine classical scholar, a pale and seemingly gentle man, as our chief swordsman and bravo. When Henley founded his weekly newspaper, first the *Scots,* afterwards the *National Observer,* this young man wrote articles and reviews notorious for savage wit; and years afterwards when the *National Observer* was dead, Henley dying, and our cavern of outlaws empty, I met him in Paris very sad and I think very poor. "Nobody will employ me now," he said. "Your master is gone," I answered, "and you are like the spear in an old Irish story that had to be kept dipped in poppy-juice that it might not go about killing people on its own account." I wrote my first good lyrics and tolerable essays for the *National Observer,* and as I always signed my work could go my own road in some measure. Henley often revised my lyrics, crossing out a line or a stanza and writing in one of his own, and I was comforted by my belief that he also rewrote Kipling then in the first flood of popularity. At first, indeed, I was ashamed of being rewritten and thought that others were not, and only began investigation when the editorial characteristics—epigrams, archaisms, and all—appeared in the article upon Paris fashions and in that upon opium by an Egyptian Pasha. I was not compelled to full conformity for verse is plainly stubborn; and in prose, that I might avoid unacceptable opinions, I wrote nothing but ghost or fairy stories, picked up from my mother or some pilot at Rosses Point and Henley saw that I must needs mix a palette fitted to my subject matter. But if he had changed every "has" into "hath" I would have let him, for had not we sunned ourselves in his generosity? "My young men outdo me and they write better than I," he wrote in some letter praising Charles Whibley's work, and to another friend with a copy of my *Man Who Dreamed of Fairyland*: "See what a fine thing has been written by one of my lads."

8

My first meeting with Oscar Wilde was an astonishment. I never before heard a man talking with perfect sentences, as if he had written them all overnight with labour and yet all spontaneous. There was present that night at Henley's, by right of propinquity or of accident, a man full of the secret spite of dullness, who interrupted from time to time, and always to check or disorder thought; and I noticed with what mastery he was foiled and thrown. I noticed, too, that the impression of artificiality that I think all Wilde's listeners have recorded came from the perfect rounding of the sentences and from the deliberation that made it possible. That very impression helped him, as the effect of metre, or of the antithetical prose of the seventeenth century, which is itself a true metre, helped its writers, for he could pass without incongruity from some unforeseen, swift stroke of wit to elaborate reverie. I heard him say a few nights later: "Give me *The Winter's Tale*, 'Daffodils that come before the swallow dare' but not *King Lear*. What is *King Lear* but poor life staggering in the fog?" and the slow, carefully modulated cadence sounded natural to my ears. That first night he praised Walter Pater's *Studies in the History of the Renaissance*: "It is my golden book; I never travel anywhere without it; but it is the very flower of decadence: the last trumpet should have sounded the moment it was written." "But," said the dull man, "would you not have given us time to read it?" "Oh no," was the retort, "there would have been plenty of time afterwards— in either world." I think he seemed to us, baffled as we were by youth, or by infirmity, a triumphant figure, and to some of us a figure from another age, an audacious Italian fifteenth-century figure. A few weeks before I had heard one of my father's friends, an official in a publishing firm that had employed both Wilde and Henley as editors, blaming Henley who was "no use except under control" and praising Wilde, "so indolent but such a genius"; and now the firm became the topic of our talk. "How often do you go to the office?" said Henley. "I used to go three times a week," said Wilde, "for an hour a day but I have since struck off one of the days." "My God," said Henley, "I went five times a week for five hours a day and when I wanted to strike off a day they had a special committee meeting." "Furthermore," was Wilde's answer, "I never answered their letters. I have known men come to London full of bright prospects and seen them complete wrecks in a few months through a habit of answering letters." He too knew how to keep our elders in their place, and his method was plainly the more successful, for Henley had been dismissed. "No he is not an aesthete," Henley commented later, being somewhat embarrassed by Wilde's pre-Raphaelite entanglement; "one soon finds that he is a scholar and a gentleman." And when I dined with Wilde a few days afterwards he began at once, "I had to strain every nerve to equal that man at all"; and I was too loyal to speak my thought: "You and not he said all the brilliant things." He like the rest of us had felt the strain of an intensity that seemed to hold life at the point of drama. He had said on that first meeting, "The basis of literary friendship is mixing the poisoned bowl"; and for a few weeks Henley and he became close friends till, the astonishment of their meeting over, diversity of character and ambition pushed them apart, and, with half the cavern helping, Henley began mixing the poisoned bowl for Wilde. Yet Henley never wholly lost that first admiration, for after Wilde's downfall he said to me: "Why did he do it? I told my lads to attack him and yet we might have fought under his banner."

9

It became the custom, both at Henley's and at Bedford Park, to say that R. A. M. Stevenson, who frequented both circles, was the better talker. Wilde had been trussed up like a turkey by undergraduates, dragged up and down a hill, his champagne emptied into the ice tub, hooted in the streets of various towns, and I think stoned, and no newspaper named him but in scorn; his manner had hardened to meet opposition and at times he allowed one to see an unpardonable insolence. His charm was acquired and systematised, a mask which he wore only when it pleased him, while the charm of Stevenson belonged to him like the colour of his hair. If Stevenson's talk became monologue we did not know it, because our one object was to show by our attention that he need never leave off. If thought failed him we would not combat what he had said, or start some new theme, but would encourage him with a question; and one felt that it had been always so from childhood up. His mind was full of fantasy for fantasy's sake and he gave us good entertainment in monologue as his cousin Robert Louis in poem or story. He was always "supposing"; "Suppose you had two millions what would you do with it?" and "Suppose you were in Spain and in love how would you propose?" I recall him one afternoon at our house at Bedford Park, surrounded by my brother and sisters and a little group of my father's friends, describing proposals in a half dozen countries. There your father did it, dressed in such and such a way with such and such words, and there a friend must wait for the lady outside the chapel door, sprinkle her with holy water and say, "My friend Jones is dying for love of you." But when it was over those quaint descriptions, so full of laughter and sympathy, faded or remained in the memory as something alien from one's own life, like a dance I once saw in a great house, where beautifully dressed children wound a long ribbon in and out as they danced. I was not of Stevenson's party mainly I think because he had written a book in praise of Velasquez, praise at that time universal wherever pre-Raphaelism was accurst, and to my mind, that had to pick its symbols where its ignorance permitted, Velasquez seemed the first bored celebrant of boredom. I was convinced from some obscure meditation that Stevenson's conversational method had joined him to my elders and to the indifferent world, as though it were right for old men, and unambitious men and all women, to be content with charm and humour. It was the prerogative of youth to take sides and when Wilde said: "Mr. Bernard Shaw has no enemies but is intensely disliked by all his friends," I knew it to be a phrase I should never forget, and felt revenged upon a notorious hater of romance, whose generosity and courage I could not fathom.

10

I saw a good deal of Wilde at that time—was it 1887 or 1888? —I have no way of fixing the date except that I had published my first book *The Wanderings of Usheen* and that Wilde had not yet published his *Decay of Lying*. He had, before our first meeting, reviewed my book and despite its vagueness of intention, and the inexactness of its speech, praised without qualification; and what was worth more than any review he had talked about it; and now he asked me to eat my Christmas dinner with him believing, I imagine, that I was alone in London. He had just renounced his velveteen, and even those cuffs turned backward over the sleeves, and had begun to dress very carefully in the fashion of the moment. He lived in a little house at Chelsea that the architect Godwin had decorated with an elegance that owed something to Whistler. There was nothing mediæval, nor pre-Raphaelite, no cupboard door with figures upon flat gold, no peacock-blue, no dark background. I remember vaguely a white drawing-room with Whistler etchings, "let in" to white panels, and a dining-room all white, chairs, walls, mantelpiece, carpet, except for a diamond-shaped piece of red cloth in the middle of the table under a terra-cotta statuette, and I think a red-shaded lamp hanging from the ceiling to a little above the statuette. It was perhaps too perfect in its unity, his past of a few years before had gone too completely, and I remember thinking that the perfect harmony of his life there, with his beautiful wife and his two young children, suggested some deliberate artistic composition.

He commended and dispraised himself during dinner by attributing characteristics like his own to his country: "We Irish are too poetical to be poets; we are a nation of brilliant failures, but we are the greatest talkers since the Greeks." When dinner was over he read me from the proofs of the *Decay of Lying* and when he came to the sentence: "Schopenhauer has analysed the pessimism that characterises modern thought, but Hamlet invented it. The world has become sad because a puppet was once melancholy," I said, "Why do you change 'sad' to 'melancholy'?" He replied that he wanted a full sound at the close of his sentence, and I thought it no excuse and an example of the vague impressiveness that spoilt his writing for me. Only when he spoke, or when his writing was the mirror of his speech, or in some simple fairy tale, had he words exact enough to hold a subtle ear. He alarmed me, though not as Henley did, for I never left his house thinking myself fool or dunce. He flattered the intellect of every man he liked; he made me tell him long Irish stories and compared my art of story-telling to Homer's; and once when he had described himself as writing in the census paper "age 19, profession genius, infirmity talent" the other guest, a young journalist fresh from Oxford or Cambridge, said, "What should I have written?" and was told that it should have been "profession talent, infirmity genius." When, however, I called, wearing shoes a little too yellow—unblackened leather had just become fashionable—I realised their extravagance when I saw his eyes fixed upon them; and another day Wilde asked me to tell his little boy a fairy story, and I had but got as far as "Once upon a time there was a giant" when the little boy screamed and ran out of the room. Wilde looked grave and I was plunged into the shame of clumsiness that afflicts the young. And when I asked for some literary gossip for some provincial newspaper, that paid me a few shillings a month, I was told that writing literary gossip was no job for a gentleman.

Though to be compared to Homer passed the time pleasantly, I had not been greatly perturbed had he stopped me with: "Is it a long story?" as Henley would certainly have done. I was abashed before him as wit and man of the world alone. I remember that he deprecated the very general belief in his success or his efficiency, and I think with sincerity. One form of success had gone: he was no more the lion of the season and he had not discovered his gift for writing comedy, yet I think I knew him at the happiest moment of his life. No scandal had touched his name, his fame as a talker was growing among his equals, and he seemed to live in the enjoyment of his own spontaneity. One day he began: "I have been inventing a Christian heresy," and he told a detailed story, in the style of some early father, of how Christ recovered after the Crucifixion, and escaping from the tomb, lived on for many years, the one man upon earth who knew the falsehood of Christianity. Once St. Paul visited his town and he alone in the carpenters' quarter did not go to hear him preach. Henceforth the other carpenters noticed that, for some unknown reason, he kept his hands covered. A few days afterwards I found Wilde with smock frocks in various colours spread out upon the floor in front of him, while a missionary explained that he did not object to the heathen going naked upon weekdays, but insisted upon clothes in church. He had brought the smock frocks in a cab that the only art-critic whose fame had reached Central Africa might select a colour; so Wilde sat there weighing all with a conscious ecclesiastic solemnity.

II

Of late years I have often explained Wilde to myself by his family history. His father was a friend or acquaintance of my father's father and among my family traditions there is an old Dublin riddle: "Why are Sir William Wilde's nails so black?" Answer, "Because he has scratched himself." And there is an old story still current in Dublin of Lady Wilde saying to a servant, "Why do you put the plates on the coal-scuttle? What are the chairs meant for?" They were famous people and there are many like stories; and even a horrible folk story, the invention of some Connaught peasant, that tells how Sir William Wilde took out the eyes of some men, who had come to consult him as an oculist, and laid them upon a plate, intending to replace them in a moment, and how the eyes were eaten by a cat. As a certain friend of mine, who has made a prolonged study of the nature of cats, said when he first heard the tale, "Cats love eyes." The Wilde family was clearly of the sort that fed the imagination of Charles Lever, dirty, untidy, daring, and what Charles Lever, who loved more normal activities, might not have valued so highly, very imaginative and learned. Lady Wilde, who when I knew her received her friends with blinds drawn and shutters closed that none might see her withered face, longed always perhaps, though certainly amid much self-mockery, for some impossible splendour of character and circumstance. She lived near her son in level Chelsea, but I have heard her say, "I want to live on some high place, Primrose Hill or Highgate, because I was an eagle in my youth." I think her son lived with no self-mockery at all, an imaginary life; perpetually performed a play which was in all things the opposite of all that he had known in childhood and early youth; never put off completely his wonder at opening his eyes every morning on his own beautiful house, and in remembering that he had dined yesterday with a duchess, and that

he delighted in Flaubert and Pater, read Homer in the original
and not as a schoolmaster reads him for the grammar. I think,
too, that because of all that half-civilised blood in his veins he
could not endure the sedentary toil of creative art and so remained a man of action, exaggerating, for the sake of immediate
effect, every trick learned from his masters, turning their easel
painting into painted scenes. He was a parvenu, but a parvenu
whose whole bearing proved that if he did dedicate every story
in *The House of Pomegranates* to a lady of title, it was but to
show that he was Jack and the social ladder his pantomime bean-
stalk. "Did you ever hear him say 'Marquess of Dimmesdale'?"
a friend of his once asked me. "He does not say 'the Duke of
York' with any pleasure."

He told me once that he had been offered a safe seat in Parliament and, had he accepted, he might have had a career like
that of Beaconsfield, whose early style resembles his, being
meant for crowds, for excitement, for hurried decisions, for immediate triumphs. Such men get their sincerity, if at all, from
the contact of events, the dinner table was Wilde's event and
made him the greatest talker of his time, and his plays and dia-
logues have what merit they possess from being now an imitation, now a record, of his talk. Even in those days I would often
defend him by saying that his very admiration for his predecessors in poetry, for Browning, for Swinburne and Rossetti, in their
first vogue while he was a very young man, made any success
seem impossible that could satisfy his immense ambition; never
but once before had the artist seemed so great, never had the
work of art seemed so difficult. I would then compare him with
Benvenuto Cellini who, coming after Michael Angelo, found
nothing left to do so satisfactory as to turn bravo and quarrel
with the man who broke Michael Angelo's nose.

12

I cannot remember who first brought me to the old stable beside Kelmscott House, William Morris's house at Hammersmith,
and to the debates held there upon Sunday evenings by the Socialist League. I was soon of the little group who had supper
with Morris afterwards. I met at these suppers very constantly

Walter Crane, Emery Walker, in association with Cobden San-
derson, the printer of many fine books, and less constantly Bernard Shaw and Cockerell, now of the Museum of Cambridge,
and perhaps but once or twice Hyndman the Socialist and the
Anarchist Prince Kropotkin. There, too, one always met certain
more or less educated workmen, rough of speech and manner,
with a conviction to meet every turn. I was told by one of them,
on a night when I had done perhaps more than my share of the
talking, that I had talked more nonsense in one evening than he
had heard in the whole course of his past life. I had merely preferred Parnell, then at the height of his career, to Michael
Davitt, who had wrecked his Irish influence by international
politics. We sat round a long unpolished and unpainted trestle
table of new wood in a room where hung Rossetti's *Pomegranate,*
a portrait of Mrs. Morris, and where one wall and part of the
ceiling were covered by a great Persian carpet. Morris had said
somewhere or other that carpets were meant for people who took
their shoes off when they entered a house and were most in
place upon a tent floor. I was a little disappointed in the house,
for Morris was an aging man content at last to gather beautiful
things rather than to arrange a beautiful house. I saw the drawing-room once or twice, and there alone all my sense of decoration, founded upon the background of Rossetti's pictures, was
satisfied by a big cupboard painted with a scene from Chaucer
by Burne-Jones; but even there were objects, perhaps a chair or
a little table, that seemed accidental, bought hurriedly perhaps
and with little thought, to make wife or daughter comfortable.
I had read as a boy, in books belonging to my father, the third
volume of *The Earthly Paradise,* and *The Defence of Guene-
vere,* which pleased me less, but had not opened either for a
long time. *The Man Who Never Laughed Again* had seemed
the most wonderful of tales till my father had accused me of
preferring Morris to Keats, got angry about it, and put me altogether out of countenance. He had spoiled my pleasure, for now
I questioned while I read and at last ceased to read; nor had
Morris written as yet those prose romances that became after his
death so great a joy that they were the only books I was ever
to read slowly that I might not come too quickly to the end. It
was now Morris himself that stirred my interest, and I took to

him first because of some little tricks of speech and body that reminded me of my old grandfather in Sligo, but soon discovered his spontaneity and joy and made him my chief of men. To-day I do not set his poetry very high, but for an odd altogether wonderful line, or thought; and yet, if some angel offered me the choice, I would choose to live his life, poetry and all, rather than my own or any other man's. A reproduction of his portrait by Watts hangs over my mantelpiece with Henley's, and those of other friends. Its grave wide-open eyes, like the eyes of some dreaming beast, remind me of the open eyes of Titian's "Ariosto," while the broad vigorous body suggests a mind that has no need of the intellect to remain sane, though it give itself to every fantasy: the dreamer of the middle ages. It is "the fool of fairy . . . wide and wild as a hill," the resolute European image that yet half remembers Buddha's motionless meditation, and has no trait in common with the wavering, lean image of hungry speculation, that cannot but because of certain famous Hamlets of our stage fill the mind's eye. Shakespeare himself foreshadowed a symbolic change, that is a change in the whole temperament of the world, for though he called his Hamlet "fat" and even "scant of breath," he thrust between his fingers agile rapier and dagger.

The dream world of Morris was as much the antithesis of daily life as with other men of genius, but he was never conscious of the antithesis and so knew nothing of intellectual suffering. His intellect, unexhausted by speculation or casuistry, was wholly at the service of hand and eye, and whatever he pleased he did with an unheard-of ease and simplicity, and if style and vocabulary were at times monotonous, he could not have made them otherwise without ceasing to be himself. Instead of the language of Chaucer and Shakespeare, its warp fresh from field and market—if the woof were learned—his age offered him a speech, exhausted from abstraction, that only returned to its full vitality when written learnedly and slowly.

The roots of his antithetical dream were visible enough; a never idle man of great physical strength and extremely irascible—did he not fling a badly baked plum pudding through the window upon Christmas Day?—a man more joyous than any intellectual man of our world, he called himself "the idle singer of an empty day," created new forms of melancholy, and faint persons, like the knights and ladies of Burne-Jones, who are never, no not once in forty volumes, put out of temper. A blunderer who had said to the only unconverted man at a Socialist picnic in Dublin, to prove that equality came easy, "I was brought up a gentleman and now as you can see associate with all sorts" and left wounds thereby that rankled after twenty years, a man of whom I have heard it said "He is always afraid that he is doing something wrong and generally is," he wrote long stories with apparently no other object than that his persons might show to one another, through situations of poignant difficulty the most exquisite tact.

He did not project like Henley or like Wilde, an image of himself, because having all his imagination set upon making and doing he had little self-knowledge. He imagined instead new conditions of making and doing; and in the teeth of those scientific generalisations that cowed my boyhood, I can see some like imagining in every great change, and believe that the first flying-fish first leaped, not because it sought "adaptation" to the air, but out of horror of the sea.

13

Soon after I began to attend the lectures a French class was started in the old coach-house for certain young Socialists who planned a tour in France, and I joined it, and was for a time a model student constantly encouraged by the compliments of the old French mistress. I told my father of the class, and he asked me to get my sisters admitted. I made difficulties and put off speaking of the matter, for I knew that the new and admirable self I was making would turn, under family eyes, into plain ragdoll. How could I pretend to be industrious, and even carry dramatisation to the point of learning my lessons, when my sisters were there and knew that I was nothing of the kind? But I had no argument I could use, and my sisters were admitted. They said nothing unkind, so far as I can remember, but in a week or two I was my old procrastinating idle self and had soon left the class altogether. My elder sister stayed on and became an embroideress under Miss May Morris, and the hangings round Morris's big bed at Kelmscott House, Oxfordshire, with their verses about lying happily in bed when "all birds sing in the town of the tree," were from her needle, though not from her design. She worked for the first few months at Kelmscott House, Hammersmith, and in my imagination I cannot always separate what I saw and heard from her report, or indeed from the report of that tribe or guild who looked up to Morris as to some worshipped mediæval king. He had no need for other people. I doubt if their marriage or death made him sad or glad, and yet no man I have known was so well loved; you saw him producing everywhere organisation and beauty, seeming, almost in the same instant, helpless and triumphant; and people loved him as children are loved. People much in his neighbourhood became gradually occupied with him or about his affairs, and, without any wish on his part, as simple people become occupied with children. I remember a man who was proud and pleased because he had distracted Morris's thoughts from an attack of gout by leading the conversation delicately to the hated name of Milton. He began at Swinburne: "Oh, Swinburne," said Morris, "is a rhetorician; my masters have been Keats and Chaucer, for they make pictures." "Does not Milton make pictures?" asked my informant. "No," was the answer, "Dante makes pictures, but Milton, though he had a great earnest mind, expressed himself as a rhetorician." "Great earnest mind" sounded strange to me, and I doubt not that were his questioner not a simple man Morris had been more emphatic. Another day the same man started by praising Chaucer, but the gout was worse, and Morris cursed Chaucer for destroying the English language with foreign words.

He had few detachable phrases, and I can remember little of his speech, which many thought the best of all good talk, except that it matched his burly body and seemed within definite boundaries inexhaustible in fact and expression. He alone of all the men I have known seemed guided by some beast-like instinct and never ate strange meat. "Balzac! Balzac!" he said to me once, "oh, that was the man the French Bourgeoisie read so much a few years ago." I can remember him at supper praising wine: "Why do people say it is prosaic to be inspired by wine? Has it not been made by the sunlight and the sap?" and his dispraising houses decorated by himself: "Do you suppose I like that kind of house? I would like a house like a big barn, where one ate in one corner, cooked in another corner, slept in the third corner, and in the fourth received one's friends"; and his complaining of Ruskin's objection to the underground railway: "If you must have a railway the best thing you can do with it is to put it in a tube with a cork at each end." I remember, too, that when I asked what led up to his movement, he replied: "Oh, Ruskin and Carlyle, but somebody should have been beside Carlyle and punched his head every five minutes." Though I remember little, I do not doubt that, had I continued going there on Sunday evenings, I should have caught fire from his words and turned my hand to some mediæval work or other.

Just before I had ceased to go there I had sent my *Wanderings of Usheen* to his daughter, hoping of course that it might meet his eyes, and soon after sending it I came upon him by chance in Holborn—"You write my sort of poetry," he said and began to praise me and to promise to send his praise to the *Commonwealth*, the League organ, and he would have said more had he not caught sight of a new ornamental cast-iron lamp-post and got very heated upon that subject.

I did not read economics, having turned socialist because of Morris's lectures and pamphlets, and I think it unlikely that Morris himself could read economics. That old dogma of mine seemed germane to the matter. If the men and women imagined by the poets were the norm, and if Morris had, in let us say "News from Nowhere," then running through the *Commonwealth,* described such men and women, living under their natural conditions, or as they would desire to live, then those conditions themselves must be the norm and could we but get rid of certain institutions the world would turn from eccentricity. Perhaps Morris himself justified himself in his own heart by as simple an argument, and was, as the socialist D—— said to me one night, walking home after some lecture, "an anarchist without knowing it." Certainly I and all about me, including D—— himself, were for chopping up the old king for Medea's pot. Morris had told us to have nothing to do with the parliamentary socialists, represented for men in general by the Fabian Society and Hyndman's Social Democratic Federation and for us in particular by D——. During the period of transition mistakes must be made, and the discredit of these mistakes must be left to "the Bourgeoisie"; and besides, when you begin to talk of this measure, or that other, you lose sight of the goal, and see, to reverse Swinburne's description of Tiresias, "Light on the way but darkness on the goal." By mistakes Morris meant vexatious restrictions and compromises—"If any man puts me into a labour squad, I will lie on my back and kick." That phrase very much expresses our idea of revolutionary tactics; we all intended to lie upon our backs and kick. D——, pale and sedentary, did not dislike labour squads and we all hated him with the left side of our heads, while admiring him immensely with the right side. He alone was invited to entertain Mrs. Morris, having many tales of his Irish uncles, more especially of one particular uncle who had tried to commit suicide by shutting his head into a carpet-bag. At that time he was an obscure man, known only for a witty speaker at street corners and in Park demonstrations. He had, with an assumed truculence and fury, cold logic, an invariable gentleness, an unruffled courtesy, and yet could never close a speech without being denounced by a journeyman hatter, with an Italian name. Converted to socialism by D——, and to anarchism by himself, with swinging arm and uplifted voice, this man put, and perhaps, exaggerated our scruple about Parliament. "I lack," said D——, "the bump of reverence"; whereon the wild man shouted: "You 'ave a 'ole." There are moments when looking back I somewhat confuse my own figure with that of the hatter, image of our hysteria, for I too became violent with the violent solemnity of a religious devotee. I can even remember sitting behind D—— and saying some rude thing or other over his shoulder.

I don't remember why I gave it up but I did quite suddenly and the push may have come from a young workman who was educating himself between Morris and Karl Marx. He had planned a history of the Navy, and when I had spoken of the battleships of Nelson's day had said, "Oh, that was the decadence of the battleship," but if his naval interests were mediæval, his ideas about religion were pure Karl Marx, and we were soon in perpetual argument. Then gradually the attitude towards religion of almost everybody but Morris, who avoided the subject altogether, got upon my nerves, for I broke out after some lecture or other with all the arrogance of raging youth. They attacked religion, I said, or some such words, and yet there must be a change of heart and only religion could make it. What was the use of talking about some new revolution putting all things right, when the change must come, if come it did, with astronomical slowness, like the cooling of the sun, or it may have been like the drying of the moon? Morris rang his chairman's bell, but I was too angry to listen, and he had to ring it a second time before I sat down. He said that night at supper, "Of course I know there must be a change of heart, but it will not come as slowly as all that. I rang my bell because you were not being understood." He did not show any vexation, but I never returned after that night; and yet I did not always believe what I had said, and only gradually gave up thinking of and planning for some near sudden change for the better.

14

I spent my days at the British Museum and must, I think, have been delicate, for I remember often putting off hour after hour consulting some necessary book because I shrank from lifting the heavy volumes of the catalogue; and yet to save money for my afternoon coffee and roll I often walked the whole way home to Bedford Park. I was compiling, for a series of shilling books, an anthology of Irish fairy stories, and, for an American publisher, a two-volume selection from the Irish novelists that would be somewhat dearer. I was not well paid, for each book cost me more than three months' reading; and I was paid for the first some twelve pounds ("Oh, Mr. E.," said publisher to editor, "you must never again pay so much!") and for the second twenty, but I did not think myself badly paid, for I had chosen the work for my own purposes.

Though I went to Sligo every summer, I was compelled to live out of Ireland the greater part of every year, and was but keeping my mind upon what I knew must be the subject-matter of my poetry. I believed that if Morris had set his stories amid the scenery of his own Wales, for I knew him to be of Welsh extraction and supposed wrongly that he had spent his childhood there, that if Shelley had nailed his *Prometheus*, or some

equal symbol, upon some Welsh or Scottish rock, their art would
have entered more intimately, more microscopically, into
our thought and given perhaps to modern poetry a breadth
and stability like that of ancient poetry. The statues of Mausolus
and Artemisia at the British Museum, private, half-animal, half-
divine figures, all unlike the Grecian athletes and Egyptian kings
in their near neighbourhood, that stand in the middle of the
crowd's applause, or sit above measuring it out unpersuadable
justice, became to me, now or later, images of an unpremedi-
tated joyous energy, that neither I nor any other man, racked
by doubt and inquiry, can achieve; and that yet, if once achieved,
might seem to men and women of Connemara or of Galway their
very soul. In our study of that ruined tomb raised by a queen
to her dead lover, and finished by the unpaid labour of great
sculptors, after her death from grief, or so runs the tale, we cannot distinguish the handiwork of Scopas from that of Praxiteles;
and I wanted to create once more an art where the artist's handiwork would hide as under those half-anonymous chisels or as
we find it in some old Scots ballads, or in some twelfth- or thir-
teenth-century Arthurian Romance. That handiwork assured, I
had martyred no man for modelling his own image upon Pallas
Athena's buckler; for I took great pleasure in certain allusions
to the singer's life one finds in old romances and ballads, and
thought his presence there all the more poignant because we discover it half lost, like portly Chaucer, behind his own maunciple
and pardoner upon the Canterbury roads. Wolfram von Eschen-
bach, singing his German Parsifal, broke off some description of
a famished city to remember that in his own house at home the
very mice lacked food, and what old ballad singer was it who
claimed to have fought by day in the very battle he sang by
night? So masterful indeed was that instinct that when the minstrel knew not who his poet was, he must needs make up a man:
"When any stranger asks who is the sweetest of singers, answer
with one voice: 'A blind man; he dwells upon rocky Chios; his
songs shall be the most beautiful for ever.'" Elaborate modern
psychology sounds egotistical, I thought, when it speaks in the
first person, but not those simple emotions which resemble the
more, the more powerful they are, everybody's emotion, and I
was soon to write many poems where an always personal emo-

tion was woven into a general pattern of myth and symbol. When the Fenian poet says that his heart has grown cold and callous—"For thy hapless fate, dear Ireland, and sorrows of my own"—he but follows tradition and if he does not move us deeply, it is because he has no sensuous musical vocabulary that comes at need, without compelling him to sedentary toil and so driving him out from his fellows. I thought to create that sensuous, musical vocabulary, and not for myself only, but that I might leave it to later Irish poets, much as a mediæval Japanese painter left his style as an inheritance to his family, and I was careful to use a traditional manner and matter, yet changed by that toil, impelled by my share in Cain's curse, by all that sterile modern complication, by my "originality," as the newspapers call it, did something altogether different. Morris set out to make a revolution that the persons of his *Well at the World's End* or his *Waters of the Wondrous Isles*, always, to my mind, in the likeness of Artemisia and her man, might walk his native scenery; and I, that my native scenery might find imaginary inhabitants, half-planned a new method and a new culture. My mind began drifting vaguely towards that doctrine of "the mask" which has convinced me that every passionate man (I have nothing to do with mechanist, or philanthropist, or man whose eyes have no preference) is, as it were, linked with another age, historical or imaginary, where alone he finds images that rouse his energy. Napoleon was never of his own time, as the naturalistic writers and painters bid all men be, but had some Roman emperor's image in his head and some condottiere's blood in his heart; and when he crowned that head at Rome with his own hands he had covered, as may be seen from David's painting, his hesitation with that emperor's old suit.

15

I had various women friends on whom I would call towards five o'clock mainly to discuss my thoughts that I could not bring to a man without meeting some competing thought, but partly because their tea and toast saved my pennies for the 'bus ride home; but with women, apart from their intimate exchanges of thought, I was timid and abashed. I was sitting on a seat in front

of the British Museum feeding pigeons when a couple of girls
sat near and began enticing my pigeons away, laughing and whispering to one another, and I looked straight in front of me, very
indignant, and presently went into the Museum without turning
my head towards them. Since then I have often wondered if they
were pretty or merely very young. Sometimes I told myself very
adventurous love-stories with myself for hero, and at other times
I planned out a life of lonely austerity, and at other times mixed
the ideals and planned a life of lonely austerity mitigated by
periodical lapses. I had still the ambition, formed in Sligo in my
teens, of living in imitation of Thoreau on Innisfree, a little island
in Lough Gill, and when walking through Fleet Street very
homesick I heard a little tinkle of water and saw a fountain in
a shop-window which balanced a little ball upon its jet, and began to remember lake water. From the sudden remembrance
came my poem *Innisfree*, my first lyric with anything in its
rhythm of my own music. I had begun to loosen rhythm as an
escape from rhetoric and from that emotion of the crowd that
rhetoric brings, but I only understood vaguely and occasionally
that I must for my special purpose use nothing but the common
syntax. A couple of years later I would not have written that first
line with its conventional archaism—"Arise and go"—nor the in-
version in the last stanza. Passing another day by the new Law
Courts, a building that I admired because it was Gothic—"It is
not very good," Morris had said, "but it is better than anything
else they have got and so they hate it"—I grew suddenly op-
pressed by the great weight of stone, and thought, "There are
miles and miles of stone and brick all round me," and presently
added, "If John the Baptist or his like were to come again and
had his mind set upon it, he could make all these people go out
into some wilderness leaving their buildings empty," and that
thought, which does not seem very valuable now, so enlightened
the day that it is still vivid in the memory. I spent a few days
at Oxford copying out a seventeenth-century translation of Pog-
gio's *Liber Facetiarum* or the *Hypnerotomachia* of Poliphili for
a publisher; I forget which, for I copied both; and returned very
pale to my troubled family. I had lived upon bread and tea because I thought that if antiquity found locust and wild honey
nutritive, my soul was strong enough to need no better. I was

always planning some great gesture, putting the whole world into
one scale of the balance and my soul into the other and imagining that the whole world somehow kicked the beam. More than
thirty years have passed and I have seen no forcible young man
of letters brave the metropolis, without some like stimulant; and
all after two or three, or twelve or fifteen years, according to
obstinacy, have understood that we achieve, if we do achieve, in
little sedentary stitches as though we were making lace. I had
one unmeasured advantage from my stimulant; I could ink my
socks, that they might not show through my shoes, with a most
haughty mind, imagining myself, and my torn tackle, somewhere else, in some far place "under the canopy . . . i' the city
of kites and crows."

In London I saw nothing good and constantly remembered
that Ruskin had said to some friend of my father's—"As I go to
my work at the British Museum I see the faces of the people
become daily more corrupt." I convinced myself for a time, that
on the same journey I saw but what he saw. Certain old women's
faces filled me with horror, faces that are no longer there, or if
they are pass before me unnoticed: the fat blotched faces, rising
above double chins, of women who have drunk too much beer
and eaten much meat. In Dublin I had often seen old women
walking with erect heads and gaunt bodies, talking to themselves
with loud voices, mad with drink and poverty, but they were
different, they belonged to romance. Da Vinci had drawn
women who looked so and so carried their bodies.

16

I attempted to restore one old friend of my father's to the practice of his youth, but failed, though he, unlike my father, had
not changed his belief. My father brought me to dine with Jack
Nettleship at Wigmore Street, once inventor of imaginative designs and now a painter of melodramatic lions. At dinner I had
talked a great deal—too much, I imagine, for so young a man, or
maybe for any man—and on the way home my father, who had
been plainly anxious that I should make a good impression, was
very angry. He said I had talked for effect and that talking for
effect was precisely what one must never do; he had always hated

rhetoric and emphasis and had made me hate it; and his anger
plunged me into great dejection. I called at Nettleship's studio
the next day to apologise, and Nettleship opened the door himself and received me with enthusiasm. He had explained to some
woman guest that I would probably talk well, being an Irishman,
but the reality had surpassed, etc., etc. I was not flattered, though
relieved at not having to apologise, for I soon discovered that
what he really admired was my volubility, for he himself was
very silent. He seemed about sixty, had a bald head, a grey beard,
and a nose, as one of my father's friends used to say, like an
opera-glass, and sipped cocoa all the afternoon and evening from
an enormous tea-cup that must have been designed for him alone,
not caring how cold the cocoa grew. Years before he had been
thrown from his horse, while hunting, and broke his arm, and
because it had been badly set suffered great pain for a long time.
A little whiskey would always stop the pain, and soon a little
became a great deal and he found himself a drunkard, but having signed his liberty away for certain months he was completely
cured. He had acquired, however, the need of some liquid
which he could sip constantly. I brought him an admiration settled in early boyhood, for my father had always said, "George
Wilson was our born painter, but Nettleship our genius," and
even had he shown me nothing I could care for, I had admired
him still because my admiration was in my bones. He showed
me his early designs, and they, though often badly drawn, fulfilled my hopes. Something of Blake they certainly did show,
but had in place of Blake's joyous, intellectual energy a Satur-
nian passion and melancholy. "God Creating Evil," the death-
like head with a woman and a tiger coming from the forehead,
which Rossetti—or was it Browning?—had described "as the most
sublime design of ancient or modern art," had been lost, but
there was another version of the same thought, and other designs never published or exhibited. They rise before me even now
in meditation, especially a blind Titan-like ghost floating with
groping hands above the tree-tops. I wrote a criticism, and arranged for reproductions with the editor of an art magazine, but
after it was written and accepted the proprietor, lifting what I
considered an obsequious caw in the Huxley, Tyndall, Carolus
Duran, Bastien-Lepage rookery, insisted upon its rejection. Net-

tleship did not mind its rejection, saying, "Who cares for such things now? Not ten people," but he did mind my refusal to show him what I had written. Though what I had written was all eulogy, I dreaded his judgment for it was my first art criticism. I hated his big lion pictures, where he attempted an art too much concerned with the sense of touch, with the softness or roughness, the minutely observed irregularity of surfaces, for his genius; and I think he knew it. "Rossetti used to call my pictures pot-boilers," he said, "but they are all—all"—and he waved his arm to the canvases—"symbols." When I wanted him to design gods, and angels, and lost spirits once more, he always came back to the point "Nobody would be pleased." "Everybody should have a *raison d'être*" was one of his phrases. "Mrs. ——'s articles are not good but they are her *raison d'être*." I had but little knowledge of art for there was little scholarship in the Dublin art school, so I overrated the quality of anything that could be connected with my general beliefs about the world. If I had been able to give angelical or diabolical names to his lions I might have liked them also and I think that Nettleship himself would have liked them better and liking them better have become a better painter. We had the same kind of religious feeling, but I could give a crude philosophical expression to mine while he could only express his in action or with brush and pencil. He often told me of certain ascetic ambitions, very much like my own, for he had kept all the moral ambition of youth, as for instance—"Yeats, the other night I was arrested by a policeman —was walking round Regent's Park barefooted to keep the flesh under—good sort of thing to do. I was carrying my boots in my hand and he thought I was a burglar and even when I explained and gave him half-a-crown, he would not let me go till I had promised to put on my boots before I met the next policeman."

He was very proud and shy and I could not imagine anybody asking him questions and so I was content to take these stories as they came: confirmations of what I had heard of him in boyhood. One story heard in boyhood had stirred my imagination particularly, for, ashamed all my boyhood of my lack of physical courage, I admired what was beyond my imitation. He thought that any weakness, even a weakness of body, had the character of sin and while at breakfast with his brother, with whom he shared a room on the third floor of a corner house, he said that his nerves were out of order. Presently he left the table, and got out through the window and on to a stone ledge that ran along the wall under the window-sills. He sidled along the ledge, and turning the corner with it, got in at a different window and returned to the table. "My nerves," he said, "are better than I thought."

Nettleship said to me: "Has Edwin Ellis ever said anything about the effect of drink upon my genius?" "No," I answered. "I ask," he said, "because I have always thought that Ellis has some strange medical insight." Though I had answered "no," Ellis had only a few days before used these words: "Nettleship drank his genius away." Ellis, but lately returned from Perugia where he had lived many years, was another old friend of my father's but some years younger than Nettleship or my father. Nettleship had found his simplifying image, but in his painting had turned away from it, while Ellis, the son of Alexander Ellis, a once famous man of science, who was perhaps the last man in England to run the circle of the sciences without superficiality, had never found that image at all. He was a painter and poet, but his painting, which did not interest me, showed no influence but that of Leighton. He had started perhaps a couple of years too late for pre-Raphaelite influence, for no great pre-Raphaelite picture was painted after 1870, and left England too soon for that of the French painters. He was, however, sometimes moving as a poet and still more often an astonishment. I have known him cast something just said into a dozen lines of musical verse, without apparently ceasing to talk; but the work once done he could not or would not amend it, and my father thought he lacked all ambition. Yet he had at times nobility of rhythm—an instinct for grandeur, and after thirty years I still repeat to myself his address to Mother Earth—

> O mother of the hills, forgive our towers,
> O mother of the clouds, forgive our dreams.

And there are certain whole poems that I read from time to time or try to make others read. There is that poem where the manner is unworthy of the matter, being loose and facile, describing Adam and Eve fleeing from Paradise. Adam asks Eve what she carries so carefully, and Eve replies that it is a little of the apple-core kept for their children. There is that vision concerning "Christ the Less," a too hurriedly written ballad, where the half of Christ sacrificed to the divine half "that fled to seek felicity" wanders wailing through Golgotha, and there is *The Saint and the Youth,* in which I can discover no fault at all. He loved complexities—"Seven silences like candles round her face" is a line of his—and whether he wrote well or ill had always a manner which I would have known from that of any other poet. He would say to me, "I am a mathematician with the mathematics left out"—his father was a great mathematician—or "A woman once said to me, 'Mr. Ellis, why are your poems like sums?'" And certainly he loved symbols and abstractions. He said once, when I had asked him not to mention something or other, "Surely you have discovered by this time that I know of no means whereby I can mention a fact in conversation."

He had a passion for Blake, picked up in pre-Raphaelite studios, and early in our acquaintance put into my hands a scrap of notepaper on which he had written some years before an interpretation of the poem that begins

> The fields from Islington to Marylebone,
>> To Primrose Hill and St. John's Wood,
> Were builded over with pillars of gold,
>> And there Jerusalem's pillars stood.

The four quarters of London represented Blake's four great mythological personages, the Zoas, and also the four elements. These few sentences were the foundation of all study of the philosophy of William Blake that requires an exact knowledge for its pursuit and that traces the connection between his system and that of Swedenborg or of Boehme. I recognised certain attributions, from what is sometimes called the Christian Cabbala, of which Ellis had never heard, and with this proof that his interpretation was more than fantasy he and I began our four years' work upon the Prophetic Books of William Blake. We took it as almost a sign of Blake's personal help when we discovered that the spring of 1889, when we first joined our knowledge, was one hundred years from the publication of *The Book of Thel,* the first published of the Prophetic Books, as though it were firmly established that the dead delight in anniversaries. After months of discussion and reading we made a concordance of all Blake's mystical terms, and there was much copying to be done in the Museum and at Red Hill, where the descendants of Blake's friend and patron, the landscape painter John Linnell, had many manuscripts. The Linnells were narrow in their religious ideas and doubtful of Blake's orthodoxy, whom they held, however, in great honour, and I remember a timid old lady who had known Blake when a child saying, "He had very wrong ideas, he did not believe in the historical Jesus." One old man sat always beside us, ostensibly to sharpen our pencils but perhaps really to see that we did not steal the manuscripts, and they gave us very old port at lunch, and I have upon my dining-room walls their present of Blake's Dante engravings. Going thither and returning Ellis would entertain me by philosophical discussion varied with improvised stories, at first folk tales which he professed to have picked up in Scotland, and, though I had read and collected many folk tales, I did not see through the deceit. I have a partial memory of two more elaborate tales, one of an Italian conspirator flying barefoot, from I forget what adventure through I forget what Italian city, in the early morning. Fearing to be recognised by his bare feet, he slipped past the sleepy porter at an hotel, calling out "number so-and-so" as if he were some belated guest. Then passing from bedroom door to door he tried on the boots, and just as he got a pair to fit, a voice cried from the room: "Who is that?" "Merely me, sir," he called back, "taking your boots." The other was of a martyr's Bible, round which the cardinal virtues had taken personal form—this is a fragment of Blake's philosophy. It was in the possession of an old clergyman when a certain jockey called upon him, and the cardinal virtues, confused between jockey and clergyman, devoted themselves to the jockey. As whenever he sinned a cardinal virtue interfered and turned him back to virtue, he lived in great credit, and made, but for one sentence, a very holy death. As his wife and family knelt round in admiration and grief he suddenly said "damn." "O my dear," said his wife, "what a dreadful expression." He answered, "I am going to heaven," and straightway died. It was a long tale, for there were all the jockey's vain attempts to sin, as well as all the adventures of the clergyman, who became very sinful indeed, but it ended happily for when the jockey died the cardinal virtues returned to the clergyman. I think he would talk to any audience that offered, one audience being the same as another in his eyes, and it may have been for this reason that my father called him unambitious. When he was a young man he had befriended a reformed thief and had asked the grateful thief to take him round the thieves' quarters of London. The thief, however, hurried him away from the worst saying, "Another minute and they would have found you out. If they were not the stupidest of men in London, they had done so already." Ellis had gone through a detailed, romantic and witty account of all the houses he had robbed and all the throats he had cut in one short life.

His conversation would often pass out of my comprehension, or indeed I think of any man's, into a labyrinth of abstraction and subtlety and then suddenly return with some verbal conceit or turn of wit. The mind is known to attain in certain conditions of trance a quickness so extraordinary that we are compelled at times to imagine a condition of unendurable intellectual intensity from which we are saved by the merciful stupidity of the body, and I think that the mind of Edwin Ellis was constantly upon the edge of trance. Once we were discussing the symbolism of sex in the philosophy of Blake and had been in disagreement all the afternoon. I began talking with a new sense of conviction and after a moment Ellis, who was at his easel, threw down his brush and said that he had just seen the same explanation in a series of symbolic visions. "In another moment," he said, "I should have been off." We went into the open air and walked up and down to get rid of that feeling, but presently we came in again and I began again my explanation, Ellis lying upon the sofa. I had been talking some time when Mrs. Ellis came into the room and said, "Why are you sitting in the dark?" Ellis answered, "But we are not," and then added in a voice of wonder, "I thought the lamp was lit, and that I was sitting up, and now I find that I am lying down and that we are in darkness." I had seen a flicker of light over the ceiling but thought it a reflection from some light outside the house.

17

I had already met most of the poets of my generation. I had said, soon after the publication of *The Wanderings of Usheen*, to the editor of a series of shilling reprints, who had set me to compile tales of the Irish fairies, "I am growing jealous of other poets and we will all grow jealous of each other unless we know each other and so feel a share in each other's triumph." He was a Welshman, lately a mining engineer, Ernest Rhys, a writer of Welsh translations and original poems, that have often moved me greatly though I can think of no one else who has read them. He was perhaps a dozen years older than myself and through his work as editor knew everybody who would compile a book for seven or eight pounds. Between us we founded The Rhymers' Club, which for some years was to meet every night in an upper room with a sanded floor in an ancient eating-house in the Strand called The Cheshire Cheese. Lionel Johnson, Ernest Dowson, Victor Plarr, Ernest Radford, John Davidson, Richard le Gallienne, T. W. Rolleston, Selwyn Image, Edwin Ellis, and John Todhunter came constantly for a time, Arthur Symons and Herbert Horne, less constantly, while William Watson joined but never came and Francis Thompson came once but never joined; and sometimes if we met in a private house, which we did occasionally, Oscar Wilde came. It had been useless to invite him to The Cheshire Cheese for he hated Bohemia. "Olive Schreiner," he said once to me, "is staying in the East End because that is the only place where people do not wear masks upon their faces, but I have told her that I live in the West End because nothing in life interests me but the mask."

We read our poems to one another and talked criticism and drank a little wine. I sometimes say when I speak of the club, "We had such and such ideas, such and such a quarrel with the great Victorians, we set before us such and such aims," as though we had many philosophical ideas. I say this because I am ashamed to admit that I had these ideas and that whenever I began to talk of them a gloomy silence fell upon the room. A young Irish poet, who wrote excellently but had the worst manners, was to say a few years later, "You do not talk like a poet, you talk like a man of letters," and if all the Rhymers had not been polite, if most of them had not been to Oxford or Cambridge, the greater number would have said the same thing. I was full of thought, often very abstract thought, longing all the while to be full of images, because I had gone to the art school instead of a university. Yet even if I had gone to a university, and learned all the classical foundations of English literature and English culture, all that great erudition which once accepted frees the mind from restlessness, I should have had to give up my Irish subject-matter, or attempt to found a new tradition. Lacking sufficient recognised precedent I must needs find out some reason for all I did. I knew almost from the start that to overflow with reasons was to be not quite wellborn; and when I could I hid them, as men hide a disagreeable ancestry; and that there was no help for it seeing that my country was not born at all. I was of those doomed to imperfect achievement, and under a curse, as it were, like some race of birds compelled to spend the time, needed for the making of the nest, in argument as to the convenience of moss and twig and lichen. Le Gallienne and Davidson, and even Symons, were provincial at their setting out, but their provincialism was curable, mine incurable; while the one conviction shared by all the younger men, but principally by Johnson and Horne, who imposed their personalities upon us, was an opposition to all ideas, all generalisations that can be explained and debated. Symons fresh from Paris would sometimes say—"We are concerned with nothing but impressions," but that itself was a generalisation and met but stony silence. Conversation constantly dwindled into "Do you like so-and-so's last book?" "No, I prefer the book before it," and I think that but for its Irish members, who said whatever came into their heads, the club would not have survived its first difficult months. I saw—now ashamed that I saw "like a man of letters," now exasperated at the indifference of these poets to the fashion of their own river-bed—that Swinburne in one way, Browning in another, and Tennyson in a third, had filled their work with what I called "impurities," curiosities about politics, about science, about history, about religion; and that we must create once more the pure work.

Our clothes were for the most part unadventurous like our conversation, though I indeed wore a brown velveteen coat, a loose tie, and a very old inverness cape, discarded by my father twenty years before and preserved by my Sligo-born mother whose actions were unreasoning and habitual like the seasons. But no other member of the club, except Le Gallienne, who wore a loose tie, and Symons, who had an inverness cape that was quite new and almost fashionable, would have shown himself for the world in any costume but "that of an English gentleman." "One should be quite unnoticeable," Johnson explained to me. Those who conformed most carefully to the fashion in their clothes, generally departed farthest from it in their handwriting, which was small, neat, and studied, one poet—which, I forget—having founded his upon the handwriting of George Herbert. Dowson and Symons I was to know better in later years when Symons became a very dear friend, and I never got behind John Davidson's Scottish roughness and exasperation, though I saw much of him, but from the first I devoted myself to Lionel Johnson. He and Horne and Image and one or two others shared a man-servant and an old house in Charlotte Street, Fitzroy Square, typical figures of transition, doing as an achievement of learning and of exquisite taste what their predecessors did in careless abundance. All were pre-Raphaelite, and sometimes one might meet in the rooms of one or other a ragged figure, as of some fallen dynasty, Simeon Solomon the pre-Raphaelite painter, once the friend of Rossetti and of Swinburne, but fresh now from some low public-house. Condemned to a long term of imprisonment for a criminal offence, he had sunk into drunkenness and misery. Introduced one night, however, to some man who mistook him, in the dim candlelight, for another Solomon, a successful academic painter and R.A., he started to his feet in a rage with, "Sir, do you dare to mistake me for that mountebank?" Though not one had hearkened to the feeblest caw, or been spattered by the smallest dropping from any Huxley, Tyndall, Carolus Duran, Bastien-Lepage bundle of old twigs I began by suspecting them of lukewarmness, and even backsliding, and I owe it to that suspicion that I never became intimate with Horne, who lived to become the greatest English authority upon Italian life in the fifteenth century and to write the one standard work on Botticelli. Connoisseur in several arts, he had designed a little church in the manner of Inigo Jones for a burial-ground near the Marble Arch. Though I now think his little church a master-piece, its style was more than a century too late to hit my fancy, at two- or three-and-twenty; and I accused him of leaning to-wards that eighteenth century

> That taught a school
> Of dolts to smooth, inlay, and clip, and fit
> Till, like the certain wands of Jacob's wit,
> Their verses tallied.

Another fanaticism delayed my friendship with two men, who are now my friends and in certain matters my chief instructors. Somebody, probably Lionel Johnson, brought me to the studio of Charles Ricketts and Charles Shannon, certainly heirs of the great generation, and the first thing I saw was a Shannon picture of a lady and child, arrayed in lace, silk and satin, suggesting that hated century. My eyes were full of some more mythologi-cal mother and child and I would have none of it and I told Shannon that he had not painted a mother and child, but elegant people expecting visitors and I thought that a great reproach. Somebody writing in the *Germ* had said that a picture of a pheasant and an apple was merely a picture of something to eat and I was so angry with the indifference to subject, which was the commonplace of all art criticism since Bastien-Lepage, that I could at times see nothing else but subject. I thought that, though it might not matter to the man himself whether he loved a white woman or a black, a female pickpocket or a regular com-municant of the Church of England, if only he loved strongly, it certainly did matter to his relations, and even under some cir-cumstances to his whole neighbourhood. Sometimes indeed, like some father in Molière, I ignored the lover's feelings altogether and even refused to admit that a trace of the devil, perhaps a trace of colour, may lend piquancy, especially if the connection be not permanent.

Among these men, of whom so many of the greatest talents were to live such passionate lives and die such tragic deaths, one serene man, T. W. Rolleston, seemed always out of place; it was I who brought him there, intending to set him to some work in Ireland later on. I have known young Dublin working men slip out of their workshop to see the second Thomas Davis passing by, and can even remember a conspiracy, by some three or four, to make him "the leader of the Irish race at home and abroad," and all because he had regular features; and when all is said Alexander the Great and Alcibiades were personable men, and the Founder of the Christian religion was the only man who was neither a little too tall nor a little too short, but exactly six feet high. We in Ireland thought as do the plays and ballads, not understanding that, from the first moment wherein nature foresaw the birth of Bastien-Lepage, she has only granted great creative power to men whose faces are contorted with extravagance or curiosity, or dulled with some protecting stupidity.

I had now met all those who were to make the 'nineties of the last century tragic in the history of literature, but as yet we were all seemingly equal, whether in talent or in luck, and scarce even personalities to one another. I remember saying one night at The Cheshire Cheese, when more poets than usual had come, "None of us can say who will succeed, or even who has or has not talent. The only thing certain about us is that we are too many."

18

I have described what image—always opposite to the natural self or the natural world—Wilde, Henley, Morris, copied or tried to copy, but I have not said if I found an image for myself. I know very little about myself and much less of that anti-self: probably the woman who cooks my dinner or the woman who sweeps out my study knows more than I. It is perhaps because nature made me a gregarious man, going hither and thither looking for conversation, and ready to deny from fear or favour his dearest conviction, that I love proud and lonely things. When I was a child and went daily to the sexton's daughter for writing lessons, I found one poem in her School Reader that delighted me beyond all others: a fragment of some metrical translation from Aristophanes wherein the birds sing scorn upon mankind. In later years my mind gave itself to gregarious Shelley's dream of a young man, his hair blanched with sorrow, studying philosophy in some lonely tower, or of his old man, master of all human knowledge, hidden from human sight in some shell-

strewn cavern on the Mediterranean shore. One passage above
all ran perpetually in my ears—

> Some feign that he is Enoch: others dream
> He was pre-Adamite, and has survived
> Cycles of generation and of ruin.
> The sage, in truth, by dreadful abstinence,
> And conquering penance of the mutinous flesh,
> Deep contemplation and unwearied study,
> In years outstretched beyond the date of man,
> May have attained to sovereignty and science
> Over those strong and secret things and thoughts
> Which others fear and know not.
>   *Mahmud.*   I would talk
> With this old Jew.
>   *Hassan.*   Thy will is even now
> Made known to him where he dwells in a sea-cavern
> 'Mid the Demonesi, less accessible
> Than thou or God! He who would question him
> Must sail alone at sunset where the stream
> Of ocean sleeps around those foamless isles,
> When the young moon is westering as now,
> And evening airs wander upon the wave;
> And, when the pines of that bee-pasturing isle,
> Green Erebinthus, quench the fiery shadow
> Of his gilt prow within the sapphire water,
> Then must the lonely helmsman cry aloud
> "Ahasuerus!" and the caverns round
> Will answer "Ahasuerus!" If his prayer
> Be granted, a faint meteor will arise,
> Lighting him over Marmora; and a wind
> Will rush out of the sighing pine-forest,
> And with the wind a storm of harmony
> Unutterably sweet, and pilot him
> Through the soft twilight to the Bosphorus:
> Thence, at the hour and place and circumstance
> Fit for the matter of their conference,
> The Jew appears. Few dare, and few who dare
> Win the desired communion.

Already in Dublin, I had been attracted to the Theosophists because they had affirmed the real existence of the Jew, or of his like, and, apart from whatever might have been imagined by Huxley, Tyndall, Carolus Duran and Bastien-Lepage, I saw nothing against his reality. Presently having heard that Madame Blavatsky had arrived from France, or from India, I thought it time to look the matter up. Certainly if wisdom existed anywhere in the world it must be in some lonely mind admitting no duty to us, communing with God only, conceding nothing from fear or favour. Have not all peoples, while bound together in a single mind and taste, believed that such men existed and paid them that honour, or paid it to their mere shadow, which they have refused to philanthropists and to men of learning?

19

I found Madame Blavatsky in a little house at Norwood, with but, as she said, three followers left—the Society of Psychical Research had just reported on her Indian phenomena—and as one of the three followers sat in an outer room to keep out undesirable visitors, I was kept a long time kicking my heels. Presently I was admitted and found an old woman in a plain loose dark dress: a sort of old Irish peasant woman with an air of humour and audacious power. I was still kept waiting, for she was deep in conversation with a woman visitor. I strayed through folding doors into the next room and stood, in sheer idleness of mind, looking at a cuckoo clock. It was certainly stopped, for the weights were off and lying upon the ground, and yet, as I stood there the cuckoo came out and cuckooed at me. I interrupted Madame Blavatsky to say, "Your clock has hooted me." "It often hoots at a stranger," she replied. "Is there a spirit in it?" I said. "I do not know," she said, "I should have to be alone to know what is in it." I went back to the clock and began examining it and heard her say: "Do not break my clock." I wondered if there was some hidden mechanism and I should have been put out, I suppose, had I found any, though Henley had said to me, "Of course she gets up fraudulent miracles, but a person of genius has to do something; Sarah Bernhardt sleeps in her coffin." Presently the visitor went away and Madame Blavatsky explained that she was a propagandist for women's rights who had called to find out "why men were so bad." "What explanation did you give her?" I said. "That men were born bad, but women made themselves so," and then she explained that I had been kept waiting because she had mistaken me for some man, whose name resembled mine and who wanted to persuade her of the flatness of the earth.

When I next saw her she had moved into a house at Holland Park, and some time must have passed—probably I had been in Sligo where I returned constantly for long visits—for she was surrounded by followers. She sat nightly before a little table covered with green baize and on this green baize she scribbled constantly with a piece of white chalk. She would scribble symbols, sometimes humorously explainable, and sometimes unintelligible figures, but the chalk was intended to mark down her score when she played patience. One saw in the next room a large table where every night her followers and guests, often a great number, sat down to their vegetable meal, while she encouraged or mocked through the folding doors. A great passionate nature, a sort of female Dr. Johnson, impressive I think to every man or woman who had themselves any richness, she seemed impatient of the formalism and the shrill abstract idealism of those about her, and this impatience broke out in railing and many nicknames: "Oh you are a flap-doodle, but then you are a theosophist and a brother." The most devout and learned of all her followers said to me, "H. P. B. has just told me that there is another globe stuck on to this at the north pole, so that the earth has really a shape something like a dumbbell." I said, for I knew that her imagination contained all the folklore of the world, "That must be some piece of Eastern mythology." "Oh no it is not," he said, "of that I am certain, and there must be something in it or she would not have said it." Her mockery was not kept for her followers alone, and her voice would become harsh, and her mockery lose fantasy and humour, when she spoke of what seemed to her scientific materialism. Once I saw this antagonism, guided by some kind of telepathic divination. I brought a very able Dublin woman to see her and this woman had a brother, a physiologist whose reputation, though known to specialists alone, was European, and because of this brother a family pride in everything scientific and modern. The Dublin woman scarcely opened her mouth the whole evening and her name was certainly unknown to Madame Blavatsky, yet I saw at once in that wrinkled old face bent over the cards, and the only time I ever saw it there, a personal hostility, the dislike of one woman for another. Madame Blavatsky seemed to bundle herself up, becoming all primeval peasant, and began complaining of her ailments, more especially of her bad leg. But of late her master—her "old Jew," her "Ahasuerus"—cured it, or set it on the way to be cured. "I was sitting here in my chair," said she, "when the master came in and brought something with him which he put over my knee, something warm which enclosed my knee—it was a live dog which he had cut open." I recognised a cure used sometimes in mediæval medicine. I did not and I do not doubt that she described an actual vision, but its use at that moment and in that company was a masterpiece of fantastic brutality. She had two masters and their portraits, ideal Indian heads, painted by some most incompetent artist, stood upon either side of the folding doors. One night when talk was impersonal and general, I sat gazing through the folding doors into the dimly lighted dining-room beyond. I noticed a curious red light shining upon a picture and got up to see where the red light came from. It was the picture of an Indian and as I came near it slowly vanished. When I returned to my seat, Madame Blavatsky said, "What did you see?" "A picture," I said. "Tell it to go away." "It is already gone." "So much the better," she said, "I was afraid it was mediumship. But it is only clairvoyance." "What is the difference?" "If it had been mediumship, it would have stayed in spite of you. Beware of mediumship; it is a kind of madness; I know for I have been through it."

I found her almost always full of gaiety that, unlike the occasional joking of those about her, was illogical and incalculable and yet always kindly and tolerant. I had called one evening to find her absent but expected every moment. She had been somewhere at the seaside for her health and arrived with a little suite of followers. She sat down at once in her big chair, and began unfolding a brown paper parcel while all looked on full of curiosity. It contained a large family Bible. "This is a present for my maid," she said. "What a Bible and not even annotated!" said some shocked voice. "Well, my children," was the answer, "what is the good of giving lemons to those who want oranges?" When I first began to frequent her house, as I soon did very constantly, I noticed a handsome clever woman of the world there, who seemed certainly very much out of place, penitent though she thought herself. Presently there was much scandal and gossip for the penitent was plainly entangled with two young men, who were expected to grow into ascetic sages. The scandal was so great that Madame Blavatsky had to call the penitent before her and to speak after this fashion, "We think that it is necessary to crush the animal nature; you should live in chastity in act and thought. Initiation is granted only to those who are entirely chaste," but after some minutes in that vehement style, the penitent standing crushed and shamed before her, she had wound up, "I cannot permit you more than one." She was quite sincere but thought that nothing mattered but what happened in the mind, and that if we could not master the mind our actions were of little importance. One young man filled her with exasperation for she thought that his settled gloom came from his chastity. I had known him in Dublin where he had been accustomed to interrupt long periods of asceticism, in which he would eat vegetables and drink water, with brief outbreaks of what he considered the devil. After an outbreak he would for a few hours dazzle the imagination of the members of the local theosophical society with poetical rhapsodies about harlots and street lamps, and then sink into weeks of melancholy. A fellow-theosophist once found him hanging from the window-pole, but cut him down in the nick of time. I said to the man who cut him down, "What did you say to each other?" He said, "We spent the night telling comic stories and laughing a great deal." This man, torn between sensuality and visionary ambition, was now the most devout of all, and told me that in the middle of the night he could often hear the ringing of the little "astral bell" whereby Madame Blavatsky's master called her attention, and that, although it was a silvery low tone, it made the whole house shake. Another night I found him waiting in the hall to show in those who had right of entrance, on some night when the discussion was private, and as I passed he whispered into my ear, "Madame Blavatsky is perhaps not a real woman at all. They say that her dead body was found many years ago upon some

Italian battlefield." She had two dominant moods, both of extreme activity, one calm and philosophic, and this was the mood always on that night in the week when she answered questions upon her system, and as I look back after thirty years I often ask myself, "Was her speech automatic? Was she a trance medium, or in some similar state, one night in every week?" In the other mood she was full of fantasy and inconsequent raillery. "That is the Greek Church, a triangle like all true religion," I recall her saying, as she chalked out a triangle on the green baize, and then as she made it disappear in meaningless scribbles, "It spread out and became a bramble bush like the Church of Rome." Then rubbing it all out except one straight line, "Now they have lopped off the branches and turned it into a broomstick and that is protestantism." And so it was night after night always varied and unforeseen. I have observed a like sudden extreme change in others, half whose thought was supernatural; and Lawrence Oliphant records somewhere or other like observations. I can remember only once finding her in a mood of reverie, something had happened to damp her spirits, some attack upon her movement, or upon herself. She spoke of Balzac, whom she had seen but once, of Alfred de Musset, whom she had known well enough to dislike for his morbidity, and George Sand, whom she had known so well that they had dabbled in magic together of which "neither knew anything at all" in those days; and she ran on, as if there was nobody there to overhear her, "I used to wonder at and pity the people who sell their souls to the devil, but now I only pity them. They do it to have somebody on their side," and added to that, after some words I have forgotten, "I write, write, write as the Wandering Jew walks, walks, walks."

Besides the devotees, who came to listen and to turn every doctrine into a new sanction for the puritanical convictions of their Victorian childhood, cranks came from half Europe and from all America, and they came that they might talk. One American said to me, "She has become the most famous woman in the world by sitting in a big chair and permitting us to talk." They talked and she played patience, and totted up her score on the green baize, and generally seemed to listen, but sometimes she would listen no more. There was a woman who talked perpetually of "the divine spark" within her, until Madame Blavatsky stopped her with—"Yes, my dear, you have a divine spark within you and if you are not very careful you will hear it snore." A certain Salvation Army captain probably pleased her, for if vociferous and loud of voice, he had much animation. He had known hardship and spoke of his visions while starving in the streets and he was still perhaps a little light in the head. I wondered what he could preach to ignorant men, his head ablaze with mild mysticism, till I met a man who had heard him near Covent Garden. "My friends," he was saying, "you have the kingdom of heaven within you and it would take a pretty big pill to get that out."

Meanwhile I had got no nearer to proving that the sage Ahasuerus "dwells in a sea cavern 'mid the Demonesi," nor did I learn any more of those "Masters" whose representative Madame Blavatsky claimed to be. All there seemed to feel their presence, and all spoke of them as if they were more important than any visible inhabitant of the house. When Madame Blavatsky was more silent, less vivid than usual, it was "because her Masters were angry"; they had rebuked her because of some error, and she professed constant error. Once I seemed in their presence, or that of some messenger of theirs. It was about nine at night, and half a dozen of us sat round her big tablecloth, when the room filled with the odour of incense. Somebody came from upstairs, but could smell nothing—had been outside the influence it seems—but to myself and the others, it was very strong. Madame Blavatsky said it was a common Indian incense, and that some pupil of her "Master's" was present; she seemed anxious to make light of the matter and turned the conversation to something else. Certainly it was a romantic house, and I did not separate myself from it by my own will. I had learned from Blake to hate all abstraction, and, irritated by the abstraction of what were called "esoteric teachings," I began a series of experiments. Some book or magazine published by the society had quoted from an essay upon magic by some seventeenth-century writer. If you burnt a flower to ashes and put the ashes under, I think, the receiver of an air pump, and stood the receiver in the moonlight for so many nights, the ghost of the flower would appear hovering over its ashes. I got together a committee which performed this experiment without results. The "esoteric teachings" had declared that a certain very pure kind of indigo was the symbol of one of the seven principles into which they divided human nature. I got with some difficulty a little of this pure indigo, and gave portions of it to members of the committee, and asked them to put it under their pillows at night and record their dreams. I argued that all natural scenery must be divided into seven types according to these principles, and by their study we could rid the mind of abstraction. Presently a secretary, a friendly, intelligent man, asked me to come and see him, and, when I did complained that I was causing discussion and disturbance. A certain fanatical hungry face had been noticed red and tearful and it was quite plain that I was not in agreement with their methods or their philosophy. "We have certain definite ideas," he said, "and we have but one duty, to spread them through the world. I know that all these people become dogmatic, that they believe what they can never prove, that their withdrawal from family life is for them a great misfortune, but what are we to do? We have been told that all spiritual influx into the society will come to an end in 1897 for exactly one hundred years; before that date our fundamental ideas must be spread in all countries." I knew the doctrine, and it made me wonder why that old woman, or the "Masters" from whom, whatever they were or were not, her genius had come, insisted upon it; for influx of some kind there must always be. Did they dread heresy, or had they no purpose but the greatest possible immediate effect?

20

At the British Museum reading-room I often saw a man of thirty-six, or thirty-seven, in a brown velveteen coat, with a gaunt resolute face, and an athletic body, who seemed before I heard his name, or knew the nature of his studies, a figure of romance. Presently I was introduced, where or by what man or woman I do not remember. He was called Liddle Mathers, but would soon, under the touch of "The Celtic Movement," become Macgregor Mathers, and then plain Macgregor. He was the author of *The Kabbala Unveiled,* and his studies were two only—magic and the theory of war, for he believed himself a born commander and all but equal in wisdom and in power to that old Jew. He had copied many manuscripts on magic ceremonial and doctrine in the British Museum, and was to copy many more in Continental libraries, and it was through him mainly that I began certain studies and experiences, that were to convince me that images well up before the mind's eye from a deeper source than conscious or subconscious memory. I believe that his mind in those early days did not belie his face and body—though in later years it became unhinged, as Don Quixote's was unhinged—for he kept a proud head amid great poverty. One that boxed with him nightly has told me that for many weeks he could knock him down, though Mathers was the stronger man, and only knew long after that during those weeks Mathers starved. He had spoken to me, I think at our first introduction, of a Society which sometimes called itself—it had a different name among its members— "The Hermetic Students," and in May or June 1887 I was initiated into that Society in a Charlotte Street studio, and being at a most receptive age, shaped and isolated. Mathers was its governing mind, a born teacher and organiser. One of those who incite —less by spoken word than by what they are—imaginative action. We paid some small annual subscription, a few shillings for rent and stationery, but no poor man paid even that and all found him generous of time and thought. With Mathers I met an old white-haired Oxfordshire clergyman, the most panic-stricken person I have ever known, though Mathers' introduction had been "he unites us to the great adepts of antiquity." This old man took me aside that he might say—"I hope you never invoke spirits —that is a very dangerous thing to do. I am told that even the planetary spirits turn upon us in the end." I said, "Have you ever seen an apparition?" "Oh yes, once," he said. "I have my alchemical laboratory in a cellar under my house where the Bishop cannot see it. One day I was walking up and down there when I heard another footstep walking up and down beside me. I turned and saw a girl I had been in love with when I was a young man, but she died long ago. She wanted me to kiss her. Oh no, I would not do that." "Why not?" I said. "Oh she might have got power over me." "Has your alchemical research had any success?" I said. "Yes, I once made the elixir of life. A French alchemist said it had the right smell and the right colour" (the alchemist may have been Eliphas Levi, who visited England in the 'sixties, and would have said anything'), "but the first effect of the elixir is that your nails fall out and your hair falls off. I was afraid that I might have made a mistake and that nothing else might happen, so I put it away on a shelf. I meant to drink it when I was an old man, but when I got it down the other day it had all dried up."

Soon after my first meeting with Mathers he emerged into brief prosperity, becoming for two or three years Curator of a private museum at Forest Hill, and marrying a young and beautiful wife, the sister of the philosopher, Henri Bergson. His house at Forest Hill was soon a romantic place to a little group, Florence Farr—she too had been initiated—myself, and some dozen fellow-students. I think that it was she, her curiosity being insatiable, who first brought a tale of marvel and that she brought it in mockery and in wonder. Mathers had taken her for a walk through a field of sheep and had said, "Look at the sheep. I am going to imagine myself a ram," and at once all the sheep ran after him; another day he had tried to quell a thunderstorm by making symbols in the air with a masonic sword, but the storm had not been quelled; and then came the crowning wonder. He had given her a piece of cardboard on which was a coloured geometrical symbol and had told her to hold it to her forehead and she had found herself walking upon a cliff above the sea, seagulls shrieking overhead. I did not think the ram story impossible, and even tried half a dozen times to excite a cat by imagining a mouse in front of its nose, but still some chance movement of the flock might have deceived her. But what could have deceived her in that final marvel? Then another brought a like report, and presently my own turn came. He gave me a cardboard symbol and I closed my eyes. Sight came slowly, there was not that sudden miracle as if the darkness had been cut with a knife, for that miracle is mostly a woman's privilege, but there rose before me mental images that I could not control: a desert and black Titan raising himself up by his two hands from the middle of a heap of ancient ruins. Mathers explained that I had seen a being of the order of Salamanders because he had shown me their symbol, but it was not necessary even to show the symbol, it would have been sufficient that he imagined it. I had already written in my diary, under some date in 1887, that Madame Blavatsky's "Masters" were "trance personalities," and I must have meant such beings as my black Titan, only more lasting and more powerful. I had found when a boy in Dublin on a table in the Royal Irish Academy a pamphlet on Japanese art and read there of an animal painter so remarkable that horses he had painted upon a temple wall had slipped down after dark and trampled the neighbours' fields of rice. Somebody had come into the temple in the early morning, had been startled by a shower of water drops, had looked up and seen painted horses still wet from the dew-covered fields, but now "trembling into stillness."

I had soon mastered Mathers' symbolic system, and discovered that for a considerable minority—whom I could select by certain unanalysable characteristics—the visible world would completely vanish, and that world, summoned by the symbol, take its place. One day when alone in a third-class carriage, in the very middle of the railway bridge that crosses the Thames near Victoria, I smelt incense. I was on my way to Forest Hill; might it not come from some spirit Mathers had called up? I had wondered when I smelt it at Madame Blavatsky's—if there might be some contrivance, some secret censer, but that explanation was no longer possible. I believed that Salamander of his but an image, and presently I found analogies between smell and image. That smell must be thought created, but what certainty had I, that what had taken me by surprise, could be from my own thought, and if a thought could affect the sense of smell, why not the sense of touch? Then I discovered among that group of students that surrounded Mathers, a man who had fought a cat in his dreams and awakened to find his breast covered with scratches. Was there an impassable barrier between those scratches and the trampled fields of rice? It would seem so, and yet all was uncertainty. What fixed law would our experiments leave to our imagination?

Mathers had much learning but little scholarship, much imagination and imperfect taste, but if he made some absurd statement, some incredible claim, some hackneyed joke, we would half consciously change claim, statement or joke, as though he were a figure in a play of our composition. He was a necessary extravagance, and he had carried farther than any one else, a claim implicit in the romantic movement from the time of Shellcy and of Goethe; and in body and in voice at least he was perfect; so might Faust have looked in his changeless aged youth. In the credulity of our youth we secretly wondered if he had not met with, perhaps even been taught by some old man who had found the elixir. Nor did he undeceive us. "If you find the elixir," he was accustomed to say, "you always look a few years younger than the age at which you found it. If you find it at sixty you will look fifty for a hundred years." None of us would have admitted that we believed in stone or elixir, the old Oxfordshire clergyman excited no belief, yet one among us certainly laboured with crucible or athanor. Ten years ago I called upon an elderly solicitor, on some business, but at his private house, and I remembered whose pupil he had been when I found among the ashes of the hearth a little earthen pot. He pretended that he studied alchemy that he might some day write its history, and I found when I questioned others, that for twenty years there had been just such a little pot among the ashes.

21

I generalised a great deal and was ashamed of it. I thought it was my business in life to be an artist and a poet, and that there could be no business comparable to that. I refused to read books and even to meet people who excited me to generalisation, all to no purpose. I said my prayers much as in childhood, though without the old regularity of hour and place, and I began to pray that my imagination might somehow be rescued from abstraction and became as preoccupied with life as had been the imagination of Chaucer. For ten or twelve years more I suffered continual remorse, and only became content when my abstractions had composed themselves into picture and dramatisation. My very remorse helped to spoil my early poetry, giving it an element of sentimentality through my refusal to permit it any share of an intellect which I considered impure. Even in practical life I only very gradually began to use generalisations, that have since become the foundation of all I have done, or shall do, in Ireland. For all I know all men may have been so timid, for I am persuaded that our intellects at twenty contain all the truths we shall ever find, but as yet we do not know truths that belong to us from opinions caught up in casual irritation or momentary fantasy. As life goes on we discover that certain thoughts sustain us in defeat, or give us victory, whether over ourselves or others, and it is these thoughts, tested by passion, that we call convictions. Among subjective men (in all those, that is, who must spin a web out of their own bowls) the victory is an intellectual daily re-creation of all that exterior fate snatches away, and so that fate's antithesis; while what I have called "the Mask" is an emotional antithesis to all that comes out of their internal nature. We begin to live when we have conceived life as tragedy.

22

A conviction that the world was now but a bundle of fragments possessed me without ceasing. I had tried this conviction on the Rhymers, thereby plunging into greater silence an already too-silent evening. "Johnson," I was accustomed to say, "you are the only man I know whose silence has beak and claw." I had lectured on it to some London Irish society, and I was to lecture upon it later on in Dublin, but I never found but one interested man, an official of the Primrose League, who was also an active member of the Fenian Brotherhood. "I am an extreme conservative apart from Ireland," I have heard him explain; and I have no doubt that personal experience made him share the sight of any eye that saw the world in fragments. I had been put into a rage by the followers of Huxley, Tyndall, Carolus Duran, and Bastien-Lepage, who not only asserted the unimportance of subject whether in art or literature, but the independence of the arts from one another. Upon the other hand, I delighted in every age where poet and artist confined themselves gladly to some inherited subject-matter known to the whole people, for I thought that in man and race alike there is something called "Unity of Being," using that term as Dante used it when he compared beauty in the *Convito* to a perfectly proportioned human body. My father, from whom I had learned the term, preferred a comparison to a musical instrument so strung that if we touch a string all the strings murmur faintly. There is not more desire, he had said, in lust than in true love, but in true love desire awakens pity, hope, affection, admiration and, given appropriate circumstance, every emotion possible to man. When I began, however, to apply this thought to the state and to argue for a law-made balance among trades and occupations my father displayed at once the violent free trader and propagandist of liberty. I thought that the enemy of this unity was abstraction, meaning by abstraction not the distinction but the isolation of occupation, or class or faculty—

> Call down the hawk from the air
> Let him be hooded, or caged,
> Till the yellow eye has grown mild,
> For larder and spit are bare,
> The old cook enraged,
> The scullion gone wild.

I knew no mediæval cathedral, and Westminster, being a part of abhorred London, did not interest me, but I thought constantly of Homer and Dante, and the tombs of Mausolus and Artemisia, the great figures of King and Queen and the lesser figures of Greek and Amazon, Centaur and Greek. I thought that all art should be a Centaur finding in the popular lore its back and its strong legs. I got great pleasure too from remembering that Homer was sung, and from that tale of Dante hearing a common man sing some stanza from *The Divine Comedy*, and from Don Quixote's meeting with some common man that sang Ariosto. Morris had never seemed to care greatly for any poet later than Chaucer and though I preferred Shakespeare to Chaucer I begrudged my own preference. Had not Europe shared one mind and heart, until both mind and heart began to break into fragments a little before Shakespeare's birth? Music and verse began to fall apart when Chaucer robbed verse of its speed that he might give it greater meditation, though for another generation or so minstrels were to sing his lengthy elaborated *Troilus and Criseyde*; painting parted from religion in the later Renaissance that it might study effects of tangibility undisturbed; while, that it might characterise, where it had once personified, it renounced, in our own age, all that inherited subject-matter which we have named poetry. Presently I was indeed to number character itself among the abstractions, encouraged by Congreve's saying that "passions are too powerful, in the fair sex to let humour" or as we say character, "have its course." Nor have we fared better under the common daylight, for pure reason has notoriously made but light of practical reason, and has been made light of in its turn from that morning when Descartes discovered that he could think better in his bed than out of it; nor needed I original thought to discover, being so late of the school of Morris, that machinery had not separated from handicraft wholly for the world's good, nor to notice that the distinction of classes had become their isolation. If the London merchants of our day competed together in writing lyrics they would not, like the Tudor merchants, dance in the open street before the house of the victor; nor do the great ladies of London finish their balls on the pavement before their doors as did the great Venetian ladies, even in the eighteenth century, conscious of an all-enfolding sympathy. Doubtless because fragments broke into even smaller fragments we saw one another in a light of bitter comedy, and in the arts, where now one technical element reigned and now another, generation hated generation, and accomplished beauty was snatched away when it had most engaged our affections. One thing I did not foresee, not having the courage of my own thought: the growing murderousness of the world.

> Turning and turning in the widening gyre
> The falcon cannot hear the falconer;
> Things fall apart; the centre cannot hold;
> Mere anarchy is loosed upon the world,
> The blood-dimmed tide is loosed and everywhere
> The ceremony of innocence is drowned;
> The best lack all conviction while the worst
> Are full of passionate intensity.

23

If abstraction had reached, or all but reached its climax escape might be possible for many, and if it had not, individual men might still escape. If Chaucer's personages had disengaged themselves from Chaucer's crowd, forgot their common goal and shrine, and after sundry magnifications became each in turn the centre of some Elizabethan play, and had after split into their

elements and so given birth to romantic poetry, must I reverse
the cinematograph? I thought that the general movement of literature must be such a reversal, men being there displayed in
casual, temporary, contact as at the Tabard door. I had lately
read Tolstoy's *Anna Karenina* and thought that where his the-
oretical capacity had not awakened there was such a turning
back: but a nation or an individual with great emotional intensity
might follow the pilgrims as it were to some unknown shrine,
and give to all those separated elements and to all that abstract
love and melancholy, a symbolical, a mythological coherence.
Not Chaucer's rough-tongued riders, but rather an ended pil-
grimage, a procession of the Gods! Arthur Symons brought back
from Paris stories of Verhaeren and Maeterlinck, and so brought
me confirmation, as I thought, and I began to announce a poetry
like that of the Sufi's. I could not endure, however, an international art, picking stories and symbols where it pleased. Might
I not, with health and good luck to aid me, create some new
Prometheus Unbound; Patrick or Columbkil, Oisin or Fion, in
Prometheus' stead; and, instead of Caucasus, Cro-Patric or Ben
Bulben? Have not all races had their first unity from a mythology,
that marries them to rock and hill? We had in Ireland imaginative stories, which the uneducated classes knew and even sang,
and might we not make those stories current among the educated
classes, rediscovering for the work's sake what I have called "the
applied arts of literature," the association of literature, that is,
with music, speech, and dance; and at last, it might be, so deepen
the political passion of the nation that all, artist and poet, craftsman and day-labourer would accept a common design? Perhaps
even these images, once created and associated with river and
mountain, might move of themselves and with some powerful,
even turbulent life, like those painted horses that trampled the
rice-fields of Japan.

24

I used to tell the few friends to whom I could speak these
secret thoughts that I would make the attempt in Ireland but
fail, for our civilisation, its elements multiplying by division like
certain low forms of life, was all-powerful; but in reality I had

the wildest hopes. To-day I add to that first conviction, to that first desire for unity, this other conviction, long a mere opinion vaguely or intermittently apprehended: Nations, races, and individual men are unified by an image, or bundle of related images, symbolical or evocative of the state of mind, which is of all states of mind not impossible, the most difficult to that man, race, or nation; because only the greatest obstacle that can be contemplated without despair rouses the will to full intensity.

A powerful class by terror, rhetoric, and organised sentimentality, may drive their people to war but the day draws near when they cannot keep them there; and how shall they face the pure nations of the East when the day comes to do it with but equal arms? I had seen Ireland in my own time turn from the bragging rhetoric and gregarious humour of O'Connell's generation and school, and offer herself to the solitary and proud Parnell as to her anti-self, buskin following hard on sock, and I had begun to hope, or to half hope, that we might be the first in Europe to seek unity as deliberately as it had been sought by theologian, poet, sculptor, architect, from the eleventh to the thirteenth century. Doubtless we must seek it differently, no longer considering it convenient to epitomise all human knowledge, but find it we well might could we first find philosophy and a little passion.

BOOK II

Ireland after Parnell

I

A couple of years before the death of Parnell, I had wound up my introduction to those selections from the Irish novelists with the prophecy of an intellectual movement at the first lull in politics, and now I wished to fulfil my prophecy. I did not put it in that way, for I preferred to think that the sudden emotion that now came to me, the sudden certainty that Ireland was to be like soft wax for years to come, was a moment of supernatural insight. How could I tell, how can I tell even now?

There was a little Irish Society of young people, clerks, shopboys, and shop-girls, called "The Southwark Irish Literary Society," and it had ceased to meet because the girls got the giggles when any member of the Committee got up to speak. Every member of it had said all he had to say many times over. I had given them a lecture about the falling asunder of the human mind, as an opening flower falls asunder, and all had professed admiration because I had made such a long speech without quotation or narrative; and now I invited the Committee to my father's house at Bedford Park, and there proposed a new organisation, "The Irish Literary Society." T. W. Rolleston came to that first meeting, and it was because he had much tact, and a knowledge of the technical business of committees, that a society was founded which was joined by every London Irish author and journalist. In a few months somebody had written its history, and published that history, illustrated by our portraits, at a shilling. When it was published I was in Dublin, founding a society there called "The National Literary Society," and affiliating it with certain Young Ireland Societies in country towns which seemed anxious to accept its leadership. I had definite plans; I wanted

to create an Irish Theatre; I was finishing my *Countess Cathleen*
in its first meagre version, and thought of a travelling company
to visit our country branches; but before that there must be a
popular imaginative literature. I arranged with Mr. Fisher Unwin and his reader, Mr. Edward Garnett—a personal friend of
mine—that when our organisation was complete Mr. Fisher Unwin was to publish for it a series of books at a shilling each. I
told only one man of this arrangement, for after I had made my
plans I heard an alarming rumour. Old Sir Charles Gavan Duffy
was coming from Australia to start an Irish publishing-house, and
publish a series of books, and I did not expect to agree with him,
but knew that I must not seek a quarrel. The two societies were
necessary because their lectures must take the place of an educated popular press, which we had not, and have not now, and
create a standard of criticism. Irish literature had fallen into contempt; no educated man ever bought an Irish book; in Dublin
Professor Dowden, the one man of letters with an international
influence, was accustomed to say that he knew an Irish book by
its smell, because he had once seen some books whose bind-
ing had been fastened together by rotten glue; and Standish
O'Grady's last book upon ancient Irish history—a book rather
wild, rather too speculative, but forestalling later research—had
not been reviewed by any periodical or newspaper in England
or in Ireland.

At first I had great success, for I brought with me a list of
names written down by some member of the Southwark Irish
Literary Society, and for six weeks went hither and thither ap-
pealing and persuading. My first conversation was over a butter-
tub in some Dublin back street, and the man agreed with me
at once; everybody agreed with me; all felt that something must
be done, but nobody knew what. Perhaps they did not understand me, perhaps I kept back my full thoughts, perhaps they
only seemed to listen; it was enough that I had a plan, and was
determined about it. When I went to lecture in a provincial
town, a workman's wife, who wrote patriotic stories in some
weekly newspaper, invited me to her house, and I found all her
children in their Sunday best. She made a little speech, very
formal and very simple, in which she said that what she wrote

had no merit, but that it paid for her children's schooling; and she finished her speech by telling her children never to forget that they had seen me. One man compared me to Thomas Davis, another said I could organise like Davitt, and I thought to succeed as they did, and as rapidly. I did not examine this applause, nor the true thoughts of those I met, nor the general condition of the country, but I examined myself a great deal, and was puzzled at myself. I knew that I was shy and timid, that I would often leave some business undone, or purchase unmade, because I shrank from facing a strange office or a shop a little grander than usual, and yet, here was I delightedly talking to strange people every day. It was many years before I understood that I had surrendered myself to the chief temptation of the artist, creation without toil. Metrical composition is always very difficult to me, nothing is done upon the first day, not one rhyme is in its place; and when at last the rhymes begin to come, the first rough draft of a six-line stanza takes the whole day. At that time I had not formed a style, and sometimes a six line stanza would take several days, and not seem finished even then and I had not learnt, as I have now, to put it all out of my head before night, and so the last night was generally sleepless, and the last day a day of nervous strain. But now I had found the happiness that Shelley found when he tied a pamphlet to a fire balloon.

2

At first I asked no help from prominent persons, and when some clerk or shop-assistant would say "Dr. So-and-so or Professor So-and-so will have nothing to do with us" I would answer, "When we prove we can gather sheep shepherds will come." Presently, come they did, old, middle-aged, or but little older than myself, but all with some authority in their town: John O'Leary, John F. Taylor, Douglas Hyde, and Standish O'Grady, and of these much presently; Dr. Sigerson, learned, artificial, unscholarly, a typical provincial celebrity, but a friendly man; Count Plunkett, Sinn Feiner of late and Minister of Dail Eireann; Dr. Coffey, now head of the National University; George Coffey, later on Curator of the Irish Antiquities at the Museum of the Royal Dublin Society; Patrick J. McCall, poet and publican of Patrick Street, and later member of the Corporation; Richard Ashe King, novelist and correspondent of *Truth*, a gentle, intelligent person, in nothing typical of the Dublin of that time; and others, known or unknown. We were now important, had our Committee room in the Mansion House, and I remember that the old Mansion House butler recognised our importance so fully, that he took us into his confidence once in every week, while we sat waiting for a quorum. He had seen many Lord Mayors, and remembered those very superior Lord Mayors who lived before the extension of the municipal franchise, and spoke of his present masters with contempt. Among our persons of authority, and among the friends and followers they had brought, there were many who at that time found it hard to refuse if anybody offered for sale a pepper-pot shaped to suggest a round tower with a wolf-dog at its foot, who would have felt it inappropriate to publish an Irish book that had not harp and shamrock and green cover, so completely did their minds move amid Young Ireland images and metaphors, and I thought with alarm of the coming of Sir Charles Gavan Duffy; while here and there I noticed that smooth, smiling face that we discover for the first time in certain pictures by Velasquez; the hungry, mediæval speculation vanished that had worn the faces of El Greco, and in its place a self-complacent certainty that all had been arranged, all provided for, all set out in clear type, in manual of devotion or of doctrine. These, however, were no true disciples of Young Ireland, for Young Ireland had sought a nation unified by political doctrine alone, a subservient art and letters aiding and abetting. The movement of thought, which had in the 'fifties and 'forties at Paris and London and Boston, filled literature, and especially poetical literature, with curiosities about science, about history, about politics, with moral purpose and educational fervour—abstractions all—had created a new instrument for Irish politics, a method of writing that took its poetical style from Campbell, Scott, Macaulay, and Beranger, with certain elements from Gaelic, its prose style—in John Mitchell, the only Young Ireland prose-writer who had a style at all—from Carlyle. To recommend this method of writing as literature with-

out much reservation and discrimination I contended was to be
deceived or to practise deception. If one examined some country
love-song, one discovered that it was not written by a man in
love, but by a patriot who wanted to prove that we did indeed
possess, in the words of Daniel O'Connell, "the finest peasantry
upon earth." Yet one well-known anthology was introduced by
the assertion that such love-poetry was superior to "affected and
artificial" English love-songs like "Drink to me only with thine
eyes"—"affected and artificial," the very words used by English
Victorians, who wrote for the newspapers, to discourage capricious, personal writing. Yet, the greater number—even of those
who thought our famous anthology, *The Spirit of the Nation*,
except for three or four songs, but good election rhyme—looked
upon such poetry as certain enlightened believers look upon the
story of Adam and Eve and the apple, or that of Jonah and the
whale, which they do not question publicly, because such stories
are an integral part of religion to simple men and women. I,
upon the other hand, being in the intemperance of my youth,
denied, as publicly as possible, merit to all but a few ballads
translated from Gaelic writers, or written out of a personal and
generally tragic experience.

3

The greater number of those who joined my society had come
under the seal of Young Ireland at that age when we are all
mere wax; the more ambitious had gone daily to some public
library to read the bound volumes of Thomas Davis's old newspaper, and tried to see the world as Davis saw it. No philosophic
speculation, no economic question of the day, disturbed an
orthodoxy which, unlike that of religion, had no philosophic
history, and the religious bigot was glad that it should be so.
Some few of the younger men were impatient, and it was these
younger men, more numerous in the London than in the Dublin
Society, who gave me support; and we had been joined by a
few older men—some personal friends of my own or my father
—who had only historical interest in Thomas Davis and his
school. Young Ireland's prose had been as much occupied with
Irish virtue, and more with the invader's vices, than its poetry,

and we were soon mired and sunk into such problems as to whether Cromwell was altogether black, the heads of the old Irish clans altogether white, the Danes mere robbers and church burners (they tell me at Rosses Point that the Danes keep to this day the maps of the Rosses fields they were driven out of in the ninth century, and plot their return) and as to whether we were or were not once the greatest orators in the world. All the past had been turned into a melodrama with Ireland for blameless hero and poet; novelist and historian had but one object, that we should hiss the villain, and only a minority doubted that the greater the talent the greater the hiss. It was all the harder to substitute for that melodrama a nobler form of art, because there really had been, however different in their form, villain and victim; yet fight that rancour I must, and if I had not made some head against it in 1892 and 1893 it might have silenced in 1907 John Synge, the greatest dramatic genius of Ireland. I am writing of disputes that happened many years ago, that led in later years to much bitterness, and I may exaggerate their immediate importance and violence, but I think I am right in saying that disputes about the merits of Young Ireland so often interrupted our discussion of rules, or of the merit of this or that lecturer, and were so aggravated and crossed by the current wrangle between Parnellite and anti-Parnellite that they delayed our public appearance for a year. Other excited persons, doubtless, seeing that we are of a race intemperate of speech, had looked up from their rancours to the dead Lord Mayors upon the wall, superior men whose like we shall not see again, but never, I think, from rancours so seemingly academic. I was preparing the way without knowing it for a great satirist and master of irony, for master works stir vaguely in many before they grow definite in one man's mind, and to help me I had already flitting through my head, jostling other ideas and so not yet established there, a conviction that we should satirise rather than praise, that original virtue arises from the discovery of evil. If we were, as I had dreaded, declamatory, loose, and bragging, we were but the better fitted—that declared and measured—to create unyielding personality, manner at once cold and passionate, daring long premeditated act; and if bitter beyond all the people of the world, we might yet lie—that too declared and measured—nearest the honeyed comb:

> Like the clangour of a bell
> Sweet and harsh, harsh and sweet,
> That is how he learnt so well
> To take the roses for his meat.

4

There were others with followers of their own, and too old or indifferent to join our society. Old men who had never accepted Young Ireland, or middle-aged men kept by some family tradition to the school of thought before it arose, to the Ireland of Daniel O'Connell and of Lever and of Thomas Moore, convivial Ireland with the traditional tear and smile. They sang Moore's *Melodies*, admitted no poetry but his, and resented Young Ireland's political objections to it as much as my generation's objection to its artificial and easy rhythm; one, an old commercial traveller, a Gaelic scholar who kept an erect head and the animal vigour of youth, frequented the houses of our leading men, and would say in a loud voice, "Thomas Moore, sir, is the greatest heroic poet of ancient or modern times." I think it was the Fire Worshippers in *Lalla Rookh* that he preferred to Homer; or, jealous for the music of the *Melodies,* he would denounce Wagner, then at the top of his vogue; "I would run ten miles through a bog to escape him," he would cry. Then there was a maker of tombstones of whom we had heard much but had seen little, an elderly fighting man, lately imprisoned for beating a wine-merchant. A young member of the London society, afterwards librarian to the National University, D. J. O'Donohue, who had published a dictionary of the Irish poets, containing, I think, two thousand names, had come to Dublin and settled there in a fit of patriotism. He had been born in London, and spoke the most Cockney dialect imaginable, and had picked up—probably from London critics—a dislike for the poetry of Thomas Moore. The tombstone-maker invited him to tea, and he arrived with a bundle of books, which he laid beside him upon the table. During tea he began expounding that dislike of his; his host was silent, but he went on, for he was an obstinate little man. Presently the tombstone-maker rose, and having said solemnly, "I have never permitted that great poet to be slandered in my presence," seized his guest by the back of the collar, and flung him out into the street, and after that flung out the books one after another. Meanwhile the guest—as he himself told the tale—stood in the middle of the street, repeating, "Nice way to treat a man in your own 'ouse."

5

I shared a lodging full of old books and magazines, covered with dirt and dust, with the head of the Fenian Brotherhood, John O'Leary. "In this country," he had said to me, "a man must have upon his side the Church or the Fenians, and you will never have the Church." He had been converted to nationality by the poems of Davis, and he wished for some analogous movement to that of Davis, but he had known men of letters, had been the friend of Whistler, and knew the faults of the old literature. We had made him the President of our Society, and without him I could do nothing, for his long imprisonment and longer exile, his magnificent appearance, and, above all, the fact that he alone had personality, a point of view not made for the crowd's sake, but for self-expression, made him magnetic to my generation. He and I had long been friends, he had stayed with us at Bedford Park, and my father had painted his portrait, but if I had not shared his lodging he would have opposed me. He was an old man, and my point of view was not that of his youth, and it often took me half the day to make him understand—so suspicious he was of all innovation—some simple thing that he would presently support with ardour. He had grown up in a European movement when the revolutionist thought that he, above all men, must appeal to the highest motive, be guided by some ideal principle, be a little like Cato or like Brutus, and he had lived to see the change Dostoievsky examined in *The Possessed*. Men who had been of his party—and oftener their sons —preached assassination and the bomb; and, worst of all, the majority of his countrymen followed after constitutional politicians who practised opportunism, and had, as he believed, such low morals that they would lie, or publish private correspondence, if it might advance their cause. He would split every practical project into its constituent elements, like a clerical casuist, to find if it might not lead into some moral error; but, were the project revolutionary, he would sometimes temper condemnation with pity. Though he would cast off his oldest acquaintance did he suspect him of rubbing shoulders with some carrier of bombs, I have heard him say of a man who blew himself up in an attempt to blow up Westminster Bridge, "He was not a bad man, but he had too great a moral nature for his intellect, not that he lacked intellect." He did not explain, but he meant, I suppose, that the spectacle of injustice might madden a good man more quickly than some common man. Such men were of his own sort, though gone astray, but the constitutional politicians he had been fighting all his life, and all they did displeased him. It was not that he thought their aim wrong, or that they could not achieve it; he had accepted Gladstone's Home Rule Bill; but that in his eyes they degraded manhood. "If England has been brought to do us justice by such men," he would say, "that is not because of our strength, but because of her weakness." He had a particular hatred for the rush of emotion that followed the announcement of Gladstone's conversion, for what was called "The Union of Hearts," and derided its sentimentality. "Nations may respect one another," he would say, "they cannot love." His ancestors had probably kept little shops, or managed little farms in County Tipperary, yet he hated democracy, though he never used the word either for praise or blame, with more than feudal hatred. "No gentleman can be a socialist," he said, and then, with a thoughtful look, "he might be an anarchist." He had no philosophy, but things distressed his palate, and two of those things were International propaganda and the Organised State, and Socialism aimed at both, nor could he speak such words as "philanthropy," "humanitarianism," without showing by his tone of voice that they offended him. The Church pleased him little better; there was an old Fenian quarrel there, and he would say, "My religion is the old Persian, to pull the bow and tell the truth." He had no self-consciousness, no visible pride, and would have hated anything that could have been called a gesture, was indeed scarce artist enough to invent a gesture; yet he would never speak of the hardship of his prison life —though abundantly enough of its humours—and once, when I pressed him, replied, "I was in the hands of my enemy, why should I complain?" A few years ago I heard that the Governor of the prison had asked why he did not report some unnecessary discomfort, and O'Leary had said, "I did not come here to complain." Now that he is dead, I wish that I could question him, and perhaps discover whether in early youth he had come across some teacher who had expounded Roman virtue, but I doubt if I would have learnt anything, for I think the wax had long forgotten the seal—if seal there were. The seal was doubtless made before the eloquent humanitarian 'forties and 'fifties, and was one kind with whatever moulded the youthful mind of Savage Landor. Stephens, the founder of Fenianism, had discovered him searching the second-hand bookstalls for rare editions, and enrolled him in his organisation. "You have no chance of success," O'Leary had said, "but it will be good for the *morale* of the country" (*morale* was his great word), "and I will join on the condition that I am never asked to enrol anybody." He still searched the second-hand bookstalls, and had great numbers of books, especially of Irish history and literature, and when I, exhausted over our morning's casuistry, would sit down to my day's work (I was writing *The Secret Rose*) he would make his tranquil way to the Dublin Quays. In the evening, over his coffee, he would write passages for his memoirs upon postcards and odd scraps of paper, taking immense trouble with every word and comma, for the great work must be a masterpiece of style. When it was finished, it was unreadable, being dry, abstract, and confused; no picture had ever passed before his mind's eye. He was a victim, I think, of a movement where opinions stick men together, or keep them apart, like a kind of bird-lime, and without any relation to their natural likes and tastes, and where men of rich nature must give themselves up to an irritation which they no longer recognise because it is always present. I often wonder why he gave me his friendship, why it was he who found almost all the subscribers for my *Wanderings of Usheen,* and why he now supported me in all I did, for how could he like verses that were all picture, all emotion, all association, all mythology? He could not have approved my criticism either, for I exalted

Mask and Image above the eighteenth century logic which he loved, and set experience before observation, emotion before fact. Yet he would say, "I have only three followers, Taylor, Yeats, and Rolleston," and presently he cast out Rolleston— "Davitt wants to convert thousands, but I want two or three." I think that perhaps it was because he no more wished to strengthen Irish Nationalism by second-rate literature than by second-rate morality, and was content that we agreed in that. "There are things a man must not do to save a Nation," he had once told me, and when I asked what things, had said, "To cry in public," and I think it probable that he would have added, if pressed, "To write oratorical or insincere verse."

O'Leary's movements and intonations were full of impulse, but John F. Taylor's voice in private discussion had no emotional quality except in the expression of scorn; if he moved an arm it moved from the shoulder or elbow alone, and when he walked he moved from the waist only, and seemed an automaton, a wooden soldier, as if he had no life that was not dry and abstract. Except at moments of public oratory, he lacked all personality, though when one saw him respectful and gentle with O'Leary, as with some charming woman, one saw that he felt its fascination. In letters, or in painting, it repelled him unless it were harsh and obvious, and, therefore, though his vast erudition included much art and letters, he lacked artistic feeling, and judged everything by the moral sense. He had great ambition, and had he joined some established party, or found some practicable policy, he might have been followed, might have produced even some great effect, but he must have known that in defeat no man would follow him, as they followed O'Leary, as they followed Parnell. His oratory was noble, strange, even beautiful, at moments the greatest I have ever listened to; but, the speech over, where there had been, as it seemed, so little of himself, all coming from beyond himself, we saw precisely as before an ungainly body in unsuitable, badly fitting clothes, and heard an excited voice speaking ill of this man or that other. We knew that he could never give us that one price we would accept, that he would never find a practicable policy; that no party would admit, no government negotiate with, a man notorious for a temper, that, if it gave him genius, could at times carry him to the edge of insanity.

Born in some country town, the son of some little watch-maker, he had been a shop assistant, put himself to college and the bar, learned to speak at temperance meetings and Young Ireland Societies, and was now a Queen's Counsel famous for his defence of country criminals, whose cases had seemed hopeless —Taylor's boys, their neighbours called them or they called themselves. He had shaped his style and his imagination from Carlyle, the chief inspirer of self-educated men in the 'eighties and early 'nineties. "I prefer Emerson's *Oversoul*," the Condalkin cobbler said to me, "but I always read Carlyle when I am wild with the neighbours"; but he used his master's style, as Mitchell had done before, to abase what his master loved, to exalt what his master scorned. His historical erudition seemed as vast as that of York Powell, but his interests were not Powell's, for he had no picture before the mind's eye, and had but one object—a plea of not guilty—entered in his country's name before a jury which he believed to be packed. O'Leary cared nothing for his country's glory, its individuality alone seemed important in his eyes; he was like some man, who serves a woman all his life without asking whether she be good or bad, wise or foolish; but Taylor cared for nothing else. He was so much O'Leary's disciple that he would say in conversation, "We are demoralised, what case for change if we are not?" for O'Leary admitted no ground for reform outside the moral life, but when he spoke to the great plea he would make no admission. He spoke to it in the most obscure places, in little halls in back streets where the white-washed walls were foul with grease from many heads, before some audience of medical students or of shop assistants, for he was like a man under a curse, compelled to hide his genius, and compelled to show in conspicuous places his ill judgment and his temper.

His distaste for myself, broken by occasional tolerance, in so far as it was not distaste for an imagination that seemed to him æsthetic rather than ethical, was because I had published Irish folklore in English reviews to the discredit, as he thought, of the Irish peasantry, and because, England within earshot, I found fault with the Young Ireland prose and poetry. He would have hated *The Playboy of the Western World,* and his death a little before its performance was fortunate for Synge and myself. His articles are nothing, and his one historical work, a life of Hugh O'Neill, is almost nothing, lacking the living voice; and now, though a most formidable man, he is forgotten, but for the fading memory of a few friends, and for what an enemy has written here and elsewhere. Did not Leonardo da Vinci warn the imaginative man against preoccupation with arts that cannot survive his death?

6

When Carleton was dying in 1870, he said there would be nothing more about Irish Literature for twenty years, and his words were fulfilled, for the land war had filled Ireland with its bitterness; but imagination had begun to stir again. I had the same confidence in the future that Lady Gregory and I had eight or nine years later, when we founded an Irish Theatre, though there were neither, as it seemed, plays or players. There were already a few known men to start my popular series, and to keep it popular until the men, whose names I did not know, had learnt to express themselves. I had met Dr. Douglas Hyde when I lived in Dublin, and he was still an undergraduate. I have a memory of meeting in college rooms for the first time a very dark young man, who filled me with surprise, partly because he had pushed a snuffbox towards me, and partly because there was something about his vague serious eyes, as in his high cheek bones, that suggested a different civilisation, a different race. I had set him down as a peasant, and wondered what brought him to college, and to a Protestant college, but somebody explained that he belonged to some branch of the Hydes of Castle Hyde, and that he had a Protestant Rector for father. He had much frequented the company of old countrymen, and had so acquired the Irish language, and his taste for snuff, and for moderate quantities of a detestable species of illegal whiskey distilled from the potato by certain of his neighbours. He had already—though intellectual Dublin knew nothing of it—considerable popularity as a Gaelic poet, mowers and reapers singing his songs from Donegal to Kerry. Years afterwards I was to stand at his side and listen

to Galway mowers singing his Gaelic words without their knowing whose words they sang. It is so in India, where peasants sing
the words of the great poet of Bengal without knowing whose
words they sing, and it must often be so where the old imaginative folk life is undisturbed, and it is so amongst schoolboys
who hand their story-books to one another without looking at the
title-page to read the author's name. Here and there, however,
the peasants had not lost the habit of Gaelic criticism, picked
up, perhaps, from the poets who took refuge among them after
the ruin of the great Catholic families, from men like that
O'Rahilly, who cries in a translation from the Gaelic that is itself a masterpiece of concentrated passion—

> The periwinkle and the tough dog-fish
> Towards evening time have got into my dish.

An old rascal was kept in food and whiskey for a fortnight by
some Connaught village under the belief that he was Craoibhin
Aoibhin, "the pleasant little branch," as Doctor Hyde signed himself in the newspapers where the villagers had found his songs.
The impostor's thirst only strengthened belief in his genius, for
the Gaelic song-writers have had the infirmitives of Robert
Burns. "It is not the drink but the company," one of the last
has sung. Since that first meeting Doctor Hyde and I had corresponded, and he had sent me in manuscript the best tale in
my *Faery and Folk Tales,* and I think I had something to do
with the London publication of his *Beside the Fire,* a book written in the beautiful English of Connaught, which is Gaelic in
idiom and Tudor in vocabulary, and indeed, the first book to
use it in the expression of emotion and romance, for Carleton
and his school had turned it into farce. Henley had praised him,
and York Powell had said, "If he goes on as he has begun, he
will be the greatest folk-loreist who has ever lived"; and I know
no first book of verse of our time that is at once so romantic and
so concrete as his Gaelic *Abhla de'n Craoibh;* but in a few years
Dublin was to laugh him, or rail him, out of his genius. He had
no critical capacity, having indeed for certain years the uncritical
folk-genius, as no educated Irish or Englishman has ever had it,
writing out of an imitative sympathy like that of a child catching a tune and leaving it to chance to call the tune; and the
failure of our first attempt to create a modern Irish literature

permitted the ruin of that genius. He was to create a great popular movement, far more important in its practical results than any movement I could have made, no matter what my luck, but, being neither quarrelsome nor vain, he will not be angry if I say—for the sake of those who come after us—that I mourn for the "greatest folk-loreist who ever lived," and for the great poet who died in his youth. The Harps and Pepperpots got him and the Harps and Pepperpots kept him till he wrote in our common English—"It must be either English or Irish," said some patriotic editor, Young Ireland practice in his head—that needs such sifting that he who would write it vigorously must write it like a learned language, and took for his model the newspaper upon his breakfast table, and became for no base reason beloved by multitudes who should never have heard his name till their schoolmasters showed it upon his tomb. That very incapacity for criticism made him the cajoler of crowds, and of individual men and women; "He should not be in the world at all," said one admiring elderly woman, "or doing the world's work"; and for certain years young Irish women were to display his pseudonym, "Craoibhin Aoibhin," in gilt letters upon their hat bands.

> Dear Craoibhin Aoibhin, . . . impart to us,
> We'll keep the secret, a new trick to please;
> Is there a bridle for this Proteus
> That turns and changes like his draughty seas,
> Or is there none, most popular of men,
> But, when they mock us, that we mock again?

7

Standish O'Grady, upon the other hand, was at once all passion and all judgment. And yet those who knew him better than I assured me he could find quarrel in a straw; and I did know that he had quarrelled a few years back with Jack Nettleship. Nettleship's account had been, "My mother cannot endure the God of the Old Testament, but likes Jesus Christ; whereas I like the God of the Old Testament, and cannot endure Jesus Christ; and we have got into the way of quarrelling about it at lunch; and once, when O'Grady lunched with us, he said it was the most disgraceful spectacle he had ever seen, and walked out."

Indeed, I wanted him among my writers, because of his quarrels, for, having much passion and little rancour, the more he quarrelled, the nobler, the more patched with metaphor, the more musical his style became, and if he were in his turn attacked, he knew a trick of speech that made us murmur, "We do it wrong, being so majestical, to offer it the show of violence." Sometimes he quarrelled most where he loved most. A Unionist in politics, a leader-writer on the *Daily Express*, the most conservative paper in Ireland, hater of every form of democracy, he had given all his heart to the smaller Irish landowners, to whom he belonged, and with whom his childhood had been spent, and for them he wrote his books, and would soon rage over their failings in certain famous passages that many men would repeat to themselves like poets' rhymes. All round us people talked or wrote for victory's sake, and were hated for their victories—but here was a man whose rage was a swan-song over all that he had held most dear, and to whom for that very reason every Irish imaginative writer owed a portion of his soul. In his unfinished *History of Ireland* he had made the old Irish heroes, Fion, and Oisin, and Cuchullan, alive again, taking them, for I think he knew no Gaelic, from the dry pages of O'Curry and his school, and condensing and arranging, as he thought Homer would have arranged and condensed. Lady Gregory has told the same tales, but keeping closer to the Gaelic text, and with greater powers of arrangement and a more original style, but O'Grady was the first, and we had read him in our 'teens. I think that, had I succeeded, a popular audience could have changed him little, and that his genius would have stayed, as it had been shaped by his youth in some provincial society, and that to the end he would have shown his best in occasional thrusts and parries. But I do think that if, instead of that one admirable little book *The Bog of Stars*, we had got all his histories and imaginative works into the hands of our young men, he might have brought the imagination of Ireland nearer the Image and the honeycomb.

Lionel Johnson was to be our critic, and above all our theologian, for he had been converted to Catholicism, and his orthodoxy, too learned to question, had accepted all that we did, and most of our plans. Historic Catholicism, with all its counsels and its dogmas, stirred his passion like the beauty of a mistress, and the unlearned parish priests who thought good literature or good criticism dangerous were in his eyes "all heretics." He belonged to a family that had, he told us, called itself Irish some generations back, and its English generations but enabled him to see as one single sacred tradition Irish nationality and Catholic religion. How should he fail to know the Holy Land? Had he not been in Egypt? He had joined our London Irish Literary Society, attended its committee meetings, and given lectures in London, in Dublin, and in Belfast, on Irish novelists and Irish poetry, reading his lectures always, and yet affecting his audience as I, with my spoken lectures, could not, perhaps because Ireland had still the shape it had received from the eighteenth century, and so felt the dignity, not the artifice, of his elaborate periods. He was very little, and at a first glance he seemed but a schoolboy of fifteen. I remember saying one night at the Rhymers', when he spoke of passing safely, almost nightly, through Seven Dials, then a dangerous neighbourhood, "Who would expect to find anything in your pockets but a pegtop and a piece of string?" But one never thought of his small stature when he spoke or read. He had the delicate strong features of a certain filleted head of a Greek athlete in the British Museum, an archaistic Græco-Roman copy of a masterpiece of the fourth century, and that resemblance seemed symbolic of the austere nobility of his verse. He was now in his best years, writing with great ease and power; neither I, nor, I think, any other, foresaw his tragedy.

He suffered from insomnia and some doctor, while he was still at the University, had recommended alcohol, and he had, in a vain hope of sleep, increased the amount as Rossetti had increased his doses of chloral, and now he drank for drinking's sake. He drank a great deal too much, and, though nothing could, it seemed, disturb his calm or unsteady his hand or foot, his doctrine, after a certain number of glasses, would become more ascetic, more contemptuous of all that we call human life. I have heard him, after four or five glasses of wine, praise some church father who freed himself from sexual passion by a surgical operation, and deny with scorn, and much historical evidence, that a gelded man lost anything of intellectual power. Even without stimulant his theology conceded nothing to human weakness, and I can remember his saying with energy, "I wish those people who deny the eternity of punishment could realise their unspeakable vulgarity."

Now that I know his end, I see him creating, to use a favourite adjective of his, "marmorean" verse, and believing the most terrible doctrines to keep down his own turbulence. One image of that stay in Dublin is so clear before me that it has blotted out most other images of that time. He is sitting at a lodging-house table, which I have just left at three in the morning, and round him lie or sit in huddled attitudes half a dozen men in various states of intoxication; and he is looking straight before him with head erect, and one hand resting upon the table. As I reach the stairs I hear him say, in a clear, unshaken voice, "I believe in nothing but the Holy Roman Catholic Church." He sometimes spoke of drink as something which he could put aside at any moment, and his friends believed, and I think he liked us to believe, that he would shortly enter a monastery. Did he deceive us deliberately? Did he himself already foresee the moment when he would write *The Dark Angel?* I am almost certain that he did, for he had already written *Mystic and Cavalier,* where the historical setting is, I believe, but masquerade.

> Go from me: I am one of those, who fall.
> What! hath no cold wind swept your heart at all,
> In my sad company? Before the end,
>   Go from me, dear my friend!
> Yours are the victories of light: your feet
> Rest from good toil, where rest is brave and sweet.
> But after warfare in a mourning gloom
>   I rest in clouds of doom.
>
> .   .   .   .   .
>
> Seek with thine eyes to pierce this crystal sphere:
> Canst read a fate there, prosperous and clear?
> Only the mists, only the weeping clouds:
>   Dimness, and airy shrouds.
>
> .   .   .   .   .
>
> O rich and sounding voices of the air!
> Interpreters and prophets of despair:
> Priests of a fearful sacrament! I come
>   To make with you my home.

8

Sir Charles Gavan Duffy arrived. He brought with him much manuscript, the private letters of a Young Ireland poetess, a dry but informing unpublished historical essay by Davis, and an unpublished novel by William Carleton, into the middle of which he had dropped a hot coal, so that nothing remained but the borders of every page. He hired a young man to read him, after dinner, Carlyle's *Heroes and Hero-Worship,* and before dinner was gracious to all our men of authority and especially to our Harps and Pepperpots. Taylor compared him to Odysseus returning to Ithaca, and every newspaper published his biography. He was a white-haired old man, who had written the standard history of Young Ireland, had emigrated to Australia, had been the first Australian Federalist, and later Prime Minister, but, in all his writings, in which there is so much honesty, so little rancour, there is not one sentence that has any meaning when separated from its place in argument or narrative, not one distinguished because of its thought or music. One imagined his youth in some little gaunt Irish town, where no building or custom is revered for its antiquity; and there speaking a language where no word, even in solitude, is ever spoken slowly and carefully because of emotional implication; and of his manhood of practical politics, of the dirty piece of orange-peel in the corner of the stairs as one climbs up to some newspaper office; of public meetings where it would be treacherous amid so much geniality to speak, or even to think of anything that might cause a moment's misunderstanding in one's own party. No argument of mine was intelligible to him, and I would have been powerless, but that fifty years ago he had made an enemy, and though the enemy was long dead, the enemy's school remained. He had attacked, why or with what result I do not remember, the only Young Ireland politician who had music and personality, though rancorous and devil-possessed. At some public meeting of ours, where he spoke amid great applause, in smooth, Gladstonian periods, of his proposed Irish publishing firm, one heard faint hostile murmurs, and at last a voice cried, "Remember Newry," and a voice answered, "There is a grave there!" and a part of the audience sang, "Here's to John Mitchell that is gone, boys, gone;

Here's to the friends that are gone." The meeting over, a group of us, indignant that the meeting we had called for his welcome should have contained those malcontents, gathered about him to apologise. He had written a pamphlet, he explained: he would give us copies. We would see that he was in the right, how badly Mitchell had behaved. But in Ireland personality, if it be but harsh and hard, has lovers, and some of us, I think may have gone home muttering, "How dare he be in the right if Mitchell is in the wrong?"

9

He wanted "to complete the Young Ireland movement"—to do all that had been left undone because of the Famine or the death of Davis, or his own emigration; and all the younger men were upon my side in resisting that. They might not want the books I wanted, but they did want books written by their own generation, and we began to struggle with him over the control of the company. Taylor became very angry, and I can understand what I looked like in his eyes, when I remember Edwin Ellis's seriously-intended warning, "It is bad manners for a man under thirty to permit himself to be in the right." But John O'Leary supported me throughout.

When Gavan Duffy had gone to London to draw up articles of association for his company, for which he had found many shareholders in Dublin the dispute became very fierce. One night members of the general public climbed the six flights of stairs to our committee room, now no longer in the Mansion House, and found seats for themselves just behind our chairs. We were all too angry to send them away, or even to notice their presence, for I was accused of saying at a public meeting in Cork, "Our books," when I should have said, "Sir Charles Gavan Duffy's books." I was not Taylor's match with the spoken word, and barely matched him with the written word. At twenty-seven or twenty-eight I was immature and clumsy, and O'Leary's support was capricious, for, being but a spectator of life, he would desert me if I used a bad argument, and would not return till I found a good one, and our chairman, Dr. Hyde, "most popular of men," sat dreaming of his old white cockatoo in far-away

Roscommon. Our very success had been a misfortune, for an opposition which had been literary and political brought, now that it had spread to the general public, religious prejudice to its aid. Suddenly, when the company seemed all but established, and a scheme had been thought out which gave some representation on its governing board to contemporary Irish writers, Gavan Duffy produced a letter from Archbishop Walsh, and threw the project up. The letter had warned him that after his death the company would fall under a dangerous influence. At this moment the always benevolent friend, to whom I had explained in confidence, when asking his support, my arrangements with my publisher, went to Gavan Duffy and suggested that they should together offer Mr. Fisher Unwin a series of Irish books, and Mr. Fisher Unwin and his reader accepted the series under the belief that it was my project that they accepted. I went to London to find the contract signed, and that all I could do was to get two sub-editors appointed, responsible to the two societies. Two or three good books were published, especially Dr. Hyde's *Short History of Gaelic Literature,* and Standish O'Grady's *Bog of Stars;* but the series was killed by its first volume, Thomas Davis's dry but informing historical essay. So important had our movement seemed that ten thousand copies had been sold before anybody had time to read it, and then came a dead stop.

Gavan Duffy knew nothing of my plans, and so was guiltless, and my friend had heard me discuss many things that evening. I had perhaps dispraised the humanitarian Stephen Phillips, already in his first vogue, and praised Francis Thompson, but half-rescued from his gutter; or flouted his belief in the perpetual marriage of genius and virtue by numbering the vices of famous men; this man's venery, that man's drink. He could not be expected to remember that where I had said so much of no account, I said one thing, and he had made one reply, that I thought of great account. He died a few months ago, and it would have surprised and shocked him if any man had told him that he was unforgiven; had he not forgotten all about it long ago? A German doctor has said that if we leave an umbrella at a friend's house it is because we have a subconscious desire to revisit that house; and he had perhaps a subconscious desire that my too tumultuous generation should not have its say.

10

I was at Sligo when I received a letter from John O'Leary, saying that I could do no more in Dublin, for even the younger men had turned against me, were "jealous," his letter said, though what they had to be jealous of God knows. He said further that it was all my own fault, that he had warned me what would happen if I lived on terms of intimacy with those I tried to influence. I should have kept myself apart and alone. It was all true; through some influence from an earlier generation, from Walt Whitman, perhaps, I had sat talking in public bars, had talked late into the night at many men's houses, showing all my convictions to men that were but ready for one, and used conversation to explore and discover among men who looked for authority. I did not yet know that intellectual freedom and social equality are incompatible; and yet, if I had, could hardly have lived otherwise, being too young for silence. The trouble came from half a dozen obscure young men, who having nothing to do attended every meeting and were able to overturn a project, that seemed my only bridge to other projects, including a travelling theatre. We had planned small libraries of Irish literature in connection with our country branches; we collected books and money, sending a lecturer to every branch and taking half the proceeds of that lecture to buy books. Maud Gonne, whose beauty could draw a great audience in any country town, had been the lecturer. The scheme was very nearly self-supporting, and six or seven bundles of books, chosen after much disputation by John O'Leary, J. F. Taylor, and myself, had been despatched to some six or seven branches. "The country will support this work," Taylor had said somewhere on some public platform, "because we are the most inflammable people on God's earth," his harsh voice giving almost a quality of style to Carlylian commonplace; but we are also a very jealous people. The half a dozen young men, if a little jealous of me, were still more jealous of those country branches which were getting so much notice, and where there was so much of that peasant mind their schoolmasters had taught them to despise. One must be English or Irish, they would have said. I returned to find a great box of books appropriated for some Dublin purpose and the whole scheme abandoned. I know that it was a bitter moment because I remember with gratitude words spoken not to my ear, but for my ear, by a young man who had lately joined our Society, Mr. Stephen McKenna, now well-known amongst scholars for his distinguished translations of Plotinus, and I seem to remember that I lost through anger what gift of persuasion I may possess, and that I was all the more helpless because I felt that even the best of us disagreed about everything at heart. I began to feel that I needed a hostess more than a society, but that I was not to find for years to come. I tried to persuade Maud Gonne to be that hostess, but her social life was in Paris, and she had already formed a new ambition, the turning of French public opinion against England. Without intellectual freedom there can be no agreement, and in Nationalist Dublin there was not—indeed there still is not—any society where a man is heard by the right ears, but never overheard by the wrong, and where he speaks his whole mind gaily, and is not the cautious husband of a part; where fantasy can play before matured into conviction; where life can shine and ring, and lack utility. Mere life lacking and protection of wealth or rank, or some beauty's privilege of caprice cannot choose its company, taking up and dropping men merely because it likes, or dislikes, their manners and their looks, and in its stead opinion crushes and rends, and all is hatred and bitterness: wheel biting upon wheel, a roar of steel or iron tackle, a mill of argument grinding all things down to mediocrity.

If, as I think, minds and metals correspond, the goldsmiths of Paris foretold the French Revolution when they substituted steel for that unserviceable gold in the manufacture of the more expensive jewel work, and made those large, flat steel buttons for men of fashion wherein the card-sharpers were able to study the reflections of the cards.

II

No country could have more natural distaste for equality, for in every circle there was some man ridiculous for posing as the type of some romantic or distinguished trait. One of our friends, a man of talent and of learning, whose ancestors had come, he

believed, from Denmark in the ninth century, looked and talked
the distinguished foreigner so perfectly that a patriotic newspaper
gave particulars of his supposed relations in contemporary Denmark! A half-mad old man who had served for a few months in
the Pope's army, many years before, still rode an old white war-
horse in all national processions, and, if their enemies were not
lying, one Town Councillor had challenged another to a duel by
flinging his glove upon the floor; while a popular Lord Mayor
had boasted in a public speech that he never went to bed at
night without reading at least twelve pages of *Sappho*. Then, too,
in those conversations of the small hours, to which O'Leary had
so much objected, whenever we did not speak of art and letters,
we spoke of Parnell. We told each other that he had admitted
no man to his counsel; that when some member of his party
found himself in the same hotel by chance, that member would
think to stay there a presumption, and move to some other
lodging; and, above all, we spoke of his pride, that made him
hide all emotion while before his enemy. Once he had seemed
callous and indifferent to the House of Commons, Foster had
accused him of abetting assassination, but when he came among
his followers his hands were full of blood, because he had torn
them with his nails. What excitement there would have been,
what sense of mystery would have stirred all our hearts, and
stirred hearts all through the country, where there was still, and
for many years to come, but one overmastering topic, had we
known the story Mrs. Parnell tells of that scene on Brighton
Pier. He and the woman that he loved stood there upon a night
of storm, when his power was at its greatest height, and still un-
threatened. He caught her from the ground and held her at
arm's length out over the water and she lay there motionless,
knowing that, had she moved, he would have drowned himself
and her. Perhaps unmotived self-immolation, were that possible,
or else at mere suggestion of storm and night, were as great evidence as such a man could give of power over self and so of the
expression of the self.

12

When I look back upon my Irish propaganda of those years I can see little but its bitterness. I never met with, or but met to quarrel with, my father's old family acquaintance; or with acquaintance I myself might have found, and kept among the prosperous educated class, who had all the great appointments at University or Castle; and this I did by deliberate calculation. If I must attack so much that seemed sacred to Irish nationalist opinion, I must, I knew, see to it that no man suspect me of doing it to flatter Unionist opinion. Whenever I got the support of some man who belonged by birth and education to University or Castle, I would say, "Now you must be baptized of the gutter." I chose Royal visits especially for demonstrations of disloyalty, rolling up with my own hands the red carpet spread by some elderly Nationalist, softened or weakened by time, to welcome Viceroyalty; and threatening, if our London Society drank to the King's health, that my friends and I would demonstrate against it by turning our glasses upside down; and was presently to discover that one can grow impassioned and fanatical about opinions, which one has chosen as one might choose a side upon the football field; and I thought many a time of the pleasant Dublin houses that would never ask me to dine; and the still pleasanter houses with trout-streams near at hand, that would never ask me upon a visit. I became absurdly sensitive, glancing about me in certain public places, the private view of our Academy, or the like, to discover imagined enemies; and even now, after twenty or thirty years, I feel at times that I have not recovered my natural manner. Yet it was in those pleasant houses, among the young men and the young girls, that we were to make our converts. When we loathe ourselves or our world, if that loathing but turn to intellect, we see self or world and its anti-self as in one vision; when loathing remains but loathing, world or self consumes itself away, and we turn to its mechanical opposite. Popular Nationalism and Unionism so changed into one another, being each but the other's headache. The nationalist opinion, I must, I knew, see to it ideas of some hysterical woman, a part of the mind turned into stone, the rest a seething and burning; and Unionist Ireland had reacted from that seething and burning to a cynical indifference, and from those fixed ideas to whatever might bring the most easy and obvious success.

I remember Taylor at some public debate, stiff of body and tense of voice; and the contrasting figure of Fitzgibbon, the Lord Justice of Appeal of the moment and his calm, flowing sentences, satisfactory to hear and impossible to remember. Taylor speaks of a little nation of antiquity, which he does not name, "set between the great Empire of Persia and the great Empire of Rome." Into the mouths of those great Empires he puts the arguments of Fitzgibbon, and such as he, "Join with our greatness! What in comparison to that is your little, beggarly nationality?" And then I recall the excitement, the shiver of the nerves, as his voice rose to an ecstatic cry, "Out of that nation came the salvation of the world." I remember, too, and grow angry, as it were yesterday, a letter from that Lord Justice of Appeal, who had changed his politics for advancement's sake, recommending a correspondent to avoid us, because we dissuaded people from the study of "Shakespeare and Kingsley."

Edward Dowden, my father's old friend, with his dark romantic face, the one man of letters Dublin Unionism possessed, was withering in that barren soil. Towards the end of his life he confessed to a near friend that he would have wished before all things to have been the lover of many women; and some careless lecture, upon the youthful Goethe, had in early life drawn down upon him the displeasure of the Protestant Archbishop. And yet he turned Shakespeare into a British Benthamite, flattered Shelley but to hide his own growing lack of sympathy, abandoned for like reason that study of Goethe that should have been his life-work, and at last cared but for Wordsworth, the one great poet who, after brief blossoms, was cut and sawn into planks of obvious utility. I called upon him from time to time out of gratitude for old encouragements, and because, among the Dublin houses open to me, his alone was pleasant to the eye, with its many books and its air of scholarship. But when O'Grady had declared, rancorous for once but under substantial provocation, that he had "a bad head and a worse heart," I found my welcome troubled and called no more.

13

The one house where nobody thought or talked politics was a house in Ely Place, where a number of young men lived together, and, for want of a better name, were called Theosophists. Besides the resident members, other members dropped in and out during the day, and the reading-room was a place of much discussion about philosophy and about the arts. The house had been taken in the name of the engineer to the Board of Works, a blackbearded young man, with a passion for Manichean philosophy, and all accepted him as host; and sometimes the conversation, especially when I was there, became too ghostly for the nerves of his young and delicate wife, and he would be made angry. I remember young men struggling, with inexact terminology and insufficient learning, for some new religious conception, on which they could base their lives, and some few strange or able men.

At the top of the house lived a medical student who read Plato and took haschisch, and a young Scotchman who owned a vegetarian restaurant, and had just returned from America, where he had gone as the disciple of the Prophet Harris, and where he would soon return in the train of some new prophet. When one asked what set him on his wanderings, he told of a young Highlander, his friend in boyhood, whose cap was always plucked off at a certain twist in the road, till the fathers of the village fastened it upon his head by recommending drink and women. When he had gone, his room was inherited by an American hypnotist, who had lived among the Zuni Indians with the explorer Cushant, and told of a Zuni Indian, who, irritated by some white man's praise of telephone and telegraph, cried out, "Can they do that?" and cast above his head two handfuls of sand that burst into flame, and flamed till his head seemed wrapped in fire. He professed to talk the philosophy of the Zuni Indians, but it seemed to me the vague Platonism that all there talked, except that he spoke much of men passing in sleep into the heart of mountains; a doctrine that was presently incorporated in the mythology of the house, to send young men and women hither and thither inquiring for sacred places. On a lower floor lived a strange red-haired girl, all whose thoughts were set upon painting and poetry, conceived as abstract images like Love and Penury in the *Symposium;* and to these images she sacrificed herself with Asiatic fanaticism. The engineer had discovered her starving somewhere in an unfurnished or half-furnished room, and that she had lived for many weeks upon bread and shell-cocoa, so that her food never cost her more than a penny a day. Born into a county family, who were so haughty that their neighbours called them the Royal Family, she had quarrelled with a mad father, who had never, his tenants declared, "unscrewed the top of his flask with any man," because she wished to study art, had run away from home, had lived for a time by selling her watch, and then by occasional stories in an Irish paper. For some weeks she had paid half-a-crown a week to some poor woman to see her to the art schools and back, for she considered it wrong for a woman to show herself in public places unattended; but of late she had been unable to afford the school fees. The engineer engaged her as a companion for his wife, and gave her money enough to begin her studies once more. She had talent and imagination, a gift for style; but, though ready to face death for painting and poetry, conceived as allegorical figures, she hated her own genius, and had not met praise and sympathy early enough to overcome the hatred. Face to face with paint and canvas, pen and paper, she saw nothing of her genius but its cruelty, and would have scarce arrived before she would find some excuse to leave the schools for the day, if indeed she had not invented over her breakfast some occupation so laborious that she could call it a duty, and so not go at all. Most watched her in mockery, but I watched in sympathy; composition strained my nerves and spoiled my sleep; and yet, for generations—and in Ireland we have long memories —my paternal ancestors had worked at some intellectual pursuit, while hers had shot and hunted. She could at any time, had she given up her profession, which her father had raged against, not because it was art, but because it was a profession, have returned to the common comfortable life of women. When, a little later, she had quarrelled with the engineer or his wife, and gone back to bread and shell-cocoa, I brought her an offer from some Dublin merchant of fairly well paid advertisement work, which would have been less laborious than artistic creation; but she said that

to draw advertisements was to degrade art, thanked me elabo-
rately, and did not disguise her indignation. She had, I believe,
returned to starvation with joy, for constant anæmia would
shortly give her an argument strong enough to silence her conscience when the allegorical images glared upon her, and, apart
from that, starvation and misery had a large share in her ritual
of worship.

14

At the top of the house, and at the time I remember best in the
same room with the young Scotchman, lived Mr. George Russell
(A. E.), and the house and the society were divided into his ad-
herents and those of the engineer; and I heard of some quarrelling between the factions. The rivalry was subconscious. Neither
had willingly opposed the other in any matter of importance. The
engineer had all the financial responsibility, and George Russell
was, in the eyes of the community, saint and genius. Had either
seen that the question at issue was the leadership of mystical
thought in Dublin, he would, I think, have given way, but the
dispute seemed trivial. At the weekly meetings, anything might
be discussed; no chairman called a speaker to order; an atheistic
workman could denounce religion, or a pious Catholic confound
theosophy with atheism; and the engineer, precise and practical,
disapproved. He had an object. He wished to make converts for
a definite form of belief, and here an enemy, if a better speaker,
might make all the converts. He wished to confine discussion to
members of the society, and had proposed in committee, I was
told, a resolution on the subject; while Russell, who had refused
to join my National Literary Society, because the party of Harp
and Pepperpot had set limits to discussion, resisted, and at last
defeated him. In a couple of years some new dispute arose; he
resigned, and founded a society which drew doctrine and method
from America or London; and Russell became, as he is today, the
one masterful influence among young Dublin men and women
who love religious speculation, but have no historical faith.

When Russell and I had been at the Art School six or seven
years before, he had been almost unintelligible. He had seemed
incapable of coherent thought, and perhaps was so at certain mo-

ments. The idea came upon him, he has told me, that, if he spoke, he would reveal that he had lost coherence; and for the three days that the idea lasted spent the hours of daylight wandering upon the Dublin mountains, that he might escape the necessity for speech. I used to listen to him at that time, mostly walking through the streets at night, for the sake of some stray sentence, beautiful and profound, amid many words that seemed without meaning; and there were others, too, who walked and listened, for he had become, I think, to all his fellow students, sacred, as the fool is sacred in the East. We copied the model laboriously, he would draw without research into the natural form, and call his study "St. John in the Wilderness"; but I can remember the almost scared look and the half-whisper of a student, now a successful sculptor, who said, pointing to the modelling of a shoulder, "That is too easy, a great deal too easy!" For with brush and pencil he was too coherent.

We derided each other, told absurd tales to one another's discredit, but we never derided him, or told tales to his discredit. He stood outside the sense of comedy his friend John Eglinton has called "the social cement" of our civilisation; and we would "gush" when we spoke of him, as men do when they praise something incomprehensible. But when he painted there was no difficulty in comprehending. How could that ease and rapidity of composition, so far beyond anything that we could attain to, belong to a man whose words seemed often without meaning?

A few months before I had come to Ireland he had sent me some verses, which I had liked till Edwin Ellis had laughed me from my liking by proving that no line had a rhythm that agreed with any other, and that, the moment one thought he had settled upon some scheme of rhyme, he would break from it without reason. But now his verse was clear in thought and delicate in form. He wrote without premeditation or labour. It had, as it were, organised itself, and grown as nervous and living as if it had, as Dante said of his own work, paled his cheek. The Society he belonged to published a little magazine, and he had asked the readers to decide whether they preferred his prose or his verse, and it was because they so willed it that he wrote the little transcendental verses afterwards published in *Homeward Songs by the Way*.

Life was not expensive in that house, where, I think, no meat was eaten; I know that out of the sixty or seventy pounds a year which he earned as accountant in a Dublin shop, he saved a considerable portion for his private charity; and it was, I think, his benevolence that gave him his lucidity of speech, and, perhaps, of writing. If he convinced himself that any particular activity was desirable in the public interest or in that of his friends, he had at once the ardour that came to another from personal ambition. He was always surrounded with a little group of infirm or unlucky persons, whom he explained to themselves and to others, turning cat to griffin, goose to swan. In later years he was to accept the position of organiser of a co-operative banking system, before he had even read a book upon economics or finance, and within a few months to give evidence before a Royal Commission upon the system, as an acknowledged expert, though he had brought to it nothing but his impassioned versatility.

At the time I write of him, he was the religious teacher, and that alone—his painting, his poetry, and his conversation all subservient to that one end. Men watched him with awe or with bewilderment; it was known that he saw visions continually, perhaps more continually than any modern man since Swedenborg, and when he painted and drew in pastel what he had seen, some accepted the record without hesitation, others, like myself, noticing the academic Græco-Roman forms, and remembering his early admiration for the works of Gustave Moreau, divined a subjective element, but no one doubted his word. One might not think him a good observer, but no one could doubt that he reported with the most scrupulous care what he believed himself to have seen; nor did he lack occasional objective corroboration. Walking with some man in his park—his demesne, as we say in Ireland—he had seen a visionary church at a particular spot, and the man had dug and uncovered its foundations; then some woman had met him with, "Oh, Mr. Russell, I am so unhappy," and he had replied, "You will be perfectly happy this evening at seven o'clock," and left her to her blushes. She had an appointment with a young man for seven o'clock. I had heard of this a day or so after the event, and I asked him about it, and was told it had suddenly come into his head to use those words; but why he did not know. He and I often quarrelled, because I wanted

him to examine and question his visions, and write them out as
they occurred; and still more because I thought symbolic what
he thought real like the men and women that had passed him
on the road. Were they so much a part of his subconscious life
that they would have vanished had he submitted them to question; were they like those voices that only speak, those strange
sights that only show themselves for an instant, when the attention has been withdrawn; that phantasmagoria of which I had
learnt something in London: and had his verse and his painting
a like origin? And was that why the same hand that painted a
certain dreamy, lovely sandy shore, now in the Dublin Municipal
Gallery, could with great rapidity fill many canvases with poetical commonplace; and why, after writing *Homeward Songs by
the Way,* where all is skilful and much exquisite, he would never
again write a perfect book? Was it precisely because in Swedenborg alone the conscious and the subconscious became one—as
in that marriage of the angels, which he has described as a contact
of the whole being—so completely one indeed that Coleridge
thought Swedenborg both man and woman?

Russell's influence, which was already great, had more to support it than his versatility, or the mystery that surrounded him,
for his sense of justice, and the daring that came from his own
confidence in it, had made him the general counsellor. He would
give endless time to a case of conscience, and no situation was
too difficult for his clarity; and certainly some of the situations
were difficult. I remember his being summoned to decide between
two ladies who had quarrelled about a vacillating admirer, and
called each other, to each other's faces, the worst names in our
somewhat anæmic modern vocabulary; and I have heard of his
success on an occasion when I think no other but Dostoievsky's
idiot could have avoided offence. The Society was very young,
and, as its members faced the world's moral complexities as
though they were the first that ever faced them, they drew up
very vigorous rules. One rule was that if any member saw a fault
growing upon any other member, it was his duty to point it out
to that member. A certain young man became convinced that a
certain young woman had fallen in love with him; and, as an
unwritten rule pronounced love and the spiritual life incompatible, that was a heavy fault. As the young man felt the delicacy

of the situation, he asked for Russell's help, and side by side they braved the offender, who, I was told, received their admonishment with surprised humility, and promised amendment. His voice would often become high, and lose its self-possession during intimate conversation, and I especially could put him in a rage; but the moment the audience became too large for intimacy, or some exciting event had given formality to speech, he would be at the same moment impassioned and impersonal. He had, and has, the capacity, beyond that of any man I have known, to put with entire justice not only the thoughts, but the emotions of the most opposite parties and personalities, as it were dissolving some public or private uproar into drama by Corneille or by Racine; and men who have hated each other must sometimes have been reconciled, because each heard his enemy's argument put into better words than he himself had found for his own; and this gift was in later years to give him political influence, and win him respect from Irish Nationalist and Unionist alike. It is, perhaps, because of it joined to a too literal acceptance of those noble images of moral tradition which are so like late Græco-Roman statues that he has come to see all human life as a mythological system, where, though all cats are griffins, the more dangerous griffins are only found among politicians he has not spoken to, or among authors he has but glanced at; while those men and women who bring him their confessions and listen to his advice, carry but the snowiest of swan's plumage. Nor has it failed to make him, as I think, a bad literary critic; demanding plays and poems where the characters must attain a stature of seven feet, and resenting as something perverse and morbid all abatement from that measure. I sometimes wonder what he would have been had he not met in early life the poetry of Emerson and Walt Whitman, writers who have begun to seem superficial precisely because they lack the Vision of Evil; and those translations of the Upanishads, which it is so much harder to study by the sinking flame of Indian tradition than by the serviceable lamp of Emerson and Walt Whitman.

We are never satisfied with the maturity of those whom we have admired in boyhood; and, because we have seen their whole circle—even the most successful life is but a segment—we remain to the end their harshest critics. One old school-fellow of mine will never believe that I have fulfilled the promise of some rough unscannable verses that I wrote before I was eighteen. Does any imaginative man find in maturity the admiration that his first half-articulate years aroused in some little circle; and is not the first success the greatest? Certainly, I demanded of Russell some impossible things, and if I had any influence upon him—and I have little doubt that I had, for we were very intimate—it may not have been a good influence for I thought there could be no aim for poet or artist except expression of a "Unity of Being" like that of a "perfectly proportioned human body"—though I would not at the time have used that phrase. I remember that I was ironic and indignant when he left the Art School because his "will was weak, and must grow weaker if he followed any emotional pursuit"; as, later, when he let the readers of a magazine decide between his prose and his verse. I now know that there are men who cannot possess "Unity of Being," who must not seek it or express it—and who, so far from seeking an anti-self, a Mask that delineates a being in all things the opposite to their natural state, can but seek the suppression of the anti-self, till the natural state alone remains. These are those who must seek no image of desire, but await that which lies beyond their mind—unities not of the mind, but unities of nature, unities of God—the man of science, the moralist, the humanitarian, the politician, St. Simon Stylites upon his pillar, St. Anthony in his cavern, all whose preoccupation is to seem nothing; to hollow their hearts till they are void and without form, to summon a creator by revealing chaos, to become the lamp for another's wick and oil; and indeed it may be that it has been for their guidance in a very special sense that the "perfectly proportioned human body" suffered crucifixion. For them Mask and Image are of necessity morbid, turning their eyes upon themselves, as though they were of those who can be law unto themselves, of whom Chapman has written, "Neither is it lawful that they should stoop to any other law," whereas they are indeed of those who can but ask, "Have I behaved as well as So-and-so?" "Am I a good man according to the commandments?" or "Do I realise my own nothingness before God?" "Have my experiments and observations excluded the personal factor with sufficient rigour?" Such men do not assume wisdom or beauty as Shelley did, when he masked himself as Ahasuerus, or as Prince Athanais, nor do they pursue an Image through a world that had else seemed an uninhabitable wilderness till, amid the privations of that pursuit, the Image is no more named Pandemos, but Urania; for such men must cast all Masks away and fly the Image, till that Image, transfigured because of their cruelties of self-abasement, becomes itself some Image or epitome of the whole natural or supernatural world, and itself pursues. The wholeness of the supernatural world can only express itself in personal form, because it has no epitome but man, nor can *The Hound of Heaven* fling itself into any but an empty heart. We may know the fugitives from other poets because, like George Herbert, like Francis Thompson, like George Russell, their imaginations grow more vivid in the expression of something which they have not themselves created, some historical religion or cause. But if the fugitive should live, as I think Russell does at times, as it is natural for a Morris or a Henley or a Shelley to live, hunters and pursuers all, his art surrenders itself to moral or poetical commonplace, to a repetition of thoughts and images that have no relation to experience.

I think that Russell would not have disappointed even my hopes had he, instead of meeting as an impressionable youth with our modern subjective romanticism, met with some form of traditional belief, which condemned all that romanticism admires and praises, indeed, all images of desire; for such condemnation would have turned his intellect towards the images of his vision. It might, doubtless, have embittered his life, for his strong intellect would have been driven out into the impersonal deeps where the man shudders; but it would have kept him a religious teacher, and set him, it may be, among the greatest of that species; politics, for a vision-seeking man, can be but half achievement, a choice of an almost easy kind of skill instead of that kind which is, of all those not impossible, the most difficult. Is it not certain that the Creator yawns in earthquake and thunder and other popular displays, but toils in rounding the delicate spiral of a shell?

15

I heard the other day of a Dublin man recognising in London an elderly man who had lived in that house in Ely Place in his youth, and of that elderly man, at the sudden memory, bursting into tears. Though I have no such poignant memories, for I was never of it, never anything but a dissatisfied critic, yet certain vivid moments come back to me as I write. . . . Russell had just come in from a long walk on the Two Rock mountain, very full of his conversation with an old religious beggar, who kept repeating, "God possesses the heavens, but He covets the earth—He covets the earth."

.   .   .   .   .

I get in talk with a young man who has taken the orthodox side in some debate. He is a stranger, but explains that he has inherited magical art from his father, and asks me to his rooms to see it in operation. He and a friend of his kill a black cock, and burn herbs in a big bowl, but nothing happens except that the friend repeats again and again, "Oh, my God," and when I ask him why he has said that, does not know that he has spoken; and I feel that there is something very evil in the room.

.   .   .   .   .

We are sitting round the fire one night and a member, a woman, tells a dream that she has just had. She dreamed that she saw monks digging in a garden. They dug down till they found a coffin, and when they took off the lid she saw that in the coffin lay a beautiful young man in a dress of gold brocade. The young man railed against the glory of the world, and when he had finished, the monks closed the coffin reverently, and buried it once more. They smoothed the ground, and then went on with their gardening.

.   .   .   .   .

I have a young man with me, an official of the National Literary Society, and I leave him in the reading-room with Russell, while I go upstairs to see the young Scotchman. I return after some minutes to find that the young man has become a Theosophist, but a month later, after an interview with a friar, to whom he gives an incredible account of his new beliefs, he goes to Mass again.

BOOK III

Hodos Chameliontos

I

When staying with Hyde in Roscommon, I had driven over to
Lough Kay, hoping to find some local memory of the old story
of Tumaus Costello, which I was turning into a story now called
Proud Costello, Macdermot's Daughter, and the Bitter Tongue.
I was rowed up the lake that I might find the island where he
died; I had to find it from Hyde's account in *The Love-Songs of
Connaught,* for when I asked the boatman, he told the story of
Hero and Leander, putting Hero's house on one island, and
Leander's on another. Presently we stopped to eat our sandwiches
at the "Castle Rock," an island all castle. It was not an old castle,
being but the invention of some romantic man, seventy or eighty
years ago. The last man who had lived there had been Dr.
Hyde's father, and he had but stayed a fortnight. The Gaelic-
speaking men in the district were accustomed, instead of calling
some specially useless thing a "white elephant," to call it "The
Castle on the Rock." The roof was, however, still sound, and
the windows unbroken. The situation in the centre of the lake,
that has little wood-grown islands, and is surrounded by wood-
grown hills, is romantic, and at one end, and perhaps at the
other too, there is a stone platform where meditative persons
might pace to and fro. I planned a mystical Order which should
buy or hire the castle, and keep it as a place where its members
could retire for a while for contemplation, and where we might
establish mysteries like those of Eleusis and Samothrace; and for
ten years to come my most impassioned thought was a vain attempt to find philosophy and to create ritual for that Order. I
had an unshakable conviction, arising how or whence I cannot
tell, that invisible gates would open as they opened for Blake,

as they opened for Swedenborg, as they opened for Boehme, and that this philosophy would find its manuals of devotion in all imaginative literature, and set before Irishmen for special manual an Irish literature which, though made by many minds, would seem the work of a single mind, and turn our places of beauty or legendary association into holy symbols. I did not think this philosophy would be altogether pagan, for it was plain that its symbols must be selected from all those things that had moved men most during many, mainly Christian, centuries.

I thought that for a time I could rhyme of love, calling it *The Rose,* because of the Rose's double meaning; of a fisherman who had "never a crack" in his heart; of an old woman complaining of the idleness of the young, or of some cheerful fiddler, all those things that "popular poets" write of, but that I must some day—on that day when the gates began to open—become difficult or obscure. With a rhythm that still echoed Morris I prayed to the Red Rose, to Intellectual Beauty:

> Come near, come near, come near—ah, leave me still
> A little space for the Rose-breath to fill,
> Lest I no more hear common things . . .
> But seek alone to hear the strange things said
> By God to the bright hearts of those long dead,
> And learn to chant a tongue men do not know.

I do not remember what I meant by "the bright hearts," but a little later I wrote of Spirits "with mirrors in their hearts."

My rituals were not to be made deliberately, like a poem, but all got by that method Mathers had explained to me, and with this hope I plunged without a clue into a labyrinth of images, into that labyrinth that we are warned against in those *Oracles* which antiquity has attributed to Zoroaster, but modern scholarship to some Alexandrian poet. "Stoop not down to the darkly splendid world wherein lieth continually a faithless depth and Hades wrapped in cloud, delighting in unintelligible images."

2

I found a supporter at Sligo in my elderly uncle, a man of fifty-three or fifty-four, with the habits of a much older man. He had never left the West of Ireland, except for a few days to London every year, and a single fortnight's voyage to Spain on board a trading schooner, in his boyhood. He was in politics a Unionist and Tory of the most obstinate kind, and knew nothing of Irish literature or history. He was, however, strangely beset by the romance of Ireland, as he discovered it among the people who served him, sailing upon his ships or attending to his horses, and, though narrow and obstinate of opinion, and puritanical in his judgment of life, was perhaps the most tolerant man I have ever known. He never expected anybody to agree with him, and if you did not upset his habits by cheating him over a horse, or by offending his taste, he would think as well of you as he did of other men, and that was not very well; and help you out of any scrape whatever. I was accustomed to people much better read than he, much more liberal-minded, but they had no life but the intellectual life, and if they and I differed, they could not take it lightly, and were often angry, and so for years now I had gone to Sligo, sometimes because I could not afford my Dublin lodging, but most often for freedom and peace. He would receive me with "I have learned that your friend So-and-so has been seen at the Gresham Hotel talking to Mr. William Redmond. What will not people do for notoriety?" He considered all Irish Nationalist Members of Parliament as outside the social pale, but after dinner, when conversation grew intimate, would talk sympathetically of the Fenians in Ballina, where he spent his early manhood, or of the Fenian privateer that landed the wounded man at Sligo in the 'sixties. When Parnell was contesting an election at Sligo a little before his death, other Unionist magistrates refused or made difficulties when asked for some assistance, what I do not remember, made necessary under election law; and so my uncle gave that assistance. He walked up and down some Town Hall assembly-room or some courtroom with Parnell, but would tell me nothing of that conversation, except that Parnell spoke of Gladstone with extravagant hatred. He would not repeat words spoken by a great man in his bitterness, yet Parnell at the moment was too angry to care who listened. I knew one other man who kept as firm a silence; he had attended Parnell's last public meeting, and after it sat alone beside him, and heard him speak of the followers that had fallen away, or were showing their faint hearts; but Parnell was the chief devotion of his life.

When I first began my visits, he had lived in the town itself, and close to a disreputable neighbourhood called the Burrough, till one evening, while he sat over his dinner, he heard a man and woman quarrelling under his window. "I mind the time," shouted the man, "when I slept with you and your daughter in the one bed." My uncle was horrified, and moved to a little house about a quarter of a mile into the country, where he lived with an old second-sighted servant, and a man-servant to look after the race-horse that was browsing in the neighbouring field, with a donkey to keep it company. His furniture had not been changed since he set up house for himself as a very young man, and in a room opposite his dining-room were the saddles of his youth, and though he would soon give up riding, they would be oiled and the stirrups kept clean and bright till the day of his death. Some love affair had gone wrong when he was a very young man; he had now no interest in women; certainly never sought favour of a woman, and yet he took great care of his appearance. He did not let his beard grow, though he had, or believed that he had, for he was hypochondriacal, a sensitiveness of the skin that forced him to spend an hour in shaving, and he would take to club and dumb-bell if his waist thickened by a hair's breadth, and twenty years after, when a very old man, he had the erect shapely figure of his youth. I often wondered why he went through so much labour, for it was not pride, which had seemed histrionic in his eyes—and certainly he had no vanity; and now, looking back, I am convinced that it was from habit, mere habit, a habit formed when he was a young man, and the best rider in his district.

Probably through long association with Mary Battle, the second-sighted servant, he had come to believe much in the supernatural world, and would tell how several times, arriving home with an unexpected guest, he had found the table set for three, and that he himself had dreamed of his brother's illness in Liverpool before he had other news of it. He saw me using images learned from Mathers to start reverie, and, though I held out for a long time, thinking him too old and habit-bound, he persuaded me to tell him their use, and from that on we experimented continually, and after a time I began to keep careful record. In summer he always had the same little house at Rosses Point, and it was at Rosses Point that he first became sensitive to the cabbalistic symbols. There are some high sandhills and low cliffs, and I adopted the practice of walking by the seashore while he walked on cliff or sandhill; I, without speaking, would imagine the symbol, and he would notice what passed before his mind's eye, and in a short time he would practically never fail of the appropriate vision. In the symbols which are used certain colours are classified as "actives," while certain other colours are "passives," and I had soon discovered that if I used "actives" George Pollexfen would see nothing. I therefore gave him exercises to make him sensitive to those colours, and gradually we found ourselves well fitted for this work, and he began to take as lively an interest, as was possible to a nature given over to habit, in my plans for the Castle on the Rock.

I worked with others, sworn to the scheme for the most part, and I made many curious observations. It was the symbol itself, or, at any rate, not my conscious intention that produced the effect, for if I made an error and told some one to gaze at the wrong symbol—they were painted upon cards—the vision would be suggested by the symbol, not by my thought, or two visions would appear side by side, one from the symbol and one from my thought. When two people, between whose minds there was even a casual sympathy, worked together under the same symbolic influence, the dream or reverie would divide itself between them, each half being the complement of the other; and now and again these complementary dreams, or reveries, would arise spontaneously. I find, for instance, in an old notebook, "I saw quite suddenly a tent with a wooden badly-carved idol, painted a dull red; a man looking like a Red Indian was prostrate before it. The idol was seated to the left. I asked X what he saw. He saw a most august immense being, glowing with a ruddy opalescent colour, sitting on a throne to the left," or, to summarise from a later notebook, . . . I am meditating in one room and my fellow student in another, when I see a boat full of tumult and movement on a still sea, and my friend sees a boat with motionless sails upon a tumultuous sea. There was nothing in the originating symbol to suggest a boat.

We never began our work until George's old servant was in her bed; and yet, when we went upstairs to our beds, we constantly heard her crying out with nightmare, and in the morning we would find that her dream echoed our vision. One night, started by what symbol I forget, we had seen an allegorical marriage of Heaven and Earth. When Mary Battle brought in the breakfast next morning, I said, "Well, Mary, did you dream anything last night?" and she replied (I am quoting from an old notebook) "indeed she had," and that it was "a dream she would not have liked to have had twice in one night." She had dreamed that her bishop, the Catholic bishop of Sligo, had gone away "without telling anybody," and had married "a very high-up lady," "and she not too young, either." She had thought in her dream, "Now all the clergy will get married, and it will be no use going to confession." There were "layers upon layers of flowers, many roses, all round the church."

Another time, when George Pollexfen had seen in answer to some evocation of mine a man with his head cut in two, she woke to find that she "must have cut her face with a pin, as it was all over blood." When three or four saw together, the dream or vision would divide itself into three or four parts, each seeming complete in itself, and all fitting together, so that each part was an adaptation of the general meaning to a particular personality. A visionary being would give, let us say, a lighted torch to one, an unlighted candle to another, an unripe fruit to a third, and to the fourth a ripe fruit. At times coherent stories were built up, as if a company of actors were to improvise, and play, not only without previous consultation, but without foreseeing at any moment what would be said or done the moment after. Who made the story? Was it the mind of one of the visionaries? Perhaps, for I have endless proof that, where two worked together, the symbolic influence commonly took upon itself, though no word was spoken, the quality of the mind that had first fixed a symbol in the mind's eye. But, if so, what part of the mind? One friend, in whom the symbolic impulse produced actual trance, described an elaborate and very strange story while the trance was upon him, but upon waking told a story that after a certain point was quite different. "They gave me a cup of wine, and after that I remembered nothing." While speaking out of trance he had said nothing of the cup of wine, which must have been offered to a portion of his mind quite early in the dream. Then, too, from whence come the images of the dream? Not always, I was soon persuaded, from the memory, perhaps never in trance or sleep. One man, who certainly thought that Eve's apple was the sort that you got from the greengrocer, and as certainly never doubted its story's literal truth, said, when I used some symbol to send him to Eden, that he saw a walled garden on the top of a high mountain, and in the middle of it a tree with great birds in the branches, and fruit out of which, if you held a fruit to your ear, came the sound of fighting. I had not at the time read Dante's *Purgatorio*, and it caused me some trouble to verify the mountain garden, and, from some passage in the Zohar, the great birds among the boughs. A young girl, on being sent to the same garden, heard "the music of heaven" from a tree, and on listening with her ear against the trunk, found that it was made by the "continual clashing of swords." Whence came that fine thought of music-making swords, that image of the garden, and many like images and thoughts? I had as yet no clear answer, but knew myself face to face with the Anima Mundi described by Platonic philosophers, and more especially in modern times by Henry More, which has a memory independent of embodied individual memories, though they constantly enrich[1] it with their images and their thoughts.

3

At Sligo we walked twice every day, once after lunch and once after dinner, to the same gate on the road to Knocknarea; and at Rosses Point, to the same rock upon the shore; and as we walked we exchanged those thoughts that never rise before me

[1] "Constantly enrich" must not be taken to mean that you can, as some suggest, separate a soul from its memory like a cockle from its shell. 1926.

now without bringing some sight of mountain or of shore. Considering that Mary Battle received our thoughts in sleep, though coarsened or turned to caricature, do not the thoughts of the scholar or the hermit, though they speak no word, or something of their shape and impulse, pass into the general mind? Does not the emotion of some woman of fashion, caught in the subtle torture of self-analysing passion, pass down, although she speak no word, to Joan with her Pot, Jill with her Pail and, it may be, with one knows not what nightmare melancholy to Tom the Fool?

Seeing that a vision could divide itself in divers complementary portions, might not the thought of philosopher or poet or mathematician depend at every moment of its progress upon some complementary thought in minds perhaps at a great distance? Is there nation-wide multiform reverie, every mind passing through a stream of suggestion, and all streams acting and reacting upon one another no matter how distant the minds, how dumb the lips? A man walked, as it were, casting a shadow, and yet one could never say which was man and which was shadow, or how many the shadows that he cast. Was not a nation, as distinguished from a crowd of chance comers, bound together by this interchange among streams or shadows; that Unity of Image, which I sought in national literature, being but an originating symbol?

From the moment when these speculations grew vivid, I had created for myself an intellectual solitude, most arguments that could influence action had lost something of their meaning. How could I judge any scheme of education, or of social reform, when I could not measure what the different classes and occupations contributed to that invisible commerce of reverie and of sleep: and what is luxury and what necessity when a fragment of gold braid, or a flower in the wallpaper may be an originating impulse to revolution or to philosophy? I began to feel myself not only solitary but helpless.

4

I had not taken up these subjects wilfully, nor through love of strangeness, nor love of excitement, nor because I found myself in some experimental circle, but because unaccountable things had happened even in my childhood, and because of an ungovernable craving. When supernatural events begin, a man first doubts his own testimony, but when they repeat themselves again and again, he doubts all human testimony. At least he knows his own bias, and may perhaps allow for it, but how trust historian and psychologist that have for some three hundred years ignored in writing of the history of the world, or of the human mind, so momentous a part of human experience? What else had they ignored and distorted? When Mesmerists first travelled about as public entertainers, a favourite trick was to tell a mesmerised man that some letter of the alphabet had ceased to exist, and after that to make him write his name upon the blackboard. Brown, or Jones, or Robinson would become upon the instant, and without any surprise or hesitation, Rown, or Ones, or Obinson.

Was modern civilisation a conspiracy of the subconscious? Did we turn away from certain thoughts and things because the Middle Ages lived in terror of the dark, or had some seminal illusion been imposed upon us by beings greater than ourselves for an unknown purpose? Even when no facts of experience were denied, might not what had seemed logical proof be but a mechanism of change, an automatic impulse? Once in London, at a dinner party, where all the guests were intimate friends, I had written upon a piece of paper, "In five minutes York Powell will talk of a burning house," thrust the paper under my neighbour's plate, and imagined my fire symbol, and waited in silence. Powell shifted conversation from topic to topic and within the five minutes was describing a fire he had seen as a young man. When Locke's French translator Coste asked him how, if there were no "innate ideas," he could explain the skill shown by a bird in making its nest, Locke replied, "I did not write to explain the actions of dumb creatures," and his translator thought the answer "very good, seeing that he had named his book *A Philosophical Essay upon Human Understanding*." Henry More, upon the other hand, considered that the bird's instinct proved the existence of the Anima Mundi, with its ideas and memories. Did modern enlightenment think with Coste that Locke had the better logic, because it was not free to think otherwise?

5

I ceased to read modern books that were not books of imagination, and if some philosophic idea interested me, I tried to trace
it back to its earliest use, believing that there must be a tradition
of belief older than any European Church, and founded upon
the experience of the world before the modern bias. It was this
search for a tradition that urged George Pollexfen and myself to
study the visions and thoughts of the country people, and some
country conversation, repeated by one or the other, often gave us
a day's discussion. These visions, we soon discovered, were very
like those we called up by symbol. Mary Battle, looking out
of the window at Rosses Point, saw coming from Knocknarea,
where Queen Maeve, according to local folklore, is buried under
a great heap of stones, "the finest woman you ever saw travelling
right across from the mountains and straight to here."—I quote
a record written at the time. "She looked very strong, but not
wicked" (that is to say, not cruel). "I have seen the Irish Giant"
(some big man shown at a fair). "And though he was a fine
man he was nothing to her, for he was round and could not
have stepped out so soldierly . . . she had no stomach on her
but was slight and broad in the shoulders, and was handsomer
than any one you ever saw; she looked about thirty." And when
I asked if she had seen others like her, she said, "Some of them
have their hair down, but they look quite different, more like
the sleepy-looking ladies one sees in the papers. Those with their
hair up are like this one. The others have long white dresses,
but those with their hair up have short dresses, so that you can
see their legs right up to the calf." And when I questioned her,
I found that they wore what might well be some kind of buskin.
"They are fine and dashing-looking, like the men one sees riding
their horses in twos and threes on the slopes of the mountains
with their swords swinging. There is no such race living now,
none so finely proportioned. . . . When I think of her and the
ladies now they are like little children running about not knowing how to put their clothes on right . . . why, I would not
call them women at all."

Not at this time, but some three or four years later, when the visions came without any conscious use of symbol for a short time, and with much greater vividness, I saw two or three forms of this incredible beauty, one especially that must always haunt my memory. Then, too, the Master Pilot told us of meeting at night close to the Pilot House a procession of women in what seemed the costume of another age. Were they really people of the past, revisiting, perhaps, the places where they lived, or must I explain them, as I explained that vision of Eden as a mountain garden, by some memory of the race, as distinct from living memory? Certainly these Spirits, as the country people called them, seemed full of personality; were they not capricious, generous, spiteful, anxious, angry, and yet did that prove them more than images and symbols? When I used a combined earth and fire and lunar symbol my seer, a girl of twenty-five, saw an obvious Diana and her dogs, about a fire in a cavern. Presently, judging from her closed eyes, and from the tone of her voice, that she was in trance, not in reverie, I wished to lighten the trance a little, and made through carelessness or hasty thinking a symbol of dismissal; and at once she started and cried out, "She says you are driving her away too quickly. You have made her angry." Then, too, if my visions had a subjective element, so had Mary Battle's, for her fairies had but one tune, *The Distant Waterfall*, and she never heard anything described in a sermon at the Cathedral that she did not "see it after," and spoke of seeing in this way the gates of Purgatory.

Furthermore, if my images could affect her dreams, the folk-images could affect mine in turn, for one night I saw between sleeping and waking a strange long-bodied pair of dogs, one black and one white, that I found presently in some country tale. How, too, could one separate the dogs of the country tale from those my uncle heard bay in his pillow? In order to keep myself from nightmare, I had formed the habit of imagining four watch-dogs, one at each corner of my room, and, though I had not told him or anybody, he said, "Here is a very curious thing; most nights now, when I lay my head upon the pillow, I hear a sound of dogs baying—the sound seems to come up out of the pillow." A friend of Strindberg's, in *delirium tremens*, was haunted by mice, and a friend in the next room heard the squealing of the mice.

6

I have much evidence that these images, or the symbols that call them up, can influence the bodily health. My uncle told me one evening that there were cases of smallpox—it turned out to be untrue—somewhere under Knocknarea, and that the doctor was coming to vaccinate him. Vaccination, probably from some infection in the lymph, brought on a very serious illness, blood-poisoning I heard it called, and presently he was delirious and a second doctor called in consultation. Between eleven and twelve one night when the delirium was at its height, I sat down beside his bed and said, "What do you see, George?" He said, "Red dancing figures," and without commenting, I imagined the cabbalistic symbol of water and almost at once he said, "There is a river running through the room," and a little later, "I can sleep now." I told him what I had done and that, if the dancing figures came again, he was to bid them go in the name of the Archangel Gabriel. Gabriel is angel of the Moon in the Cabbala and might, I considered, command the waters at a pinch. The doctor found him much better and heard that I had driven the delirium away and given him such a word of command that when the red men came again in the middle of the night, they looked greatly startled, and fled.

The doctor came, questioned, and said, "Well, I suppose it is a kind of hypnotism, but it is very strange, very strange." The delirium did not return.

7

To that multiplicity of interest and opinion, of arts and sciences, which had driven me to conceive a Unity of Culture defined and evoked by Unity of Image, I had but added a multiplicity of images, and I was the more troubled because, the first excitement over, I had done nothing to rouse George Pollexfen from the gloom and hypochondria always thickening about him. I asked no help of books, for I believed that the truth I sought would come to me like the subject of a poem, from some moment of passionate experience, and that if I filled my exposition with other men's thought, other men's investigation, I would sink into all that multiplicity of interest and opinion. That passionate experience could never come—of that I was certain—until I had found the right image or right images. From what but the image of Apollo, fixed always in memory and passion, did his priest-hood get that occasional power, a classical historian has described, of lifting great stones and snapping great branches; and did not Gemma Galgani, like many others that had gone before, in 1889 cause deep wounds to appear in her body by contemplating her crucifix? In the essay that Wilde read to me one Christmas Day, occurred these words—"what does not the world owe to the imita-tion of Christ, what to the imitation of Cæsar?" and I had seen Macgregor Mathers paint little pictures combining the forms of men, animals, and birds, according to a rule which provided a combination for every possible mental condition, and I had heard him say, upon what authority I do not remember, that citizens of ancient Egypt assumed, when in contemplation, the images of their gods.

But now image called up image in an endless procession, and I could not always choose among them with any confidence; and when I did choose, the image lost its intensity, or changed into some other image. I had but exchanged the temptation of Flau-bert's *Bouvard et Pecuchet* for that of his *St. Anthony,* and I was lost in that region a cabbalistic manuscript, shown me by Macgregor Mathers, had warned me of; astray upon the Path of the Chameleon, upon *Hodos Chameliontos.*[1]

8

Now that I am a settled man and have many birds—the ca-naries have just hatched out five nestlings—I have before me the problem that Locke waved aside. As I gave them an artificial nest, a hollow vessel like a saucer, they had no need of that skill the wild bird shows, each species having its own preference among the lichen, or moss; but they could sort out wool and hair and a certain soft white down that I found under a big

[1] *Hodos Camelionis,* not *Hodos Chameliontos,* were the words, a mixture of Greek and Latin typical of such documents.

tree. They would twist a stem of grass till it was limber, and would wind it all about the centre of the nest, and when the five grey eggs were laid, the mother bird knew how to turn them over from time to time, that they might be warmed evenly; and how long she must leave them uncovered, that the white might not be dried up, and when to return that the growing bird might not take cold. Then the young birds, even when they had all their feathers, were very still as compared with the older birds, as though any habit of movement would disturb the nest or make them tumble out. One of them would now and again pass on the food that he had received from his mother's beak to some other nestling. The father had often pecked the mother bird before the eggs were laid, but now, until the last nestling was decently feathered, he took his share in the feeding, and was very peaceable, and it was only when the young could be left to feed themselves that he grew jealous and had to be put into another cage.

When I watch my child, who is not yet three years old, I can see so many signs of knowledge from beyond her own mind; why else should she be so excited when a little boy passes outside the window, and take so little interest in a girl; why should she put a cloak about her, and look over her shoulder to see it trailing upon the stairs, as she will some day trail a dress; and why, above all, as she lay against her mother's side, and felt the unborn child moving within, did she murmur, "Baby, baby"?

When a man writes any work of genius, or invents some creative action, is it not because some knowledge or power has come into his mind from beyond his mind? It is called up by an image, as I think; all my birds' adventures started when I hung a little saucer at one side of the cage, and at the other a bundle of hair and grass; but our images must be given to us, we cannot choose them deliberately.

9

I know now that revelation is from the self, but from that age-long memoried self, that shapes the elaborate shell of the mollusc and the child in the womb, that teaches the birds to make their nest; and that genius is a crisis that joins that buried self for certain moments to our trivial daily mind. There are, indeed, personifying spirits that we had best call but Gates and Gate-keepers, because through their dramatic power they bring our souls to crisis, to Mask and Image, caring not a straw whether we be Juliet going to her wedding, or Cleopatra to her death; for in their eyes nothing has weight but passion. We have dreamed a foolish dream these many centuries in thinking that they value a life of contemplation, for they scorn that more than any possible life, unless it be but a name for the worst crisis of all. They have but one purpose, to bring their chosen man to the greatest obstacle he may confront without despair. They contrived Dante's banishment, and snatched away his Beatrice, and thrust Villon into the arms of harlots, and sent him to gather cronies at the foot of the gallows, that Dante and Villon might through passion become conjoint to their buried selves, turn all to Mask and Image, and so be phantoms in their own eyes. In great lesser writers like Landor and like Keats we are shown that Image and that Mask as something set apart; Andromeda and her Perseus—though not the sea-dragon—but in a few in whom we recognise supreme masters of tragedy, the whole contest is brought into the circle of their beauty. Such masters—Villon and Dante, let us say—would not, when they speak through their art, change their luck; yet they are mirrored in all the suffering of desire. The two halves of their nature are so completely joined that they seem to labour for their objects, and yet to desire whatever happens, being at the same instant predestinate and free, creation's very self. We gaze at such men in awe, because we gaze not at a work of art, but at the re-creation of the man through that art, the birth of a new species of man, and, it may even seem that the hairs of our heads stand up, because that birth, that re-creation, is from terror. Had not Dante and Villon understood that their fate wrecked what life could not rebuild, had they lacked their Vision of Evil, had they cherished any species of optimism, they could but have found a false beauty, or some momentary instinctive beauty, and suffered no change at all, or but changed as do the wild creatures, or from devil well to devil sick, and so round the clock.

They and their sort alone earn contemplation, for it is only when the intellect has wrought the whole of life to drama, to crisis, that we may live for contemplation, and yet keep our intensity.

And these things are true also of nations, but the Gate-keepers who drive the nation to war or anarchy that it may find its Image are different from those who drive individual men, though I think at times they work together. And as I look backward upon my own writing, I take pleasure alone in those verses where it seems to me I have found something hard and cold, some articulation of the Image, which is the opposite of all that I am in my daily life, and all that my country is; yet man or nation can no more make this Mask or Image[1] than the seed can be made by the soil into which it is cast.

Ille.

What portion in the world can the artist have,
Who has awakened from the common dream,
But dissipation and despair?

Hi.

                        And yet
No one denies to Keats, love of the world.
Remember his deliberate happiness.

Ille.

His art is happy, but who knows his mind?
I see a schoolboy, when I think of him,
With face and nose pressed to a sweet-shop window.
For certainly he sank into his grave
His senses and his heart unsatisfied,
And made, being poor, ailing, and ignorant . . .
Shut out from all the luxury of the world,
Luxuriant song.

[1] There is a form of Mask or Image that comes from life and is fated, but there is a form that is chosen.

BOOK IV

The Tragic Generation

I

Two or three years after our return to Bedford Park *A Doll's House* had been played at the Royalty Theatre in Dean Street, the first Ibsen play to be played in England, and somebody had given me a seat for the gallery. In the middle of the first act, while the heroine was asking for macaroons, a middle-aged washerwoman who sat in front of me, stood up and said to the little boy at her side, "Tommy, if you promise to go home straight, we will go now"; and at the end of the play, as I wandered through the entrance hall, I heard an elderly critic murmur, "A series of conversations terminated by an accident." I was divided in mind, I hated the play; what was it but Carolus Duran, Bastien-Lepage, Huxley and Tyndall all over again; I resented being invited to admire dialogue so close to modern educated speech that music and style were impossible.

"Art is art because it is not nature," I kept repeating to myself, but how could I take the same side with critic and washerwoman? As time passed Ibsen became in my eyes the chosen author of very clever young journalists, who, condemned to their treadmill of abstraction, hated music and style; and yet neither I nor my generation could escape him because, though we and he had not the same friends, we had the same enemies. I bought his collected works in Mr. Archer's translation out of my thirty shillings a week and carried them to and fro upon my journeys to Ireland and Sligo, and Florence Farr, who had but one great gift, the most perfect poetical elocution, became prominent as an Ibsen actress and had almost a success in *Rosmersholm*, where there is symbolism and a stale odour of spilt poetry. She and I and half our friends found ourselves involved in a quarrel with the supporters of old-fashioned melodrama, and conventional romance, in the support of the new dramatists who wrote in what the Daily Press chose to consider the manner of Ibsen. In 1894 she became manageress of the Avenue Theatre with a play of Dr. Todhunter's, called *The Comedy of Sighs,* and Mr. Bernard Shaw's *Arms and the Man.* She asked me to write a one-act play that her niece, Miss Dorothy Paget, a girl of eight or nine, might make her first stage appearance, and I, with my Irish Theatre in mind, wrote *The Land of Heart's Desire,* in some discomfort when the child was theme, for I knew nothing of children, but with an abundant mind when Mary Bruin was, for I knew an Irish woman whose unrest troubled me. When Florence Farr opened her theatre she had to meet a hostile audience, almost as violent as that Synge met in January 1907, and certainly more brutal, for the Abbey audience had no hatred for the players, and I think but little for Synge himself. Nor had she the certainty of final victory to give her courage, for *The Comedy of Sighs* was a rambling story told with a little paradoxical wit. She had brought the trouble upon herself perhaps, for always in revolt against her own poetical gift, which now seemed obsolete, and against her own Demeter-like face in the mirror, she had tried when interviewed by the Press to shock and startle; and yet, unsure of her own judgment being out of her own trade, had feared to begin with Shaw's athletic wit; and now outraged convention saw its chance. For two hours and a half, pit and gallery drowned the voices of the players with boos and jeers that were meant to be bitter to the author who sat visible to all in his box surrounded by his family, and to the actress struggling bravely through her weary part; and then pit and gallery went home to spread their lying story that the actress had a fit of hysterics in her dressing-room.

Todhunter had sat on to the end, and there were, I think, four acts of it, listening to the howling of his enemies, while his friends slipped out one by one, till one saw everywhere their empty seats, but nothing could arouse the fighting instincts of that melancholy man. Next day I tried to get him to publish his book of words with satirical designs and illustrations, by Beardsley, who was just rising into fame, and an introduction attacking the public, but though petulant and irascible he was incapable of any emotion that could give life to a cause. He shared the superstition still current in the theatre, that the public wants sincere drama, but is kept from it by some conspiracy of managers or newspapers, and could not get out of his head that the actors were to blame. Shaw, whose turn came next, had foreseen all months before, and had planned an opening that would confound his enemies. For the first few minutes *Arms and the Man* is crude melodrama and then just when the audience are thinking how crude it is, it turns into excellent farce. At the dress rehearsal, a dramatist who had his own quarrel with the public, was taken in the noose; at the first laugh he stood up, turned his back on the stage, scowled at the audience, and even when everybody else knew what turn the play had taken, continued to scowl, and order those nearest to be silent.

On the first night the whole pit and gallery, except certain members of the Fabian Society, started to laugh at the author and then, discovering that they themselves were being laughed at, sat there not converted their hatred was too bitter for that —but dumbfounded, while the rest of the house cheered and laughed. In the silence that greeted the author after the cry for a speech one man did indeed get his courage and boo loudly. "I assure the gentleman in the gallery," was Shaw's answer, "that he and I are of exactly the same opinion, but what can we do against a whole house who are of the contrary opinion?" And from that moment Bernard Shaw became the most formidable man in modern letters, and even the most drunken of medical students knew it. My own play, which had been played with *The Comedy of Sighs*, had roused no passions, but had pleased a sufficient minority for Florence Farr to keep it upon the stage with *Arms and the Man*, and I was in the theatre almost every night for some weeks. "Oh yes, the people seem to like *Arms and the Man*," said one of Mr. Shaw's players to me, "but we have just found out that we are all wrong. Mr. Shaw did really mean it quite seriously, for he has written a letter to say so, and we must not play for laughs any more." Another night I found the manager, triumphant and excited, the Prince of Wales and the Duke of Edinburgh had been there, and the Duke of Edinburgh had spoken his dislike out loud so that the whole stalls could hear, but the Prince of Wales had been "very pleasant" and "got the Duke of Edinburgh away as soon as possible." "They asked for me," he went on, "and the Duke of Edinburgh kept on repeating, 'The man is mad,' meaning Mr. Shaw, and the Prince of Wales asked who Mr. Shaw was, and what he meant by it." I myself was almost as bewildered for though I came mainly to see how my own play went, and for the first fortnight to vex my most patient actors with new lines, I listened to *Arms and the Man* with admiration and hatred. It seemed to me inorganic, logical straightness and not the crooked road of life, yet I stood aghast before its energy as to-day before that of the Stone Drill by Mr. Epstein or of some design by Mr. Wyndham Lewis. He was right to claim Samuel Butler for his master, for Butler was the first Englishman to make the discovery, that it is possible to write with great effect without music, without style, either good or bad, to eliminate from the mind all emotional implication and to prefer plain water to every vintage, so much metropolitan lead and solder to any tendril of the vine. Presently I had a nightmare that I was haunted by a sewing machine, that clicked and shone, but the incredible thing was that the machine smiled, smiled perpetually. Yet I delighted in Shaw the formidable man. He could hit my enemies and the enemies of all I loved, as I could never hit, as no living author that was dear to me could ever hit.

Florence Farr's way home was mine also for a part of the way, and it was often of this that we talked, and sometimes, though not always, she would share my hesitations, and for years to come I was to wonder whenever Shaw became my topic, whether the cock crowed for my blame or for my praise.

2

Shaw and Wilde, had no catastrophe come, would have long divided the stage between them, though they were most unlike— for Wilde believed himself to value nothing but words in their emotional associations, and he had turned his style to a parade as though it were his show, and he Lord Mayor.

I was at Sligo again and I saw the announcement of his action against Lord Queensberry, when starting from my uncle's home to walk to Knocknarea to dine with Cochrane of the Glen, as he was called, to distinguish him from others of that name, an able old man. He had a relation, a poor mad girl, who shared our meals, and at whom I shuddered. She would take a flower from the vase in front of her and push it along the tablecloth towards any male guest who sat near. The old man himself had strange opinions, born not from any mental eccentricity, but from the solitude of his life; and a freedom from all prejudices that were not of his own discovery. "The world is getting more manly," he would say, "it has begun to drink port again," or "Ireland is going to become prosperous. Divorced couples now choose Ireland for a retreat, just as before Scotland became prosperous they began to go there. There are a divorced wife and her lover living at the other side of the mountain." I remember that I spoke that night of Wilde's kindness to myself, said I did not believe him guilty, quoted the psychologist Bain, who has attributed to every sensualist "a voluminous tenderness," and described Wilde's hard brilliance, his dominating self-possession. I considered him essentially a man of action, that he was a writer by perversity and accident, and would have been more important as soldier or politician; and I was certain that, guilty or not guilty, he would prove himself a man. I was probably excited, and did most of the talking, for if Cochrane had talked, I would have remembered an amusing sentence or two; but he was certainly sympathetic. A couple of days later I received a letter from Lionel Johnson, denouncing Wilde with great bitterness. He had "a cold scientific intellect"; he got a "sense of triumph and power, at every dinner-table he dominated, from the knowledge that he was guilty of that sin which, more than any other possible to man, would turn all those people against him if they but knew." He wrote in the mood of his poem, *To the Destroyer of a Soul,* addressed to Wilde, as I have always believed, though I know nothing of the circumstance that made him write it.

I might have known that Wilde's fantasy had taken some tragic turn, and that he was meditating upon possible disaster, but one took all his words for play—had he not called insincerity "a mere multiplication of the personality" or some such words? I had met a man who had found him in a barber's shop in Venice, and heard him explain, "I am having my hair curled that I may resemble Nero"; and when, as editor of an Irish anthology, I had

asked leave to quote "Tread gently, she is near under the snow,"
he had written that I might do so if I pleased, but his most characteristic poem was that sonnet with the lines

> Lo! with a little rod
> I did but touch the honey's romance—
> And must I lose a soul's inheritance.

When in London for my play I had asked news from an actor
who had seen him constantly. "He is in deep melancholy," was
the answer. "He says that he tries to sleep away as much of life as
possible, only leaving his bed at two or three in the afternoon,
and spending the rest of the day at the Café Royal. He has written what he calls the best short story in the world, and will have it
that he repeats to himself on getting out of bed and before every
meal. 'Christ came from a white plain to a purple city, and as he
passed through the first street, he heard voices overhead, and saw
a young man lying drunk upon a window-sill, "Why do you
waste your soul in drunkenness?" He said. "Lord, I was a leper
and You healed me, what else can I do?" A little further through
the town he saw a young man following a harlot, and said, "Why
do you dissolve your soul in debauchery?" and the young man
answered, "Lord, I was blind, and You healed me, what else
can I do?" At last in the middle of the city He saw an old man
crouching, weeping upon the ground, and when He asked why
he wept, the old man answered, "Lord, I was dead and You raised
me into life, what else can I do but weep?"'"

Wilde published that story a little later, but spoiled it with the
verbal decoration of his epoch, and I have to repeat it to myself
as I first heard it, before I can see its terrible beauty. I no more
doubt its sincerity than I doubt that his parade of gloom, all that
late rising, and sleeping away his life, that elaborate playing with
tragedy, was an attempt to escape from an emotion by its exaggeration. He had three successful plays running at once; he had
been almost poor, and now, his head full of Flaubert, found himself with ten thousand a year:—"Lord, I was dead, and You
raised me into life, what else can I do but weep." A comedian,
he was in the hands of those dramatists who understand nothing
but tragedy.

A few days after the first production of my *Land of Heart's*

Desire, I had my last conversation with him. He had come into the theatre as the curtain fell upon my play, and I knew that it was to ask my pardon that he overwhelmed me with compliments; and yet I wonder if he would have chosen those precise compliments, or spoken so extravagantly, but for the turn his thoughts had taken: "Your story in *The National Observer, The Crucifixion of the Outcast,* is sublime, wonderful, wonderful."

Some business or other brought me to London once more and I asked various Irish writers for letters of sympathy, and I was refused by none but Edward Dowden, who gave me what I considered an irrelevant excuse—his dislike for everything that Wilde had written. I heard that Wilde was at his mother's house in Oakley Street, and I called there, but the Irish servant said, her face drawn and tragic as in the presence of death, that he was not there, but that I could see his brother. Willie Wilde received me with, "Who are you; what do you want?" but became all friendship when I told him that I had brought letters of sympathy. He took the bundle of letters in his hand, but said, "Do these letters urge him to run away? Every friend he has is urging him to, but we have made up our minds that he must stay and take his chance." "No," I said, "I certainly do not think that he should run away, nor do those letters advise it." "Letters from Ireland," he said. "Thank you, thank you. He will be glad to get those letters, but I would keep them from him if they advised him to run away." Then he threw himself back in his chair and began to talk with incoherent emotion, and in phrases that echoed now and again his brother's style at its worst; there were tears in his eyes, and he was, I think, slightly intoxicated. "He could escape, oh, yes, he could escape—there is a yacht in the Thames, and five thousand pounds to pay his bail—well not exactly in the Thames, but there is a yacht—oh, yes, he could escape, even if I had to inflate a balloon in the back-yard with my own hand, but he has resolved to stay, to face it out, to stand the music like Christ. You must have heard—it is not necessary to go into detail —that he and I have not been friends; but he came to me like a wounded stag, and I took him in." "After his release"—after he had been bailed out I suppose—"Stewart Headlam engaged a room at an hotel and brought him there under another name, but the manager came up and said, 'Are you Mr. Wilde?' You know what my brother is, you know how he would answer that. He said, 'Yes, I am Oscar Wilde,' and the manager said he must not stay. The same thing happened in hotel after hotel, and at last he made up his mind to come here. It is his vanity that has brought all this disgrace upon him; they swung incense before him." He dwelt upon the rhythm of the words as his brother would have done—"They swung it before his heart." His first emotion at the thought of the letters over, he became more simple, and explained that his brother considered that his crime was not the vice itself, but that he should have brought such misery upon his wife and children, and that he was bound to accept any chance, however slight, to re-establish his position. "If he is acquitted," he said, "he will stay out of England for a few years, and can then gather his friends about him once more—even if he is condemned he will purge his offence—but if he runs away he will lose every friend that he has." I heard later, from whom I forget now, that Lady Wilde had said, "If you stay, even if you go to prison, you will always be my son, it will make no difference to my affection, but if you go, I will never speak to you again." While I was there, some woman who had just seen him —Willie Wilde's wife, I think—came in, and threw herself in a chair, and said in an exhausted voice, "It is all right now, he has made up his mind to go to prison if necessary." Before his release, two years later, his brother and mother were dead, and a little later his wife, struck by paralysis during his imprisonment, I think, was dead, too; and he himself, his constitution ruined by prison life, followed quickly; but I have never doubted, even for an instant, that he made the right decision, and that he owes to that decision half of his renown.

Cultivated London, that before the action against Lord Queensberry had mocked his pose and his affected style, and refused to acknowledge his wit, was now full of his advocates, though I did not meet a single man who considered him innocent. One old enemy of his overtook me in the street and began to praise his audacity, his self-possession. "He has made," he said, "of infamy a new Thermopylæ." I had written in reply to Lionel Johnson's letter that I regretted Wilde's downfall but not that of his imitators, but Johnson had changed with the rest. "Why do you not regret the fall of Wilde's imitators"—I had but tried to share what I thought his opinion—"They were worthless, but should have been left to criticism." Wilde himself was a martyr in his eyes, and when I said that tragedy might give his art a greater depth, he would not even grant a martyr's enemies that poor merit, and thought Wilde would produce, when it was all over, some comedy exactly like the others, writing from an art where events could leave no trace. Everywhere one met writers and artists who praised his wit and eloquence in the witness-box, or repeated some private saying. Willie Redmond told of finding him, to his astonishment, at the conversazione of some theatrical society, standing amid an infuriated crowd, mocking with more than all his old satirical wit the actors and their country. He had said to a well-known painter during one or other of the trials, "My poor brother writes to me that he is defending me all over London; my poor, dear brother, he could compromise a steam engine." His brother, too, had suffered a change, for, if rumour did not wrong him, "the wounded stag" had not been at all graciously received. "Thank God my vices were decent," had been his comment, and refusing to sit at the same table, he had dined at some neighbouring hotel at his brother's expense. His successful brother who had scorned him for a drunken ne'er-do-well was now at his mercy, and besides, he probably shared, until tragedy awoke another self, the rage and contempt that filled the crowds in the street, and all men and women who had an over-abundant normal sexual instinct. "Wilde will never lift his head again," said the art critic, Gleeson White, "for he has against him all men of infamous life." When the verdict was announced the harlots in the street outside danced upon the pavement.

3

Somewhere about 1450, though later in some parts of Europe by a hundred years or so, and in some earlier, men attained to personality in great numbers, "Unity of Being," and became like a "perfectly proportioned human body," and as men so fashioned held places of power, their nations had it too, prince and ploughman sharing that thought and feeling. What afterwards showed for rifts and cracks were there already, but imperious impulse held all together. Then the scattering came, the seeding of the poppy, bursting of pea-pod, and for a time personality seemed but the stronger for it. Shakespeare's people make all things serve their passion, and that passion is for the moment the whole energy of their being—birds, beasts, men, women, landscape, society, are but symbols, and metaphors, nothing is studied in itself, the mind is a dark well, no surface, depth only. The men that Titian painted, the men that Jongsen painted, even the men of Van Dyck, seemed at moments like great hawks at rest. In the Dublin National Gallery there hung, perhaps there still hang, upon the same wall, a portrait of some Venetian gentleman by Strozzi and Mr. Sargent's painting of President Wilson. Whatever thought broods in the dark eyes of that Venetian gentleman, has drawn its life from his whole body; it feeds upon it as the flame feeds upon the candle—and should that thought be changed, his pose would change, his very cloak would rustle for his whole body thinks. President Wilson lives only in the eyes, which are steady and intent; the flesh about the mouth is dead, and the hands are dead, and the clothes suggest no movement of his body, nor any movement but that of the valet, who has brushed and folded in mechanical routine. There, all was an energy flowing outward from the nature itself; here, all is the anxious study and slight deflection of external force; there man's mind and body were predominantly subjective; here all is objective, using those words not as philosophy uses them, but as we use them in conversation.

The bright part of the moon's disk, to adopt the symbolism of a certain poem, is subjective mind, and the dark, objective mind, and we have eight and twenty Phases for our classification of mankind, and of the movement of its thought. At the first Phase —the night where there is no moonlight—all is objective, while when, upon the fifteenth night, the moon comes to the full, there is only subjective mind. The mid-renaissance could but approximate to the full moon "For there's no human life at the full or the dark," but we may attribute to the next three nights of the moon the men of Shakespeare, of Titian, of Strozzi, and of Van Dyck, and watch them grow more reasonable, more orderly, less turbulent, as the nights pass; and it is well to find before the fourth—the nineteenth moon counting from the start—a sudden change, as when a cloud becomes rain, or water freezes, for the great transitions are sudden; popular, typical men have grown more ugly and more argumentative; the face that Van Dyck called a fatal face has faded before Cromwell's warty opinionated head. Henceforth no mind made like "a perfectly proportioned human body" shall sway the public, for great men must live in a portion of themselves, become professional and abstract; but seeing that the moon's third quarter is scarce passed; that abstraction has attained but not passed its climax; that a half, as I affirm it, of the twenty-second night still lingers, they may subdue and conquer, cherish even some Utopian dream, spread abstraction ever further till thought is but a film, and there is no dark depth any more, surface only. But men who belong by nature to the nights near to the full are still born, a tragic minority, and how shall they do their work when too ambitious for a private station, except as Wilde of the nineteenth Phase, as my symbolism has it, did his work? He understood his weakness, true personality was impossible, for that is born in solitude, and at his moon one is not solitary; he must project himself before the eyes of others, and, having great ambition, before some great crowd of eyes; but there is no longer any great crowd that cares for his true thought. He must humour and cajole and pose, take worn-out stage situations, for he knows that he may be as romantic as he please, so long as he does not believe in his romance, and all that he may get their ears for a few strokes of contemptuous wit in which he does believe.

We Rhymers did not humour and cajole; but it was not wholly from demerit, it was in part because of different merit, that he refused our exile. Shaw, as I understand him, has no true quarrel with his time, its moon and his almost exactly coincide. He is quite content to exchange Narcissus and his Pool for the signal-box at a railway junction, where goods and travellers pass perpetually upon their logical glittering road. Wilde was a monarchist, though content that monarchy should turn demagogue for its own safety, and he held a theatre by the means whereby he held a London dinner-table. "He who can dominate a London dinner-table," he had boasted, "can dominate the world." While Shaw has but carried his street-corner socialist eloquence on to the stage, and in him one discovers, in his writing and his public speech, as once—before their outline had been softened by prosperity or the passage of the years—in his clothes and in his stiff joints, the civilisation that Sargent's picture has explored. Neither his crowd nor he have yet made a discovery that brought President Wilson so near his death, that the moon draws to its fourth quarter. But what happens to the individual man whose moon has come to that fourth quarter, and what to the civilisation . . . ?

I can but remember pipe music to-night, though I can half hear beyond it in the memory a weightier music, but this much at any rate is certain—the dream of my early manhood, that a modern nation can return to Unity of Culture, is false; though it may be we can achieve it for some small circle of men and women, and there leave it till the moon bring round its century.

> The cat went here and there
> And the moon spun round like a top,
> And the nearest kin of the moon
> The creeping cat looked up.
>
> .   .   .   .   .
>
> Minnaloushe creeps through the grass
> From moonlit place to place;
> The sacred moon overhead
> Has taken a new phase.
>
> Does Minnaloushe know that his pupils
> Will pass from change to change,
> And that from round to crescent
> From crescent to round they range?
> Minnaloushe creeps through the grass
> Alone, important and wise,
> And lifts to the changing moon
> His changing eyes.

4

Henley's troubles and infirmities were growing upon him. He, too, an ambitious, formidable man, who showed alike in his practice and in his theory—in his lack of sympathy for Rossetti and Landor, for instance—that he never understood how small a fragment of our own nature can be brought to perfect expression, nor that even but with great toil, in a much divided civilisation; though, doubtless, if our own Phase be right, a fragment may be an image of the whole, the moon's still scarce crumbled image, as it were, in a glass of wine. He would be, and have all poets be, a true epitome of the whole mass, a Herrick and Dr. Johnson in the same body and because this—not so difficult before the Mermaid closed its door—is no longer possible, his work lacks music, is abstract, as even an actor's movement can be when the thought of doing is plainer to his mind than the doing itself: the straight line from cup to lip, let us say, more plain than the hand's own sensation weighed down by that heavy spillable cup. I think he was content, when he had called before our eyes—before the too understanding eyes of his chosen crowd—the violent burly man that he had dreamed, content with the mere suggestion, and so did not work long enough at his verses. He disliked Victor Hugo as much as he did Rossetti, and yet Rossetti's translation from *Les Burgraves*, because of its mere technical mastery, out-sings Henley in his own song—

> My mother is dead; God's patience wears;
> It seems my Chaplain will not have done.
>   Love on: who cares?
>   Who cares? Love on.

I can read his poetry with emotion, but I read it for some glimpse of what he might have been as Border balladist, or Cavalier, or of what he actually was, not as poet but as man. He had what Wilde lacked, even in his ruin, passion, was maybe as passionate as some great man of action, as Parnell, let us say. When he and Stevenson quarrelled, he cried over it with some woman or other, and his notorious article was but for vengeance upon Mrs. Stevenson, who had arranged for the public eye, what he considered an imaginary figure, with no resemblance to the gay companion who had founded his life, to that life's injury, upon "The august, the immortal musketeers." She had caused the quarrel, as he believed, and now she had robbed him over again, by blotting from the world's memory the friend of his youth; and because he believed in the robbery I read those angry exaggerated paragraphs with deep sympathy; and I think that the man who has left them out of Henley's collected writings has wronged his memory, as Mrs. Stevenson may have wronged that of Stevenson.

He was no contemplative man, no pleased possessor of wooden models, and paper patterns, but a great passionate man, and no friend of his would have him pictured otherwise. I saw little of him in later years, but I doubt if he was ever the same after the death of his six-year-old daughter. Few passages of his verse touch me as do those few mentions of her though they lack precision of word and sound. When she is but a hope, he prays that she may have his "gift of life" and his wife's "gift of love," and when she is but a few months old he murmurs over her sleep—

> When you wake in your crib,
> You an inch of experience—
> Vaulted about
> With the wonder of darkness;
> Wailing and striving
> To reach from your feebleness
> Something you feel
> Will be good to and cherish you.

And now he commends some friend "boyish and kind, and shy," who greeted him, and greeted his wife, "that day we brought our beautiful one to lie in the green peace" and who is now dead himself; and after that he speaks of love "turned by death to longing" and so, to an enemy.

When I spoke to him of his child's death he said, "she was a person of genius; she had the genius of the mind, and the genius of the body." And later I heard him talk of her as a man talks of something he cannot keep silence over because it is in all his thoughts. I can remember, too, his talking of some book of natural history he had read, that he might be able to answer her questions.

He had a house now at Mortlake on the Thames with a great ivy tod shadowing door and window, and one night there he shocked and startled a roomful of men by showing that he could be swept beyond our reach in reveries of affection. The dull man, who had tried to put Wilde out of countenance, suddenly said to the whole room, roused by I cannot remember what incautious remark meant for the man at my side: "Yeats believes in magic; what nonsense." Henley said, "No, it may not be nonsense; black magic is all the go in Paris now." And then turning towards me with a changed sound in his voice, "It is just a game, isn't it?" I replied, not noticing till too late his serious tone, and wishing to avoid discussion in the dull man's company, "One has had a vision; one wants to have another, that is all." Then Henley said, speaking in a very low voice, "I want to know how I am to get to my daughter. I was sitting here the other night when she came into the room and played round the table and went out again. Then I saw that the door was shut and I knew that I had seen a vision." There was an embarrassed silence, and then somebody spoke of something else and we began to discuss it hurriedly and eagerly.

5

I came now to be more in London, never missing the meetings of the Rhymers' Club, nor those of the council of the Irish Literary Society, where I constantly fought out our Irish quarrels and pressed upon the unwilling Gavan Duffy the books of our new movement. The Irish members of Parliament looked upon us with some hostility because we had made it a matter of principle never to put a politician in the chair, and upon other grounds. One day, some old Irish member of Parliament made perhaps his only appearance at a gathering of members. He recited with great emotion a ballad of his own composition in the manner of Young Ireland, repeating over his sacred names, Wolfe Tone, Emmet, and Owen Roe, and mourning that new poets and new movements should have taken something of their sacredness away. The ballad had no literary merit, but I went home with a troubled conscience; and for a dozen years perhaps, till I began to see the result of our work in a deepened perception of all those things that strengthen race, that trouble remained. I had in mind that old politician as I wrote but the other day—

> Our part
> To murmur name upon name
> As a mother names her child.

The Rhymers had begun to break up in tragedy, though we did not know that till the play had finished. I have never found a full explanation of that tragedy; sometimes I have remembered that, unlike the Victorian poets, almost all were poor men, and had made it a matter of conscience to turn from every kind of money-making that prevented good writing, and that poverty meant strain, and for the most part, a refusal of domestic life. Then I have remembered that Johnson had private means, and that others who came to tragic ends, had wives and families. Another day I think that perhaps our form of lyric, our insistence upon emotion which has no relation to any public interest, gathered together, overwrought, unstable men; and remember, the moment after, that the first to go out of his mind had no lyrical gift, and that we valued him mainly because he seemed a witty man of the world; and that a little later another who seemed, alike as man and writer, dull and formless, went out of his mind, first burning poems which I cannot believe would have proved him as the one man who saw them claims, a man of genius. The meetings were always decorous and often dull; some one would read out a poem and we would comment, too politely for the criticism to have great value; and yet that we read out our poems, and thought that they could be so tested, was a definition of our aims. *Love's Nocturne* is one of the most beautiful poems in the world, but no one can find out its beauty, so intricate its thought and metaphor, till he has read it over several times, or stopped several times to re-read a passage, and the *Faustine* of Swinburne, where much is powerful and musical, could not, were it read out, be understood with pleasure, however clearly it were read, because it has no more logical structure than a bag of shot. I shall, however, remember all my life that evening when Lionel Johnson read or spoke aloud in his musical monotone, where meaning and cadence found the most precise elocution, his poem suggested "by the Statue of King Charles at Charing Cross." It was as though I listened to a great speech. Nor will that poem be to me again what it was that first night. For long I only knew Dowson's *O Mors,* to quote but the first words of its long title, and his *Villanelle of Sunset* from his reading, and it was because of the desire to hold them in my hand that I suggested the first *Book of The Rhymers' Club.* They were not speech but perfect song, though song for the speaking voice. It was perhaps our delight in poetry that was, before all else, speech or song, and could hold

the attention of a fitting audience like a good play or good conversation, that made Francis Thompson, whom we admired so
much—before the publication of his first poem I had brought to
The Cheshire Cheese the proof sheets of his *Ode to the Setting
Sun,* his first published poem—come but once and refuse to contribute to our book. Preoccupied with his elaborate verse, he
may have seen only that which we renounced, and thought what
seemed to us simplicity, mere emptiness. To some members this
simplicity was perhaps created by their tumultuous lives, they
praised a desired woman and hoped that she would find amid
their praise her very self, or at worst, their very passion; and
knew that she, ignoramus that she was, would have slept in the
middle of *Love's Nocturne,* lofty and tender though it be.
Woman herself was still in our eyes, for all that, romantic and
mysterious, still the priestess of her shrine, our emotions remembering the *Lilith* and the *Sybilla Palmifera* of Rossetti; for as yet
that sense of comedy, which was soon to mould the very fashion
plates, and, in the eyes of men of my generation, to destroy at
last the sense of beauty itself, had scarce begun to show here
and there, in slight subordinate touches among the designs of
great painters and craftsmen. It could not be otherwise, for Johnson's favourite phrase, that life is ritual, expressed something that
was in some degree in all our thoughts, and how could life be
ritual if woman had not her symbolical place?

If Rossetti was a subconscious influence, and perhaps the most
powerful of all, we looked consciously to Pater for our philosophy. Three or four years ago I re-read *Marius the Epicurean,*
expecting to find I cared for it no longer, but it still seemed to
me, as I think it seemed to us all, the only great prose in modern
English, and yet I began to wonder if it, or the attitude of mind
of which it was the noblest expression, had not caused the disaster of my friends. It taught us to walk upon a rope, tightly
stretched through serene air, and we were left to keep our feet
upon a swaying rope in a storm. Pater had made us learned;
and, whatever we might be elsewhere, ceremonious and polite,
and distant in our relations to one another, and I think none
knew as yet that Dowson, who seemed to drink so little and had
so much dignity and reserve, was breaking his heart for the
daughter of the keeper of an Italian eating house, in dissipation

and drink; and that he might that very night sleep upon a six-penny bed in a doss house. It seems to me that even yet, and I am speaking of 1894 and 1895, we knew nothing of one another, but the poems that we read and criticised; perhaps I have for-gotten or was too much in Ireland for knowledge, but of this I am certain, we shared nothing but the artistic life. Sometimes Johnson and Symons would visit our sage at Oxford, and I re-member Johnson, whose reports however were not always to be trusted, returning with a sentence that long ran in my head. He had noticed books on political economy among Pater's books, and Pater had said, "Everything that has occupied man, for any length of time, is worthy of our study." Perhaps it was because of Pater's influence that we with an affectation of learn-ing, claimed the whole past of literature for our authority, in-stead of finding it like the young men in the age of comedy that followed us, in some new, and so still unrefuted authority; that we preferred what seemed still uncrumbled rock, to the still un-spotted foam; that we were traditional alike in our dress, in our manner, in our opinions, and in our style.

Why should men, who spoke their opinions in low voices, as though they feared to disturb the readers in some ancient library, and timidly as though they knew that all subjects had long since been explored, all questions long since decided in books whereon the dust settled—live lives of such disorder and seek to rediscover in verse the syntax of impulsive common life? Was it that we lived in what is called "an age of transition" and so lacked co-herence, or did we but pursue antithesis?

6

All things, apart from love and melancholy, were a study to us; Horne already learned in Botticelli had begun to boast that when he wrote of him there would be no literature, all would be but learning; Symons, as I wrote when I first met him, studied the music halls, as he might have studied the age of Chaucer; while I gave much time to what is called the Christian Cabbala; nor was there any branch of knowledge Johnson did not claim for his own. When I had first gone to see him in 1888 or 1889, at the Charlotte Street house, I had called about five in the afternoon, but the man-servant that he shared with Horne and Image, told me that he was not yet up, adding with effusion "he is always up for dinner at seven." This habit of breakfasting when others dined had been started by insomnia, but he came to defend it for its own sake. When I asked if it did not separate him from men and women he replied, "In my library I have all the knowledge of the world that I need." He had certainly a considerable library, far larger than that of any young man of my acquaintance, so large that he wondered if it might not be possible to find some way of hanging new shelves from the ceiling like chandeliers. That room was always a pleasure to me, with its curtains of grey corduroy over door and window and book case, and its walls covered with brown paper, a fashion invented, I think, by Horne, that was soon to spread. There was a portrait of Cardinal Newman, looking a little like Johnson himself, some religious pictures by Simeon Solomon, and works upon theology in Greek and Latin and a general air of neatness and severity; and talking there by candlelight it never seemed very difficult to murmur Villiers de L'Isle Adam's proud words, "As for living —our servants will do that for us." Yet I can now see that Johnson himself in some half-conscious part of him desired the world he had renounced. I was often puzzled as to when and where he could have met the famous men or beautiful women, whose conversation, often wise, and always appropriate, he quoted so often, and it was not till a little before his death that I discovered that these conversations were imaginary. He never altered a detail of speech, and would quote what he had invented for Gladstone or Newman for years without amplification or amendment, with what seemed a scholar's accuracy. His favourite quotations were from Newman, whom, I believe, he had never met, though I can remember nothing now but Newman's greeting to Johnson, "I have always considered the profession of a man of letters a third order of the priesthood!" and these quotations became so well known that at Newman's death, the editor of *The Nineteenth Century* asked them for publication. Because of his delight in all that was formal and arranged he objected to the public quotation of private conversation even after death, and this scruple helped his refusal. Perhaps this dreaming was made a necessity by his artificial life, yet before that life began he wrote

from Oxford to his Tory but flattered family, that as he stood
mounted upon a library ladder in his rooms taking a book from a
shelf, Gladstone, about to pass the open door on his way upstairs to some college authority, had stopped, hesitated, come
into the room and there spent an hour of talk. Presently it was
discovered that Gladstone had not been near Oxford on the date
given; yet he quoted that conversation without variation of a word
until the end of his life, and I think believed in it as firmly as
did his friends. These conversations were always admirable in
their drama, but never too dramatic or even too polished to lose
their casual accidental character; they were the phantasmagoria
through which his philosophy of life found its expression. If he
made his knowledge of the world out of his fantasy, his knowledge of tongues and books was certainly very great; and yet was
that knowledge as great as he would have us believe? Did he
really know Welsh, for instance, had he really as he told me,
made his only love song his incomparable *Morfydd* out of three
lines in Welsh, heard sung by a woman at her door on a walking
tour in Wales, or did he but wish to hide that he shared in their
emotion?

> O, what are the winds?
> And what are the waters?
> Mine are your eyes.

He wanted us to believe that all things, his poetry with its Latin
weight, his religion with its constant reference to the Fathers of
the Church, or to the philosophers of the Church, almost his very
courtesy were a study and achievement of the intellect. Arthur
Symons' poetry made him angry, because it would substitute for
that achievement, Parisian impressionism, "a London fog, the
blurred tawny lamplight, the red omnibus, the dreary rain, the
depressing mud, the glaring gin shop, the slatternly shivering
women, three dexterous stanzas telling you that and nothing
more." I, on the other hand, angered him by talking as if art existed for emotion only, and for refutation he would quote the
close of the Aeschylean Trilogy, the trial of Orestes on the
Acropolis. Yet at moments the thought came to him that intellect,
as he conceived it, was too much a thing of many books, that it
lacked lively experience. "Yeats," he has said to me, "you need

ten years in a library, but I have need of ten years in the wilderness." When he said "Wilderness" I am certain, however, that he thought of some historical, some bookish desert, the Thebaid, or the lands about the Mareotic sea. Though his best poetry is natural and impassioned, he spoke little of it, but much about his prose, and would contend that I had no right to consider words made to read, less natural than words made to be spoken; and he delighted in a sentence in his book on Thomas Hardy, that kept its vitality, as he contended, though two pages long. He punctuated after the manner of the seventeenth century and was always ready to spend an hour discussing the exact use of the colon. "One should use a colon where other people use a semi-colon, a semi-colon where other people use a comma," was, I think, but a condescension to my ignorance for the matter was plainly beset with many subtleties.

7

Not till some time in 1895 did I think he could ever drink too much for his sobriety—though what he drank would certainly be too much for that of most of the men whom I knew— I no more doubted his self-control, though we were very intimate friends, than I doubted his memories of Cardinal Newman. The discovery that he did was a great shock to me, and, I think, altered my general view of the world. I had, by my friendship with O'Leary, by my fight against Gavan Duffy, drawn the attention of a group of men, who at that time controlled what remained of the old Fenian movement in England and Scotland; and at a moment when an attempt, that came to nothing, was being made to combine once more our constitutional and unconstitutional politics, I had been asked to represent this group at some convention in the United States. I went to consult Johnson, whom I found sitting at a table with books about him. I was greatly tempted, because I was promised complete freedom of speech; and I was at the time enraged by some wild articles published by some Irish American newspaper, suggesting the burning down of the houses of Irish landlords. Nine years later I was lecturing in America, and a charming old Irishman came to see me with an interview to write, and we spent, and as I think in entire neglect of his interview, one of the happiest hours I have ever spent, comparing our tales of the Irish fairies, in which he very firmly believed. When he had gone I looked at his card, to discover that he was the writer of that criminal incitement. I told Johnson that if I had a week to decide in I would probably decide to go, but as they had only given me three days, I had refused. He would not hear of my refusal with so much awaiting my condemnation; and that condemnation would be effective with Catholics, for he would find me passages in the Fathers, condemning every kind of political crime, that of the dynamiter and the incendiary especially. I asked how could the Fathers have condemned weapons they had never heard of, but those weapons, he contended, were merely developments of old methods and weapons; they had decided all in principle; but I need not trouble myself about the matter, for he would put into my hands before I sailed the typewritten statement of their doctrine, dealing with the present situation in the utmost detail. He seemed perfectly logical, though a little more confident and impassioned than usual, and I had, I think, promised to accept—when he rose from his chair, took a step towards me in his eagerness, and fell on to the floor; and I saw that he was drunk. From that on, he began to lose control of his life; he shifted from Charlotte Street, where, I think, there was fear that he would overset lamp or candle and burn the house, to Gray's Inn, and from Gray's Inn to old rambling rooms in Lincoln's Inn Fields, and at last one called to find his outer door shut, the milk on the doorstep sour. Sometimes I would urge him to put himself, as Jack Nettleship had done, into an Institute. One day when I had been very urgent, he spoke of "a craving that made every atom of his body cry out" and said the moment after, "I do not want to be cured," and a moment after that, "In ten years I shall be penniless and shabby, and borrow half-crowns from friends." He seemed to contemplate a vision that gave him pleasure, and now that I look back, I remember that he once said to me that Wilde's pleasure and excitement were perhaps increased by the degradation of that group of beggars and blackmailers where he sought his pathics, and I remember, too, his smile at my surprise, as though he spoke of psychological depths I could never enter. Did the austerity, the melancholy of his thoughts, that spiritual ecstasy which he touched at times, heighten, as complementary colours heighten one another, not only the Vision of Evil, but its fascination? Was it only Villon, or did Dante also feel the fascination of evil, when shown in its horror, and, as it were, judged and lost; and what proud man does not feel temptation strengthened from the certainty that his intellect is not deceived?

8

I began now to hear stories of Dowson, whom I knew only at the Rhymers, or through some chance meeting at Johnson's. I was indolent and procrastinating, and when I thought of asking him to dine, or taking some other step towards better knowledge, he seemed to be in Paris, or at Dieppe. He was drinking, but, unlike Johnson, who, at the autopsy after his death, was discovered never to have grown, except in the brain, after his fifteenth year, he was full of sexual desire. Johnson and he were close friends, and Johnson lectured him out of the Fathers upon chastity, and boasted of the great good done him thereby. But the rest of us counted the glasses emptied in their talk. I began to hear now in some detail of the restaurant-keeper's daughter, and of her marriage to the waiter, and of that weekly game of cards with her that filled so great a share of Dowson's emotional life. Sober, he would look at no other woman, it was said, but drunk, desired whatever woman chance brought, clean or dirty.

Johnson was stern by nature, strong by intellect, and always, I think, deliberately picked his company, but Dowson seemed gentle, affectionate, drifting. His poetry shows how sincerely he felt the fascination of religion, but his religion had certainly no dogmatic outline, being but a desire for a condition of virginal ecstasy. If it is true, as Arthur Symons, his very close friend, has written, that he loved the restaurant-keeper's daughter for her youth, one may be almost certain that he sought from religion some similar quality, something of that which the angels find who move perpetually, as Swedenborg has said, towards "the day-spring of their youth." Johnson's poetry, like Johnson himself before his last decay, conveys an emotion of joy, of intellectual clearness, of hard energy; he gave us of his triumph; while Dowson's poetry is sad, as he himself seemed, and pictures his life of temptation and defeat,

> Unto us they belong
> Us the bitter and gay,
> Wine and women and song.

Their way of looking at their intoxication showed their characters. Johnson, who could not have written *Dark Angel* if he did not suffer from remorse, showed to his friends an impenitent face, and defeated me when I tried to prevent the foundation of an Irish convivial club—it was brought to an end after one meeting by the indignation of the members' wives—whereas the last time I saw Dowson he was pouring out a glass of whiskey for himself in an empty corner of my room and murmuring over and over in what seemed automatic apology "The first to-day."

9

Two men are always at my side, Lionel Johnson and John Synge whom I was to meet a little later; but Johnson is to me the more vivid in memory, possibly because of the external finish, the clearly-marked lineament of his body, which seemed but to express the clarity of his mind. I think Dowson's best verse immortal, bound, that is, to outlive famous novels and plays and learned histories and other discursive things, but he was too vague and gentle for my affections. I understood him too well, for I had been like him but for the appetite that made me search out strong condiments. Though I cannot explain what brought others of my generation to such misfortune, I think that (falling backward upon my parable of the moon) I can explain some part of Dowson's and Johnson's dissipation—

> What portion in the world can the artist have,
> Who has awaked from the common dream,
> But dissipation and despair?

When Edmund Spenser described the islands of Phædria and of Acrasia he aroused the indignation of Lord Burleigh, "that rugged forehead" and Lord Burleigh was in the right if morality were our only object.

In those islands certain qualities of beauty, certain forms of sensuous loveliness were separated from all the general purposes of life, as they had not been hitherto in European literature— and would not be again, for even the historical process has its ebb and flow, till Keats wrote his *Endymion*. I think that the movement of our thought has more and more so separated certain images and regions of the mind, and that these images grow in beauty as they grow in sterility. Shakespeare leaned, as it were, even as craftsman, upon the general fate of men and nations, had about him the excitement of the playhouse; and all poets, including Spenser in all but a few pages, until our age came, and when it came almost all, have had some propaganda or traditional doctrine to give companionship with their fellows. Had' not Matthew Arnold his faith in what he described as the best thought of his generation? Browning his psychological curiosity, Tennyson, as before him Shelley and Wordsworth, moral values that were not æsthetic values? But Coleridge of the *Ancient Mariner*, and *Kubla Khan*, and Rossetti in all his writing made what Arnold has called that "morbid effort," that search for "perfection of thought and feeling, and to unite this to perfection of form," sought this new, pure beauty, and suffered in their lives because of it. The typical men of the classical age (I think of Commodus, with his half-animal beauty, his cruelty and his caprice), lived public lives, pursuing curiosities of appetite, and so found in Christianity, with its Thebaid and its Mareotic Sea the needed curb. But what can the Christian confessor say to those who more and more must make all out of the privacy of their thought, calling up perpetual images of desire, for he cannot say "Cease to be artist, cease to be poet," where the whole life is art and poetry, nor can he bid men leave the world, who suffer from the terrors that pass before shut-eyes. Coleridge, and Rossetti though his dull brother did once persuade him that he was an agnostic, were devout Christians, and Steinbock and Beardsley were so towards their lives' end, and Dowson and Johnson always, and yet I think it but deepened despair and multiplied temptation.

> Dark Angel, with thine aching lust,
> To rid the world of penitence:

Malicious angel, who still dost
My soul such subtil violence!

When music sounds, then changest thou
A silvery to a sultry fire:
Nor will thine envious heart allow
Delight untortured by desire.

Through thee, the gracious Muses turn
To Furies, O mine Enemy!
And all the things of beauty burn
With flames of evil ecstasy.

Because of thee, the land of dreams
Becomes a gathering place of fears:
Until tormented slumber seems
One vehemence of useless tears.

Why are these strange souls born everywhere to-day? with hearts
that Christianity, as shaped by history, cannot satisfy. Our love
letters wear out our love; no school of painting outlasts its founders, every stroke of the brush exhausts the impulse, pre-Raphaelitism had some twenty years; impressionism thirty perhaps. Why
should we believe that religion can never bring round its antithesis? Is it true that our air is disturbed, as Mallarmé said, by "the
trembling of the veil of the temple," or "that our whole age is
seeking to bring forth a sacred book"? Some of us thought that
book near towards the end of last century, but the tide sank
again.

10

I do not know whether John Davidson, whose life also was
tragic, made that "morbid effort," that search for "perfection of
thought and feeling," for he is hidden behind failure, to unite it
"to perfection of form." At eleven one morning I met him in the
British Museum reading-room, probably in 1894, when I was in
London for the production of *The Land of Heart's Desire*, but
certainly after some long absence from London. "Are you working here?" I said; "No," he said, "I am loafing, for I have finished
my day's work." "What, already?" "I work an hour a day—I can-

not work longer without exhaustion, and even as it is, if I meet anybody and get into talk, I cannot write the next day; that is why I loaf when my work is finished." No one had ever doubted his industry; he had supported his wife and family for years by "devilling" many hours a day for some popular novelist. "What work is it?" I said. "I am writing verse," he answered. "I had been writing prose for a long time, and then one day I thought I might just as well write what I liked, as I must starve in any case. It was the luckiest thought I ever had, for my agent now gets me forty pounds for a ballad, and I made three hundred out of my last book of verse."

He was older by ten years than his fellow Rhymers; a national schoolmaster from Scotland, he had been dismissed, he told us, for asking for a rise in his salary, and had come to London with his wife and children. He looked older than his years. "Ellis," he had said, "how old are you?" "Fifty," Edwin Ellis replied, or whatever his age was. "Then I will take off my wig. I never take off my wig when there is a man under thirty in the room." He had endured and was to endure again, a life of tragic penury, which was made much harder by the conviction that the world was against him, that he was refused for some reason his rightful position. Ellis thought that he pined even for social success, and I that his Scots jealousy kept him provincial and but half articulate.

During the quarrel over Parnell's grave a quotation from Goethe ran through the papers, describing our Irish jealousy: "The Irish seem to me like a pack of hounds, always dragging down some noble stag." But I do not think we object to distinction for its own sake; if we kill the stag, it is that we may carry off his head and antlers. "The Irish people," O'Leary used to say, "do not know good from bad in any art, but they do not hate the good once it is pointed out to them because it is good." An infallible Church, with its Mass in Latin, and its mediæval Philosophy, and our Protestant social prejudice, have kept our ablest men from levelling passions; but Davidson with a jealousy, which may be Scottish, seeing that Carlyle had it, was quick to discover sour grapes. He saw in delicate, laborious, discriminating taste, an effeminate pedantry, and would, when that mood was on him, delight in all that seemed healthy, popular, and bustling. Once when I had praised Herbert Horne for his knowledge and his taste, he burst out, "If a man must be a connoisseur, let him be a connoisseur in women." He, indeed, was accustomed, in the most characteristic phrase of his type, to describe the Rhymers as lacking in "blood and guts," and very nearly brought us to an end by attempting to supply the deficiency by the addition of four Scotsmen. He brought all four upon the same evening, and one read out a poem upon the Life Boat, evidently intended for a recitation; another described how, when gold-digging in Australia, he had fought and knocked down another miner for doubting the rotundity of the earth; while of the remainder I can remember nothing except that they excelled in argument. He insisted upon their immediate election, and the Rhymers, through that complacency of good manners whereby educated Englishmen so often surprise me, obeyed, though secretly resolved never to meet again; and it cost me seven hours' work to get another meeting, and vote the Scotsmen out. A few days later I chanced upon Davidson at some restaurant; he was full of amiability, and when we parted shook my hand, and proclaimed enthusiastically that I had "blood and guts." I think he might have grown to be a successful man had he been enthusiastic instead about Dowson or Johnson, or Horne or Symons, for they had what I still lacked, conscious deliberate craft, and what I must lack always, scholarship. They had taught me that violent energy, which is like a fire of straw, consumes in a few minutes the nervous vitality, and is useless in the arts. Our fire must burn slowly, and we must constantly turn away to think, constantly analyse what we have done, be content even to have little life outside our work, to show, perhaps, to other men, as little as the watch-mender shows, his magnifying glass caught in his screwed-up eye. Only then do we learn to conserve our vitality, to keep our mind enough under control and to make our technique sufficiently flexible for expression of the emotions of life as they arise. A few months after our meeting in the Museum, Davidson had spent his inspiration. "The fires are out," he said, "and I must hammer the cold iron." When I heard a few years ago that he had drowned himself, I knew that I had always expected some such end. With enough passion to make a great poet, through meeting no man of culture in early life, he lacked intellectual receptivity, and, anarchic and indefinite, lacked pose and gesture, and now no verse of his clings to my memory.

II

Gradually Arthur Symons came to replace in my intimate friendship, Lionel Johnson from whom I was slowly separated by a scruple of conscience. If he came to see me he sat tongue-tied unless I gave him the drink that seemed necessary to bring his vitality to but its normal pitch, and if I called upon him he drank so much that I became his confederate. Once, when a friend and I had sat long after our proper bed-time at his constantly repeated and most earnest entreaty, knowing what black melancholy would descend upon him at our departure, and with the unexpressed hope of getting him to his bed, he fixed upon us a laughing and whimsical look, and said:—"I want you two men to understand that you are merely two men that I am drinking with." That was the only time that I was to hear from him an imaginary conversation that had not an air of the most scrupulous accuracy. He gave two accounts of a conversation with Wilde in prison; in one Wilde wore his hair long, and in the other it had been cropped by the prison barber. He was gradually losing, too, the faculty of experience, and in his prose and verse repeated the old ideas and emotions, but faintly, as though with fading interest. I am certain that he prayed much, and on those rare days that I came upon him dressed and active before mid-day or but little after, I concluded that he had been to morning Mass at Farm Street.

When with Johnson I had turned myself to his mood, but Arthur Symons, more than any man I have ever known, could slip as it were into the mind of another, and my thoughts gained in richness and in clearness from his sympathy, nor shall I ever know how much my practice and my theory owe to the passages that he read me from Catullus and from Verlaine and Mallarmé. I had read *Axel* to myself or was still reading it, so slowly, and with so much difficulty, that certain passages had an exaggerated importance, while all remained so obscure that I could without much effort imagine that here at last was the Sacred Book I longed for. An Irish friend of mine lives in a house where beside a little old tower rises a great new Gothic hall and stair, and I have sometimes got him to extinguish all light but a little Roman lamp, and in that faint light and among great vague shadows, blotting away the unmeaning ornament, have imagined myself partaking in some incredible romance. Half a dozen times, beginning in boyhood with Shelley's *Prometheus Unbound,* I have in that mood possessed for certain hours or months the book that I long for; and Symons, without ever being false to his own impressionist view of art and of life, deepened as I think my longing.

It seems to me, looking backward, that we always discussed life at its most intense moment, that moment which gives a common sacredness to the Song of Songs, and to the Sermon on the Mount, and in which one discovers something supernatural, a stirring as it were of the roots of the hair. He was making those translations from Mallarmé and from Verlaine, from Calderon, from St. John of the Cross, which are the most accomplished metrical translations of our time, and I think that those from Mallarmé may have given elaborate form to my verses of those years, to the later poems of *The Wind Among the Reeds,* to *The Shadowy Waters,* while Villiers de L'Isle Adam had shaped whatever in my *Rosa Alchemica* Pater had not shaped. I can remember the day in Fountain Court when he first read me Herodiade's address to some Sibyl who is her nurse and it may be the moon also:

> The horror of my virginity
> Delights me, and I would envelope me
> In the terror of my tresses, that, by night,
> Inviolate reptile, I might feel the white
> And glimmering radiance of thy frozen fire,
> Thou that are chaste and diest of desire,
> White night of ice and of the cruel snow!
> Eternal sister, my lone sister, lo
> My dreams uplifted before thee! now, apart,
> So rare a crystal is my dreaming heart,
> And all about me lives but in mine own
> Image, the idolatrous mirror of my pride,
> Mirroring this Herodiade diamond-eyed.

Yet I am certain that there was something in myself compelling me to attempt creation of an art as separate from everything heterogeneous and casual, from all character and circumstance, as some Herodiade of our theatre, dancing seemingly alone in her narrow moving luminous circle. Certainly I had gone a great distance from my first poems, from all that I had copied from the folk-art of Ireland, as from the statue of Mausolus and his Queen, where the luminous circle is motionless and contains the entire popular life; and yet why am I so certain? I can imagine an Aran Islander who had strayed into the Luxembourg Gallery, turning bewildered from Impressionist or Post-Impressionist, but lingering at Moreau's "Jason," to study in mute astonishment the elaborate background, where there are so many jewels, so much wrought stone and moulded bronze. Had not lover promised mistress in his own island song, "A ship with a gold and silver mast, gloves of the skin of a fish, and shoes of the skin of a bird, and a suit of the dearest silk in Ireland?"

12

Hitherto when in London I had stayed with my family in Bedford Park, but now I was to live for some twelve months in chambers in the Temple that opened through a little passage into those of Arthur Symons. If anybody rang at either door, one or other would look through a window in the connecting passage, and report. We would then decide whether one or both should receive the visitor, whether his door or mine should be opened, or whether both doors were to remain closed. I have never liked London, but London seemed less disagreeable when one could walk in quiet, empty places after dark, and upon a Sunday morning sit upon the margin of a fountain almost as alone as if in the country. I was already settled there, I imagine, when a publisher called and proposed that Symons should edit a Review or Magazine, and Symons consented on the condition that Beardsley were Art Editor—and I was delighted at his condition, as I think were all his other proposed contributors. Aubrey Beardsley had been dismissed from the Art editorship of *The Yellow Book* under circumstances that had made us indignant. He had illustrated Wilde's *Salome*, his strange satiric art had raised the popular press to fury, and at the height of the excitement aroused by Wilde's condemnation, a popular novelist, a woman who had great influence among the most conventional part of the British public, had written demanding his dismissal. "She owed it to her position before the British people," she had said. Beardsley was not even a friend of Wilde's—they even disliked each other—he had no sexual abnormality, but he was certainly unpopular, and the moment had come to get rid of unpopular persons. The public at once concluded—they could hardly conclude otherwise, he was dismissed by telegram—that there was evidence against him, and Beardsley, who was some twenty-three years old, being embittered and miserable, plunged into dissipation. We knew that we must face an infuriated press and public, but being all young we delighted in enemies and in everything that had an heroic air.

13

We might have survived but for our association with Beardsley; perhaps, but for his *Under the Hill,* a Rabelaisian fragment promising a literary genius as great maybe as his artistic genius; and for the refusal of the bookseller who controlled the railway bookstalls to display our wares. The bookseller's manager, no doubt looking for a design of Beardsley's, pitched upon Blake's *Anteus setting Virgil and Dante upon the verge of Cocytus* as the ground of refusal, and when Arthur Symons pointed out that Blake was considered "a very spiritual artist," replied, "O, Mr. Symons, you must remember that we have an audience of young ladies as well as an audience of agnostics." However, he called Arthur Symons back from the door to say, "If contrary to our expectations the *Savoy* should have a large sale, we should be very glad to see you again." As Blake's design illustrated an article of mine, I wrote a letter upon that remarkable saying to a principal daily newspaper. But I had mentioned Beardsley, and I was told that the editor had made it a rule that his paper was never to mention Beardsley's name. I said upon meeting him later, "Would you have made the same rule in the case of Hogarth?" against whom much the same objection could be taken, and he replied with what seemed to me a dreamy look, as though suddenly reminded of a lost opportunity—"Ah, there was no popular press in Hogarth's day." We were not allowed to forget that in our own day there was a popular press, and its opinions began to affect our casual acquaintance, and even our comfort in public places. At some well-known house, an elderly man to whom I had just been introduced, got up from my side and walked to the other end of the room; but it was as much my reputation as an Irish rebel as the evil company that I was supposed to keep, that excited some young men in a railway carriage to comment upon my general career in voices raised that they might catch my attention. I discovered, however, one evening that we were perhaps envied as well as despised. I was in the pit at some theatre, and had just noticed Arthur Symons a little in front of me, when I heard a young man, who looked like a shop-assistant or clerk, say, "There is Arthur Symons. If he can't get an order, why can't he pay for a stall?" Clearly we were supposed to prosper upon iniquity, and to go to the pit added a sordid parsimony. At another theatre I caught sight of a woman that I once liked, the widow of some friend of my father's youth, and tried to attract her attention, but she had no eyes for anything but the stage curtain; and at some house where I met no hostility to myself, a popular novelist snatched out of my hand a copy of the *Savoy*, and opening it at Beardsley's drawing, called *The Barber*, expounded what he called its bad drawing and wound up with, "Now if you want to admire really great black and white art, admire the *Punch* cartoons of Mr. Lindley Sambourne." Our hostess, after making peace between us, said, "O, Mr. Yeats, why do you not send your poems to the *Spectator* instead of to the *Savoy*?" The answer, "My friends read the *Savoy* and they do not read the *Spectator*," called up a puzzled, disapproving look.

Yet, even apart from Beardsley, we were a sufficiently distinguished body: Max Beerbohm, Bernard Shaw, Ernest Dowson, Lionel Johnson, Arthur Symons, Charles Conder, Charles Shannon, Havelock Ellis, Selwyn Image, Joseph Conrad; but nothing counted but the one hated name. I think that had we been challenged we might have argued something after this fashion: "Science through much ridicule and some persecution has won its right to explore whatever passes before its corporeal eye, and merely because it passes: to set as it were upon an equality the beetle and the whale though Ben Jonson could find no justification for the entomologist in *The New Inn*, but that he had been crossed in love. Literature now demands the same right of exploration of all that passes before the mind's eye, and merely because it passes." Not a complete defence, for it substitutes a spiritual for a physical objectivity, but sufficient it may be for the moment, and to settle our place in the historical process.

The critic might well reply that certain of my generation delighted in writing with an unscientific partiality for subjects long forbidden. Yet is it not most important to explore especially what has been long forbidden, and to do this not only "with the highest moral purpose," like the followers of Ibsen, but gaily, out of sheer mischief, or sheer delight in that play of the mind? Donne could be as metaphysical as he pleased, and yet never seemed unhuman and hysterical as Shelley often does, because he could be as physical as he pleased; and besides who will thirst for the metaphysical, who have a parched tongue, if we cannot recover the Vision of Evil?

I have felt in certain early works of my own which I have long abandoned, and here and there in the work of others of my generation, a slight, sentimental sensuality which is disagreeable, and does not exist in the work of Donne, let us say, because he, being permitted to say what he pleased, was never tempted to linger, or rather to pretend that we can linger, between spirit and sense. How often had I heard men of my time talk of the meeting of spirit and sense, yet there is no meeting but only change upon the instant, and it is by the perception of a change, like the sudden "blacking out" of the lights of the stage, that passion creates its most violent sensation.

14

Dowson was now at Dieppe, now at a Normandy village. Wilde, too, was at Dieppe; and Symons, Beardsley, and others would cross and recross, returning with many tales, and there were letters and telegrams. Dowson wrote a protest against some friend's too vivid essay upon the disorder of his life, and explained that in reality he was living a life of industry in a little country village; but before the letter arrived that friend received a wire, "arrested, sell watch and send proceeds." Dowson's watch had been left in London—and then another wire, "Am free." Dowson, or so ran the tale as I heard it ten years after, had got drunk and fought the baker, and a deputation of villagers had gone to the magistrate and pointed out that Monsieur Dowson was one of the most illustrious of English poets. "Quite right to remind me," said the magistrate, "I will imprison the baker."

A Rhymer had seen Dowson at some café in Dieppe with a particularly common harlot, and as he passed, Dowson, who was half drunk, caught him by the sleeve and whispered, "She writes poetry—it is like Browning and Mrs. Browning." Then there came a wonderful tale, repeated by Dowson himself, whether by word of mouth or by letter I do not remember. Wilde had arrived in Dieppe, and Dowson pressed upon him the necessity of acquiring "a more wholesome taste." They emptied their pockets on to the café table, and though there was not much, there was enough if both heaps were put into one. Meanwhile the news had spread, and they set out accompanied by a cheering crowd. Arrived at their destination, Dowson and the crowd remained outside, and presently Wilde returned. He said in a low voice to Dowson, "The first these ten years, and it will be the last. It was like cold mutton"—always, as Henley had said, "a scholar and a gentleman" he now remembered that the Elizabethan dramatists used the words "Cold mutton"—and then aloud so that the crowd might hear him, "But tell it in England, for it will entirely restore my character."

15

When the first few numbers of the *Savoy* had been published, the contributors and the publisher gave themselves a supper, and Symons explained that certain among us were invited afterwards to the publisher's house, and if I went there that once I need never go again. I considered the publisher a scandalous person, and had refused to meet him; we were all agreed as to his character, and only differed as to the distance that should lie between him and us. I had just received two letters, one from T. W. Rolleston protesting with all the conventional moral earnestness of an article in the *Spectator* newspaper, against my writing for such a magazine; and one from A. E. denouncing with the intensity of a personal conviction that magazine, which he called the "Organ of the Incubi and the Succubi." I had forgotten that Arthur Symons had borrowed the letters until as we stood about the supper table waiting for the signal to be seated, I heard the infuriated voice of the publisher shouting, "Give me the letter, give me the letter, I will prosecute that man," and I saw Symons waving Rolleston's letter just out of reach. Then Symons folded it up and put it in his pocket, and began to read out A. E. and the publisher was silent, and I saw Beardsley listening. Presently Beardsley came to me and said, "Yeats, I am going to surprise you very much. I think your friend is right. All my life I have been fascinated by the spiritual life—when a child I saw a vision of a Bleeding Christ over the mantelpiece—but after all to do one's work when there are other things one wants to do so much more, is a kind of religion."

Something, I forget what, delayed me a few minutes after the supper was over, and when I arrived at our publisher's I found Beardsley propped up on a chair in the middle of the room, grey and exhausted, and as I came in he left the chair and went into another room to spit blood, but returned immediately. Our publisher, perspiration pouring from his face, was turning the handle of a hurdy gurdy piano—it worked by electricity, I was told, when the company did not cut off the supply—and very plainly had had enough of it, but Beardsley pressed him to labour on, "The tone is so beautiful," "It gives me such deep pleasure," etc., etc. It was his method of keeping our publisher at a distance.

Another image competes with that image in my memory. Beardsley has arrived at Fountain Court a little after breakfast with a young woman who belongs to our publisher's circle and certainly not to ours, and is called "twopence coloured," or is it "penny plain." He is a little drunk and his mind has been running upon his dismissal from *The Yellow Book,* for he puts his hand upon the wall and stares into a mirror. He mutters, "Yes, yes. I look like a Sodomite," which he certainly did not. "But no, I am not that," and then begins railing, against his ancestors, accusing them of that and this, back to and including the great Pitt, from whom he declares himself descended.

16

I can no more justify my convictions in these brief chapters than Shakespeare could justify within the limits of a sonnet his conviction that the soul of the wide world dreams of things to come; and yet as I have set out to describe nature as I see it, I must not only describe events but those patterns into which they fall, when I am the looker-on. A French miracle-working priest once said to Maud Gonne and myself and to an English Catholic who had come with us, that a certain holy woman had been the "victim" for his village, and that another holy woman who had been "victim" for all France, had given him her Crucifix, because he, too, was doomed to become a "victim."

French psychical research has offered evidence to support the historical proofs that such saints as Lydwine of Schiedam, whose life suggested to Paul Claudel his *L'Annonce faite à Marie*, did really cure disease by taking it upon themselves. As disease was considered the consequence of sin, to take it upon themselves was to copy Christ. All my proof that mind flows into mind, and that we cannot separate mind and body, drives me to accept the thought of victimage in many complex forms, and I ask myself if I cannot so explain the strange, precocious genius of Beardsley. He was in my Lunar metaphor a man of the thirteenth Phase, his nature on the edge of Unity of Being, the understanding of that Unity by the intellect his one overmastering purpose; whereas Lydwine de Schiedam and her like, being of the saints, are at the seven and twentieth Phase, and seek a unity with a life beyond individual being; and so being all subjective he would take upon himself not the consequences, but the knowledge of sin. I surrender myself to the wild thought that by so doing he enabled persons who had never heard his name, to recover innocence. I have so often, too, practised meditations, or experienced dreams, where the meditations or dreams of two or three persons contrast with and complement one another, in so far as those persons are in themselves complementary or contrasting, that I cannot but see him gathering his knowledge from the saint or potential saint. I see in his fat women and shadowy, pathetic girls, his horrible children, half child, half embryo, in all the lascivious monstrous imagery of the privately published designs, the phantasms that from the beginning have defied the scourge and the hair shirt. I once said to him half seriously, "Beardsley, I was defending you last night in the only way in which it is possible to defend you, by saying that all you draw is inspired by rage against iniquity," and he answered, "If it were so inspired the work would be in no way different," meaning, as I think, that he drew with such sincerity that no change of motive could change the image.

I know that some turn of disease had begun to parade erotic images before his eyes, and I do not doubt that he drew these images. "I make a blot upon the paper," he said to me; "and I begin to shove the ink about and something comes." But I was wrong to say that he drew these things in rage against iniquity, for to know that rage he must needs be objective, concerned with other people, with the Church or the Divinity, with something outside his own head, and responsible not for the knowledge but for the consequence of sin. His preparation had been the exhaustion of sin in act, while the preparation of the Saint is the exhaustion of his pride, and instead of the Saint's humility, he had come to see the images of the mind in a kind of frozen passion, the virginity of the intellect.

Does not all art come when a nature, that never ceases to judge itself, exhausts personal emotion in action or desire so completely that something impersonal, something that has nothing to do with action or desire, suddenly starts into its place, something which is as unforeseen, as completely organised, even as unique, as the images that pass before the mind between sleeping and waking?

But all art is not victimage; and much of the hatred of the art of Beardsley came from the fact that victimage, though familiar under another name to French criticism since the time of Baudelaire, was not known in England. He pictures almost always disillusion, and apart from those privately published drawings which he tried upon his deathbed to have destroyed, there is no representation of desire. Even the beautiful women are exaggerated into doll-like prettiness by a spirit of irony, or are poignant with a thwarted or corrupted innocence. I see his art with more understanding now, than when he lived, for in 1895 or 1896, I was in despair at the new breath of comedy that had begun to wither the beauty that I loved, just when that beauty seemed to have united itself to mystery. I said to him once, "You have never done anything to equal your Salome with the head of John the Baptist." I think, that for the moment he was sincere when he replied, "Yes, yes; but beauty is so difficult." It was for the moment only, for as the popular rage increased and his own disease increased, he became more and more violent in his satire, or created out of a spirit of mockery a form of beauty where his powerful logical intellect eliminated every outline that suggested meditation or even satisfied passion.

The distinction between the Image, between the apparition as it were, and the personal action and desire, took a new form at the approach of death. He made two or three charming and blasphemous designs; I think especially of a Madonna and Child, where the Child has a foolish, doll-like face, and an elaborate modern baby's dress; and of a St. Rose of Lima in an expensive gown decorated with roses, ascending to Heaven upon the bosom of the Madonna, her face enraptured with love, but with that form of it which is least associated with sanctity. I think that his conversion to Catholicism was sincere, but that so much of impulse as could exhaust itself in prayer and ceremony, in formal action and desire, found itself mocked by the antithetical image; and yet I am perhaps mistaken, perhaps it was merely his recognition that historical Christianity had dwindled to a box of toys, and that it might be amusing to empty the whole box on to the counterpane.

17

I had been a good deal in Paris, though never very long at any time; my later visits with a member of the Rhymers' Club whose curiosity or emotion was roused by every pretty girl. He treated me with a now admiring, now mocking wonder, because being in love, and in no way lucky in that love, I had grown exceedingly puritanical so far as my immediate neighbourhood was concerned. One night, close to the Luxembourg, a strange young woman in bicycling costume, came out of a side street, threw one arm around his neck, walked beside us in perfect silence for a hundred yards or so, and then darted up another side street. He had a red and white complexion and fair hair, but how she discovered that in the dark I could not understand. I became angry and reproachful, but he defended himself by saying, "You never meet a stray cat without caressing it: I have similar instincts." Presently we found ourselves at some café—the Café D'Harcourt, I think—and when I looked up from my English newspaper, I found myself surrounded with painted ladies and saw that he was taking vengeance. I could not have carried on a conversation in French, but I was able to say, "That gentleman over there has never refused wine or coffee to any lady," and in a little they had all settled about him like greedy pigeons.

I had put my ideal of those years, an ideal that passed away with youth, into my description of *Proud Costello*. "He was of those ascetics of passion, who keep their hearts pure for love or for hatred, as other men for God, for Mary and for the Saints." My friend was not interested in passion. A woman drew him to her by some romantic singularity in her beauty or her circumstance, and drew him the more if the curiosity she aroused were half intellectual. A little after the time I write of, throwing himself into my chair after some visit to a music-hall or hippodrome, he began, "O, Yeats, I was never in love with a serpent-charmer before." He was objective. For him "the visible world existed" as he was fond of quoting, and I suspect him of a Moon that had entered its fourth quarter.

18

At first I used to stay with Macgregor Mathers and his gracious young wife near the Champ de Mars, or in the Rue Mozart, but later by myself in a student's hotel in the Latin Quarter, and I cannot remember always where I stayed when this or that event took place. Macgregor Mathers, or Macgregor, for he had now shed the "Mathers," would come down to breakfast one day with his Horace, the next day with his Macpherson's Ossian, and read out fragments during breakfast, considering both books of equal authenticity. Once when I questioned that of Ossian, he got into a rage—what right had I to take sides with the English enemy— and I found that for him the eighteenth-century controversy still raged. At night he would dress himself in Highland dress, and dance the sword dance, and his mind brooded upon the ramifications of clans and tartans. Yet I have at moments doubted whether he had seen the Highlands, or even, until invited there by some White Rose Society, Scotland itself. Every Sunday he gave to the evocation of Spirits, and I noted that upon that day he would spit blood. That did not matter, he said, because it came from his head, not his lungs; what ailed him I do not know, but I think that he lived under some great strain, and presently I noted that he was drinking too much neat brandy, though not to drunkenness. It was in some measure a Scottish pose and whether he carried it into later life like his Jacobite opinions I do not know.

He began to foresee changes in the world, announcing in 1893 or 1894, the imminence of immense wars, and was it in 1895 or 1896 that he learned ambulance work, and made others learn it? He had a sabre wound on his wrist—or perhaps his forehead, for my memory is not clear—got in some student riot that he had mistaken for the beginning of war. It may have been some talk of his that made me write the poem that begins:

> The dews drop slowly and dreams gather;
>   unknown spears
> Suddenly hurtle before my dream awakened eyes,
> And then the clash of fallen horsemen and the cries
> Of unknown perishing armies beat about my ears.

Was this prophecy of his, which would shortly be repeated by mediums and clairvoyants all over the world, an unconscious inference taken up into an imagination brooding upon war or was it prevision? An often-repeated statement that anarchy would follow and accompany war suggests prevision, and so too does that unreasoning confidence in his own words. His dream whether prevision or inference was doubtless vague in outline, and as he attempted to make it definite nations and individuals seemed to change into the arbitrary symbols of his desires and fears. He imagined a Napoleonic rôle for himself, a Europe transformed according to his fancy, Egypt restored, a Highland Principality, and even offered subordinate posts to unlikely people. I was soon to quarrel with him, but up to his death in the middle of the Great War heard of him from time to time. Somewhere in 1914 or 1915 he turned his house into a recruiting office and raised six hundred volunteers for the Foreign Legion—they were used in some other way—from Englishmen or Americans born in France, or from Frenchmen born in England, and had some part in their training. He had lost the small income he had lived on when I first knew him, and had sunk into great poverty, but to set the balance right remembered a title Louis XV had conferred upon a Jacobite ancestor who had fought at Pondicherry and called himself Comte de Glenstrae, and gathered about him Frenchmen and Spaniards whose titles were more shadowy perhaps, an obscure claimant to the French throne among the rest, the most as poor as he and some less honest, and in that dream-court cracked innumerable mechanical jokes—to hide discouragement—and yet remained to the end courageous in thought and kind in act. He had tried to prolong his youthful dream, had mounted into *Hodos Chameliontos,* and I have known none mount there and come to good that lacked philosophy. All that he knew of that was a vague affirmation, a medicinal phrase that he would repeat and have friends repeat in all moments of adversity: "There is no part of me that is not of the Gods."

Once, when Mathers had told me that he met his Teachers in some great crowd, and only knew that they were phantoms by a shock that was like an electric shock to his heart, I asked him how he knew that he was not deceived or hallucinated. He said, "I had been visited by one of them the other night, and I followed him out, and followed him down that little lane to the right. Presently I fell over the milk boy, and the milk boy got in a rage because he said that not only I but the man in front had fallen over him." He like all that I have known, who have given themselves up to images, and to the speech of images, thought that when he had proved that an image could act independently of his mind, he had proved also that neither it, nor what it had spoken, had originated there. Yet had I need of proof to the contrary, I had it while under his roof. I was eager for news of the Spanish-American War, and went to the Rue Mozart before breakfast to buy a *New York Herald.* As I went out past the young Normandy servant who was laying breakfast, I was telling myself some schoolboy romance, and had just reached a place where I carried my arm in a sling after some remarkable escape. I bought my paper and returned, to find Mathers on the doorstep. "Why, you are all right," he said. "What did the Bonne mean by telling me that you had hurt your arm and carried it in a sling?"

Once when I met him in the street in his Highland clothes, with several knives in his stocking, he said, "When I am dressed like this I feel like a walking flame," and I think that everything he did was but an attempt to feel like a walking flame. Yet at heart he was, I think, gentle, and perhaps even a little timid. He had some impediment in his nose that gave him a great deal of trouble, and it could have been removed had he not shrunk from the slight operation; and once when he was left in a mouse-infested flat with some live traps, he collected his captives into a large birdcage, and to avoid the necessity of their drowning, fed them there for a couple of weeks. Being an un-scholarly, though learned man, he was bound to express the fundamental antithesis in the most crude form, and being arrogant, to prevent as far as possible that alternation between the two natures which is, it may be, necessary to sanity. When the nature turns to its spiritual opposite alone there can be no alternation, but what nature is pure enough for that?

I see Paris in the Eighteen-nineties as a number of events separated from one another, and without cause or consequence, without lot or part in the logical structure of my life; I can often as little find their dates as I can those of events in my early childhood. William Sharp, who came to see me there, may have come in 1895, or on some visit four or five years later, but certainly I was in an hotel in the Boulevard Raspail. When he stood up to go he said, "What is that?" pointing to a geometrical form painted upon a little piece of cardboard that lay upon my window-sill. And then before I could answer, looked out of the window, saying, "There is a funeral passing." I said, "That is curious, as the Death symbol is painted upon the card." I did not look, but I am sure there was no funeral. A few days later he came back and said, "I have been very ill; you must never allow me to see that symbol again." He did not seem anxious to be questioned, but years later he said, "I will now tell you what happened in Paris. I had two rooms at my hotel, a front sitting-room and a bedroom leading out of it. As I passed the threshold of the sitting-room, I saw a woman standing at the bureau writing, and

presently she went into my bedroom. I thought somebody had got
into the wrong room by mistake, but when I went to the bureau
I saw the sheet of paper she had seemed to write upon, and there
was no writing upon it. I went into my bedroom and I found
nobody, but as there was a door from the bedroom on to the stairs
I went down the stairs to see if she had gone that way. When I
got out into the street I saw her just turning a corner, but when
I turned the corner there was nobody there, and then I saw her
at another corner. Constantly seeing her and losing her like that
I followed till I came to the Seine, and there I saw her standing
at an opening in the wall, looking down into the river. Then she
vanished, and I cannot tell why, but I went to the opening in
the wall and stood there, just as she had stood, taking just the
same attitude. Then I thought I was in Scotland, and that I
heard a sheep bell. After that I must have lost consciousness,
for I knew nothing till I found myself lying on my back, drip-
ping wet, and people standing all around. I had thrown myself
into the Seine."

I did not believe him, and not because I thought the story impossible, for I knew he had a susceptibility beyond that of any
one I had ever known, to symbolic or telepathic influence, but
because he never told one anything that was true; the facts of
life disturbed him and were forgotten. The story had been created
by the influence but it had remained a reverie, though he may
in the course of years have come to believe that it happened as
an event. The affectionate husband of his admiring and devoted
wife, he had created an imaginary beloved, had attributed to her
the authorship of all his books that had any talent, and though
habitually a sober man, I have known him to get drunk, and at
the height of his intoxication when most men speak the truth, to
attribute his state to remorse for having been unfaithful to Fiona
Macleod.

Paul Verlaine alternated between the two halves of his nature
with so little apparent resistance that he seemed like a bad child,
though to read his sacred poems is to remember perhaps that the
Holy Infant shared His first home with the beasts. In what month
was it that I received a note inviting me to "coffee and cigarettes
plentifully," and signed "Yours quite cheerfully, Paul Verlaine"?
I found him at the top of a tenement house in the Rue St.

Jacques, sitting in an easy chair, his bad leg swaddled in many bandages. He asked me, speaking in English, if I knew Paris well, and added, pointing to his leg, that it had scorched his leg for he knew it "well, too well" and "lived in it like a fly in a pot of marmalade." He took up an English dictionary, one of the few books in the room, and began searching for the name of his disease, selecting after a long search and with, as I understood, only comparative accuracy "Erysipelas." Meanwhile his homely middle-aged mistress made the coffee and found the cigarettes; it was obviously she who had given the room its character; her canaries in several cages hanging in the window, and her sentimental lithographs nailed here and there among the nude drawings and newspaper caricatures of her lover as various kinds of monkey, which he had pinned upon the wall. A slovenly, ragged man came in, his trousers belted with a piece of rope and an opera hat upon his head. She drew a box over to the fire, and he sat down, now holding the opera hat upon his knees, and I think he must have acquired it very lately for he kept constantly closing and opening it. Verlaine introduced him by saying, "He is a poor man, but a good fellow, and is so like Louis XI to look at that we call him Louis the XIth." I remember that Verlaine talked of Victor Hugo who was "a supreme poet, but a volcano of mud as well as of flame," and of Villiers de L'Isle Adam who was "exalté" and wrote excellent French; and of *In Memoriam*, which he had tried to translate and could not. "Tennyson is too noble, too Anglais; when he should have been broken-hearted, he had many reminiscences."

At Verlaine's burial, but a few months after, his mistress quarrelled with a publisher at the graveside as to who owned the sheet by which the body had been covered, and Louis XI stole fourteen umbrellas that he found leaning against a tree in the Cemetery.

19

I am certain of one date, for I have gone to much trouble to get it right. I met John Synge for the first time in the Autumn of 1896, when I was one and thirty, and he four and twenty. I was at the Hotel Corneille instead of my usual lodging, and why I cannot remember for I thought it expensive. Synge's biographer says that you boarded there for a pound a week, but I was accustomed to cook my own breakfast, and dine at an anarchist restaurant in the Boulevard St. Jacques for little over a shilling. Some one, whose name I forget, told me there was a poor Irishman at the top of the house, and presently introduced us. Synge had come lately from Italy, and had played his fiddle to peasants in the Black Forest; six months of travel upon fifty pounds; and was now reading French literature and writing morbid and melancholy verse. He told me that he had learned Irish at Trinity College, so I urged him to go to the Aran Islands and find a life that had never been expressed in literature, instead of a life where all had been expressed. I did not divine his genius, but I felt he needed something to take him out of his morbidity and melancholy. Perhaps I would have given the same advice to any young Irish writer who knew Irish, for I had been that summer upon Inishmaan and Inishmore, and was full of the subject. My friends and I had landed from a fishing boat to find ourselves among a group of islanders, one of whom said he would bring us to the oldest man upon Inishmaan. This old man, speaking very slowly, but with laughing eyes, had said, "If any gentleman has done a crime, we'll hide him. There was a gentleman that killed his father, and I had him in my own house six months till he got away to America."

From that on I saw much of Synge, and brought him to Maud Gonne's, under whose persuasion perhaps, he joined the "Young Ireland Society of Paris," the name we gave to half a dozen Parisian Irish, but resigned after a few months because "it wanted to stir up Continental nations against England, and England will never give us freedom until she feels she is safe," the one political sentence I ever heard him speak. Over a year was to pass before he took my advice and settled for a while in an Aran cottage, and became happy, having escaped at last, as he wrote, "from the squalor of the poor and the nullity of the rich." I almost forget the prose and verse he showed me in Paris, though I read it all through again when after his death I decided, at his written request, what was to be published and what not. Indeed, I have but a vague impression, as of a man trying to look out of a window and blurring all that he sees by breathing upon the window.

According to my Lunar parable, he was a man of the twenty-third Phase; a man whose subjective lives—for a constant return to our life is a part of my dream—were over; who must not pursue an image, but fly from it, all that subjective dreaming, that had once been power and joy, now corrupting within him. He had to take the first plunge into the world beyond himself, the first plunge away from himself that is always pure technique, the delight in doing, not because one would or should, but merely because one can do.

He once said to me, "a man has to bring up his family and be as virtuous as is compatible with so doing, and if he does more than that he is a puritan; a dramatist has to express his subject and to find as much beauty as is compatible with that, and if he does more he is an æsthete," that is to say, he was consciously objective. Whenever he tried to write drama without dialect he wrote badly, and he made several attempts, because only through dialect could he escape self-expression, see all that he did from without, allow his intellect to judge the images of his mind as if they had been created by some other mind. His objectivity was, however, technical only, for in those images paraded all the desires of his heart. He was timid, too shy for general conversation, an invalid and full of moral scruple, and he was to create now some ranting braggadocio, now some tipsy hag full of poetical speech, and now some young man or girl full of the most abounding health. He never spoke an unkind word, had admirable manners, and yet his art was to fill the streets with rioters, and to bring upon his dearest friends enemies that may last their lifetime.

No mind can engender till divided into two, but that of a Keats or a Shelley falls into an intellectual part that follows, and a hidden emotional flying image, whereas in a mind like that of Synge the emotional part is dreaded and stagnant, while the intellectual part is a clear mirror-like technical achievement.

But in writing of Synge I have run far ahead, for in 1896 he was but one picture among many. I am often astonished when I think that we can meet unmoved some person, or pass some house, that in later years is to bear a chief part in our life. Should there not be some flutter of the nerve or stopping of the heart

like that Macgregor Mathers experienced at the first meeting
with a phantom?

20

Many pictures come before me without date or order. I am
walking somewhere near the Luxembourg Gardens when Synge,
who seldom generalises and only after much thought, says,
"There are three things any two of which have often come together but never all three; ecstasy, asceticism, austerity; I wish to
bring all three together."

.   .   .   .

I notice that Macgregor Mathers considers William Sharp
vague and sentimental, while Sharp is repelled by Mathers' hard-
ness and arrogance. William Sharp met Mathers in the Louvre,
and said, "No doubt considering your studies you live upon
milk and fruit." And Mathers replied, "No, not exactly milk and
fruit, but very nearly so"; and now Sharp has lunched with
Mathers and been given nothing but brandy and radishes.

.   .   .   .

Mathers is much troubled by ladies who seek spiritual advice,
and one has called to ask his help against phantoms who have the
appearance of decayed corpses, and try to get into bed with her
at night. He has driven her away with one furious sentence,
"Very bad taste on both sides."

.   .   .   .

I take haschisch with some followers of the eighteenth-century
mystic Saint-Martin. At one in the morning, while we are talking
wildly, and some are dancing, there is a tap at the shuttered window; we open it and three ladies enter, the wife of a man of letters who thought to find no one but a confederate, and her husband's two young sisters whom she has brought secretly to some
disreputable dance. She is very confused at seeing us, but as she
looks from one to another understands that we have taken some
drug and laughs; caught in our dream we know vaguely that she
is scandalous according to our code and to all codes, but smile
at her benevolently and laugh.

.   .   .   .

I am at Stuart Merrill's, and I meet there a young Jewish Persian scholar. He has a large gold ring, seemingly very rough, made by some amateur, and he shows me that it has shaped itself to his finger, and says, "That is because it contains no alloy—it is alchemical gold." I ask who made the gold, and he says a certain Rabbi, and begins to talk of the Rabbi's miracles. We do not question him—perhaps it is true—perhaps he has imagined it all—we are inclined to accept every historical belief once more.

.   .   .   .   .   .

I am sitting in a café with two French Americans, a German poet Douchenday, and a silent man whom I discover to be Strindberg, and who is looking for the Philosopher's Stone. The French American reads out a manifesto he is about to issue to the Latin Quarter; it proposes to establish a communistic colony of artists in Virginia, and there is a footnote to explain why he selects Virginia, "Art has never flourished twice in the same place. Art has never flourished in Virginia."

Douchenday, who has some reputation as a poet, explains that his poems are without verbs, as the verb is the root of all evil in the world. He wishes for an art where all things are immovable, as though the clouds should be made of marble. I turn over the page of one of his books which he shows me, and find there a poem in dramatic form, but when I ask if he hopes to have it played he says: "It could only be played by actors before a black marble wall, with masks in their hands. They must not wear the masks for that would not express my scorn for reality."

.   .   .   .   .   .

I go to the first performance of Alfred Jarry's *Ubu Roi*, at the Théâtre de L'Œuvre, with the Rhymer who had been so attractive to the girl in the bicycling costume. The audience shake their fists at one another, and the Rhymer whispers to me, "There are often duels after these performances," and he explains to me what is happening on the stage. The players are supposed to be dolls, toys, marionettes, and now they are all hopping like wooden frogs, and I can see for myself that the chief personage, who is some kind of King, carries for Sceptre a brush of the kind that we use to clean a closet. Feeling bound to support the most spirited party, we have shouted for the play, but that night at the Hotel Corneille I am very sad, for comedy, objectivity, has displayed its growing power once more. I say, "After Stephane Mallarmé, after Paul Verlaine, after Gustave Moreau, after Puvis de Chavannes, after our own verse, after all our subtle colour and nervous rhythm, after the faint mixed tints of Conder, what more is possible? After us the Savage God."

BOOK V

The Stirring of the Bones

I

It may have been the spring of 1897 that Maud Gonne, who was passing through London, told me that for some reason unknown to her, she had failed to get a Dublin authorisation for an American lecturing tour. The young Dublin Nationalists planned a monument to Wolfe Tone which, it was hoped, might exceed in bulk and in height that of the too compromised and compromising Daniel O'Connell, and she proposed to raise money for it by these lectures. I had left the Temple and taken two rooms in Bloomsbury, and in Bloomsbury lived important London Nationalists, elderly doctors, who had been medical students during the Fenian movement. So I was able to gather a sufficient committee to pass the necessary resolution. She had no sooner sailed than I found out why the Dublin committee had refused it, or rather put it off by delay and vague promises. A prominent Irish American had been murdered for political reasons, and another Irish American had been tried and acquitted, but was still accused by his political opponents, and the dispute had spread to London and to Ireland, and had there intermixed itself with current politics and gathered new bitterness. My committee, and the majority of the Nationalist Irish Societies throughout England were upon one side, and the Dublin com-

mittee and the majority of the Nationalist Societies in Ireland
upon the other, and feeling ran high. Maud Gonne had the same
political friends that I had, and the Dublin committee could not
be made to understand that whatever money she collected would
go to the movement, not to her friends. It seemed to me that
if I accepted the Presidency of the '98 Commemoration Association of Great Britain, I might be able to prevent a public quarrel, and so make a great central council possible; and a public
quarrel I did prevent, though with little gain perhaps to anybody,
for at least one active man assured me that I had taken the heart
out of his work, and no gain at all perhaps to the movement,
for our central council had commonly to send two organisers or
to print two pamphlets, that both parties might be represented
when one pamphlet or one organiser had served.

2

It was no business of mine, and that was precisely why I
could not keep out of it. Every enterprise that offered, allured
just in so far as it was not my business. I still think that in a
species of man, wherein I count myself, nothing so much matters as Unity of Being, but if I seek it as Goethe sought, who
was not of that species, I but combine in myself, and perhaps
as it now seems, looking backward, in others also, incompatibles.
Goethe, in whom objectivity and subjectivity were intermixed I
hold, as the dark is mixed with the light at the eighteenth Lunar
Phase, could but seek it as Wilhelm Meister seeks it intellectually, critically, and through a multitude of deliberately chosen
experiences; events and forms of skill gathered as if for a collector's cabinet; whereas true Unity of Being, where all the nature murmurs in response if but a single note be touched, is
found emotionally, instinctively, by the rejection of all experience not of the right quality, and by the limitation of its quan-
tity. Of all this I knew nothing, for I saw the world by the light
of what my father had said, speaking about some Frenchman
who frequented the dissecting rooms to overcome his dread in
the interest of that Unity. My father had mocked, but had not
explained why he had mocked, and I, for my unhappiness had
felt a shuddering fascination. Nor did I understand as yet how

little that Unity, however wisely sought, is possible without a Unity of Culture in class or people that is no longer possible at all.

> The fascination of what's difficult
> Has dried the sap out of my veins, and rent
> Spontaneous joy and natural content
> Out of my heart.

3

I went hither and thither speaking at meetings in England and Scotland and occasionally at tumultuous Dublin conventions, and endured some of the worst months of my life. I had felt years before that I had made a great achievement when the man who trained my uncle's horses invited me to share his Christmas dinner, which we roasted in front of his harness-room fire; and now I took an almost equal pride in an evening spent with some small organiser into whose spittoon I secretly poured my third glass of whiskey. I constantly hoped for some gain in self-possession, in rapidity of decision, in capacity for disguise, and am at this moment, I dare say, no different for it all, having but burgeoned and withered like a tree.

When Maud Gonne returned she became our directing mind both in England and in Ireland, and it was mainly at her bidding that our movement became a protest against the dissensions, the lack of dignity, of the Parnellite and the Anti-Parnellite parties, who had fought one another for seven or eight years, till busy men passed them by, as they did those performing cats that in my childhood I used to see, pretending to spit at one another on a table, outside Charing Cross station. Both parliamentary parties seeing that all young Ireland, and a good part of old, were in the movement, tried to join us, the Anti-Parnellite without abandoning its separate identity. They were admitted I think, but upon what terms I do not remember. I and two or three others had to meet Michael Davitt, and a member of Parliament called F. X. O'Brien to talk out the question of separate identity, and I remember nothing of what passed but the manner and image of Michael Davitt. He seemed hardly more unfitted for such negotiation, perhaps even for any possible present politics, than I myself, and I watched him with sympathy. One knows by the way a man sits in his chair if he have emotional intensity, and Davitt's suggested to me a writer, a painter, an artist of some kind, rather than a man of action. Then, too, F. X. O'Brien did not care whether he used a good or a bad argument, whether he seemed a fool or a clever man, so that he carried his point, but if he used a bad argument Davitt would bring our thought back to it though he had to wait several minutes and restate it. One felt that he had lived always with small unimaginative, effective men whom he despised; and that perhaps through some lack of early education, perhaps because nine years' imprisonment at the most plastic period of his life had jarred or broken his contact with reality, he had failed, except during the first months of the Land League, to dominate those men. He told me that if the split in the Irish Party had not come he would have carried the Land League into the Highlands, and recovered for Ireland as much of Scotland as was still Gaelic in blood or in language. Our negotiations, which interested so much F. X. O'Brien and my two negotiators, a barrister and a doctor, bored him I thought, even more than they did me, to whom they were a novelty; but the Highland plan with its historical foundation and its vague possibilities excited him, and it seemed to me that what we said or did stirred him, at other moments also, to some similar remote thought and emotion. I think he returned my sympathy, for a little before his death he replied to some words of congratulation I sent him after the speech in which he resigned his seat in the House of Commons, with an account of some project of his for improving the quality of the Irish representation there.

4

I think that he shared with poet and philosopher the necessity of speaking the whole mind or remaining silent or ineffective, and he had been for years in a movement, where, to adapt certain words of a friend of mine, it was as essential to carry the heart upon the sleeve as the tongue in the cheek. The founders of the Irish Agrarian movement had acted upon the doctrine, contradicted by religious history, that ignorant men will not work for an idea, or feel a political passion for its own sake, and that you must find "a lever" as it was called, some practical grievance; and I do not think that I am fantastic in believing that this faith in "levers," universal among revolutionaries, is but a result of that mechanical philosophy of the Eighteenth Century, which has, as Coleridge said, turned the human mind into the quick-silver at the back of a mirror, though it still permits a work of art to seem "a mirror dawdling along a road."

O'Leary had told me the story, not I think hitherto published. A prominent Irish American, not long released from the prison where Fenianism had sent him, cabled to Parnell: "Take up Land Reform side by side with the National Question and we will support you. See Kickham." What had Parnell, a land-owner and a haughty man, to do with the peasant or the peas-ant's grievance? And he was indeed so ignorant of both that he asked Kickham, novelist and Fenian leader, if he thought the people would take up land agitation, and Kickham answered: "I am only afraid they would go to the Gates of Hell for it"; and O'Leary's comment was, "and so they have."

And so was founded an agitation where some men pretended to national passion for the land's sake; some men to agrarian passion for the nation's sake; some men to both for their own advancement, and this agitation at the time I write of had but old men to serve it, who found themselves after years of labour, some after years of imprisonment, derided for unscrupulous rascals. Unscrupulous they certainly were, for they had grown up amid make-believe, and now because their practical grievance was too near settlement to blind and to excite, their make-believe was visible to all. They were as eloquent as ever, they had never indeed shared anything in common but the sentimental imagery, the poetical allusions inherited from a still earlier generation, but were faced by a generation that had turned against all oratory. I recall to my memory a member of Parliament who had fought for Parnell's policy after Parnell's death, and much against his own interest, who refused to attend a meeting my friends had summoned at the declaration of the Boer War, because he thought "England was in the right," and yet a week later when the Dublin mob had taken the matter up, advised Irish soldiers to shoot their officers and join President Kruger. I recall another and more distinguished politician who supported the Anti-Parnellite Party in his declining years, and in his vigorous years had raked up some scandal about some Colonial Governor. A friend of mine, after advising that Governor's son to write his father's life, had remembered the scandal and called in her alarm upon the politician; "I do beseech you," he had said and with the greatest earnestness, "to pay no attention whatever to anything I may have said during an election."

Certain of these men, public prepossessions laid aside, were excellent talkers, genial and friendly men, with memories enriched by country humour, much half sentimental, half practical philosophy, and at moments by a poetical feeling not all an affectation—found moving by English sympathisers—of the tear and the smile in Erin's eye. They may even have had more sincerity than their sort elsewhere, but they had inherited a cause men had died for, and they themselves had gone to jail for it, and so worn their hereditary martyrdom that they had seemed for a time no common men, and now must pay the penalty. "I have just told Mahaffy," Wilde had said to me, "that it is a party of men of genius," and now John O'Leary, Taylor, and many obscure sincere men had pulled them down; and yet, should what followed, judged by an eye that thinks most of the individual soul, be counted as more clearly out of the common? A movement first of poetry, then of sentimentality, and land hunger, had struggled with, and as the nation passed into the second period of all revolutions given way before a movement of abstraction and hatred; and after some twenty years of the second period, though abstraction and hatred have won their victory, there is no clear sign, of a third, a *tertium quid,* and a reasonable frame of mind.

Seeing that only the individual soul can attain to its spiritual opposite, a nation in tumult must needs pass to and fro between mechanical opposites, but one hopes always that those opposites may acquire sex and engender. At moments when I have thought of the results of political subjection upon Ireland I have remembered a story told me by Oscar Wilde who professed to have found it in a book of magic, "if you carve a Cerberus upon an emerald," he said, "and put it in the oil of a lamp and carry it into a room where your enemy is, two new heads will come upon his shoulders and all three devour one another."

Instead of sharing our traditional sentimental rhetoric with every man who had found a practical grievance, whether one care a button for the grievance or not, most of us were prosecuting heretics. Nationality was like religion, few could be saved, and meditation had but one theme—the perfect nation and its perfect service. "Public opinion," said an anonymous postcard sent to a friend of mine, "will compel you to learn Irish," and it certainly did compel many persons of settled habits to change tailor and cloth. I believed myself dressed according to public opinion, until a letter of apology from my tailor informed me that "It takes such a long time getting Connemara cloth as it has to come all the way from Scotland."

The Ireland of men's affections must be, as it were, self-moving, self-creating, though as yet (avoiding a conclusion that seemed hopeless) but few added altogether separate from England politically. Men for the moment were less concerned with the final achievement than with independence from English parties and influence during the struggle for it. We had no longer any leaders, abstractions were in their place; and our Conventions, where O'Leary presided, interrupting discussion when the moment came for his cup of coffee, without the least consideration for rules of procedure, were dominated by little groups, the Gaelic propagandists being the most impassioned, which had the intensity and narrowness of theological sects.

I had in my head a project to reconcile old and new that gave Maud Gonne and myself many stirring conversations upon journeys by rail to meetings in Scotland, in Dublin, or in the Midlands. Should we not persuade the organisations in Dublin and in London, when the time drew near for the unveiling of our statue, or even perhaps for the laying of its foundation stone, to invite the leaders of Parnellite or Anti-Parnellite, of the new group of Unionists who had almost changed sides in their indignation at the over-taxation of Ireland, to lay their policy before our Convention—could we not then propose and carry that the Convention sit permanently, or appoint some Executive Committee to direct Irish policy and report from time to time. The total withdrawal from Westminster had been proposed in the 'Seventies, before the two devouring heads were of equal strength —for our Cerberus had but two—and now that the abstract head seemed the strongest, would be proposed again, but the Convention could send them thither, not as an independent power, but as its delegation, and only when, and for what purpose the Convention might decide. I dreaded some wild Fenian movement, and with literature perhaps more in my mind than politics, dreamed of that Unity of Culture which might begin with some few men controlling some form of administration. I began to talk my project over with various organisers, who often interrupted their attention, which was perhaps only politeness, with some new jibe at Mr. Dillon or Mr. Redmond. I thought I had Maud Gonne's support, but when I overheard her conversation, she commonly urged the entire withdrawal of the Irish Members, or if she did refer to my scheme, it was to suggest the sending to England of eighty ragged and drunken Dublin beggars or eighty pugilists "to be paid by results."

She was the first who spoke publicly or semi-publicly of the withdrawal of the Irish Members as a practical policy for our time, so far as I know, but others may have been considering it. A nation in crisis becomes almost like a single mind, or rather like those minds I have described that become channels for parallel streams of thought, each stream taking the colour of the mind it flows through. These streams are not set moving, as I think, through conversation or publication, but through "telepathic contact" at some depth below that of normal consciousness; and it is only years afterwards, when future events have shown the themes' importance, that we discover that they are different expressions of a common theme. That self-moving, self-creating nation necessitated an Irish centre of policy, and I planned a premature impossible peace between those two devouring heads because I was sedentary and thoughtful; but Maud Gonne was not sedentary, and I noticed that before some great event she did not think but became exceedingly superstitious. Are not such as she aware, at moments of great crisis, of some power beyond their own minds; or are they like some good portrait painter of my father's generation and only think when the model

is under their eye? Once upon the eve of some demonstration,
I found her with many caged larks and finches which she was
about to set free for the luck's sake.

I abandoned my plans on discovering that our young men,
not yet educated by Mr. Birrell's university, would certainly
shout down every one they disagreed with, and that their finance
was so extravagant that we must content ourselves with a foundation stone and an iron rail to protect it, for there could never be
a statue; while she carried out every plan she made.

Her power over crowds was at its height, and some portion
of the power came because she could still, even when pushing
an abstract principle to what seemed to me an absurdity, keep
her own mind free, and so when men and women did her bidding they did it not only because she was beautiful, but because
that beauty suggested joy and freedom. Besides there was an element in her beauty that moved minds full of old Gaelic stories
and poems, for she looked as though she lived in an ancient civilisation where all superiorities whether of the mind or the body
were a part of public ceremonial, were in some way the crowd's
creation, as the entrance of the Pope into St. Peter's is the crowd's
creation. Her beauty, backed by her great stature, could instantly
affect an assembly and not as often with our stage beauties because obvious and florid, for it was incredibly distinguished, and
if—as must be that it might seem that assembly's very self, fused,
unified, and solitary—her face, like the face of some Greek statue,
showed little thought, her whole body seemed a master work of
long labouring thought, as though a Scopas had measured and
calculated, consorted with Egyptian sages, and mathematicians
out of Babylon, that he might outface even Artemisia's sepulchral
image with a living norm.

But in that ancient civilisation abstract thought scarce existed,
while she but rose partially and for a moment out of raging abstraction; and for that reason, as I have known another woman
do, she hated her own beauty, not its effect upon others, but its
image in the mirror. Beauty is from the antithetical self, and a
woman can scarce but hate it, for not only does it demand a
painful daily service, but it calls for the denial or the dissolution
of the self.

How many centuries spent
The sedentary soul,
In toil of measurement
Beyond eagle or mole
Beyond hearing and seeing
Or Archimedes' guess,
To raise into being
That loveliness?

5

On the morning of the great procession, the greatest in living memory, the Parnellite and Anti-Parnellite members of Parliament, huddled together like cows in a storm, gather behind our carriage, and I hear John Redmond say to certain of his late enemies, "I went up nearer the head of the Procession, but one of the Marshals said, 'This is not your place, Mr. Redmond; your place is further back.' 'No,' I said, 'I will stay here.' 'In that case,' he said, 'I will lead you back'." Later on I can see by the pushing and shouldering of a delegate from South Africa how important place and precedure is; and noticing that Maud Gonne is cheered everywhere, and that the Irish Members march through street after street without welcome, I wonder if their enemies have not intended their humiliation.

. . . . .

We are at the Mansion House Banquet, and John Dillon is making the first speech he has made before a popular Dublin audience since the death of Parnell; and I have several times to keep my London delegates from interrupting. Dillon is very nervous, and as I watch him the abstract passion begins to rise within me, and I am almost overpowered by an instinct of cruelty; I long to cry out, "Had Zimri peace who slew his master?"

. . . . .

Is our Foundation Stone still unlaid when the more important streets are decorated for Queen Victoria's Jubilee?

I find Maud Gonne at her hotel talking to a young working-man who looks very melancholy. She had offered to speak at one of the regular meetings of his socialist society about Queen

Victoria, and he has summoned what will be a great meeting in the open air. She has refused to speak, and he says that her refusal means his ruin, as nobody will ever believe that he had any promise at all. When he has left without complaint or anger, she gives me very cogent reasons against the open-air meeting, but I can think of nothing but the young man and his look of melancholy. He has left his address, and presently at my persuasion, she drives to his tenement, where she finds him and his wife and children crowded into a very small space—perhaps there was only one room—and, moved by the sight, promises to speak. The young man is James Connolly who, with Padraic Pearce, is to make the Insurrection of 1916 and to be executed.

.   .   .   .   .

The meeting is held in College Green and is very crowded, and Maud Gonne speaks, I think, standing upon a chair. In front of her is an old woman with a miniature of Lord Edward Fitzgerald, which she waves in her excitement, crying out, "I was in it before she was born." Maud Gonne tells how that morning she had gone to lay a wreath upon a martyr's tomb at St. Michael's Church, for it is the one day in the year when such wreaths are laid, but had been refused admission because it is the Jubilee. Then she pauses, and after that her voice rises to a cry, "Must the graves of our dead go undecorated because Victoria has her Jubilee?"

.   .   .   .   .

It is eight or nine at night, and she and I have come from the City Hall, where the Convention has been sitting, that we may walk to the National Club in Rutland Square, and we find a great crowd in the street, who surround us and accompany us. Presently I hear a sound of breaking glass, the crowd has begun to stone the windows of decorated houses, and when I try to speak that I may restore order, I discover that I have lost my voice through much speaking at the Convention. I can only whisper and gesticulate, and as I am thus freed from responsibility I share the emotion of the crowd, and perhaps even feel as they feel when the glass crashes. Maud Gonne has a look of exultation and she walks with her laughing head thrown back.

Later that night Connolly carries in procession a coffin with the words "British Empire" upon it, and police and mob fight for its ownership, and at last that the police may not capture, it is thrown into the Liffey. And there are fights between police and window-breakers, and I read in the morning papers that many have been wounded; some two hundred heads have been dressed at the hospitals; an old woman killed by baton blows, or perhaps trampled under the feet of the crowd; and that two thousand pounds worth of decorated plate-glass windows have been broken. I count the links in the chain of responsibility, run them across my fingers, and wonder if any link there is from my workshop.

.   .   .   .

Queen Victoria visits the city, and Dublin Unionists have gathered together from all Ireland some twelve thousand children and built for them a grandstand, and bought them sweets and buns that they may cheer. A week later Maud Gonne marches forty thousand children through the streets of Dublin, and in a field beyond Drumcondra, and in the presence of a Priest of their Church, they swear to cherish towards England until the freedom of Ireland has been won, an undying enmity.

How many of these children will carry bomb or rifle when a little under or a little over thirty?

.   .   .   .

Feeling is still running high between the Dublin and London organisations, for a London doctor, my fellow-delegate, has called a little after breakfast to say he was condemned to death by a certain secret society the night before. He is very angry, though it does not seem that his life is in danger, for the insult is beyond endurance.

.   .   .   .

We arrive at Chancery Lane for our Committee meeting, but it is Derby Day, and certain men who have arranged a boxing match are in possession of our rooms. We adjourn to a neighbouring public-house where there are little panelled cubicles as in an old-fashioned eating house, that we may direct the secretary how to answer that week's letters. We are much interrupted by a committee man who has been to the Derby, and now, half lying on the table, keeps repeating, "I know what you all think.

Let us hand on the torch, you think; let us hand it on to our children; but I say no! I say, let us order an immediate rising."

Presently one of the boxers arrives, sent up to apologise it seems, and to explain that we had not been recognised. He begins his apology but stops, and for a moment fixes upon us a meditative critical eye. "No, I will not," he cries. "What do I care for any one now but Venus and Adonis and the other Planets of Heaven."

.   .   .   .   .

French sympathisers have been brought to see the old buildings in Galway, and with the towns of Southern France in their mind's eye, are not in the least moved. The greater number are in a small crowded hotel. Presently an acquaintance of mine, peeping, while it is still broad day, from his bedroom window, sees the proprietress of the hotel near the hall door, and in the road a serious-minded, quixotic Dublin barrister, with a little boy who carries from a stick over his shoulder twelve chamber pots. He hears one angry, and one soft pleading explanatory voice, "But, Madam, I feel certain that at the unexpected arrival of so many guests; so many guests of the Nation, I may say; you must have found yourself unprepared." "Never have I been so insulted." "Madam, I am thinking of the honour of my country."

.   .   .   .   .

I am at Maud Gonne's hotel, and an Italian sympathiser Cipriani, the friend of Garibaldi, is there, and though an old man now, he is the handsomest man I have ever seen. I am telling a ghost story in English at one end of the room, and he is talking politics in French at the other. Somebody says, "Yeats believes in ghosts," and Cipriani interrupts for a moment his impassioned declamation to say in English, and with a magnificent movement and intonation, "As for me, I believe in nothing but cannon."

.   .   .   .   .

I call at the office of the Dublin organisation in Westmoreland Street, and I find the front door open, and the office door open, and though the office is empty the cupboard door open and eighteen pounds in gold upon the shelf.

.   .   .   .   .

At a London Committee meeting I notice a middle-aged man who slips into the room for a moment, whispers something to the secretary, lays three or four shillings on a table, and slips out. I am told that he is an Irish board-school teacher who, in early life, took an oath neither to drink nor smoke, but to contribute the amount so saved weekly to the Irish Cause.

.   .   .   .   .

6

When in my twenty-second year I had finished *The Wanderings of Usheen,* my style seemed too elaborate, too ornamental, and I thought for some weeks of sleeping upon a board. Had I been anywhere but at Sligo, where I was afraid of my grandfather and grandmother, I would have made the attempt. When I had finished *Rosa Alchemica* for the *Savoy,* I had a return of the old trouble and went to consult a friend who, under the influence of my cabbalistic symbols, could pass into a condition between meditation and trance. A certain symbolic personality who called herself, if I remember rightly, Megarithma, said that I must live near water and avoid woods "because they concentrate the solar ray." I believed that this enigmatic sentence came from my own daimon, my own buried self speaking through my friend's mind. "Solar," according to all that I learnt from Mathers, meant elaborate, full of artifice, rich, all that resembles the work of a goldsmith, whereas "water" meant "lunar" and "lunar" all that is simple, popular, traditional, emotional. But why should woods concentrate the solar ray? I did not understand why, nor do I now, and I decided to reject that part of the message as an error. I accepted the rest without difficulty, for after *The Wanderings of Usheen,* I had simplified my style by filling my imagination with country stories. My friends believed that the dark portion of the mind—the subconscious—had an incalculable power, and even over events. To influence events or one's own mind, one had to draw the attention of that dark portion, to turn it, as it were, into a new direction. Mathers described how as a boy he had drawn over and over again some event that he longed for; and called those drawings an instinctive magic. But for the most part one repeated certain names and drew or imagined certain symbolic forms which had acquired a precise meaning, and not only to the dark portion of one's own mind, but to the mind of the race. I decided to repeat the names associated with the moon in the cabbalistic tree of life. The divine name, the name of the angelic order, the name of the planetary sphere, and so on, and probably, though my memory is not clear upon the point, to draw certain geometrical forms. As Arthur Symons and I were about to stay with Mr. Edward Martyn at Tullyra Castle, in Galway, I decided that it was there I must make my invocation of the moon. I made it night after night just before I went to bed, and after many nights—eight or nine perhaps—I saw between sleeping and waking, as in a kinematograph, a galloping centaur, and a moment later a naked woman of incredible beauty, standing upon a pedestal and shooting an arrow at a star. I still remember the tint of that marvellous flesh which makes all human flesh seem unhealthy, and remember that others who have seen such forms have remembered the same characteristic. Next morning before breakfast Arthur Symons took me out on to the lawn to recite a scrap of verse, the only verse he had ever written to a dream. He had dreamt the night before of a woman of great beauty, but she was clothed and had not a bow and arrow. When he got back to London, he found awaiting him a story sent to the *Savoy* by Fiona Macleod and called, I think, *The Archer*. Some one in the story had a vision of a woman shooting an arrow into the sky and later of an arrow shot at a faun that pierced the faun's body and remained, the faun's heart torn out and clinging to it, embedded in a tree. Some weeks later I too was in London, and found among Mathers' pupils a woman whose little child—perhaps at the time of my vision, perhaps a little later—had come running in from the garden calling out, "Oh, mother, I have seen a woman shooting an arrow into the sky and I am afraid that she has killed God." I have somewhere among my papers a letter from a very old friend describing how her little cousin—perhaps a few months later—dreamed of a man who shot at a star with a gun and that the star fell down, but "I do not think," the child said, "it minded dying because it was so very old," and how presently the child saw the star lying in a cradle. Had some great event taken place in some world where myth is reality and had we seen some portion of it? One of my fellow-students quoted a Greek saying, "Myths are the activities of the daimons," or had we but seen in the memory of the race something believed thousands of years ago, or had somebody— I myself perhaps—but dreamed a fantastic dream which had come to those others by transference of thought? I came to no conclusion, but I was sure there was some symbolic meaning could I but find it. I went to my friend who had spoken to Megarithma, and she went once more into her trance-like meditation and heard but a single unexplained sentence: "There were three that saw; three will attain a wisdom older than the serpent, but the child will die." Did this refer to myself, to Arthur Symons, to Fiona Macleod, to the child who feared that the archer had killed God? I thought not, for Symons had no deep interest in the subject, and there was the second child to account for. It was probably some new detail of the myth or an interpretation of its meaning. There was a London coroner in those days, learned in the cabbala, whom I had once known though we had not met for some years. I called upon him and told all that I have set down here. He opened a drawer and took out of it two water-colour paintings, made by a clumsy painter who had no object but a symbolical record; one was of a centaur, the other of a woman standing upon a stone pedestal and shooting her arrow at what seemed a star. He asked me to look carefully at the star, and I saw that it was a little golden heart. He said: "You have hit upon things that you can never have read of in any book; these symbols belong to a part of the Christian Cabbala" —perhaps this was not his exact term—"that you know nothing of. The centaur is the elemental spirit and the woman the divine spirit of the path Samekh, and the golden heart is the central point upon the cabbalistic Tree of Life and corresponds to the Sephiroth Tippereth." I was full of excitement, for now at last I began to understand. The "Tree of Life" is a geometrical figure made up of ten circles or spheres called Sephiroth joined by straight lines. Once men must have thought of it as like some great tree covered with its fruit and its foliage, but at some period, in the thirteenth century perhaps, touched by the mathematical genius of Arabia in all likelihood, it had lost its natural form. The Sephiroth Tippereth, attributed to the sun, is joined to the Sephiroth Yesod, attributed to the moon, by a straight line

called the path Samekh, and this line is attributed to the constellation Sagittarius. He would not or could not tell me more,
but when I repeated what I had heard to one of my fellow-
students, a yachtsman and yachts-designer and cabbalist, he said:
"Now you know what was meant by a wisdom older than the
serpent." He reminded me that the cabbalistic tree has a green
serpent winding through it which represents the winding path
of nature or of instinct, and that the path Samekh is part of the
long straight line that goes up through the centre of the tree,
and that it was interpreted as the path of "deliberate effort." The
three who saw must, he said, be those who could attain to wisdom by the study of magic, for that was "deliberate effort." I
remember that I quoted Balzac's description of the straight line
as the line of man, but he could not throw light on the other
symbols except that the shot arrow must symbolise effort, nor did
I get any further light.[1]

·   ·   ·   ·   ·

A couple of weeks after my vision, Lady Gregory, whom I had
met once in London for a few minutes, drove over to Tullyra,
and after Symons' return to London I stayed at her house.
When I saw her great woods on the edge of a lake, I remembered the saying about avoiding woods and living near the water. Had this new friend come because of my invocation, or had
the saying been but prevision and my invocation no act of will,
but prevision also? Were those unintelligible words—"avoid
woods because they concentrate the solar ray"—but a dream confusion, an attempt to explain symbolically an actual juxtaposition
of wood and water? I could not say nor can I now. I was in poor
health, the strain of youth had been greater than it commonly
is, even with imaginative men, who must always, I think, find
youth bitter, and I had lost myself besides as I had done periodically for years, upon *Hodos Chameliontos*. The first time was
in my eighteenth or nineteenth year, when I tried to create a
more multitudinous dramatic form, and now I had got there
through a novel that I could neither write nor cease to write
which had *Hodos Chameliontos* for its theme. My chief person

[1] See, however, Note II.

was to see all the modern visionary sects pass before his bewildered eyes, as Flaubert's St. Anthony saw the Christian sects, and I was as helpless to create artistic, as my chief person to create philosophic order. It was not that I do not love order, or that I lack capacity for it, but that—and not in the arts and in thought only—I outrun my strength. It is not so much that I choose too many elements, as that the possible unities themselves seem without number, like those angels, that in Henry More's paraphrase of the Schoolman's problem, dance spurred and booted upon the point of a needle. Perhaps fifty years ago I had been in less trouble, but what can one do when the age itself has come to *Hodos Chameliontos?*

Lady Gregory seeing that I was ill brought me from cottage to cottage to gather folk-belief, tales of the fairies, and the like, and wrote down herself what we had gathered, considering that this work, in which one let others talk, and walked about the fields so much, would lie, to use a country phrase, "Very light upon the mind." She asked me to return there the next year, and for years to come I was to spend my summers at her house. When I was in good health again, I found myself indolent, partly perhaps because I was affrighted by that impossible novel, and asked her to send me to my work every day at eleven, and at some other hour to my letters, rating me with idleness if need be, and I doubt if I should have done much with my life but for her firmness and her care. After a time, though not very quickly, I recovered tolerable industry, though it has only been of late years that I have found it possible to face an hour's verse without a preliminary struggle and much putting off.

Certain woods at Sligo, the woods above Dooney Rock and those above the waterfall at Ben Bulben, though I shall never perhaps walk there again, are so deep in my affections that I dream about them at night; and yet the woods at Coole, though they do not come into my dream are so much more knitted to my thought, that when I am dead they will have, I am persuaded, my longest visit. When we are dead, according to my belief, we live our lives backward for a certain number of years, treading the paths that we have trodden, growing young again, even childish again, till some attain an innocence that is no longer a mere accident of nature, but the human intellect's crowning achievement. It was at Coole that the first few simple thoughts that now, grown complex through their contact with other thoughts, explain the world, came to me from beyond my own mind. I practised meditations, and these, as I think, so affected my sleep that I began to have dreams that differed from ordinary dreams in seeming to take place amid brilliant light, and by their invariable coherence, and certain half-dreams, if I can call them so, between sleep and waking. I have noticed that such experiences come to me most often amid distraction, at some time that seems of all times the least fitting, as though it were necessary for the exterior mind to be engaged elsewhere, and it was during 1897 and 1898, when I was always just arriving from or just setting out to some political meeting, that the first dreams came. I was crossing a little stream near Inchy Wood and actually in the middle of a stride from bank to bank, when an emotion never experienced before swept down upon me. I said, "That is what the devout Christian feels, that is how he surrenders his will to the will of God." I felt an extreme surprise for my whole imagination was preoccupied with the pagan mythology of ancient Ireland, I was marking in red ink upon a large map, every sacred mountain. The next morning I awoke near dawn, to hear a voice saying, "The love of God is infinite for every human soul because every human soul is unique, no other can satisfy the same need in God."

Lady Gregory and I had heard many tales of changelings, grown men and women as well as children, who as the people believe are taken by the fairies, some spirit or inanimate object bewitched into their likeness remaining in their stead, and I constantly asked myself what reality there could be in these tales, often supported by so much testimony. I woke one night to find myself lying upon my back with all my limbs rigid, and to hear a ceremonial measured voice, which did not seem to be mine, speaking through my lips, "We make an image of him who sleeps," it said, "and it is not him who sleeps, and we call it Emmanuel." After many years that thought, others often found as strangely being added to it, became the thought of the Mask, which I have used in these memoirs to explain men's characters. A few months ago at Oxford I was asking myself why it should be "An image of him who sleeps," and took down from the shelf, not knowing what I did, Burkitt's *Early Eastern Christianity,* and opened it at random. I had opened it at a Gnostic Hymn that told of a certain King's son who being exiled, slept in Egypt—a symbol of the natural state—and how an Angel while he slept brought him a royal mantle; and at the bottom of the page I found a footnote saying that the word mantle did not represent the meaning properly for that which the Angel gave had the exile's own form and likeness. I did not, however, find in the Gnostic Hymn my other conviction that Egypt and that which the Mask represents are antithetical. That, I think, became clear when a countryman told Lady Gregory and myself that he had heard the crying of new-dropped lambs in November—Spring in the world of Fairy, being November with us.

.   .   .   .   .

On the sea coast at Duras, a few miles from Coole, an old French Count, Florimond de Basterot, lived for certain months in every year. Lady Gregory and I talked over my project of an Irish Theatre looking out upon the lawn of his house, watching a large flock of ducks that was always gathered for his arrival from Paris, and that would be a very small flock, if indeed it were a flock at all, when he set out for Rome in the autumn. I told her that I had given up my project because it was impossible to get the few pounds necessary for a start in little halls, and she promised to collect or give the money necessary. That was her first great service to the Irish intellectual movement. She reminded me the other day that when she first asked me what she could do to help our movement I suggested nothing; and, certainly, I no more foresaw her genius than I foresaw that of John Synge, nor had she herself foreseen it. Our theatre had been established before she wrote or had any ambition to write, and yet her little comedies have merriment and beauty, an unusual combination, and those two volumes where the Irish heroic tales are arranged and translated in an English so simple and so noble, may do more than other books to deepen Irish imagination. They contain our ancient literature, are something better than our *Mabinogion,* are almost our *Morte D'Arthur.* It is more fitting, however, that in a book of memoirs I should speak of her personal influence, and especially as no witness is likely to arise better qualified to speak. If that influence were lacking, Ireland would be greatly impoverished, so much has been planned out in the library, or among the woods at Coole; for it was there that John Shawe-Taylor found the independence from class and family that made him summon the conference between landlord and tenant, that brought land purchase, and it was there that Hugh Lane formed those Irish ambitions that led to his scattering many thousands, and gathering much ingratitude; and where, but for that conversation at Florimond de Basterot's, had been the genius of Synge?

I have written these words instead of leaving all to posterity, and though my friend's ear seems indifferent to praise or blame, that young men to whom recent events are often more obscure than those long past, may learn what debts they owe and to what creditor.

Dramatis Personae

1896–1902

When I was thirty years old the three great demesnes of three Galway houses, Coole House, Tullyra Castle, Roxborough House, lay within a half-hour or two hours' walk of each other. They were so old they seemed unchanging; now all have been divided among small farmers, their great ancient trees cut down. Roxborough House was burnt down during the civil war; Coole House has passed to the Forestry Department, but Tullyra Castle is inhabited by blood relatives of those who built it. I went there for the first time with Arthur Symons, then editor of the *Savoy* magazine. I was taking him here and there through Ireland. We had just been sight-seeing in Sligo. Edward Martyn, met in London, perhaps with George Moore, had seemed so heavy, uncouth, countrified that I said as we turned in at the gate: "We shall be waited on by a bare-footed servant." I was recalling a house seen at Sligo when a child. Then I saw the great trees, then the grey wall of the Castle.

Edward Martyn brought us up the wide stairs of his Gothic hall decorated by Crace and showed us our rooms. "You can take your choice," he said. I took out a penny to toss, shocking Symons, who was perhaps all the more impressed by his surroundings because of what I had said about bare feet. I think the man of letters has powers of make-believe denied to the painter or the architect. We both knew that those pillars, that stair and varnished roof with their mechanical ornament, were among the worst inventions of the Gothic revival, but upon several evenings we asked Edward Martyn to extinguish all light except that of a little Roman lamp, sat there in the shadows, as though upon a stage set for *Parsifal*; Edward Martyn sat at his harmonium, so placed among the pillars that it seemed some ancient instrument, and played Palestrina. He hated that house in all its detail—it had been built by his mother when he was a very young man to replace some plain eighteenth-century house —all except an ancient tower where he had his study. A fire had destroyed the old house, and whatever old furniture or pictures the family possessed, as though fate had deliberately prepared for an abstract mind that would see nothing in life but its vulgarity and temptations. In the tower room, in a light filtered through small stained glass windows, without any quality of design, made before Whall rediscovered the methods of medieval glass-workers, he had read Saint Chrysostom, Ibsen, Swift, because they made abstinence easy by making life hateful in his eyes. He drank little, ate enormously, but thought himself an ascetic because he had but one meal a day, and suffered, though a courteous man, from a subconscious hatred of women. His father had been extravagantly amorous; I was later to collect folklore from one of his father's peasant mistresses, then an old woman. I have heard of his getting from his horse to chase a girl for a kiss. Edward's mother who still lived, and is a frail, pinched figure in my memory, had tried to marry him to women who did not share or even understand his tastes and were perhaps chosen for that reason. Edward, who admired Beardsley for his saturnine genius, had commissioned from him a great stained-glass window for the hall. And had Beardsley lived another year, his fat women, his effeminate men, his children drawn so as to suggest the foetus, would have fed Edward's hatred of life. I can remember his mother's current selection, a pretty somewhat ruddy girl, saying: "I never could stand those Beardsleys," fixing her eye on an incomparable Utamaro. The drawing-room furniture was vulgar and pretentious, because he thought himself bound to satisfy what he believed to be the taste of women. Only his monklike bedroom, built over the stables and opening into the tower on the opposite side to the house, his study in the tower, and the pictures, showed his own improving taste. His first purchase, a large, coffee-coloured sea picture by Edwin Ellis —not my friend the Blake scholar, but the Academician—had been a mistake; then, perhaps under the influence of George Moore, a relative on his father's side, came Degas, Monet, Corot, Utamaro, and of these pictures he talked with more intelligence, more feeling than when he talked of literature. His Degas showed the strongly-marked shoulder-blades of a dancing-girl, robbing her of voluptuous charm. Degas had said to him: "Cynicism is the only sublimity." It hung somewhere near the Utamaro, which pleased him because of its almost abstract pattern, or because the beautiful women portrayed do not stir our Western senses.

2

When Symons and I paid our visit, Martyn had just finished *The Heather Field*. Alexander had praised it and refused it, and he talked of having it produced in Germany. He sat down daily to some task, perhaps *Maeve*, but I was certain even then, I think, that though he would find subjects, construct plots, he would never learn to write; his mind was a fleshless skeleton. I used to think that two traditions met and destroyed each other in his blood, creating the sterility of a mule. His father's family was old and honoured; his mother but one generation from the peasant. Her father, an estate steward, earned money in some way that I have forgotten. His religion was a peasant religion; he knew nothing of those interpretations, casuistries, whereby my Catholic acquaintances adapt their ancient rules to modern necessities. What drove him to those long prayers, those long meditations, that stern Church music? What secret torture?

3

Presently, perhaps, after Arthur Symons had gone, Lady Gregory called, reminded me that we had met in London though but for a few minutes at some fashionable house. A glimpse of a long vista of trees, over an undergrowth of clipped laurels, seen for a moment as the outside car approached her house on my first visit, is a vivid memory. Coole House, though it has lost its great park full of ancient trees, is still set in the midst of a thick wood, which spreads out behind the house in two directions, in one along the edges of a lake which, as there is no escape for its water except a narrow subterranean passage, doubles or trebles its size in winter. In later years I was to know the edges of that lake better than any spot on earth, to know it in all the changes of the seasons, to find there always some new beauty. Wondering at myself, I remember that when I first saw that house I was so full of the medievalism of William Morris that I did not like the gold frames, some deep and full of ornament, round the pictures in the drawing-room; years were to pass before I came to understand the earlier nineteenth and later eighteenth century, and to love that house more than all other houses. Every generation had left its memorial; every generation had been highly educated; eldest sons had gone the grand tour, returning with statues or pictures; Mogul or Persian paintings had been brought from the Far East by a Gregory chairman of the East India Company, great earthenware ewers and basins, great silver bowls, by Lady Gregory's husband, a famous Governor of Ceylon, who had married in old age, and was now some seven years dead; but of all those Gregorys, the least distinguished, judged by accepted standards, most roused my interest—a Richard who at the close of the eighteenth century was a popular brilliant officer in the Guards. He was accused of pleading ill-health to escape active service, and though exonerated by some official inquiry, resigned his commission, gave up London and his friends. He made the acquaintance of a schoolgirl, carried her off, put her into a little house in Coole demesne, afterwards the steward's house, where she lived disguised as a boy until his father died. They married, and at the end of last century the people still kept the memory of her kindness and her charity. One of the latest planted of the woods bore her name, and is, I hope, still called, now that the Government Foresters are in possession, "The Isabella Wood." While compelled to live in boy's clothes she had called herself "Jack the Sailor" from a song of Dibdin's. Richard had brought in bullock-carts through Italy the marble copy of the Venus de' Medici in the drawing-room, added to the library the Greek and Roman Classics bound by famous French and English binders, substituted for the old straight avenue two great sweeping avenues each a mile or a little more in length. Was it he or his father who had possessed the Arab horses, painted by Stubbs? It was perhaps Lady Gregory's husband, a Trustee of the English National Gallery, who had bought the greater number of the pictures. Those that I keep most in memory are a Canaletto, a Guardi, a Zurbarán. Two or three that once hung there had, before I saw those great rooms, gone to the National Gallery, and the fine portraits by Augustus John and Charles Shannon were still to come. The mezzotints and engravings of the masters and friends of the old Gregorys that hung round the small downstairs breakfast room, Pitt, Fox, Lord Wellesley, Palmerston, Gladstone, many that I have forgotten, had increased generation by generation, and amongst them Lady Gregory had hung a letter from Burke to the Gregory that was chairman of the East India Company saying that he committed to his care, now that he himself had grown old, the people of India. In the hall, or at one's right hand as one ascended the stairs, hung Persian helmets, Indian shields, Indian swords in elaborate sheaths, stuffed birds from various parts of the world, shot by whom nobody could remember, portraits of the members of Grillion's Club, illuminated addresses presented in Ceylon or Galway, signed photographs or engravings of Tennyson, Mark Twain, Browning, Thackeray, at a later date paintings of Galway scenery by Sir Richard Burton, bequeathed at his death, and etchings by Augustus John. I can remember somebody saying: "Balzac would have given twenty pages to the stairs." The house itself was plain and box-like, except on the side towards the lake where somebody, probably Richard Gregory, had enlarged the drawing-room and dining-room with great bow windows. Edward Martyn's burnt house had been like it doubtless, for it was into such houses men moved, when it was safe to leave their castles, or the thatched cottages under castle walls; architecture did not return until the cut stone Georgian houses of a later date.

4

Lady Gregory, as I first knew her, was a plainly dressed woman of forty-five, without obvious good looks, except the charm that comes from strength, intelligence and kindness. One who knew her at an earlier date speaks of dark skin, of an extreme vitality, and a portrait by Mrs. Jopling that may have flattered shows considerable beauty. When her husband died, she had given up her London house, had devoted herself to the estate and to her son, spending little that mortgages might be paid off. The house had become her passion. That passion grew greater still when the house took its place in the public life of Ireland. She was a type that only the superficial observer could identify with Victorian earnestness, for her point of view was founded, not on any narrow modern habit but upon her sense of great literature, upon her own strange feudal, almost medieval youth. She was a Persse—a form of the name Shakespeare calls Percy—descended from some Duke of Northumberland; her family had settled in the seventeenth century somewhere in the midlands, but finding, the legend declares, the visits of Lord Clanricarde, going and returning between his estate and Dublin, expensive, they had moved that they might be no longer near the high road and bought vast tracts of Galway land. Roxborough House small and plain, but interesting for its high-pitched roof—the first slate roof built in Galway—was beside the road from Gort to Loughrea, a few yards from the bounding wall of a demesne that was nine miles round. Three or four masons were, during Lady Gregory's girlhood, continually busy upon the wall. On the other side of the road rose the Slievoughter range, feeding grouse and wild deer. The house contained neither pictures nor furniture of historic interest. The Persses had been soldiers, farmers, riders to hounds and, in the time of the Irish Parliament, politicians; a bridge within the wall commemorated the victory of the Irish Volunteers in 1782, but all had lacked intellectual curiosity until the downfall of their class had all but come. In the last half of the nineteenth century Lady Gregory was born, an older and a younger sister gave birth to Sir Hugh Lane and to that John Shawe-Taylor who, by an act of daring I must presently describe, made the settlement of the Land Question possible.

Popular legend attributes to all the sons of the house daring and physical strength; some years ago, Free State Ministers were fond of recounting the adventures of Lady Gregory's "Seven Brothers" who, no matter who objected to their rents, or coveted their possessions, were safe "because had one been killed, the others would have run down and shot the assassin"; how the wildest of the brothers, excluded by some misdemeanour from a Hunt Ball, had turned a hose on the guests; how, a famous shot, he had walked into a public-house in a time of disturbance and put a bullet through every number on the clock. They had all the necessities of life on the mountain, or within the walls of their demesne, exporting great quantities of game, ruling their tenants, as had their fathers before, with a despotic benevolence, were admired, and perhaps loved, for the Irish people, however lawless, respect a rule founded upon some visible supremacy. I heard an old man say once to Lady Gregory "There was never a man that could hold a bow with your brothers." Those brothers were figures from the eighteenth century. Sir John Barrington might have celebrated their lives, but their mother and the mother of John Shawe-Taylor were of the nineteenth in one of their characteristics. Like so many Irish women of the upper classes, who reacted against the licence, the religious lassitude of the immediate past, they were evangelical Protestants, and set out to convert their neighbourhood. Few remember how much of this movement was a genuine enthusiasm; that one of its missionaries who travelled Ireland has written her life, has described meetings in peasant cottages where everybody engaged in religious discussion, has said that she was everywhere opposed and slandered by the powerful and the wealthy because upon the side of the poor. I can turn from the pages of her book with sympathy. Were I a better man and a more ignorant I had liked just such a life. But that missionary would have met with no sympathy at Roxborough, except, it may be, amongst those boisterous brothers or from one studious girl, for Roxborough Protestantism was on the side of wealth and power. All there had an instinctive love for their country or their neighbourhood, the mailboat had not yet drawn the thoughts of the wealthy classes elsewhere. My great-grandmother Corbet, the mistress of Sandymount Castle, had been out of Ireland but once. She had visited her son, afterwards Governor of Penang, at his English school, carrying a fortnight's provisions, so great were the hazards of the crossing; but that was some two generations earlier. Their proselytism expressed their love, they gave what they thought best. But the born student of the great literature of the world cannot proselytise, and Augusta Persse, as Lady Gregory was then named, walked and discussed Shakespeare with a man but little steadier than her brothers, a scholar of Trinity, in later years a famous botanist, a friendship ended by her alarmed mother. Was it earlier or later that she established a little shop upon the estate and herself sold there that she might compel the shopkeepers to bring down their exorbitant prices? Other well-born women of that time, Ruskin's Rose amongst them, did the same. Born in 1852, she has passed her formative years in comparative peace, Fenianism a far-off threat; and her marriage with Sir William Gregory in her twenty-seventh year, visits to Ceylon, India, London, Rome, set her beyond the reach of the bitter struggle between landlord and tenant of the late 'seventies and early 'eighties. She knew Ireland always in its permanent relationships, associations—violence but a brief interruption—never lost her sense of feudal responsibility, not of duty as the word is generally understood, but of burdens laid upon her by her station and her character, a choice constantly renewed in solitude. "She has been," said an old man to me, "like a serving-maid among us. She is plain and simple, like the Mother of God, and that was the greatest lady that ever lived." When in later years her literary style became in my ears the best written by woman, she had made the people a part of her soul; a phrase of Aristotle's had become her motto: "To think like a wise man, but to express oneself like the common people."

5

When I went to Coole the curtain had fallen upon the first act of my drama. In 1891 I had founded in London the Irish Literary Society, joined by most London journalists of Irish birth, a couple of years later in Dublin, the National Literary Society; these societies had given, as I intended, opportunity to a new generation of critics and writers to denounce the propagandist verse and prose that had gone by the name of Irish literature, and to substitute for it certain neglected writers: Sir Samuel Ferguson, a writer of ballads dry in their eighteenth-century sincerity; Standish O'Grady, whose *History of Ireland* retold the Irish heroic tales in romantic Carlylian prose; the Clarence Mangan of

The Dark Rosaleen and *O'Hussey's Ode to The Maguire*, our one poet raised to the first rank by intensity, and only that in these or perhaps in the second of these poems. No political purpose informed our meetings; no Lord Mayor, no Member of Parliament, was elected to the Chair. John O'Leary, the old Fenian, since his return from his Parisian exile more scholar than politician, first president of the National Literary Society, was succeeded by Dr. Douglas Hyde. His famous presidential lecture upon what he called "The De-Anglicisation of Ireland" led to the foundation of the Gaelic League, which, though not yet the great movement it became, was soon stronger than the movement in English. Irishmen who wrote in the English language were read by the Irish in England, by the general public there, nothing was read in Ireland except newspapers, prayer-books, popular novels; but if Ireland would not read literature it might listen to it, for politics and the Church had created listeners. I wanted a Theatre—I had wanted it for years, but knowing no way of getting money for a start in Ireland, had talked to Florence Farr, that accomplished speaker of verse, less accomplished actress, of some little London hall, where I could produce plays. I first spoke to Lady Gregory of my abandoned plan for an Irish Theatre, if I can call anything so hopeless a plan, in the grounds of a little country house at Duras, on the sea coast, where Galway ends and Clare begins. She had brought me to see the only person in Galway, perhaps I should say in Ireland, who was in any real sense her friend. His romantic name is written on the frame of a picture by Stott of Oldham in the Dublin Municipal Gallery: "Given by A. Gregory and W. R. Gregory"—Lady Gregory's son, at the time of my first visit a boy of seventeen—"in memory of Count Florimond de Basterot." He was a Catholic, an old man crippled by the sins of his youth, much devoted to his prayers, but an accomplished man of the world. He had flats in Paris and in Rome and divided his year between them and his little Galway house, passing through Dublin as quickly as possible because he thought it "a shabby England." Ancestors had fled from the French Revolution, bought a considerable Galway estate long since sold to some other landlord or divided among the tenants. In a few years, seven or eight, he was to speak to Lady Gregory and to myself, and for the first time, of estate and house, to drive us through what had once been park, show where the walls had stood, what had been garden, an aviary in the midst of it, where the avenue had wound, where upon that avenue he, a boy in his teens, and his father's men-servants had thrown a barricade across it and stood with guns in their hands. His father had died in debt, and at that time a creditor could seize a body and prevent its burial until paid. The creditor arrived, but at the sight of armed men fled. De Basterot fulfilled a saying I have heard somewhere: "Things reveal themselves passing away." We never saw him again. In five or six weeks, several men and women with old French titles announced upon a black-edged card the death of "Florimond, Alfred Jacques, Comte de Basterot, Chevalier de l'Ordre du Saint Sépulcre, leur Cousin Germain et Cousin." In his garden under his friendly eyes, the Irish National Theatre, though not under that name, was born. I may then have used for the first time the comparison which in later years I turned into a proverb. Except during certain summer months, when they roost in the fields, crows at nightfall return to the vast rookeries round Tullyra Castle, whirling, counter-whirling, clamorous; excited, as it seems, by the sublime dance. It was the one unforgettable event of my first visit as of other visits there. And I was accustomed to say to Lady Gregory when it seemed that some play of mine must be first performed outside Ireland, or when it seemed, as it did once or twice, that I myself might find it impossible to live in Ireland: "The crows of Tullyra return to their trees in winter" or "The crows return at nightfall," meaning that, after my death, my books would be a part of Irish literature. She, however, with her feeling for immediate action, for the present moment, disapproved of my London project. She offered to collect or give the money for the first Irish performances. My *Countess Cathleen* was ready, and either I or Lady Gregory spoke to Edward Martyn, who gave up a proposed German performance and became enthusiastic. Then came an unexpected difficulty. Dublin had two theatres, the Royal and the Gaiety, that had been granted patents, a system obsolete everywhere else. No performance, except for charity, could be given but at these two theatres; they were booked for the best months of the year by English travelling companies and in the

worst months were expensive. We had to change the law, which
we did with the assistance of an old friend of Lady Gregory's
husband, Lecky the historian, representative in Parliament of
Trinity College. The writing of letters, talks in the Lobby of
the House of Commons, seemed to take up all our time.

6

I must have spent the summer of 1897 at Coole. I was involved in a miserable love affair, that had but for one brief interruption absorbed my thoughts for years past, and would for
some years yet. My devotion might as well have been offered to
an image in a milliner's window, or to a statue in a museum,
but romantic doctrine had reached its extreme development.
Dowson was in love with a girl in an Italian restaurant, courted
her for two years; at first she was too young, then he too disreputable; she married the waiter and his life went to wreck.
Sober, he looked on no woman; drunk, he picked the cheapest
whore. "He did not even want them clean," said a friend. "I
have been faithful to thee, Cynara, in my fashion." My health
was giving way, my nerves had been wrecked. Finding that I
could not work, and thinking the open air salutary, Lady Gregory brought me from cottage to cottage collecting folklore. Every
night she wrote out what we had heard in the dialect of the cottages. She wrote, if memory does not deceive me, two hundred
thousand words, discovering that vivid English she was the first
to use upon the stage. My object was to find actual experience
of the supernatural, for I did not believe, nor do I now, that
it is possible to discover in the text-books of the schools, in the
manuals sold by religious booksellers, even in the subtle reverie
of saints, the most violent force in history. I have described elsewhere our discovery that when we passed the door of some peasant's cottage, we passed out of Europe as that word is understood. "I have longed," she said once, "to turn Catholic, that I
might be nearer to the people, but you have taught me that pa-
ganism brings me nearer still." Yet neither she nor those peasants
were pagans. Christianity begins to recognise the validity of experiences that preceded its birth and were, in some sense, shared
by its founders. When later she asked me to annotate and intro-

duce her book, *Visions and Beliefs,* I began a study of "Spiritu-
alism" not only in its scientific form but as it is found among
the London poor, and discovered that there was little difference
except that the experience of the cottagers was the richer. Re-
quiring no proof that we survive the grave, they could turn to
what was dramatic or exciting and, though more ignorant than
the townsmen, lacked vulgarity. Do the cottagers still live that
mysterious life? Has it been driven away by exciting tales of am-
bush and assassination or has it become more inaccessible? When
I was yet a very young man Sligo people told me whatever I
asked, because all knew my mother's father, and some still remembered my father's grandfather. The people of South Galway
did the same because Lady Gregory was my friend; an old witch-
doctor in Clare said to us both: "I have told you now what I
have not told my own wife"; but if a stranger, or a neighbour
that might mock, questioned them, they would say that all such
things had long disappeared through the influence of the school.
Once when I heard an old shepherd at Doneraile, where I spent
a few days, give Lord Castletown such an answer, I said: "Has
anybody ever gone from here to consult Biddy Earley?"—a famous Clare witch—and in a moment the man's face became excited; he himself had stood at the roadside, watching spirits playing hurley in a field, until one came and pulled the cap over
his eyes. What he saw, what he did not see but thought he saw,
does not concern me here, being but a part of that traditional experience which I have discussed only too much elsewhere. That
experience is my obsession, as Coole and its history, her hope that
her son or her grandson might live there, were Lady Gregory's.

7

It was now that George Moore came into our affairs, brought
by Edward Martyn, who invited him to find a cast for *The
Heather Field.* They were cousins and inseparable friends,
bound one to the other by mutual contempt. When I told Martyn that Moore had good points, he replied: "I know Moore a
great deal longer than you do. He has no good points." And a
week or two later Moore said: "That man Martyn is the most
selfish man alive. He thinks that I am damned and he doesn't

care." I have described their friendship in a little play called *The Cat and the Moon;* the speaker is a blind beggar-man, and Laban is a townland where Edward Martyn went to chapel: . . . "Did you ever know a holy man but had a wicked man for his comrade and his heart's darling? There is not a more holy man in the barony than the man who has the big house at Laban, and he goes knocking about the roads day and night with that old lecher from the county of Mayo, and he a woman-hater from the day of his birth. And well you know and all the neighbours know what they talk of by daylight and candlelight. The old lecher does be telling over all the sins he committed, or maybe never committed at all, and the man of Laban does be trying to head him off and quiet him down that he may quit telling them." Moore and Martyn were indeed in certain characteristics typical peasants, the peasant sinner, the peasant saint. Moore's grandfather or great-grandfather had been a convert, but there were Catholic marriages. Catholic families, beaten down by the Penal Laws, despised by Irish Protestants, by the few English Catholics they met, had but little choice as to where they picked their brides; boys, on one side of old family, grew up squireens, halfsirs, peasants who had lost their tradition, gentlemen who had lost theirs. Lady Gregory once told me what marriage coarsened the Moore blood, but I have forgotten.

George Moore had a ceaseless preoccupation with painting and the theatre, within certain limits a technical understanding of both; whatever idea possessed him, courage and explosive power; but sacrificed all that seemed to other men good breeding, honour, friendship, in pursuit of what he considered the root facts of life. I had seen him once in The Cheshire Cheese. I had with me some proof-sheets of the Ellis and Yeats study of Blake's philosophy, and the drooping tree on the second page of *The Book of Thel* stirred him to eloquence. His "How beautiful, how beautiful!" is all I can remember. Then one evening, in a narrow empty street between Fleet Street and the river, I heard a voice resounding as if in a funnel, someone in a hansom cab was denouncing its driver, and Moore drove by. Then I met him in Arthur Symons' flat in the Temple. He threw himself into a chair with the remark: "I wish that woman would wash." He had just returned from an assignation with his mistress, a woman known to Symons personally, to me by repute, an accomplished, witty, somewhat fashionable woman. All his friends suffered in some way; good behaviour was no protection, for it was all chance whether the facts he pursued were in actual life or in some story that amused him. Had "that woman" prided herself upon her cleanliness, he would, had he decided upon a quarrel, have said with greater publicity: "I wish that woman would wash." His pursuit had now and then unfortunate results. "What has depressed you, Moore?" said an acquaintance. "I have been paying attention to a certain woman. I had every reason to think she liked me. I came to the point to-day and was turned down completely." "You must have said something wrong." "No, what I said was all right." "What was it?" "I said I was clean and healthy and she could not do better." Upon occasion it made him brutal and witty. He and I went to the town of Galway for a Gaelic festival that coincided with some assembly of priests. When we lunched at the Railway Hotel the room was full of priests. A Father Moloney, supposed to know all about Greek Art, caught sight of Moore and introduced himself. He probably knew nothing about Moore, except that he was some kind of critic, for he set out upon his favourite topic with: "I have always considered it a proof of Greek purity that though they left the male form uncovered, they invariably draped the female." "Do you consider, Father Moloney," said Moore in a voice that rang through the whole room, "that the female form is inherently more indecent than the male?" Every priest turned a stern and horrified eye upon Father Moloney, who sat hunched up and quivering.

I have twice known Moore alarmed and conscience-struck, when told that he had injured somebody's financial prospects—a financial prospect is a root fact—but he attacked with indifference so long as nothing suffered but his victim's dignity or feelings. To injure a famous scholar in a quarrel not his he had printed all the scandalous stories he could rake together, or invent, in a frenzy of political hatred. I had remonstrated in vain, except that he cut out a passage describing his victim as "a long pink pig," yet when he thought he might have deprived that scholar of a post he was miserable.

He had gone to Paris straight from his father's racing stables, from a house where there was no culture, as Symons and I under-

stood that word, acquired copious inaccurate French, sat among
art students, young writers about to become famous, in some café;
a man carved out of a turnip, looking out of astonished eyes. I see
him as that circle saw him, for I have in memory Manet's caricature. He spoke badly and much in a foreign tongue, read nothing, and was never to attain the discipline of style. "I wrote a
play in French," he said, "before I had seen dialogue on paper."
I doubt if he had read a play of Shakespeare's even at the end
of his life. He did not know that style existed until he returned
to Ireland in middle life; what he learned, he learned from conversation, from acted plays, from pictures. A revolutionary in
revolt against the ignorant Catholicism of Mayo, he chose for
master Zola as another might have chosen Karl Marx. Even to
conversation and acted plays, he gave an inattentive ear, instincts
incapable of clear expression deafened him and blinded him; he
was Milton's lion rising up, pawing out of the earth, but, unlike that lion, stuck halfway. He reached to middle life ignorant
even of small practical details. He said to a friend: "How do you
keep your pants from falling about your knees?" "Oh," said the
friend, "I put my braces through the little tapes that are sewn
there for the purpose." A few days later, he thanked the friend
with emotion. Upon a long country bicycle ride with another
friend, he had stopped because his pants were about his knees,
had gone behind a hedge, had taken them off, and exchanged
them at a cottage for a tumbler of milk. Only at pictures did he
look undeafened and unblinded, for they impose their silence
upon us. His *Modern Painting* has colloquial animation and surprise that might have grown into a roundness and ripeness of
speech that is a part of style had not ambition made him in later
life prefer sentences a Dublin critic has compared to ribbons of
tooth-paste squeezed out of a tube. When the Irish Theatre was
founded, he had published *A Mummer's Wife*, which had made
a considerable sensation, for it was the first realistic novel in the
language, the first novel where every incident was there not because the author thought it beautiful, exciting or amusing, but
because certain people who were neither beautiful, exciting, nor
amusing must have acted in that way: the root facts of life, as
they are known to the greatest number of people, that and nothing else. Balzac would have added his wisdom. Moore had but

his blind ambition. *Esther Waters* should have been a greater novel, for the scene is more varied. Esther is tempted to steal a half-crown; Balzac might have made her steal it and keep our sympathy, but Moore must create a personification of motherly goodness, almost an abstraction. Five years later he begged a number of his friends to read it; "I have just read it," he said. "It has done me good, it radiates goodness." He had wanted to be good as the mass of men understand goodness. In later life he wrote a long preface to prove that he had a mistress in Mayfair.

8

I knew nothing of Moore at the time I write of except what Symons or Martyn told me, or I had learnt from his occasional articles. I had read no book of his, nor would I, had he not insisted, for my sympathies were narrow. I cared for nothing but poetry or prose that shared its intensity. Florence Farr and I had just begun that attempt described in "Speaking to the Psaltery" to revive the ancient art of minstrelsy. Florence Farr had ruined her career by premature success. For ten years she had played a series of parts, which had through their association with controversial movements attained great publicity. I remember most vividly her performance in *Arms and the Man* and in *Rosmersholm*, but most of all her first success in Dr. Todhunter's *Sicilian Idyll*. Because she could not accept less than twenty pounds a week without loss of status and got it but rarely, she was doomed to remain an amateur. Yet her voice was among the most beautiful of her time, her elocution, her mastery of poetical rhythm incomparable.

9

To remind myself of these and other events I have been looking through the letters I wrote to Lady Gregory during those first years of our friendship. She was now at Coole, now at Queen Anne's Mansions, now in Paris, I at 18 Woburn Buildings, London, or with an uncle at Sligo. On the ground floor at Woburn Buildings lived a shoemaker; on the first floor a workman and his family; I on the second floor; in the attic an old pedlar, who painted a little in water colours. I wrote in one of the earliest letters: "I have measured the window." (Lady Gregory must have given me the great blue curtain that was a principal feature there for twenty years.) "Ought I to let you do all these kind things for me? . . . I have reasoned myself out of the instincts and rules by which one mostly surrounds oneself. I have nothing but reason to trust to, and so am in continual doubt about simple things."

Presently she gave me a great leather arm chair which is before my eyes at this moment. From her came the great collection of folklore that, turned into essays for the monthly reviews, brought ten or fifteen pounds at a time. Then one night when she and the other guests had gone I found twenty pounds behind my clock. I went to see her and tried to return it. "You must take this money," she said. "You should give up journalism. The only wrong act that matters is not doing one's best work." She had that test for everyone. We were all like packets of herbs, each with its special quality. From time to time from that on she gave me money. I was not to consider it a loan, though I might return it some day if well off. When I finished my first lecture tour in the United States, the winter of 1903–4, I tried to return it, but she said: "Not until I think you have enough money to feel independent." I inherited a little money from a relative, but she still refused. Four or five years later she consented. I asked how much; she said, "Five hundred." It was a shock to find I owed so much. I wrote to an American lecture agent, earned the money and paid it back. That I am ashamed of that long debt to so dear a friend, that I have told it after a struggle with myself, puts me to shame. Of still greater service were those summers at Coole. For twenty years I spent two or three months there in every year. Because of those summers, because of that money, I was able through the greater part of my working life to write without thought of anything but the beauty or the utility of what I wrote. Until I was nearly fifty, my writing never brought me more than two hundred a year, and most often less, and I am not by nature economical.

I wrote from Sligo of my uncle George Pollexfen (I have described him in *The Trembling of the Veil*): "He is just at this moment in one of his bad fits owing to the fact that the inhabitants attack him as they cannot get at me. He brought me to a Masonic concert on Thursday. Somebody sang a stage Irishman's song—the usual whiskey, shillelagh kind of thing—and I hissed him, and lest my hiss might be lost in the general applause, waited until the applause had died down and hissed again. That gave somebody else also courage, and we both hissed. My uncle defends me, but says that he makes a poor hand of it and gets beaten."

Then I wrote about "A great battle with George Armstrong" (Professor of Literature at Cork; author of a trilogy, *Saul, David, Solomon*). "He lectured on the *Two Irelands, or Ireland in Literature,* and his whole lecture was an attack on the 'Celtic Movement,' full of insinuations about conspiracies to prevent his success as a poet, to keep him out of anthologies, etc. I replied with a great deal of fierceness, described the barrenness of the so-called intellect of Ireland, told him that all the cleverest of the young men were leaving him and coming to us. I then attacked his scholarship and showed that his knowledge of Irish things was of the most obsolete kind. I believe I was unanswerable. At any rate Armstrong made no attempt to reply, but excused himself because of the lateness of the hour, which was weak as he had brought the contest upon himself, and made the hour late by speaking for two hours. Father Barry who was in the Chair said afterwards: 'Thank you for your speech. I agree with almost every word of it.' I was glad of this, as it was probably the fiercest the Society had ever heard."

Then I told how I had taken the chair at some public meeting in London where speakers talked open sedition: "A principal speaker was the Vicar of Plumpton, who advised everybody to buy a breechloader and prepare for the day of battle and wound up by singing a patriotic song, apparently of his own making. . . . I was in such a rage that I forgot to put the Resolutions." Then I described old Cipriani, who spoke as though he stood "on a battlefield, and he has stood on fifty." A magnificent-looking old man, a friend of Garibaldi, he had gone all over the world fighting for liberty, and Maud Gonne had brought him to Ireland to work out a scheme for insurrection, then to some London Irish to make his report. In one letter I used a phrase Lady Gregory was often to chaff me about, though never to repudiate: "In a battle like Ireland's which is one of poverty against wealth, we must prove our sincerity by making ourselves unpopular to wealth. We must accept the baptism of the gutter. Have not all the leaders done that?"

Then an adventure: "Yesterday I was in a tea-shop," I wrote from London, "when a woman with an obvious look of the country introduced herself to me as a Gaelic Leaguer, and straightway introduced me to two friends, a man and a woman who had an equally country look. They told me with wonderful brogues that they were on their way to the Paris Exhibition, and wanted to shake hands with me. They had a great deal to say about the Movement and talked very fast for fear I might go before they had said it. What they said was chiefly about a play in Irish to be acted in Macroom next Monday. It is by one Father Peter O'Leary, and is about a man who lived in Macroom and arranged his own funeral to escape the bailiff. There was immense local enthusiasm over it, and deep indignation among the descendants of the bailiff."

There is an allusion to the Cabbalistic Society, which had taught me methods of meditation that had greatly affected my thought. A talented girl I had tried to find work for had after years of victorious prudery become the mistress of a drunken scoundrel, and advertised the fact everywhere, even pouring out tea with his arm round her waist. "Because she has enough genius," I wrote, "to make her thirst for reality, and not enough intellect to understand the temporal use of unreal things, she is throwing off every remnant of respectability." Presently, from excitability, shock, bewilderment at her private circle which had no objection to lovers but much to that particular lover, her health broke down. Then the Cabbalistic Society took her affairs in hand, a rich member had "collected all her unpaid bills . . . another mystic sees her to-day and will give her whatever help may be wanted. These mystics will not demoralise her, which her other friends have been doing, especially Lady ——." (She had denounced the crime of picking the wrong man. Her own entanglement was notorious but exalted.) "For their faith makes them look on everything in the world as so wrong that the conventional errors seem to them trivial, and all defiance meritorious. They keep their morality for each other, and are firmly divided

just now into the compassionate who lack idealism, and the
idealists who lack compassion—Moore 'Idle Devout'; and ——
has been handed over to the Compassionate, to the joy of the
'Idle Devout' who are anxious to be forgotten by their enemies."
A year or two later I was to describe her crying over Wilde's
death: " 'He was so kind, nobody ever lived who was so kind.'
As she said it I thought of Homer's description of the captive
women: 'Weeping in seeming for Patroclus, yet each weeping
for her own sorrow, because he was ever kind.' " I wrote to Lady
Gregory about this girl, because I was certain of her sympathy,
yet those who did not know her thought her stern. A beautiful
woman, whose love affairs were notorious, once said to me:
"When I got into the train at Broadstone, there were only two
vacant places, one next Lady Gregory and one next the Bishop
of Tuam. I thought 'I am in for a lecture from somebody' and
took the place next the Bishop, and all he said was: 'Well, my
child, you know a great deal more of the world than when I
confirmed you.' "

10

I invited Florence Farr to find players for my *Countess Cathleen*. I do not remember whether it was Florence Farr or I or
Edward Martyn who asked a Dublin amateur actor to play a
principal part in both plays, but it was certainly Edward Martyn
who invited George Moore to a rehearsal of *The Heather Field*.
I wrote to Lady Gregory in March or April 1899: "Moore first
got rid of practically the whole cast," putting X (the Dublin
amateur actor) out of the part of Usher. "He ran at the chairs,
kicked them and called Moore names, upon which the prompter
threatened him with personal violence if he used such language
in the presence of ladies."

Then Moore descended upon my rehearsals. I was relieved,
for I was rehearsing in the part of Countess Cathleen a young
girl who had made a great success some years before as the Faery
Child in my *Land of Heart's Desire*. She had a beautiful speaking voice but lacked experience. I describe the result: "Moore has
put a Miss Whitty to act Countess Cathleen. She acts admirably,
and has no sense of rhythm whatever. . . . She enrages me

every moment, but will make the part a success. I am getting the others to speak with a little, a very little music. Mrs. Emery [Florence Farr] alone satisfies my ear." Perhaps I should have insisted upon the young girl, for after Miss Whitty's dress rehearsal somebody said: "Miss Whitty brought tears into my eyes because she had them in her voice, but that young girl brought them into my eyes with beauty."

When "The Antient Concert Rooms" had been taken, the rehearsals almost begun, Edward Martyn wrote to Lady Gregory and myself withdrawing financial support. Some monk, I never learned the name, had called *The Countess Cathleen* heretical. She sells her soul to certain demons for money that the people may not be compelled by starvation to sell theirs. She dies. The demons had deceived themselves, had trusted to bond and signature, but God sees "the motive and not the deed." My error was doubly dangerous, for I had put the thought into the mouth of an angel. A political enemy wrote a pamphlet against the play, quoting the opinions of the demons as if they were the author's, sold it in the shops, in the streets, dropped copies into every doctor's letter-box, but Edward Martyn was not disturbed. No popular agitation disturbed him. Somebody had read or shown the pamphlet to old Cardinal Logue, and he had written to the newspapers that if the play was as represented, no Catholic should go to it. And that, too, did not disturb him, because Cardinal Logue had not seen the play. Lady Gregory and I thought that two ecclesiastics might be got to outvote one; Martyn agreed to accept the verdict, and Lady Gregory made Moore promise silence for a fortnight. I have lost Father Finlay's letter, it approved the play, but I have Father Barry's. He was the author of *The New Antigone,* a famous book in those days, and what is more, a learned, accomplished man. "From the literal point of view," he wrote, "theologians, Catholic or other, could object that no one is free to sell his soul in order to buy bread even for the starving, but Saint Paul says: 'I wish to be anathema for my people,' which is another way for expressing what you have put into the story. I would give the play and the explanation afterwards." Edward Martyn was quite content, but not Moore. "Martyn," I wrote to Lady Gregory, "is in excellent spirits, but says that if any person in authority were to speak, he would withdraw again." (The votes would be equal.) Moore, upon the other hand, lamented his lost row. He had meant to write an article called "Edward Martyn and his Soul." He said: "It was the best opportunity I ever had. What a sensation it would have made! Nobody has ever written that way about his most intimate friend. What a chance! It would have been heard of everywhere." As Florence Farr and I sat at breakfast in a Dublin hotel, having just arrived by the mailboat to make some final arrangements, Martyn came wiping the perspiration from his face in great excitement. His first sentence was: "I withdraw again." He had just received by post "Edward Martyn and his Soul" in the form of a letter. We comforted him all we could, and before twelve o'clock all was well. Before the first performance, to the charge of heresy was added that of representing Irish men and women as selling their souls, whereas "their refusal to change their religion, even when starving, proved that they would not." On the night of the performance, there was a friendly house drawn from the general public, but many interrupters in the gallery. I had asked for police protection and found twenty or thirty police awaiting my arrival. A sergeant explained that they could not act unless called upon. I turned to a friend, once Secretary to the Land League, and said: "Stay with me, I have no experience." All the police smiled, and I remembered a lying rumour that I had organised the Jubilee riots, people had even told each other what sum I paid for every rioter. The selling of the souls; the lines—

> The Light of Lights
> Looks always on the motive not the deed;

and

> Sign with this quill.
> It was a feather growing on the cock
> That crowed when Peter dared deny his Master,
> And all who use it have great honour in Hell;

the last four considered an attack on the Pope, caused disturbances. Every disturbance was drowned by cheers. Arthur Griffith, afterwards slanderer of Lane and Synge, founder of the Sinn Fein Movement, first President of the Irish Free State, and at that time an enthusiastic anti cleric, claimed to have brought "a lot of men from the Quays and told them to applaud everything the Church would not like." I did not want my play turned into an anti-clerical demonstration, and decided from the general feeling of discomfort when an evil peasant in my first act trampled upon a Catholic shrine that the disturbances were in part my own fault. In using what I considered traditional symbols I forgot that in Ireland they are not symbols but realities. But the attacks in the main, like those upon Synge and O'Casey, came from the public ignorance of literary method. The play itself was ill-constructed, the dialogue turning aside at the lure of word or metaphor, very different, I hope, from the play as it is to-day after many alterations, every alteration tested by performance. It was not, nor is it now, more than a piece of tapestry. The Countess sells her soul, but she is not transformed. If I were to think out that scene to-day, she would, the moment her hand has signed, burst into loud laughter, mock at all she has held holy, horrify the peasants in the midst of their temptations. Nothing satisfied me but Florence Farr's performance in the part of Aleel. Dublin talked of it for years, and after five-and-thirty years I keep among my unforgettable memories the sense of coming disaster she put into the words:

> . . . but now
> Two grey horned owls hooted above our heads.

I telegraphed to Moore: "Play a success"; he arrived in time for *The Heather Field.* He says in *Ave* that Martyn telegraphed: "The sceptre of intellect has passed from England to Ireland," but that sounds more like Moore than the economical, tongue-tied Martyn, and suggests the state of exaltation he arrived in. *The Heather Field* was a much greater success than *The Countess Cathleen*, being in the manner of Ibsen, the manner of the moment. The construction seemed masterly. I tried to believe that a great new dramatist had appeared. Miss Whitty, who in *The Countess Cathleen* had been effective and commonplace, moving us to tears by the tears in her own voice, was now acrid, powerful, original; an actor who played the hero driven to madness by his too practical wife (Mrs. Martyn's attempts to find a wife for her son came into my head) was perhaps even better.

At the end of the performance, Moore forced his way through the crowded lobby triumphant (I did not know until months afterwards that the masterly construction had been his), and catching sight of a tall friend near the street door shouted: "I see by the morning paper that . . . has provided Lord . . . with an heir," thereby starting a scandal that ran for months from village to village, disturbing several circles, private and official.

II

A couple of years before, it had seemed for a few months that the old political groupings were about to break up, everywhere people had looked forward, expecting, speculating. A Royal Commission, its members drawn from all parties, appointed by a Conservative Government, presided over by Gladstone's Lord Chancellor, had reported that the over-taxation of Ireland for the last fifty years amounted to some three hundred millions. The Irish Landlord Party, which based its politics upon the conviction that Ireland had gained by the Union, had a revulsion of conscience. Lord Castletown made a famous speech declaring that Ireland must imitate the colonists, who flung the tea into Boston Harbour. Landlord committees were appointed in every county. Then Lord Salisbury appointed a second Royal Commission to consider the wrongs of landlords, and not one of those committees met again. There was deep disappointment. Protestant Ireland had immense prestige, Burke, Swift, Grattan, Emmet, Fitzgerald, Parnell, almost every name sung in modern song, had been Protestant; Dublin's dignity depended upon the gaunt magnificence of buildings founded under the old Parliament; but wherever it attempted some corporate action, wherein Ireland stood against England, the show, however gallant it seemed, was soon over. It sold its Parliament for solid money, and now it sold this cause for a phantom. Nobody was the better or worse for Lord Salisbury's new Commission. Protestant Ireland could not have done otherwise; it lacked hereditary passion. Parnell, its last great figure, finding that this lack had made the party of my father's old friend Isaac Butt powerless, called in the peasants' tenacity and violence, but for months now the peasants had stood aside and waited, hoping that their old masters might take the leadership again. Standish O'Grady, a man past middle life, was now principal leader-writer of the *Daily Express*, the most uncompromising of the Dublin Unionist newspapers. He was of landlord stock, based all his hopes for Ireland upon that stock. He resigned his position in despair, bought a provincial newspaper, hoped, having made it a success, to buy up other provincial newspapers till he had all the provincial newspapers in Ireland. They would keep their local news, but all would contain his articles, all would rouse the gentry to their duty. He wrote pamphlets, published a weekly review, the same theme recurring. A famous passage described the downfall and flight of the Catholic aristocracy, lamented by the poor, sung by poets, but their successors, he cried out, would pass unlamented, unsung. In another, fixing his thought upon the poorer gentry, he compared them to the lean hounds that are the best hunters: "Oh, lean hounds, when will you begin to hunt?" His plans brought him misfortune. A certain man had, in his opinion, wronged and slandered a county family. He denounced him, and because the county took no notice wrote lofty essays upon its lack of public spirit. He wrote for his equals, wrote as Grattan spoke, not for the mob that he scorned. Hearing a great noise under his window, he looked out; men were marching to take ship for South Africa, cheering for Kruger, at their head the man he had denounced. His words had destroyed that man's influence among those O'Grady scorned without affecting it anywhere else. He lost his head and in fierce melancholy wrote that he no longer condemned "the poor wretch himself, but the three bad men who supported him," naming the Master of the Foxhounds, the Bishop and the principal nobleman of that district. After that an action for libel and financial disaster. The Bishop—or was it the Master of Foxhounds?—never heard of the essays, never knew that there was a charge against "the poor wretch himself," and as O'Grady was unable to prove the contrary, friends arranged for his apology and mitigated his bankruptcy. All that, however, was yet to come.

Horace Plunkett had bought the *Daily Express*. Under T. P. Gill, an ex-Parnellite Member and London journalist, it expounded Plunkett's agricultural policy, avoiding all that might excite passion. Gill had spent his life manipulating incompatibles; at the Parnellite split he took neither side. I think of him as making toy houses with little bits of pasteboard, gummed together with stamp-paper. "So-and-so is flat-footed," he would say, characterising some person whose heavy step might shake the table, and the flat-footed abounded at the moment. The relations of England and France were disturbed, a French officer, batoned in the Dublin streets, reported to the French War Office that Ireland was ready for insurrection. Maud Gonne had persuaded that Office to take from a pigeon-hole a scheme for an invasion of Ireland. A man I met in Sligo dreamed that he was entrenched in a swamp, fighting against invaders. "What will you do," somebody asked the *Express* Editor, "if the French land at Killala?" "I will write the best article of my life," was the answer. "I will call upon my readers to remember their great traditions, to remember their own ancestors, to make up their minds with the utmost resolution, without a moment's hesitation, which side they are going to take."

The *Daily Express* was almost as unsuccessful financially as Standish O'Grady's paper. When it wrote of a Protestant and of a Catholic Archbishop, old subscribers withdrew because the first, being the only true Archbishop, required no prefix. New subscribers bought little but the Friday number, which reviewed books, avoided contemporary politics, but contained articles that made people say: "Something is going to happen." In its correspondence column, controversies were fought out that are still remembered.

Then Horace Plunkett told Gill to give a public dinner to Edward Martyn and myself. I do not remember who took the chair, or the names of more than half a dozen of the guests. Moore has described it in *Ave*, but our memories differ. I doubt even his first sentence: "Not an opera hat amongst them, and no one should be seen without one . . . perhaps they have not even changed their socks." He was thinking of taking up politics, wanted to go into Parliament as an Irish patriot, had suggested, with that ingenuous way of his, that I should do the same, he would even accept me as his leader, and when I would not, wrote—or did that come later?—to John Redmond, then in control of the reunited Party, and offered himself as a candidate. He came to the dinner carrying in his hand the only political speech he was ever to deliver, an attack on William O'Brien, then about to return to public life at the head of his Mayo peasants. A little before he stood up, J. F. Taylor came, late for the dinner, but in time for his main interest, the speeches. He was Moore's opposite, a great orator, the greatest I have heard, doomed by the violence of his temper to speak before Law Students' Debating Societies, obscure Young Ireland Societies, Workmen's Clubs. His body was angular, often rigid with suppressed rage, his gaze fixed upon some object, his clothes badly made, his erect attitude suggesting a firm base. Moore's body was insinuating, upflowing, circulative, curvicular, pop-eyed. What brought Taylor, I do not know. He hated me, partly because his mind, trained in Catholic schools, where formal logic had importance, was dry and abstract, except in the great flights of his rhetoric, mine romantic, but mainly because jealous of my influence with the old Fenian John O'Leary. O'Leary used to say: "I have three followers—Taylor, Yeats, and Rolleston." But now that Rolleston had taken office under the Crown, he had but Taylor and me. He came perhaps because *The Heather Field's* lack of sensuous form, or its logical structure, attracted him. Moore seemed timid, and was certainly all but inaudible. Taylor alone seemed to listen, but he listened stiffening. William O'Brien was his special private butt, he had denounced him for ten years as the type of an unscrupulous, reckless demagogue. How dared anybody touch his pheasant, his partridge, his snipe? What Moore said, I do not remember. I remember Taylor, though, lacking the crowd of young men, the instrument on which he had learned to play, he was not at his best. "When William O'Brien was making the sacrifice of Mr. Yeats' *Countess Cathleen,* damning his soul for his country, where was Mr. Moore? In London, in Paris?" Thereon he described Moore's life, in phrases that were perhaps influenced by Carlyle's description at the opening of his *French Revolution,* of the "Scarlet Woman" Dubarry. Moore has written that I tried to make him answer, but I was at the other side of the table, and had learnt from defeats of my own not to rouse that formidable man. Moore with *Esther Waters* and *A Mummer's Wife* to his account, one or other in the mind of every man there, had no need to answer. Towards the end of the evening, when everybody was more or less drunk, O'Grady spoke. He was very drunk, but neither his voice nor his manner showed it. I had never heard him speak, and at first he reminded me of Cardinal Manning. There was the same simplicity, the same gentleness. He stood between two tables, touching one or the other for support, and said in a low penetrating voice: "We have now a literary movement, it is not very important; it will be followed by a political movement, that will not be very important; then must come a military movement, that will be important indeed." Tyrrell, Professor of Greek in Trinity College, known to scholars for his share in the Tyrrell-Purser edition of Cicero's Letters, a Unionist, but very drunk, led the applause. Then O'Grady described the Boy Scout Act, which had just passed, urged the landlords of Ireland to avail themselves of that Act and drill the sons of their tenants—"paying but little attention to the age limit"— then, pointing to where he supposed England to be, they must bid them "march to the conquest of that decadent nation." I knew what was in his mind. England was decadent because, democratic and so without fixed principles, it had used Irish landlords, his own ancestors or living relatives, as its garrison, and later left them deserted among their enemies. Tyrrell, understanding nothing but the sweetness of that voice, the nobility of that gesture, continued to lead the applause. Moore for all his toil had never style. Taylor had it in flights of oratorical frenzy, but drunk or sober, idle or toiling, this man had it; their torch smoked, their wine had dregs, his element burned or ran pure. When in later years compelled to answer some bitter personal attack, he showed that alone among our public men he could rise above bitterness, use words that, for all their convincing logic, made his reader murmur:

> Ye do it wrong, being so majestical,
> To offer it the show of violence.

When I try to recall his physical appearance, my father's picture in the Municipal Gallery blots out my own memory. He comes before me with a normal robust body, dim obsessed eyes, upon the wall above his head the title of a forgotten novel: *Ye Loste Lande.*

12

The Countess Cathleen and *The Heather Field* were performed in the week commencing May 8th, 1899, and such was
our faith in the author of *The Heather Field* that, though we
had not seen his unfinished play, we engaged the Gaiety Theatre
for a week in 1900. His play, understood to be satirical and
topical, was to be the main event. *Maeve*, originally published
with *The Heather Field*, would accompany it, but was, we
thought, too poetical, too remote from normal life to draw the
crowd. I spent the summer at Coole; George Moore was at Tullyra, but on Sunday mornings Edward Martyn's old coachman
would drive up by the Gort Avenue, George Moore behind him
on the old outside car. Moore had been to Mass. As Moore had
been brought up a Catholic, Martyn insisted upon Mass; how they
avoided the Ardrahan church and Martyn's company I cannot
remember; perhaps Martyn went to early Mass; but Gort suited
them both. Moore would listen for a minute, would slip out,
meet his coachman at the side door of a public-house which ignored the Act of Parliament for its more valuable customers, find
the outside car in some yard. Coole was but two miles off, one
mile of road, one mile of demesne under great trees. Devotion
to Parnell had made the coachman an anti-cleric. A couple of
years later I saw him for the last time, he wanted an introduction
to somebody he knew of that lacked a coachman. When Lady
Gregory asked about his dismissal he said: "I think Mr. Martyn
thought I must soon die because I am an old man, and that he
might see my ghost." Lady Gregory remembered that Mrs.
Martyn had died the year before, that Martyn, whose conscience
tortured him because he had opposed her plans, perhaps because
he had refused to marry, had seen some sight or heard some
sound that terrified him. Sometimes Moore drove over in the
afternoon. One afternoon he asked to see me alone. I brought
him to the path by the lakeside. He had constructed *The
Heather Field*, he said, telling Martyn what was to go into every
speech but writing nothing, had partly constructed *Maeve*—I
heard only the other day that Arthur Symons had revised the
style for a fee, setting it high above Martyn's level—but that

Martyn now refused his help. "He can find subjects," Moore said, "and I cannot, but he will never write a play alone; I am ready to collaborate all my life and say nothing about it. You must go to Tullyra and persuade Martyn." This was a Moore I had known nothing of; he had certainly kept silent; it was improbable he could do so now that the play was a success, but it did not seem so at the moment. Moore in his moments of self-abnegation was convinced and convincing. I do not remember whether he had brought the new play as Martyn had written it or whether Martyn sent it later, but I know that my interview with Martyn was postponed until Lady Gregory and I had read it. It seemed to us crude throughout, childish in parts, a play to make our movement and ourselves ridiculous. I was now Moore's advocate and, unlike Lady Gregory, unable to see with Martyn's eyes. I went to Tullyra and there denounced the play. I seem to remember Moore as anxious and subdued. Later when he described the scene he compared me to Torquemada. Martyn told us to do what we liked with the play. Moore asked for my collaboration as it was a satire upon contemporary Irish politics and of these he knew nothing. I moved from Coole to Tullyra. The finished work was Moore's in its construction and characterisation, but most of the political epigrams and certain bitter sentences put into the mouth of Deane, a dramatisation of Standish O'Grady, were mine. A rhetorical, undramatic second act about the Celtic Movement, which I had begun to outlive, was all Moore's; as convert he was embarrassing, unsubduable, preposterous.

Lady Gregory thought that no man could endure the sight of others altering all that he had done and discussing the alterations within earshot. She was doubtless right, for Martyn suddenly took the play back. If he could not write his own plays he was no use, he said; but when the position of the theatre was put before him, my determination and Lady Gregory's to refuse his play, his loss of money, for he was to pay for all, if we had only *Maeve,* he gave way once more. Moore, however, must sign the play; he would not sign with him "because Moore would put in what he liked." Moore was unwilling, he thought little could be made of such material; but being for the moment all self-abnegation, agreed, and was soon convinced that he had written a masterpiece.

There were continual quarrels, sometimes because both were woman-mad, Martyn with contempt, sometimes because Moore did not want to go to Mass, once because he had over-slept himself "on purpose." Yet Moore was at this time neither anti-clerical nor anti-Catholic. He had written not only *Evelyn Innes* but *Sister Teresa,* a sympathetic study of a convent; nor was he ever to lose an understanding of emotions and beliefs remembered from childhood. He did not want to go to Mass, because his flesh was unwilling, as it was a year later when the teacher, engaged to teach him Gaelic, was told that he was out.

He had exhausted his England in *A Mummer's Wife* and *Esther Waters,* and had turned to us, seeking his new task with an ungovernable childlike passion. In later years he attributed his distaste for England to his work upon *The Bending of the Bough,* his name for Martyn's rewritten play, and it is possible that it made him aware of change. Violent and coarse of temper, he was bound to follow his pendulum's utmost swing; hatred of Queen Victoria, admiration of Catholicism, hatred of the English language, love of everything Gaelic, were bound to follow one upon another till he had found his new limit. His relations to men and women ran through like alternations, in his relations to women he touched madness. On a visit to Coole, during some revising of *The Bending of the Bough,* or to begin *Diarmuid and Grania,* its successor, he behaved well till there came a long pause in the conversation one night after dinner. "I wonder," said Moore, "why Mrs. —— threw me over; was it because she wanted to marry ——" —he named a famous woman and a famous peer—"or was it conscience?" I followed Moore to his room and said, "You have broken the understanding?" "What understanding?" "That your conversation would be fit for Robert." Robert, Lady Gregory's son, was on holiday there from Harrow. "The word conscience can have only one meaning." "But it's true." "There is a social rule that bars such indiscretions." "It has gone out." "Not here." "But it is the only thing I can say about her that she would mind." Mrs. —— had been much taken with Moore, I had heard her talk of him all evening, but was of strict morals: I knew from the friend who had listened to Moore's daily complaints and later to his contradictory inventions, that he had courted her in vain. Two or three years after his Coole transgression, he was accustomed to say: "Once she and I were walking in the Green Park. 'There is nothing more cruel than lust,' she said. 'There is,' I said. 'What is that?' 'Vanity,' and I let her go a step or two ahead and gave her a kick behind."

13

On February 19th, *The Bending of the Bough* and a narrative undramatic play by Alice Milligan, *The Last Feast of the Fianna;* on February 20th, *Maeve,* were performed at the Gaiety Theatre. The actors had been collected by Moore in London. Our audiences, which seemed to us very large, did not fill the house, but were enthusiastic; we worked, perhaps I still work, for a small fanatical sect. *The Bending of the Bough* was badly constructed, had never become a single thought or passion, but was the first dramatisation of an Irish problem. Lady Gregory wrote in her diary: "M. is in great enthusiasm over it, says it will cause a revolution. [Whoever M. was he was not Martyn, who hated the play.] H. says no young man who sees that play will leave the house as he came into it. . . . The Gaelic League, in great force, sang 'Fainne geal an lae' between the acts, and 'The Wearing of the Green' in Irish. . . . The play hits so impartially all round that no one is really offended." Edward Martyn had shaped Peg Inerny, a principal character in *Maeve,* under the influence of stories gathered by Lady Gregory and myself. She is one of those women who in sleep pass into another state, are "away" as the people say, seem to live among people long dead, in the midst of another civilisation. We had thought the play dim and metaphysical, but it did not seem so in performance. *Maeve,* Lady Gregory wrote, "which we did not think a nationalist play at all, has turned out to be one, the audience understanding and applauding the allegory. There is such applause at 'I am only an old woman, but I tell you that Erin will never be subdued,' Lady —— reported to the Castle that they had better boycott it, which they have done."

14

I disliked Moore's now sentimental, now promiscuous amours, the main matter of his talk. A romantic, when romanticism was in its final extravagance, I thought one woman, whether wife, mistress, or incitement to platonic love, enough for a life-time: a Parsifal, Tristram, Don Quixote, without the intellectual prepossessions that gave them solidity. I disliked almost as much the manner of his talk, I told him that he was more mob than man, always an enthusiastic listener or noisy interrupter. Yet I admired him and found myself his advocate. I wrote to Lady Gregory: "He is constantly so likeable that one can believe no evil of him, and then in a moment a kind of devil takes hold of him, his voice changes, his look changes, and he becomes hateful. . . . It is so hard not to trust him, yet he is quite untrustworthy. He has what Talleyrand calls 'the terrible gift familiarity.' One must look upon him as a mind that can be of service to one's cause." Moore, driven to frenzy by the Boer War, had some project of lecturing in America against an Anglo-American alliance, much talked of at the time. "I shall be glad," I wrote, "if he himself goes." (I had refused to go with him.) "Less because of any harm he may do the Anglo-American alliance than because it will help to make our extremists think about the foundations of life and letters, which they certainly do not at present. To transmute the anti-English passion into a passion of hatred against the vulgarity and materialism whereon England has founded her worst life and the whole life that she sends us, has always been a dream of mine, and Moore may help in that transmutation." Moore, accustomed by his journalism to an immediate sensation contact with public opinion, was always urging Lady Gregory and me to do this or do that, that we might be more notorious, more popular. "How Moore lives in the present," I wrote. "If the National Theatre is ever started" (the company of players that was to succeed to the annual dramatic event with English players) "what he is and what I am will be weighed, and very little what we have said or done. A phrase more or less matters little. . . . Yet I suppose we would both be more popular if I could keep from saying what I think, and Moore from saying what he does not think.

You may tell him that the wisest of men does not know what is expedient, but that we can all know what is our particular truth, cajolery never lit the fire." Yet to friends who complained by letter or word of mouth against my bringing such a man into the movement, I defended him and attacked his enemies. George Russell (A. E.), afterwards Moore's chief Dublin friend, had complained much, and I wrote—too much aware of what I thought my own quality—"He and I are the opposite of one another. I think I understand people easily, easily sympathise with all kinds of character, easily forgive all kinds of defects. Apart from opinions which I judge too sternly, I scarcely judge people at all, am altogether lax in my attitude towards conduct. He understands nobody but himself, so must be always condemning or worshipping. He is a good judge of right and wrong so long as they can be judged apart from people, so long as they are merely action to be weighed by the moral sense. His moral enthusiasm is an inspiration, but it makes him understand ideas and not human nature. One pays a price for everything." My advocacy had threatened to disrupt the Irish Literary Society which I had founded and still thought a useful instrument. Early in the year its treasurer, Charles Russell, the famous lawyer, invited Moore to become a member, forgot he had done so, proposed that the Committee should blackball him—there was some anti-Catholic passage in *A Drama in Muslin*—and was supported by Barry O'Brien who could not abide *Parnell and his Island*. I got rid of Charles Russell by producing his letter of invitation, but Barry O'Brien remained, and after a long fight I withdrew Moore's name and resigned rather than force his resignation. He and I had given the Society what energy it had, keeping it out of the commonplace that was bound to overtake it in the end.

It was Moore's own fault that everybody hated him except a few London painters. In one of Dostoievsky's novels there is a man who proposes that everybody present should tell his worst action. Nobody takes the proposal seriously; everybody is witty or amusing until his turn comes. He confesses that he once stole half-a-crown and left a servant girl to bear the blame. Moore might have so confessed, but his confession would have been a plagiarism or a whole lie. I met a man who hated Moore because Moore told some audience that he had selected a Parisian street-boy, for one day dressed him in good clothes, housed him in an expensive hotel, gave him all that he wanted, then put him back into rags and turned him out to discover what would happen: a plagiarism from a well-known French author. "Yeats," he said to me once, "I was sitting here in my room the other night when there was a ring. My servant was out; when I opened the door a woman ran in and threw her arms round my neck. 'At last I have found you. There were thirteen George Moores in the *London Directory*. You're the ninth I have called on. What? Not recollect me—not recollect the woman you raped in Paris twenty years ago?'" She had called about her daughter's musical education, he said. Had I been more sympathetic I would have heard of a new Evelyn Innes. He was jealous of his own Sir Owen Asher. He was all self and yet had so little self that he would destroy his reputation, or that of some friend, to make his audience believe that the story running in his head at the moment had happened, had only just happened.

15

I saw Moore daily, we were at work on *Diarmuid and Grania*. Lady Gregory thought such collaboration would injure my own art, and was perhaps right. Because his mind was argumentative, abstract, diagrammatic, mine sensuous, concrete, rhythmical, we argued about words. In later years, through much knowledge of the stage, through the exfoliation of my own style, I learnt that occasional prosaic words gave the impression of an active man speaking. In dream poetry, in *Kubla Khan*, in *The Stream's Secret*, every line, every word, can carry its unanalysable, rich associations; but if we dramatise some possible singer or speaker we remember that he is moved by one thing at a time, certain words must be dull and numb. Here and there in correcting my early poems I have introduced such numbness and dullness, turned, for instance, "the curd-pale moon" into the "brilliant moon," that all might seem, as it were, remembered with indifference, except some one vivid image. When I began to rehearse a play I had the defects of my early poetry; I insisted upon obvious all-pervading rhythm. Later on I found myself saying that only in those lines or words where the beauty of the passage came to its climax, must rhythm be obvious. Because Moore thought all drama should be about possible people set in their appropriate surroundings, because he was fundamentally a realist ("Who are his people?" he said after a performance of George Russell's *Deirdre*. "Ours were cattle merchants") he required many dull, numb words. But he put them in more often than not because he had no feeling for words in themselves, none for their historical associations. He insisted for days upon calling the Fianna "soldiers." In *A Story-teller's Holiday* he makes a young man in the thirteenth century go to the "salons" of "the fashionable ladies" in Paris, in his last story men and women of the Homeric age read books. Our worst quarrels, however, were when he tried to be poetical, to write in what he considered my style. He made the dying Diarmuid say to Fionn: "I will kick you down the stairway of the stars." My letters to Lady Gregory show that we made peace at last, Moore accepting my judgment upon words, I his upon construction. To that he would sacrifice what he had thought the day before not only his best scene but "the best scene in any modern play," and without regret: all must receive its being from the central idea; nothing be in itself anything. He would have been a master of construction, but that his practice as a novelist made him long for descriptions and reminiscences. If *Diarmuid and Grania* failed in performance, and I am not sure that it did, it failed because the second act, instead of moving swiftly from incident to incident, was reminiscent and descriptive; almost a new first act. I had written enough poetical drama to know this and to point it out to Moore. After the performance and just before our final quarrel the letters speak of an agreement to re-write this act. I had sent Moore a scenario.

16

When in later years some play after months of work grew more and more incoherent, I blamed those two years' collaboration. My father began life a pre-Raphaelite painter; when past thirty he fell under the influence of contemporary French painting. Instead of finishing a picture one square inch at a time, he kept all fluid, every detail dependent upon every other, and remained a poor man to the end of his life, because the more anxious he was to succeed, the more did his pictures sink through innumerable sittings into final confusion. Only when he was compelled to finish in eight or nine sittings were his pictures the work of a great painter. *Deirdre* and *Baile's Strand,* unified after I had torn up many manuscripts, are more profound than the sentimental *Land of Heart's Desire,* than the tapestry-like *Countess Cathleen,* finished scene by scene, but that first manner might have found its own profundity. It is not far from popular songs and stories with their traditional subject-matter and treatment, it travels a narrow path. A painter or poet can from the first carry the complete work in his head and so finish scene by scene, but when the puppet-play becomes Goethe's *Faust,* Parts I and II, when *Gil Blas* is transformed into *Wilhelm Meister,* the *Waverley Novels* into the *Comédie Humaine,* he must, unhelped by tradition, all nature there to tempt him, try, fail perhaps, to impose his own limits. *Hodos Chameliontos* had no terrors for Moore; he was more simple, more naïve, more one-idea'd than a Bank-holiday schoolboy. Yet whatever effect that collaboration had on me, it was unmixed misfortune for Moore, it set him upon a pursuit of style that made barren his later years. I no longer underrate him, I know that he had written, or was about to write, five great novels. But *A Mummer's Wife, Esther Waters, Sister Teresa* (everything is there of the convent, a priest said to me, except the religious life), *Muslin, The Lake,* gained nothing from their style. I may speak later of the books he was to write under what seems to me a misunderstanding of his powers.

England had turned from style, as it has been understood from the translators of the Bible to Walter Pater, sought mere clarity in statement and debate, a journalistic effectiveness, at the moment when Irish men of letters began to quote the saying of Sainte-Beuve: "There is nothing immortal in literature except style." Style was his growing obsession, he would point out all the errors of some silly experiment of mine, then copy it. It was from some such experiment that he learnt those long, flaccid, structureless sentences, "and, and and, and and"; there is one of twenty-eight lines in *Muslin.* Sometimes he rebelled: "Yeats, I have a deep distrust of any man who has a style," but it was generally I who tried to stop the obsession. "Moore, if you ever get a style," I would say, "it will ruin you. It is coloured glass and you need a plate-glass window." When he formed his own circle he found no escape; the difficulties of modern Irish literature, from the loose, romantic, legendary stories of Standish O'Grady to James Joyce and Synge, had been in the formation of a style. He heard those difficulties discussed. All his life he had learnt from conversation, not from books. His nature, bitter, violent, discordant, did not fit him to write the sentences men murmur again and again for years. Charm and rhythm had been denied him. Improvement makes straight roads; he pumice-stoned every surface because will had to do the work for nature. I said once: "You work so hard that, like the Lancelot of Tennyson, you will almost see the Grail." But now, his finished work before me, I am convinced that he was denied even that "almost."

17

Douglas Hyde was at Coole in the summer of 1899. Lady Gregory, who had learnt Gaelic to satisfy her son's passing desire for a teacher, had founded a branch of the Gaelic League; men began to know the name of the poet whose songs they had sung for years. Lady Gregory and I wanted a Gaelic drama, and I made a scenario for a one-act play founded upon an episode in my *Stories of Red Hanrahan;* I had some hope that my invention, if Hyde would but accept it, might pass into legend as though he were an historical character. In later years Lady Gregory and I gave Hyde other scenarios and I always watched him with astonishment. His ordinary English style is without charm; he explores facts without explaining them, and in the language of the newspapers—Moore compared one of his speeches to frothing porter. His Gaelic, like the dialect of his *Love Songs of Connacht,* written a couple of years earlier, had charm, seemed all spontaneous, all joyous, every speech born out of itself. Had he shared our modern preoccupation with the mystery of life, learnt our modern construction, he might have grown into another and happier Synge. But emotion and imagery came as they would, not as he would, somebody else had to put them together. He had the folk mind as no modern man has had it, its qualities and its defects, and for a few days in the year Lady Gregory and I

shared his absorption in that mind. When I wrote verse, five or
six lines in two or three laborious hours were a day's work, and
I longed for somebody to interrupt me; but he wrote all day,
whether in verse or prose, and without apparent effort. Effort
was there, but in the unconscious. He had given up verse writing
because it affected his lungs or his heart. Lady Gregory kept
watch, to draw him from his table after so many hours; the gamekeeper had the boat and the guns ready; there were ducks upon
the lake. He wrote in joy and at great speed because emotion
brought the appropriate word. Nothing in that language of his
was abstract, nothing worn-out; he need not, as must the writer
of some language exhausted by modern civilisation, reject word
after word, cadence after cadence; he had escaped our perpetual,
painful, purification. I read him, translated by Lady Gregory or
by himself into that dialect which gets from Gaelic its syntax
and keeps its still partly Tudor vocabulary; little was, I think,
lost.

> I was myself one time a poor barnacle goose;
> The night was not plain to me more than the day
> Till I got sight of her.

That does not impress me to-day; it is too easy to copy, too many
have copied it; when I first read it, I was fresh from my struggle
with Victorian rhetoric. I began to test my poetical inventions by
translating them into like speech. Lady Gregory had already, I
think, without knowing it, begun a transformation of her whole
mind into the mind of the people, begun "to think like a wise
man" but to express herself like "the common people." I proposed that *Diarmuid and Grania* should be turned or half turned
into dialect, the rough, peasant-like characters using much, the
others using little or none. But Moore was impatient and would
not listen. Later on this method was more clearly defined by
Lady Gregory. The more educated characters should use as much
dialect as would seem natural in the mouth of some country gentleman who had spent all his life on his estate. It was first tested
in *The White Cockade*. *Deirdre of the Sorrows,* had Synge lived
to weave, as he had intended, a grotesque peasant element
through the entire play, would have justified it by a world-
famous masterpiece. It should have been obvious from the first;

Shakespeare made his old man with the ass talk "Somerset." The distant in time and space live only in the near and present. Lady Gregory's successful translations from Molière are in dialect. The Indian yogi sinks into a trance, his thought, like his eye, fixed upon the point of his tongue, symbolical of all the senses. He must not meditate upon abstractions, nor, because unseen, upon eye and ear. Yet when I made my suggestion to Moore I was not sure, I was easily put off it. A movement develops in darkness and timidity, nor does it follow that Lady Gregory remembered my suggestion when she began *The White Cockade;* a movement is like an animal, its shape is from the seed.

18

Diarmuid and Grania was read to famous actors and actresses, was greatly admired; a famous actress offered some hundreds as a first payment; but there was always the difficulty; there must be a simultaneous or first performance in Dublin. The actress said: "If you make a failure there, it will be no use coming to me." I was in negotiation with her, but took to my bed with influenza. After a fortnight Moore came: "I have withdrawn the play. She asked me to call upon her manager. I said that her manager should call upon me. Am I not right?" I said: "The naturalist Waterton climbed to the top of St. Peter's at Rome and put his glove on the lightning-conductor; such feats make me dizzy." "But don't you see it?" he replied. "I thought her manager was going to refuse the play; now instead of that refusal getting into the papers there will be weeks of controversy as to whether a manager should call upon an author or an author upon a manager." "And now," I said, "in spite of all that, you want me to call upon her, repudiate you, and give the play back." Yes, that was what he wanted. He was repudiated, and all seemed well. I cannot remember, and my letters to Lady Gregory do not record, what arrangements were made or unmade except that Benson undertook the Dublin performance, with Mrs. Benson as Grania. "She will be all right," said Moore. "She will play her body." Moore had behaved well; although convinced that the play was worth "two thousand pounds"—I learnt later that al-

ways when writing a play, he valued it at that sum—he risked
it for the sake of the Irish Literary Theatre. On October 2nd,
1901, *Diarmuid and Grania*, preceded by *The Twisting of the
Rope*, was produced for a week by the Benson Company in the
Gaiety Theatre, Dublin. Theatre managers must have thought it
failed, or that the newspapers' comments had taken freshness
from it, for the London managers who had admired it in MS.
were silent. Yet it did not seem to fail; when Maud Gonne and
I got into our cab to go to some supper party after the performance, the crowd from the gallery wanted to take the horse out
of the cab and drag us there, but Maud Gonne, weary of public
demonstrations, refused. What was it like? York Powell, Scandinavian scholar, historian, an impressionable man, preferred it to
Ibsen's *Vikings at Helgeland*. I do not know. I have but a draft
of some unfinished scenes, and of the performance I can but recall Benson's athletic dignity in one scene and the notes of the
horn in Elgar's dirge over the dead Diarmuid. *The Twisting
of the Rope*, Hyde as the chief character—he had always acted
his speeches—the enthusiasm of his Gaelic Leaguers for the first
Gaelic play ever acted in a theatre, are still vivid. But then Lady
Gregory's translation of the Gaelic text has renewed my memory.

19

Moore had inherited a large Mayo estate, and no Mayo country gentleman had ever dressed the part so well. He lacked manners, but had manner; he could enter a room so as to draw your
attention without seeming to, his French, his knowledge of painting, suggested travel and leisure. Yet nature had denied to him
the final touch: he had a coarse palate. Edward Martyn alone
suspected it. When Moore abused the waiter or the cook, he had
thought, "I know what he is hiding." In a London restaurant on a
night when the soup was particularly good, just when Moore
had the spoon at his lip, he said: "Do you mean to say you are
going to drink that?" Moore tasted the soup, then called the
waiter, and ran through the usual performance. Martyn did not
undeceive him, content to chuckle in solitude. Moore had taken
a house in Upper Ely Place; he spent a week at our principal
hotel while his furniture was moving in: he denounced the food

to the waiter, to the manager, went down to the kitchen and denounced it to the cook. "He has written to the proprietress," said the manager, "that the steak is like brown paper. How can you believe a word such a man would say, a steak cannot be like brown paper." He had his own bread sent in from the baker and said on the day he left: "How can these people endure it?" "Because," said the admiring headwaiter, "they are not *comme il faut*." A little later I stayed with him and wrote to Lady Gregory: "He is boisterously enduring the sixth cook." Then from Sligo a few days later: "Moore dismissed the sixth cook the day I left —six in three weeks. One brought in a policeman, Moore had made so much noise. He dragged the policeman into the dining-room and said: 'Is there a law in this country to compel me to eat this abominable omelette?'"

Sometimes Moore, instead of asking us to accept for true some monstrous invention, would press a spontaneous action into deliberate comedy; starting in bad blood or blind passion, he would all in a moment see himself as others saw him. When he arrived in Dublin, all the doors in Upper Ely Place had been painted white by an agreement between the landlord and the tenants. Moore had his door painted green, and three Miss Beams—no, I have not got the name quite right—who lived next door protested to the landlord. Then began a correspondence between Moore and the landlord wherein Moore insisted on his position as an art critic, that the whole decoration of his house required a green door—I imagine that he had but wrapped the green flag around him—then the indignant young women bought a copy of *Esther Waters*, tore it up, put the fragments into a large envelope, wrote thereon: "Too filthy to keep in the house," dropped it into his letter-box. I was staying with Moore, I let myself in with a latch-key some night after twelve, and found a note on the hall table asking me to put the door on the chain. As I was undressing, I heard Moore trying to get in; when I had opened the door and pointed to the note he said: "Oh, I forgot. Every night I go out at eleven, at twelve, at one, and rattle my stick on the railing to make the Miss Beams' dogs bark." Then I saw in the newspapers that the Miss Beams had hired organ-grinders to play under Moore's window when he was writing, that he had prosecuted the organ-grinders. Moore had a large garden on the other side of the street, a blackbird sang there; he received his friends upon Saturday evening and made a moving speech upon the bird. "I enjoy its song. If I were the bad man people say I am, could I enjoy its song?" He wrote every morning at an open window on the ground floor, and one morning saw the Miss Beams' cat cross the street, and thought, "That cat will get my bird." He went out and filled his pocket with stones, and whenever he saw the cat, threw a stone. Somebody, perhaps the typist, must have laughed, for the rest of the tale fills me with doubt. I was passing through Dublin just on my way to Coole; he came to my hotel. "I remembered how early that cat got up. I thought it might get the blackbird if I was not there to protect it, so I set a trap. The Miss Beams wrote to the Society for the Prevention of Cruelty to Animals, and I am carrying on a correspondence with its secretary, cat versus bird." (Perhaps after all, the archives of the Society do contain that correspondence. The tale is not yet incredible.) I passed through Dublin again, perhaps on my way back. Moore came to see me in seeming great depression. "Remember that trap?" "Yes." "Remember that bird?" "Yes." "I have caught the bird."

Moore gave a garden party during the annual festival of the Gaelic League; there was a Gaelic play by Douglas Hyde based upon a scenario of Moore's, and to this garden party he invited the Catholic Archbishop, beginning the letter with: "Cher confrère." The Archbishop did not answer. He had already in a letter to the Press invited the Archbishop to institute a stage censorship. "But, my dear Yeats, Archbishops are educated men. If there is some difficulty about a play, I will call upon him. I will explain. He will approve the play. No more mob rule. No more such trouble as we had about *The Countess Cathleen*. No more letters to the Press signed 'Father of a Family'."

20

I was depressed; we had promised, seeing no other way, to bring over English actors for a week in every year for three years, and now the three years were up. Moore wanted to negotiate with Benson for a stock company, taught by English actors, or made up of actors chosen by Benson, or with such actors in the principal parts. At first it seemed probable that Martyn would find the money; I urged him to employ Gordon Craig, a young unknown man who had staged a Purcell opera at his own or his friends' expense. But Martyn said with characteristic decision: "Henceforth I will pay for nobody's plays but my own." Perhaps somebody, or some committee, would take his place, negotiation dragged on; perhaps Moore's unpopularity, or mine, made Benson hesitate. We had attacked Queen Victoria, said that she came to Ireland recruiting, that she had, in Moore's words, driven through the city "a shilling between her finger and thumb, a bag of shillings under the seat." William Fay and his brother, whose company of amateurs played in a Lockhart's coffee-house, were putting their case, and all my Nationalist friends backing it. I summarised their arguments in *Samhain,* a little annual published in the interests of the movement. Any project that needed much money would have to promise good behaviour, and Ireland was turning towards revolution, but I did not give my own opinion. As yet I had none, and if I had I would have held it back.

I felt that Moore wanted the professional stage that he had known all his life. I wanted to keep him in good humour till *Diarmuid and Grania* was finished; we had learnt from the performance, and he had just accepted my sketch of a new second act. Then I wanted to write; I had been organising for ten years and if I joined Fay I saw no end to it. I felt acutely my unpopularity and told my publisher not to send my books for review in Ireland, a decision kept for many years. A. H. Bullen, Elizabethan scholar, a handsome man with a great mass of curly grey hair, at that time my publisher, came to Dublin. "He told me," I wrote to Lady Gregory, "that he was amazed to find the hostility of the booksellers. A——, he declared, seemed hardly to like to speak my name. I am looked upon as heterodox. *The Secret Rose* was particularly disapproved of, but they spoke with hostility, too, of *The Shadowy Waters.* . . . Memory of the *Countess Cathleen* dispute accounts for a great deal. Bullen found the Protestant booksellers little better, asked if T. C. D. disliked me. B——, the College bookseller, said, 'What is he doing here? Why doesn't he go away and leave us in peace?' Bullen was rather drunk, but his travellers gave the same account. He had tried to sell a book of Carleton's, too, and said that Carleton and I were received with the same suspicion. This was, of course, because of Carleton's early stories. I imagine that as I withdraw from politics my friends among the Nationalists grow less and my foes more numerous. What I have heard confirms the idea that I had at the time of the *Countess Cathleen* row, that it would make a serious difference in my position." I had withdrawn from politics because I could not bear perplexing, by what I said about books, the simple patriotic men whose confidence I had gained by what I said about nationality.

Some work connected with our theatrical project brought Lady Gregory to Dublin. Bullen asked to be introduced, and until we arrived at her hotel I did not notice how drunk he was. When he sat down he was on the verge of tears. "Yeats is an astrologer. He knows the moment of my death. No, no, it is no use denying it, he knows the moment of my death." Presently I wrote from Sligo that my uncle, the High Sheriff, had been warned that I must keep away from a certain Club. Moore was constantly attacked in the English Press, and every attack reached Dublin. I found that certain of our enemies were passing round some article in a monthly review, pointing out the plagiarisms in his *Modern Painting*, and I, not knowing how well-founded the attack was, had suggested a reply. "The man I object to," said Moore, "is the man who plagiarises without knowing it; I always know; I took ten pages." To Lady Gregory he said, "We both quote well, but you always put inverted commas, I never do."

21

I saw William Fay's amateur company play Miss Milligan's *Red Hugh*, an historical play in two scenes in the style of Walter Scott. "Yonder battlements," all the old rattle-traps acquired modernity, reality, spoken by those voices. I came away with my head on fire. I wanted to hear my own unfinished *Baile's Strand*, to hear Greek tragedy, spoken with a Dublin accent. After consulting with Lady Gregory I gave William Fay my *Cathleen ni Houlihan*, the first play where dialect was not used with an exclusively comic intention, to be produced in April 1902, in a hall attached to a church in a back street. A. E. gave his *Deirdre*, a protest against *Diarmuid and Grania* because the play had made mere men out of heroes. It was well constructed (A. E. in later years gave plots, or incidents that suggested plots, to several dramatists), but all its male characters resembled Lord Tennyson's King Arthur. Five or six years earlier he had published his lovely *Homeward Songs by the Way,* and because of those poems and what he was in himself, writers or would-be writers, among them James Stephens, who has all my admiration to-day, gathered at his house upon Sunday nights, making it a chief centre of literary life in Dublin. I was not friendly with that centre, considering it made up for the most part of "barren rascals"— critics as Balzac saw critics. For the next few years it seemed to lead the opposition, not the violent attacks, but the sapping and mining. A. E. himself, then as always, I loved and hated, and when I read or saw his play, I distrusted my judgment, fearing it mere jealousy, or some sort of party dislike. It was admired by everybody, hurt no national susceptibility, but in a few years A. E. himself abandoned it as Moore and I abandoned *Diarmuid and Grania.* I wrote to Lady Gregory, who was then in Italy: "They took to *Deirdre* from the first. The hall was crowded and great numbers could not get in. I hated *Deirdre*. In fact I did not remain in the theatre because I was nervous about it. I still hate it, but I suppose Moore is the only person who shares my opinion. When I saw it in rehearsal I thought it superficial and sentimental as I thought when it came out in the *All Ireland Review.* *Cathleen ni Houlihan* was also enthusiastically received. The one defect was that the mild humour of the part before Cathleen came in kept them in such delighted laughter that it took them some little while to realise the tragic meaning of Cathleen's part though Maud Gonne played it magnificently and with weird power. I should have struck a tragic note at the start." Then two days later: "The plays are over. Last night was the most enthusiastic of all. The audience now understands *Cathleen ni Houlihan* and there is no difficulty in getting from humour to tragedy. There is continual applause, and strange to say I like *Deirdre*. The absence of character is like the absence of individual expression in wall decoration. It was acted with great simplicity; the actors kept very quiet, often merely posing and speaking. The result was curiously dreamlike and gentle. Russell is plan-

ning a play on the Children of Tuireann and will, I imagine,
do quite a number of plays. The costumes and scenery from designs of his were beautiful; there was a thin gauze veil in front.
It was really a wonderful sight to see crowds of people standing
up at the back of the hall where they could hardly see because
there were people in front, yet patient, and enthusiastic." I gave
Fay a little farce, *The Pot of Broth*, written with Lady Gregory's
help but showing that neither Lady Gregory nor I could yet distinguish between the swift-moving town dialect—the dialect of
the Irish novelists no matter what part of Ireland they wrote of
—and the slow-moving country dialect. In *Cathleen ni Houlihan*,
written too with Lady Gregory's help, the dialect is as it were
neutral, neither predominantly town nor country; my stage technique, swifter than Lady Gregory's when a tragic crisis is the
theme, had pared it to the bone. It was, I think, this spareness,
or barrenness, that made Arthur Symons tell me after he had
seen Synge's first play to write no more peasant plays.

I had joined Fay's dramatic society but had as yet no authority.
I wrote to Lady Gregory that I had not marked my scornful analysis of one of Fay's dramatists "private" because "the sooner I
have that man for an enemy the better." When *The Pot of Broth*
was played in the Antient Concert Rooms in October, that trivial, unambitious retelling of an old folk-tale showed William Fay
for the first time as a most lovable comedian. He could play dirty
tramp, stupid countryman, legendary fool, insist on dirt and im-
becility, yet play—paradox of the stage—with indescribable personal distinction.

22

In the early autumn Zola died, asphyxiated by a charcoal
stove. Innumerable paragraphs and leading articles made Moore
jealous and angry; he hated his own past in Zola. He talked much
to his friends on Saturday nights. "Anybody can get himself asphyxiated." Then after some six weeks announced that he himself had awakened that very morning to smell gas, a few minutes more and he would have been dead; the obsession was over.
But there had been another torture earlier in the year. A brother
of his, Augustus Moore, a London journalist, had taken an ac-

tion about a scenario, whether against an actor, a writer or a manager, I cannot remember; he would appear in the witness-box, be examined, cross-examined, re-examined, and would not, could not, rise to the occasion, whereas he, George Moore, could have been amusing, profound, all the world looking on. When it seemed likely that Benson, or some company brought together by Martyn, would continue the Irish Literary Theatre, I had told Moore a fantastic plot for a play, suggested collaboration, and for twenty minutes or half an hour walked up and down a path in his garden discussing it. He proposed that my hero's brother should seduce the housemaid. When I had decided to work with Fay, Moore had withdrawn from the movement. I had written him regretting that I must write that play without his help. He did not answer, the letter required no answer. Weeks or months passed, then at some Gaelic festival in the town of Galway we met. I saw that he had something on his mind, he was gloomy and silent. I pointed out the number of young women with Douglas Hyde's pseudonym in gilt letters round their hats: "No woman, Moore, has ever done that for you," I said. He took my banter well, threw off his gloom; had I not started his favourite theme? But on his return to Dublin he telegraphed: "I have written a novel on that scenario we composed together. Will get an injunction if you use it." Had I known about his brother's law-case I would have known that Moore had not written a line and that his telegram was drama; knowing nothing, I wrote or telegraphed that I would use nothing of his but would certainly use my own plot. I went to Coole, asked the assistance of Lady Gregory and of a certain cautious friend, whose name must be left out of this narrative, and in a fortnight they and I dictated or wrote a five-act tragedy. I called it *Where there is Nothing* and published it as a supplement to *The United Irishman,* afterwards the organ of the Sinn Fein movement. Moore had been talking and his talk had reached me, he was expecting a London trial, and this was checkmate. Boys were shouting the supplement in the streets as he came out of the Antient Concert Rooms, where he had seen Fay's company. He bought a copy, spoke to nobody about it, always declared that he never read it, nor any other edition of the play.

"Has Yeats' hero got a brother?" he said to somebody. "Yes."
"Then Yeats has stolen the spoons." But my hero's brother was
in a monastery. Some months later an American friend, John
Quinn, a strong supporter and helper of our movement, brought
us together, but we were never cordial again; on my side distrust
remained, on his disgust. I look back with some remorse. "Yeats,"
Moore had said, "a man can only have one conscience, mine is
artistic." Had I abandoned my plot and made him write the
novel, he might have put beside *Muslin* and *The Lake* a third
masterpiece, but I was young, vain, self-righteous, and bent on
proving myself a man of action. *Where there is Nothing* is a
bad play; I had caught sight of Tolstoy's essay about the Sermon
on the Mount lying on a chair and made the most important
act pivot upon pacifist commonplace. I soon came to my senses,
refused a distinguished Frenchman permission to translate it, and
in later years with Lady Gregory's help turned it into *The Uni-
corn from the Stars.* For the moment it was successful; it could
not be played in Ireland for religious reasons, but the Stage Society found an approving audience and it set the tinkers of Mayo
rioting. My anonymous collaborator, when asked to name a
tinker in the play, had named him after a real tinker. A farmer
who had read the *United Ireland* supplement reproached that
tinker for letting his daughter marry a man with no visible means
of subsistence and permitting her to solemnise the marriage by
jumping over a bucket. The angry parent called God to witness
that he had done no such thing, other farmers and tinkers joined
what grew into a considerable fight, and all were brought up
before the magistrate.

23

During these first years Lady Gregory was friend and hostess,
a centre of peace, an adviser who never overestimated or under-
estimated trouble, but neither she nor we thought her a possible
creator. And now all in a moment, as it seemed, she became the
founder of modern Irish dialect literature. When her husband
died she had sold her London house, hiring instead a small flat
in Queen Anne's Mansions, lived most of the year at Coole, cut-

ting down expenses that her son might inherit an unencumbered
estate. In early life she had written two or three articles, such as
many clever fashionable women write, more recently had edited
her husband, Sir William Gregory's, *Autobiography* and *Mr.
Gregory's Letter-Box*, a volume of letters to Richard Gregory,
Irish Under-Secretary at the beginning of the nineteenth century, from Palmerston, Wellesley, many famous men, drawn
from the Coole archives. Some slight desire to create had been
put aside until her son reached manhood; but now he had left
the university and she was fifty. I told her that Alfred Nutt had
offered to supply me with translations of the Irish heroic cycles
if I would pick the best versions and put my English upon them,
attempting what Malory had done for the old French narratives.
I told her that I was too busy with my own work. Some days
later she asked if I would object to her attempting it, making or
finding the translations herself. An eminent Trinity College professor had described ancient Irish literature as "silly, religious, or
indecent," and she thought such work necessary for the dignity
of Ireland. "We work to add dignity to Ireland" was a favourite
phrase of hers. I hesitated, I saw nothing in her past to fit her
for that work; but in a week or two she brought a translation
of some heroic tale, what tale I cannot now remember, in the
dialect of the neighbourhood, where one discovers the unem-
phatic cadence, the occasional poignancy of Tudor English.
Looking back, *Cuchulain of Muirthemne* and *Gods and Fighting Men* at my side, I can see that they were made possible by
her past; semi-feudal Roxborough, her inherited sense of caste,
her knowledge of that top of the world where men and women
are valued for their manhood and their charm, not for their
opinions, her long study of Scottish Ballads, of Percy's *Reliques*,
of the *Morte d'Arthur*. If she had not found those tales, or finding them had not found the dialect of Kiltartan, that past could
not, as it were, have drawn itself together, come to birth as present personality. Sometimes in her letters, in her books when she
wrote ordinary English, she was the late-Victorian woman turning aside from reality to what seems pleasing, or to a slightly
sentimental persiflage as to a form of politeness—in society, to
discover "eternity glaring," as Carlyle did when he met Charles

Lamb for the first time, is scarcely in good taste—but in her last years, when speaking in her own character, she seemed always her greater self. A writer must die every day he lives, be reborn, as it is said in the Burial Service, an incorruptible self, that self opposite of all that he has named "himself." George Moore, dreading the annihilation of an impersonal bleak realism, used life like a medieval ghost making a body for itself out of drifting dust and vapour; and have I not sung in describing guests at Coole—"There one that ruffled in a manly pose, For all his timid heart"—that one myself? Synge was a sick man picturing energy, a doomed man picturing gaiety; Lady Gregory, in her life much artifice, in her nature much pride, was born to see the glory of the world in a peasant mirror. "I saw the household of Finn; it was not the household of a soft race; I had a vision of that man yesterday. . . . A King of heavy blows; my law; my adviser, my sense and my wisdom, prince and poet, braver than kings, King of the Fianna, brave in all countries; golden salmon of the sea, clean hawk of the air . . . a high messenger in bravery and in music. His skin lime-white, his hair golden; ready to work, gentle to women. His great green vessels full of rough sharp wine, it is rich the king was, tho head of his people." And then Grania's song over the sleeping Diarmuid:—

"'Sleep a little, sleep a little, for there is nothing at all to fear, Diarmuid, grandson of Duibhne; sleep here soundly, soundly, Diarmuid, to whom I have given my love. It is I will keep watch for you, grandchild of shapely Duibhne; sleep a little, a blessing on you, beside the well of the strong field; my lamb from above the lake, from the banks of the strong streams. Let your sleep be like the sleep in the North of fair comely Fionnchadh of Ess Ruadh, the time he took Slaine with bravery as we think, in spite of Failbhe of the Hard Head.

'Let your sleep be like the sleep in the West of Aine, daughter of Gailian, the time she went on a journey in the night with Dubhthach from Dorinis, by the light of torches.

'Let your sleep be like the sleep in the East of Deaghadh the proud, the brave fighter, the time he took Coincheann, daughter of Binn, in spite of fierce Decheall of Duibdreann.

'O heart of the valour of the world to the west of Greece, my heart will go near to breaking if I do not see you every day.

The parting of us two will be the parting of two children of the one house; it will be the parting of life from the body.' "

"And then to rouse him she would make another song, and it is what she would say: 'Caoinche will be loosed on your track; it is not slow the running of Caoilte will be; do not let death reach to you, do not give yourself to sleep forever.

'The stag to the East is not asleep, he does not cease from bellowing; the bog lark is not asleep to-night on the high stormy bogs; the sound of her clear voice is sweet; she is not sleeping between the streams.' "

Estrangement

The Death of Synge

The Bounty of Sweden

Estrangement

EXTRACTS FROM A DIARY KEPT IN 1909

1

To keep these notes natural and useful to me I must keep one note from leading on to another, that I may not surrender myself to literature. Every note must come as a casual thought, then it will be my life. Neither Christ nor Buddha nor Socrates wrote a book, for to do that is to exchange life for a logical process.

2

Last night there was a debate in the Arts Club on a political question. I was for a moment tempted to use arguments merely to answer something said, but did not do so, and noticed that every argument I had been tempted to use was used by somebody or other. Logic is a machine, one can leave it to itself; unhelped it will force those present to exhaust the subject, the fool is as likely as the sage to speak the appropriate answer to any statement, and if an answer is forgotten somebody will go home miserable. You throw your money on the table and you receive so much change.

Style, personality—deliberately adopted and therefore a mask —is the only escape from the hot-faced bargainers and the money-changers.

3

I have been talking to a man typical of a class common elsewhere but new in Ireland: often not ill-bred in manner and therefore the more manifestly with the ill-breeding of the mind, every thought made in some manufactory and with the mark upon it of its wholesale origin—thoughts never really thought out in their current form in any individual mind, but the creation of impersonal mechanism—of schools, of textbooks, of newspapers, these above all. He had that confidence which the first thinker of anything never has, for all thinkers are alike in that they approach the truth full of hesitation and doubt. Confidence comes from repetition, from the breath of many mouths. This ill-breeding of the mind is a far worse thing than the mere bad manners that spit on the floor. Is not all charm inherited, whether of the intellect, of the manners, of the character, or of literature? A great lady is as simple as a good poet. Neither possesses anything that is not ancient and their own, and both are full of uncertainty about everything but themselves, about everything that can be changed, about all that they merely think. They assume convictions as if they were a fashion in clothes and remould all slightly.

4

The articles upon *The Miser* in to-day's paper show the old dislike of farce and dialect; written by men who are essentially parvenus in intellectual things, they shudder at all that is not obviously and notoriously refined—the objection to the word "shift" over again. Our Abbey secretary has a deep hatred of Molière. None of these people can get it out of their heads that we are exaggerating the farce of Molière. We reduce it. Years ago Dr. Sigerson said of the last verse of my "Moll Magee," "Why candles? Surely tapers?"

5

To oppose the new ill-breeding of Ireland, which may in a few years destroy all that has given Ireland a distinguished name in the world—"Mother of the bravest soldiers and the most beautiful women," cried Borrow, or some such words, remembering the hospitality shown to him, a distributor of Bibles, by the Irish Monks of Spain—I can only set up a secondary or interior personality created out of the tradition of myself, and this personality (alas, only possible to me in my writings) must be always gracious and simple. It must have that slight separation from interests which makes charm possible, while remaining near enough for passion. Is not charm what it is because an escape from mechanism? So much of the world as is dominated by the contest of interests is a mechanism. The newspaper is the roar of the machine. Argument, the moment acknowledged victory is sought, becomes a clash of interests. One should not—above all in books, which sigh for immortality—argue at all if not ready to leave to another apparent victory. In daily life one becomes rude the moment one grudges to the clown his perpetual triumph.

6

My father says, "A man does not love a woman because he thinks her clever or because he admires her, but because he likes the way she has of scratching her head."

7

It seems to me that true love is a discipline, and it needs so much wisdom that the love of Solomon and Sheba must have lasted, for all the silence of the Scriptures. Each divines the secret self of the other, and refusing to believe in the mere daily self, creates a mirror where the lover or the beloved sees an image to copy in daily life; for love also creates the Mask.

8

Our modern poetry is imaginative. It is the poetry of the young. The poetry of the greatest periods is a sustained expression of the appetites and habits. Hence we select where they exhausted.

9

I have remembered to-day that the Brahmin Mohini said to me, "When I was young I was happy. I thought truth was something that could be conveyed from one man's mind to another. I now know that it is a state of mind."

10

Last night I met A——.[1] There was some rich man there, and some person spoke of the great power that wealth might have for good. The rich man was talking of starting a deer forest in Connaught. A—— said, "Wealth has very little power, it can really do very little." I said, "Yet every now and then one meets some charming person who likes all fine things and is quite delightful and who would not have had these qualities if some great-grandfather had not sold his country for gold." A—— answered, "I admit that wealth occasionally—Darwin is an example—enables someone to write a great book." I answered, "O, I was not thinking of that. I meant that it creates the fine life which we look at with affectionate eyes out of our garret windows. We must not leave our garrets, but we could not write well but for what we see from their windows." A—— answered, "Then writers are parasites." I noticed that most of the guests seemed, besides A—— and the rich man, too sympathetic and anxious to please; I myself among the rest. We talked, they were talked to. Dean B—— was there too, a charming and intelligent man with an ingratiating manner like that of certain well-educated Catholic priests, a manner one does not think compatible with deep spiritual experience. We discussed self-realisation and self-sacrifice. He said the classic self-realisation had failed and yet the victory of Christian self-sacrifice had plunged the world into the Dark Ages. I reminded him of some Norse God, who was hung over an abyss for three days, "a sacrifice to himself," to show that the two were not incompatible, but he answered, "Von Hartmann discusses the question whether the soul may not sacrifice itself, even to the losing of itself, for some good end." I said, "That is the problem of my *Countess Cathleen*," and he said, "It is a further problem whether a nation may make this sacrifice." He must have been thinking of Ireland.

[1] The initials used in these extracts are never those of the persons quoted or described. With the exception of A. E., George Russell's pseudonym, they are copied from a dictionary of painters, the initials or initial of the first name under A, then of the second under A or of the first under B and so on.

11

I see clearly that when I re-write *The Adoration of the Magi* the message given to the old men must be a series of seemingly arbitrary commands: A year of silence, certain rules of diet, and so on. Without the arbitrary there cannot be religion, because there cannot be the last sacrifice, that of the spirit. The old men should refuse to record the message on hearing that it contains not wisdom but the supernaturally sanctioned arbitrary, the commanded pose that makes all definite. The tree has to die before it can be made into a cross.

12

I have noticed that when these men (certain disciples of A. E.) take to any kind of action it is to some kind of extreme politics. Partly, I think, because they have never learned the discipline which enables the most ardent nature to accept obtainable things, even if a little sadly; but still more because they cannot believe in any success that is not in the unconditioned future, and because, like an artist described by Balzac, they long for popularity that they may believe in themselves.

13

A. E. endures them because he has the religious genius, for to the religious genius all souls are of equal value: the queen is not more than an old apple-woman. His poetical genius does not affect his mind as a whole, and probably he puts aside as unworthy every suggestion of his poetical genius which would separate man from man. The most fundamental of divisions is that between the intellect, which can only do its work by saying continually "thou fool," and the religious genius which makes all equal. That is why we have discovered that the mountain-top and the monastery are necessary to civilisation. Civilisation dies of all those things that feed the soul, and both die if the Remnant refuse the wilderness.

14

One of their errors is to continually mistake a philosophical idea for a spiritual experience. The very preoccupation of the intellect with the soul destroys that experience, for everywhere impressions are checked by opinion.

15

The real life being despised is only prized when sentimentalised over, and so the soul is shut off alike from earth and Heaven.

16

I heard Miss A—— B—— speak this the other day: "We have such a wonderful cat and it is so full of dignity that if the kitten goes to take its food it leaves the dish. It will not struggle. It will not assert itself. And what's more our cat won't eat at all if there is not a perfectly clean napkin spread under the plate. I assure you it is quite true. I have often noticed it. It will not eat if there is even a spot on the napkin."

17

When A. E. and I were fellow-students at the art schools there was a strange mad pious student who used to come sometimes with a daisy chain round his neck. A. E. lent him a little theosophical book, *Light on the Path*. He stayed away for several days and then came one day looking very troubled. He gave the book back saying, "You will drift into a penumbra."

18

In Christianity what was philosophy in Eastern Asia became life, biography and drama. A play passes through the same process in being written. At first, if it has psychological depth, there is a bundle of ideas, something that can be stated in philosophical terms; my *Countess Cathleen,* for instance, was once the moral question, may a soul sacrifice itself for a good end? but gradually philosophy is eliminated until at last the only philosophy audible, if there is even that, is the mere expression of one character or another. When it is completely life it seems to the hasty reader a mere story. Was the *Bhagavad Gita* the "scenario" from which the Gospels were made?

19

One reason for the tendency of the A. E. group to extreme political opinion is that a taste fed for long on milk diet thirsts for strong flavours. In England the reaction would be vice, in Ireland it is politics.

20

I have once more met Miss A—— B——. "O, it is not because of the pictures that I said I liked Mr. Lane's Gallery. I like it because it has such a beautiful atmosphere, because of the muffed glass."

21

All empty souls tend to extreme opinion. It is only in those who have built up a rich world of memories and habits of thought that extreme opinions affront the sense of probability. Propositions, for instance, which set all the truth upon one side can only enter rich minds to dislocate and strain, if they can enter at all, and sooner or later the mind expels them by instinct.

22

There is a relation between discipline and the theatrical sense. If we cannot imagine ourselves as different from what we are and assume that second self, we cannot impose a discipline upon ourselves, though we may accept one from others. Active virtue as distinguished from the passive acceptance of a current code is therefore theatrical, consciously dramatic, the wearing of a mask. It is the condition of arduous full life. One constantly notices in very active natures a tendency to pose, or if the pose has become a second self a preoccupation with the effect they are producing. One notices this in Plutarch's *Lives,* and every now and then in some modern who has tried to live by classical ideas, in Oscar Wilde, for instance, and less obviously in men like Walt Whitman. Wordsworth is often flat and heavy, partly because his moral sense has no theatrical element, it is an obedience to a discipline which he has not created. This increases his popularity with the better sort of journalists, writers in the *Spectator,* for instance, with all who are part of the machine and yet care for poetry.

23

All my life I have been haunted with the idea that the poet should know all classes of men as one of themselves, that he should combine the greatest possible personal realisation with the greatest possible knowledge of the speech and circumstances of the world. Fifteen or twenty years ago I remember longing, with this purpose, to disguise myself as a peasant and wander through the West, and then to ship as sailor. But when one shrinks from all business with a stranger, and is unnatural with all who are not intimate friends, because one underrates or overrates unknown people, one cannot adventure forth. The artist grows more and more distinct, more and more a being in his own right as it were, but more and more loses grasp of the always more complex world. Some day setting out to find knowledge, like some pilgrim to the Holy Land, he will become the most romantic of characters. He will play with all masks.

24

Tragedy is passion alone, and rejecting character, it gets form from motives, from the wandering of passion; while comedy is the clash of character. Eliminate character from comedy and you get farce. Farce is bound together by incident alone. In practice most works are mixed: Shakespeare being tragi-comedy. Comedy is joyous because all assumption of a part, of a personal mask, whether of the individualised face of comedy or of the grotesque

face of farce, is a display of energy, and all energy is joyous.
A poet creates tragedy from his own soul, that soul which is
alike in all men. It has not joy, as we understand that word, but
ecstasy, which is from the contemplation of things vaster than
the individual and imperfectly seen, perhaps, by all those that
still live. The masks of tragedy contain neither character nor personal energy. They are allied to decoration and to the abstract
figures of Egyptian temples. Before the mind can look out of
their eyes the active will perishes, hence their sorrowful calm.
Joy is of the will which labours, which overcomes obstacles,
which knows triumph. The soul knows its changes of state alone,
and I think the motives of tragedy are not related to action but
to changes of state. I feel this but do not see clearly, for I am
hunting truth into its thicket and it is my business to keep close
to the impressions of sense, to common daily life. Yet is not
ecstasy some fulfilment of the soul in itself, some slow or sudden expansion of it like an overflowing well? Is not this what is
meant by beauty?

25

Allingham and Davis have two different kinds of love of Ireland. In Allingham I find the entire emotion for the place one
grew up in which I felt as a child. Davis on the other hand was
concerned with ideas of Ireland, with conscious patriotism. His
Ireland was artificial, an idea built up in a couple of generations
by a few commonplace men. This artificial idea has done me as
much harm as the other has helped me. I tried to free myself
from it, and all my enemies come from my fighting it in others.
The beauty of peasant thought is partly from a spontaneity un-
spoiled by the artificial town-made thought. One cannot sum up
a nation intellectually, and when the summing up is made by
half-educated men the idea fills one with alarm. I remember
when I was nine or ten years old walking along Kensington High
Street so full of love for the fields and roads of Sligo that I
longed—a strange sentiment for a child—for earth from a road
there that I might kiss it. I had no politics; a couple of years
before, I had read with delight a volume of Orange verses belonging to my grandmother's stable-boy, and my mother, who

loved Sligo where she had been born and bred with the same passion, was, if she had any politics, Unionist. This love was instinctive and left the soul free. If I could have kept it and yet never felt the influence of Young Ireland I had given a more profound picture of Ireland in my work. Synge's purity of genius comes in part from having kept this instinct and this alone. Emotion is always justified by time, thought hardly ever. It can only bring us back to emotion. I went to see Synge yesterday and found him ill: if he dies it will set me wondering if he could have lived had he not had his long misunderstanding with the wreckage of Young Ireland. Even a successful performance of one of his plays seems to have made him ill. My sister reminded me of this the other day and urged me not to revive the *Playboy* while he is ill. In one thing he and Lady Gregory are the strongest souls I have ever known. He and she alike have never for an instant spoken to me the thoughts of their inferiors as their own thoughts. I have never known them to lose the self-possession of their intellects. The others here—even Moore for all his defiance—possess their own thoughts above the general flood only for a season, and Moore has in addition an automatic combativeness that makes even his original thought a reaction not a creation. Both Synge and Lady Gregory isolate themselves, Synge instinctively and Lady Gregory consciously, from all contagious opinions of poorer minds: Synge so instinctively and naturally—helped certainly by the habits of an invalid—that no one is conscious of rejection. Lady Gregory's life is too energetic and complex for her rejections to be other than deliberate. I do neither the one nor the other, being too talkative, too full of belief in whatever thought lays hold on me to reject people from my company, and so keep by angry outbreaks which are pure folly, from these invasions of the soul. One must agree with the clown or be silent, for he has in him the strength and confidence of the multitudes.

Lady Gregory is planting trees; for a year they have taken up much of her time. Her grandson will be fifty years old before they can be cut. We artists, do not we also plant trees and it is only after some fifty years that we are of much value? Every day I notice some new analogy between the long-established life of the well-born and the artist's life. We come from the permanent things and create them, and instead of old blood we have old emotions and we carry in our heads always that form of society aristocracies create now and again for some brief moment at Urbino or Versailles. We too despise the mob and suffer at its hands, and when we are happiest we have some little post in the house of Duke Frederick where we watch the proud dreamless world with humility, knowing that our knowledge is invisible and that at the first breath of ambition our dreams vanish. If we do not see daily beautiful life at which we look as old men and women do at young children, we become theorists —thinkers as it is called—or else give ourselves to strained emotions, to some overflow of sentiment "sighing after Jerusalem in the regions of the grave." How can we sing without our bush of whins, our clump of heather, and does not Blake say that it takes a thousand years to create a flower?

26

Blake talking to Crabb Robinson said once that he preferred to any man of intellect a happy thoughtless person, or some such phrase. It followed, I suppose, from his praise of life—"all that lives is holy"—and from his dislike of abstract things. Balzac, though when he is praising some beautiful high-bred woman he makes one think he had the same preference, is too much taken up with his worship of the will, which cannot be thoughtless even if it can be happy, to be aware of the preference if he has it. Nietzsche had it doubtless at the moment when he imagined the "Superman" as a child. We artists suffer in our art if we do not love most of all life at peace with itself and doing without forethought what its humanity bids it and therefore happily. We are, as seen from life, an artifice, an emphasis, an uncompleted arc perhaps. Those whom it is our business to cherish and celebrate are complete arcs. Because the life man sees is not the final end of things, the moment we attain to greatness of any kind by personal labour and will we become fragmentary, and find no task in active life which can use our finest faculties. We are compelled to think and express and not to do. Faust in the end was only able to reclaim land like some official of the Agricultural Board. It is right that Romeo should not be a man of intellect

or learning, it is enough for us that there is nature in him. We
see all his arc, for in literature we need completed things. Men
of action, our celebrators of life and passion, should be in all
men's eyes, but it is not well that we should be too much talked
of. Plutarch was right when he said the artist should not be too
prominent in the State because no young man, born for war and
love, desires to be like Phidias. Life confesses to the Priest and
honours him, but we confess to Life and tell it all that we would
do if we were young, beautiful and rich, and Life answers, "I
could never have thought of all that for myself, I have so little
time." And it is our praise that it goes upon its way with shining
eyes forgetting us.

27

I have to speak to-night at the Arts Club and have no time
for much preparation. I will speak, I think, of the life of a young
Irishman, his gradual absorption in some propaganda. How the
very nature of youth makes this come readily. Youth is always
giving itself, expending itself. It is only after years that we begin the supreme work, the adapting of our energies to a chosen
end, the disciplining of ourselves. A young man in Ireland meets
only crude, impersonal things, things that make him like others.
One cannot discuss his ideas or ideals, for he has none. He has
not the beginning of aesthetic culture. He never tries to make
his rooms charming, for instance. The slow perfecting of the
senses which we call taste has not even begun. When he throws
himself into the work of some league he succeeds just in so far
as he puts aside all delicate and personal gifts. I myself know
the sense of strain that comes when one speaks to ignorant or,
still worse, half-ignorant men. There is a perpetual temptation
not merely to over-simplification but to exaggeration, for all ignorant thought is exaggerated thought. I can only wish that a young
Irishman of talent and culture may spend his life, from eighteen
to twenty-five, outside Ireland. Can one prescribe duties to a developed soul?—and I suppose him to grow conscious of himself
in those years. If one can, I would wish him to return. I will then
describe the idea of modern culture as I see it in some young Oxford man: to have perfect taste; to have felt all the finest emo-

tions that art can give. The young Dublin man who sticks to his books becomes a pedant because he only believes in external things. I will then describe a debate at Oxford a few years ago when I felt so much pity for that young brilliant man full of feminine sensitiveness. Surely the ideal of culture expressed by Pater can only create feminine souls. The soul becomes a mirror not a brazier. This culture is self-knowledge in so far as the self is a calm, deliberating, discriminating thing, for when we have awakened our tastes, and criticised the world in tasting it, we have come to know ourselves; ourselves, not as misers, or spendthrifts, or magistrates, or pleaders, but as men, face to face with what is permanent in the world. Newman defines culture as wise receptivity, though I do not think he uses these words. Culture of this kind produces the most perfect flowers in a few highbred women. It gives to its sons an exquisite delicacy. I will then compare the culture of the Renaissance, which seems to me founded not on self-knowledge but on knowledge of some other self, Christ or Caesar, not on delicate sincerity but on imitative energy.

28

This morning I got a letter telling me of A—— C——'s illness. I did not recognise her son's writing at first, and my mind wandered, I suppose because I was not well. I thought my mother was ill and that my sister was asking me to come at once: then I remembered that my mother died years ago and that more than kin was at stake. She has been to me mother, friend, sister and brother. I cannot realise the world without her—she brought to my wavering thoughts steadfast nobility. All the day the thought of losing her is like a conflagration in the rafters. Friendship is all the house I have.

29

A—— C—— is better but writes in pencil that she "very nearly slipped away." All Wednesday I heard Castiglione's phrase ringing in my memory, "Never be it spoken without tears, the Duchess, too, is dead," and that phrase, which—coming

where it did among the numbering of his dead—often moved
me till my eyes dimmed, brought before me now all his sorrow
and my own, as though one saw the worth of life fade for ever.

> Sickness brought me this
> Thought, in that scale of his:
> Why should I be dismayed
> Though flame had burned the whole
> World, as it were a coal,
> Now I have seen it weighed
> Against a soul?

30

I went for a walk in the woods with little E—— and we
talked of religion. He said, "There is no longer belief, nobody
with belief ever comes to my Bible Class but you yourself. If
people believed, they would talk of God and Christ. They think
it good taste not to talk of such things, and yet people always
talk of what they care for. Belief makes a mind abundant." I
thought of the perpetual desire of all lovers to talk of their love
and how many lovers' quarrels have come from it. I said, "What
of the Dublin theosophists?" He said fiercely, "They are thieves.
They pick up names and thoughts all over the world and these
never become being in their minds, never become their own, because they have no worship." He is not easy to understand, but I
gradually drew from him these thoughts. "They are all self, all
presumption. They do not know what it is to abase themselves
before Christ, or their own Gods, or anything. If one does that,
one is filled with life. Christ is so full of life that it flows into
us. The whole world is vivid to us. They are all self, and so
they despise the foundation." He means by the foundation, life,
nature. I said, "But what are the forms they see?" He answered,
"They can only be lesser spirits—part of what they call the Astral
—creatures that live on them and draw away their life." I said,
"Must one therefore either feed or be fed?" He said, "Yes, surely.
Have you not noticed that they are all fluid, tenuous, flimsy-
minded? You know Miss A—— B——? They are all like that. It
is the astral fluid. There is no life, the life has been sucked out.

They despise the foundation, and that no one can do till after the resurrection. They are all self, and so they live on stolen goods. Of course there are a few chosen spirits who need not enter into life, but they are very few. Ah if only one could see all boys and girls after nineteen married." He told me earlier in the day that once when mountaineering he was in great danger. Some one had slipped and dragged another with him, and he had the weight of two men hanging from the rope—but he felt a great being descending into him and strengthening him. Even when the danger was over he felt no loss of nerve as he looked back on the danger. He had been filled with life. On the way back E—— said, "There is so little life now. Look at the modern soldier—he is nothing—and the ancient soldier was something—he had to be strong and skilful, they fought man to man." I said, "There are some books like that—ideas as wonderful as a campaign by Moltke, but no man. The plan of campaign was not so impressive in the old books, but all was human!" He answered, "When races cease to believe in Christ, God takes the life out of them, at last they cease to procreate." E—— himself, all muscular force and ardour, makes me think of that line written, as one believes, of Shakespeare by Ben Jonson—"So rammed with life that he can but grow in life with being." The irregular line of his thought which makes him obscure is itself a sign of this. He is as full of twists and turns as a tree.

31

The other day when I was speaking at the Arts Club someone asked me what life I would recommend to young Irishmen, the thought my whole speech if it were logical should have led up to. I was glad to be able to reply, "I do not know, though I have thought much about it." Who does not distrust complete ideas?

32

There is an astrological sense in which a man's wife or sweetheart is always an Eve made from a rib of his body. She is drawn to him because she represents a group of stellar influences in the radical horoscope. These influences also create an element in his character, and his destiny, in things apart from love or marriage. Whether this element be good or evil she is therefore its external expression. The happiest have such horoscopes that they find what they have of good in their wives, others must find what they have of evil, or a man may have both affinities. Sometimes a man may find the evil of his horoscope in a woman, and in rescuing her from her own self may conquer his own evil, as with Simon Magus who married a harlot. Others may find in a woman the good that conquers them and shapes them. All external events of life are of course an externalisation of character in the same way, but not to the same degree as the wife, who may represent the gathering up of an entire web of influences. A friend represented by a powerful star in the eleventh house may be the same, especially if the sun apply to the star. We are mirrors of the stellar light and we cast this light outward as incidents, magnetic attractions, characterisations, desires. This casting outward of the light is that fall into the circumference the mystics talk of.

33

By implication the philosophy of Irish faery lore declares that all power is from the body, all intelligence from the spirit. Western civilisation, religion and magic insist on power and therefore on body, and hence these three doctrines—efficient rule —the Incarnation—thaumaturgy. Eastern thoughts answer to these with indifference to rule, scorn of the flesh, contemplation of the formless. Western minds who follow the Eastern way become weak and vapoury, because unfit for the work forced upon them by Western life. Every symbol is an invocation which produces its equivalent expression in all worlds. The Incarnation invoked modern science and modern efficiency, and individualised emotion. It produced a solidification of all those things that grow from individual will. The historical truth of the Incarnation is indifferent, though the belief in that truth was essential to the power of the invocation. All civilisation is held together by the suggestions of an invisible hypnotist—by artificially created illusions. The knowledge of reality is always in some measure a secret knowledge. It is a kind of death.

34

While Lady Gregory has brought herself to death's door with overwork, to give us, while neglecting no other duty, enough plays, translated or original, to keep the Theatre alive, our base half-men of letters, or rather half-journalists, that coterie of patriots who have never been bought because no one ever thought them worth a price, have been whispering everywhere that she takes advantage of her position as director to put her own plays upon the stage. When I think, too, of Synge dying at this moment of their bitterness and ignorance, as I believe, I wonder if I have been right to shape my style to sweetness and serenity, and there comes into my mind that verse that Fergus spoke, "No man seeks my help because I be not of the things I dream." On the night of the *"Playboy* debate" they were all there, silent and craven, but not in the stalls for fear they might be asked to speak and face the mob. A—— D—— even refused by a subterfuge and joined the others in the gallery. No man of all literary Dublin dared show his face but my own father, who spoke to, or rather in the presence of, that howling mob with sweetness and simplicity. I fought them, he did a finer thing—forgot them.

35

Those who accuse Synge of some base motive are the great-grandchildren of those Dublin men who accused Smith O'Brien of being paid by the Government to fail. It is of such as these Goethe thought when he said, "The Irish always seem to me like a pack of hounds dragging down some noble stag."

36

Last night, Miss Allgood, who has been bad hitherto, gave a good performance in *Kincora*. This play in its new form gives me the greatest joy—colour, speech, all has its music, and the scenes with the servants make one feel intimate and friendly with those great people who otherwise would be far off—mere figures of speech. The joy that this play gives makes me understand how much I dislike plays like —— and —— and ——. If at all possible I will now keep at the Theatre till I have seen produced a mass of fine work. If we can create a taste for translated work—which we have not yet done—we can carry on the Theatre without vulgarity. If not, the mere growth of the audience will make all useless, for the Irish town mind will by many channels, public and private, press its vulgarity upon us. If we should feel that happening, if the Theatre is not to continue as we have shaped it, it must, for the sake of our future influence, for the sake of our example, be allowed to pass out of our hands, or cease. We must not be responsible for a compromise.

37

Last night I read E—— a passage in which Coventry Patmore says we cannot teach another religious truth; we can only point out to him a way whereby he may find it for himself. E—— said, "If one could show another religious experience, which is of the whole being, one would have to give one's whole being, one would be Christ. He alone can give Himself."

38

I often wonder if my talent will ever recover from the heterogeneous labour of these last few years. The younger Hallam says that vice does not destroy genius but that the heterogeneous does. I cry out vainly for liberty and have ever less and less inner life. Evil comes to us men of imagination wearing as its mask all the virtues. I have certainly known more men destroyed by the desire to have wife and child and to keep them in comfort than I have seen destroyed by drink and harlots. L—— E—— at the Rhymers' Club used to say that he meant to have a butler and that he thought it his duty to his wife to keep a house on that scale. Harlots in his case finished what the virtues began, but it was the virtues and not the harlots that killed his knack of verse. I thought myself loving neither vice nor virtue; but virtue has come upon me and given me a nation instead of a home. Has it left me any lyrical faculty? Whatever happens I must go on that

there may be a man behind the lines already written; I cast the
die long ago and must be true to the cast.

39

Two hours' idleness—because I have no excuse but to begin
creative work, an intolerable toil. Little D—— F—— of Hyderabad
told me that in her father's garden one met an opium-eater who
made poems in his dreams and wrote the title-pages when he
awoke but forgot the rest. He was the only happy poet.

40

A couple of days ago I went to see Dr. F—— F——. He spoke
of the attacks on both him and myself in *Sinn Fein* and of their
untruthfulness. He said, "I congratulated Edward Martyn some
time ago on being leader of an important political party, and he
answered, 'I don't want to be, I want to do my own work.' Says
I, 'I want to do my own work also,' and then says he, 'The worst
of it is that those fellows would not leave either of us there for
five minutes if they thought we liked it.'"

41

The root of it all is that the political class in Ireland—the
lower-middle class from whom the patriotic associations have
drawn their journalists and their leaders for the last ten years—
have suffered through the cultivation of hatred as the one energy
of their movement, a deprivation which is the intellectual equivalent to a certain surgical operation. Hence the shrillness of their
voices. They contemplate all creative power as the eunuchs contemplate Don Juan as he passes through Hell on the white horse.

42

To-night G—— said that he has always thought that the bad
luck of Ireland comes from hatred being the foundation of our
politics. It is possible that emotion is an evocation and in ways
beyond the senses alters events—creating good and evil luck. Cer-

tain individuals who hate much seem to be followed by violent events outside their control. B—— G—— has been so followed always. It is possible to explain it by saying that hatred awakens hatred in others and in oneself a tendency to violent action; but there are times when there seems more than this—an actual stream of ill-luck. Certainly evocation with symbol has taught me that much that we think limited to certain obvious effects influences the whole being. A meditation on sunlight, for instance, affects the nature throughout, producing all the effects which follow from the symbolical nature of the sun. Hate must, in the same way, create sterility, producing many effects which would follow from meditation on a symbol. Such a symbol would produce not merely hate but associated effects. An emotion produces a symbol—sensual emotion dreams of water, for instance —just as a symbol produces emotion. The symbol without emotion is more precise and, perhaps, more powerful than an emotion without symbol. Hatred as a basis of imagination, in ways which one could explain even without magic, helps to dry up the nature and make the sexual abstinence, so common among young men and women in Ireland, possible. This abstinence reacts in its turn on the imagination, so that we get at last that strange eunuch-like tone and temper. For the last ten or twenty years there has been a perpetual drying of the Irish mind with the resultant dust-cloud.

43

I saw Synge to-day and asked how much of his *Deirdre* was done. He said the third act was right, that he had put a grotesque character, a new character, into the second act and intended to weave him into Act One. He was to come in with Conchubor, carrying some of his belongings, and afterwards at the end of the act to return for a forgotten knife—just enough to make it possible to use him in Act Two. He spoke of his work this winter doubtfully, thought it not very good, seemed only certain of the third act. I did not like to ask more questions lest he should understand that I wished to know if another could complete the work if he died. He is certainly too ill to work himself, and will be for a long time.

44

Met MacDonagh[1] yesterday—a man with some literary faculty
which will probably come to nothing through lack of culture and
encouragement. He had just written an article for *The Leader*,
and spoke much as I do myself of the destructiveness of journalism here in Ireland, and was apologetic about his article. He is
managing a school on Irish and Gaelic League principles but
says he is losing faith in the League. Its writers are infecting Irish
not only with the English idiom but with the habits of thought
of current Irish journalism, a most un-Celtic thing. "The
League," he said, "is killing Celtic civilisation." I told him that
Synge about ten years ago foretold this in an article in the *Academy*. He thought the National Movement practically dead, that
the language would be revived but without all that he loved it
for. In England this man would have become remarkable in some
way, here he is being crushed by the mechanical logic and commonplace eloquence which give power to the most empty mind,
because, being "something other than human life," they have no
use for distinguished feeling or individual thought. I mean that
within his own mind this mechanical thought is crushing as with
an iron roller all that is organic.

45

The soul of Ireland has become a vapour and her body a stone.

46

Ireland has grown sterile, because power has passed to men
who lack the training which requires a certain amount of wealth
to ensure continuity from generation to generation, and to free
the mind in part from other tasks. A gentleman is a man whose
principal ideas are not connected with his personal needs and his
personal success. In old days he was a clerk or a noble, that is
to say, he had freedom because of inherited wealth and position,

[1] Executed in 1916.

or because of a personal renunciation. The names are different
to-day, and I would put the artist and the scholar in the category
of the clerk, yet personal renunciation is not now sufficient or
the *hysterica passio* of Ireland would be inspiration, or perhaps
it is sufficient but is impossible without inherited culture. For
without culture or holiness, which are always the gift of a very
few, a man may renounce wealth or any other external thing,
but he cannot renounce hatred, envy, jealousy, revenge. Culture
is the sanctity of the intellect.

47

I have been talking of the literary element in painting with
Miss E—— G—— and turning over the leaves of Binyon's book on
Eastern Painting, in which he shows how traditional, how literary
that is. The revolt against the literary element in painting was
accompanied by a similar revolt in poetry. The doctrine of what
the younger Hallam called the Aesthetic School was expounded
in his essay on Tennyson, and when I was a boy the unimportance of subject was a canon. A French poet had written of
girls taking lice out of a child's hair. Henley was supposed to
have founded a new modern art in the "hospital poems," though
he would not have claimed this. Hallam argued that poetry was
the impression on the senses of certain very sensitive men. It
was such with the pure artists, Keats and Shelley, but not so with
the impure artists who, like Wordsworth, mixed up popular
morality with their work. I now see that the literary element in
painting, the moral element in poetry, are the means whereby
the two arts are accepted into the social order and become a part
of life and not things of the study and the exhibition. Supreme
art is a traditional statement of certain heroic and religious truths,
passed on from age to age, modified by individual genius, but
never abandoned. The revolt of individualism came because the
tradition had become degraded, or rather because a spurious copy
had been accepted in its stead. Classical morality—not quite natural in Christianised Europe—dominated this tradition at the Renaissance, and passed from Milton to Wordsworth and to Arnold,
always growing more formal and empty until it became a vulgarity in our time—just as classical forms passed on from Raphael

to the Academicians. But Anarchic revolt is coming to an end, and the arts are about to restate the traditional morality. A great work of art, the "Ode to a Nightingale" not less than the "Ode to Duty," is as rooted in the early ages as the Mass which goes back to savage folklore. In what temple garden did the nightingale first sing?

48

No art can conquer the people alone—the people are conquered by an ideal of life upheld by authority. As this ideal is rediscovered, the arts, music and poetry, painting and literature, will draw closer together.

49

The Abbey Theatre will fail to do its full work because there is no accepted authority to explain why the more difficult pleasure is the nobler pleasure. The fascination of the National Movement for me in my youth was, I think, that it seemed to promise such authority. One cannot love a nation struggling to realise itself without an idea of that nation as a whole being present in our mind. One could always appeal to that idea in the mind of others. National spirit is, for the present, dying, because the influence of *The Nation* newspaper, which first gave popular expression to that idea in English, has passed away. *Kincora,* which should have certain poems and traditions to help it, and at its first production caused so much excitement, rouses now but slight interest, while H——'s plays grow more and more popular. H—— alone requires nothing but his own thought.

50

I cry continually against my life. I have sleepless nights, thinking of the time that I must take from poetry—last night I could not sleep—and yet, perhaps, I must do all these things that I may set myself into a life of action and express not the traditional poet but that forgotten thing, the normal active man.

51

We require a new statement of moral doctrine, which shall be accepted by the average man, but be at the same time beyond his power in practice. Classical morality in its decay became an instrument in the hands of commonplace energy to overthrow distinguished men. A true system of morals is from the first a weapon in the hands of the most distinguished. The Catholic Church created a system only possible for saints, hence its prolonged power. Its definition of the good was narrow, but it did not set out to make shopkeepers. A lofty morality should be tolerant, for none declare its laws but those worn out with its warfare, and they must pity sinners. Besides, it must needs take a personal form in their minds and give to those minds the timidity of discoverers, not less than the courtesy of soldiers.

52

A few days ago my sister Lolly dreamed that she saw three dead bodies on a bed. One had its face to the wall, one had a pink mask like a child's toy mask, and before she could look at the third, somebody put a mask on that too. While she was looking at them the body with its face to the wall suddenly moved. The same night J—— dreamed that she saw three very long funerals and that she saw what she thought a body on a bed. She thought it the body of a brother of hers who had died lately. She lay down on the bed by it, and it suddenly moved. The same night my sister Lily dreamed that she had received three telegrams.

53

There is a dying-out of national feeling very simple in its origin. You cannot keep the idea of a nation alive where there are no national institutions to reverence, no national success to admire, without a model of it in the mind of the people. You can call it "Cathleen ni Houlihan" or the "Shan van Voght" in a mood of simple feeling, and love that image, but for the general purposes of life you must have a complex mass of images, something like an architect's model. The Young Ireland poets created a mass of obvious images that filled the minds of the young—Wolfe Tone, King Brian, Emmet, Owen Roe, Sarsfield, the Fisherman of Kinsale—answered the traditional slanders on Irish character and entered so into the affections that it followed men on to the scaffold. The ethical ideas implied were of necessity very simple, needing neither study nor unusual gifts for their understanding. Our own movement thought to do the same thing in a more profound and therefore more enduring way. When I was twenty-five or twenty-six I planned a *Légende des Siècles* of Ireland that was to set out with my *Wanderings of Oisin*, and show something of every century. Lionel Johnson's work and, later, Lady Gregory's, carried on the dream in a different form; and I did not see, until Synge began to write, that we must renounce the deliberate creation of a kind of Holy City in the imagination, and express the individual. The Irish people were not educated enough to accept images more profound, more true to human nature, than the schoolboy thoughts of Young Ireland. You can only create a model of a race to inspire the action of that race as a whole, apart from exceptional individuals, when you and it share the same simple moral understanding of life. Milton and Shakespeare inspire the active life of England, but they do it through exceptional individuals. Having no understanding of life that we can teach to others, we must not seek to create a school. Could we create a vision of the race as noble as that of Sophocles and of Aeschylus, it would be attacked upon some trivial ground by minds that prefer Young Ireland rhetoric, or the obvious sentiment of popular English literature, a few Irish thoughts and feelings added for conscience' sake.

Meanwhile, the need of a model of the nation, of some moral diagram, is as great as in the early nineteenth century, when national feeling was losing itself in a religious feud over tithes and emancipation. Neither the grammars of the Gaelic League nor the industrialism of the *Leader,* nor the *Sinn Fein* attacks upon the Irish Party, give sensible images to the affections. Yet in the work of Lady Gregory, of Synge, of O'Grady, of Lionel Johnson, in my own work, a school of journalists with simple moral ideas could find right building material to create an historical and literary nationalism as powerful as the old and nobler. That done, they could bid the people love and not hate.

54

Nobody running at full speed has either a head or a heart.

55

I told my sister that I was to spend the night in the K—— Street haunted house. She said, "O, I know about that house. I saw a furniture-van there one day and furniture going in, and ten days after, the house was empty again; and somebody I know was passing by in the early morning and saw an old woman on a window-sill, clinging to the sash. She was the caretaker. The ghost had driven her out and there was a policeman trying to get her down. But the pious Protestants say that there is no ghost or anything but the young novices in the Convent opposite 'screaming in the nighttime'."

The Death of Synge

EXTRACTS FROM A DIARY KEPT IN 1909

1

Why does the struggle to come at truth take away our pity, and the struggle to overcome our passions restore it again?

2

National feeling could be roused again if some man of good education—if a Catholic, he should have been educated outside Ireland—gathered about him a few men like himself, and founded a new *Nation* newspaper, forbidding it all personal attacks, all arguments that assume a base motive in an opponent, and choosing for its national policy, not what seems most desirable in the abstract, but such policy as may stir the imagination and yet gather to its support the greatest possible number of educated men. Ireland is ruined by abstractions, and should prefer what may seem a worse policy if it gathers better men. So long as all is ordered for attack, and that alone, leaders will instinctively increase the number of enemies that they may give their followers something to do, and Irish enemies rather than English because they are the more easily injured. The greater the enemy, the greater the hatred, and therefore the greater seems the power. They would give a nation the frenzy of a sect. A sign that this method, powerful in the time of Parnell, no longer satisfies the nation is that parties are drifting into the hands of feebler and more ignorant men.

3

The education of our Irish secondary schools, especially the Catholic schools, substitutes pedantry for taste. Men learn the dates of writers, the external facts of masterpieces and not sense of style or feeling for life. I have met no young man out of these schools who has not been injured by the literature and the literary history learned there. The arts have nothing to give but that joy of theirs which is the other side of sorrow, that exhausting contemplation: and in youth before habits have been formed—unless our teachers be wise men—we turn from it to pedantry, which opens to the mind a kind of sensual ease. The young Catholic men and women who have not been through the secondary schools are upon the other hand more imaginative than Protestant boys and girls of the same age. Catholic secondary education destroys, I think, much that the Catholic religion gives. Provincialism destroys the nobility of the Middle Ages.

4

March 17.

As I go to and from my bedroom, here at Coole, I pass a wall covered with Augustus John's etchings and drawings. I notice a woman with strongly marked shoulder-blades and a big nose, and a pencil drawing called "Epithalamium." In the "Epithalamium" an ungainly, ill-grown boy holds out his arms to a tall woman with thin shoulders and a large stomach. Near them is a vivid etching of a woman with the same large stomach and thin shoulders. There is not one of these fifty or sixty clerks and seamstresses and students that has not been broken by labour or wasted by sedentary life. A gymnast would find in all something to amend; and the better he mended the more would those bodies, as with the voice of Dürer, declare that ancient canon discovered in the Greek gymnasium, which, whenever present in painting or sculpture, shows a compact between the artist and society. John is not interested in the social need, in the perpetual thirst for greater health, but in character, in the revolt from all that makes one man like another. The old art, if carried to its logical conclusion, would have led to the creation of one single type of man, one single type of woman; gathering up by a kind of deification a capacity for all energy and all passion, into a Krishna, a Christ, a Dionysus; and at all times a poetical painter, a Botticelli, a Rossetti, creates as his supreme achievement one type of face, known afterwards by his name. The new art can create innumerable personalities, but in each of these the capacity for passion has been sacrificed to some habit of body or of mind. That woman with the big shoulder-blades has, for instance, a nature too keen, too clever for any passion, with the cleverness of people who cannot rest, and that young lad with his arms spread out will sink back into disillusionment and exhaustion after the brief pleasure of a passion which is in part curiosity. Some limiting environment or idiosyncrasy is displayed; man is studied as an individual fact, and not as that energy which seems measureless and hates all that is not itself. It is a powerful but prosaic art, celebrating the "fall into division" not the "resurrection into unity." Did not even Balzac, who looked at the world so often with similar eyes, find it necessary to deny character to his great ladies and young lovers that he might give them passion? What beautiful woman delights us by her look of character? That shows itself when beauty is gone, being the creation of habit, the bare stalk when the flower of spring has withered. Beauty consumes character with what Patmore calls "the integrity of fire."

It is this lack of the capacity for passion which makes women dislike the schools of characterisation, and makes the modern artist despise woman's judgment. Women, for the same reason, dislike pure comedy. How few women like Molière!

Here at Coole my room is hung with Arundel prints from Botticelli, Benozzo Gozzoli, Giorgione, Mantegna and the Van Eycks. Here everywhere is the expression of desire, though in the Van Eycks the new interest has begun. All display bodies to please an amorous woman's eyes or the eyes of a great King. The martyrs and saints even must show the capacity for all they have renounced.

5

These notes are morbid, but I heard a man of science say that all progress is at the outset pathological, and I write for my own good.

The pain others give passes away in their later kindness, but that of our own blunders, especially when they hurt our vanity, never passes away. Our own acts are isolated and one act does not buy absolution for another. They are always present before a strangely abstract judgment. We are never a unity, a personality to ourselves. Small acts of years ago are so painful in the memory that often we start at the presence a little below "the threshold of consciousness" of a thought that remains unknown. It sheds a vague light like that of the moon before it rises, or after its setting. Vanity is so intimately associated with our spiritual identity that whatever hurts it, above all if it came from it, is more painful in the memory than serious sin, and yet I do not think it follows that we are very vain. The harm we do to others is lost in changing events and passes away and so is healed by time, unless it was very great. Looking back I find only one offence which is as painful to me as a hurt to vanity. It was done to a man who died shortly after. Because of his death, it has not been touched by the transforming hand—tolerant Nature has not rescued it from Justice.

6

I think that all happiness depends on the energy to assume the mask of some other self; that all joyous or creative life is a re-birth as something not oneself, something which has no memory and is created in a moment and perpetually renewed. We put on a grotesque or solemn painted face to hide us from the terrors of judgment, invent an imaginative Saturnalia where one forgets reality, a game like that of a child, where one loses the infinite pain of self-realisation. Perhaps all the sins and energies of the world are but its flight from an infinite blinding beam.

7

F—— is learning Gaelic. I would sooner see her in the Gaelic movement than in any Irish movement I can think of. I fear some new absorption in political opinion. Women, because the main event of their lives has been a giving themselves and giving birth, give all to an opinion as if it were some terrible stone doll. Men take up an opinion lightly and are easily false to it, and when faithful keep the habit of many interests. We still see the world, if we are of strong mind and body, with considerate eyes, but to women opinions become as their children or their sweethearts, and the greater their emotional capacity the more do they forget all other things. They grow cruel, as if in defence of lover or child, and all this is done for "something other than human life." At last the opinion is so much identified with their nature that it seems a part of their flesh becomes stone and passes out of life. It was a part of F——'s power in the past that though she made this surrender with her mind, she kept the sweetness of her voice and much humour, and yet I am afraid. Women should have their play with dolls finished in childish happiness, for if they play with them again it is amid hatred and malice.

8

Women should find in the mask enough joy to forget the doll without regret. There is always a living face behind the mask.

9

Last night at "The Theatre of Ireland" I talked to the man next to me. "I have been to your theatre also," he said. "I like your popular plays, *The Suburban Groove* and those plays by the Frenchman, I do not remember his name" (evidently Molière), "but I don't like your mysteries." I thought he meant something of mine, as the word "mystery" is a popular reproach since *The Shadowy Waters*, but I found he meant *Kincora*. I said, "Why do you find that mysterious?" He said, "O, I know nothing about all that history." I replied, "When I was young every Irish Nationalist young man knew as much about King Brian as about Saint Patrick." He thought I was talking of the peasants and said he was afraid that sort of knowledge was dying out amongst them. He evidently thought it their business alone, like the rath and the blessed well.

10

March 23.

MacDonagh called to-day. Very sad about Ireland. Says that he finds a barrier between himself and the Irish-speaking peasantry, who are "cold, dark and reticent" and "too polite." He watches the Irish-speaking boys at his school, and when nobody is looking, or when they are alone with the Irish-speaking gardener, they are merry, clever and talkative. When they meet an English speaker or one who has learned Gaelic, they are stupid. They are in a different world. Presently he spoke of his nine years in a monastery and I asked what it was like. "O," he said, "everybody is very simple and happy enough. There is a little jealousy sometimes. If one brother goes into a town with a Superior, another brother is jealous." He then told me that the Bishop of Raphoe had forbidden anybody in his See to contribute to the Gaelic League because its Secretary "has blasphemed against the holy Adamnan." The Secretary had said, "The Bishop is an enemy, like the founder of his See, S. Adamnan, who tried to injure the Gaelic language by writing in Latin." MacDonagh says, "Two old countrymen fell out and one said, 'I have a brother who will make you behave,' meaning the Bishop of Raphoe, and the other said, 'I have a son who will put sense into you,' meaning Cardinal Logue."

11

Molly Allgood came to-day to ask where I would be to-morrow, as Synge wishes to send for me if strong enough. He wants "to make arrangements." He is dying. They have ceased to give him food. Should we close the Abbey or keep it open while he still lives? Poor Molly is going through her work as always. Perhaps that is best for her. I feel Synge's coming death less now than when he first became ill. I am used to the thought of it and I do not find that I pity him. I pity her. He is fading out of life. I felt the same when I saw M—— in the madhouse. I pitied his wife. He seemed already dead. One does not feel that death is evil when one meets it—evil, I mean, for the one who dies. Our Daimon is silent as was that other before the death of Socrates. The wildest sorrow that comes at the thought of death is, I think, "Ages will pass over and no one ever again look on that nobleness or that beauty." What is this but to pity the living and to praise the dead?

12

March 24.

Synge is dead. In the early morning he said to the nurse, "It is no use fighting death any longer," and he turned over and died. I called at the hospital this afternoon and asked the assistant matron if he knew he was dying. She answered, "He may have known it for weeks, but he would not have said so to anyone. He would have no fuss. He was like that." She added, with emotion in her voice, "We were devoted to him."

13

March 28.

Mr. Stephens, Synge's brother-in-law, said he suffered no pain but only great weakness. On Sunday he questioned the doctor and convinced himself that he was dying. He told his brother-in-law next day and was quite cheerful, even making jokes. In the evening he saw Molly and told her to be brave and sent her to me that I might arrange about his writings. On the morning when I heard of his death a heavy storm was blowing and I doubt not when he died that it had well begun. That morning Lady Gregory felt a very great depression and was certain that some evil was coming but feared for her grandchild, feared it was going to be ill. On the other hand, my sister Lolly said at breakfast, "I think it will be all right with Synge, for last night I saw a galley struggling with a storm and then it shot into calm and bright sunlight and I heard the keel grate on the shore." One remembers the voyages to Tir-nan-oge, certainly the voyages of souls after death to their place of peace.

14

I have been looking through his poems and have read once more that on page 21, "I asked if I grew sick and died." Certainly they were there at the funeral, his "idiot" enemies: A—— who against all regulations rushed up to the dressing-rooms during the *Playboy* riot to tell the actors they should not have played in so disgraceful a play; B—— who has always used his considerable influence with the Company against Synge, and has spoken against him in public; there, too, were the feeble friends who pretended to believe but gave no help. And there was C—— whose obituary notice speaks of Synge's work as only important in promise, of the exaggeration of those who praise it, and then claims that its writer spent many hours a day with Synge in Paris (getting the date wrong by two years, however), with Synge who was proud and lonely, almost as proud of his old blood as of his genius, and had few friends. There was D—— the Secretary of the Society—it had sent a wreath—whose animosity had much to do with the attacks in *Sinn Fein*. It was, to quote E——, a funeral "small but select." A good friend of Synge's quoted to me:

> How shall the ritual then be read,
> The requiem how be sung
> By you, by yours the evil eye,
> By yours the slanderous tongue,
> That did to death the innocence,
> That died, and died so young?

Yet these men came, though but in remorse; they saw his plays, though but to dislike; they spoke his name, though but to slander. Well-to-do Ireland never saw his plays nor spoke his name. Was he ever asked to any country house but Coole? Was he ever asked to a dinner party? How often I have wished that he might live long enough to enjoy that communion with idle, charming and cultivated women which Balzac in one of his dedications calls "the chief consolation of genius"!

15

In Paris Synge once said to me, "We should unite stoicism, asceticism and ecstasy. Two of them have often come together, but the three never."

16

I believe that some thing I said may have suggested "I asked if I got sick and died." S—— had frequently attacked his work while admitting him a man of genius. He attacked it that he might remain on good terms with the people about him. When Synge was in hospital to be operated upon, S—— was there too as a patient, and I told Synge that whenever I spoke of his illness to any man that man said, "And isn't it sad about S——?" until I could stand it no longer and burst out with "I hope he will die," and now, as someone said, I was "being abused all over the town as without heart." I had learned that people were calling continually to inquire how S—— was, but hardly anybody called to ask for Synge. Two or three weeks later Synge wrote this poem. Had my words set his mind running on the thought that fools flourish, more especially as I had prophesied that S—— would flourish, and in my mood at the moment it seemed that for S—— to be operated on at the same time with Synge was a kind of insolence? S——'s illness did, indeed, win for him so much sympathy that he came out to lucrative and honourable employment, and now when playing golf he says with the English accent he has acquired of late, to some player who needs a great man's favour, "I know him well, I will say a word in that quarter."

The Irish weekly papers notice Synge's death with short and for the most part grudging notices. There was an obscure Gaelic League singer who was a leader of the demonstration against the *Playboy*. He died on the same day. *Sinn Fein* notices both deaths in the same article and gives three-fourths of it to the rioter. For Synge it has but grudging words, as was to be expected.

Molly tells me that Synge went to see Stephen McKenna and

his wife before going into hospital and said good-bye with "You
will never see me again."

17

CELEBRATIONS

1. He was one of those unmoved souls in whom there is a
perpetual "Last Day," a perpetual trumpeting and coming up for
judgment.

2. He did not speak to men and women, asking judgment, as
lesser writers do; but knowing himself part of judgment he was
silent.

3. We pity the living and not such dead as he. He has gone
upward out of his ailing body into the heroical fountains. We
are parched by time.

4. He had the knowledge of his coming death and was cheerful to the end, even joking a little when that end had all but
come. He had no need of our sympathies. It was as though we
and the things about us died away from him and not he from us.

18

DETRACTIONS

He had that egotism of the man of genius which Nietzsche
compares to the egotism of a woman with child. Neither I nor
Lady Gregory had ever a compliment from him. After *Hyacinth*
Lady Gregory went home the moment the curtain fell, not waiting for the congratulation of friends, to get his supper ready. He
was always ailing and weakly. All he said of the triumphant
Hyacinth was, "I expected to like it better." He had under charming and modest manners, in almost all things of life, a complete
absorption in his own dream. I have never heard him praise any
writer, living or dead, but some old French farce-writer. For him
nothing existed but his thought. He claimed nothing for it
aloud. He never said any of those self-confident things I am enraged into saying, but one knew that he valued nothing else. He
was too confident for self-assertion. I once said to George Moore,
"Synge has always the better of you, for you have brief but

ghastly moments during which you admit the existence of other writers; Synge never has." I do not think he disliked other writers —they did not exist. One did not think of him as an egotist. He was too sympathetic in the ordinary affairs of life and too simple. In the arts he knew no language but his own.

I have often envied him his absorption as I have envied Verlaine his vice. Can a man of genius make that complete renunciation of the world necessary to the full expression of himself without some vice or some deficiency? You were happy or at least blessed, "blind old man of Scio's rocky isle."

19

Two plays last night, *Time,* a play of suggestion, *Cross-roads,* a logical play. We accepted this last play because of its central idea, a seeming superstition of its creator, a promise of a new attitude towards life, of something beyond logic. In the four morning papers *Time* is cursed or ignored and *Cross-roads* given great praise, but praise that is never for the central idea, and the only critic who speaks of that idea misunderstands it completely. State a logical proposition and the most commonplace mind can complete it. Suggestion is richest to the richest and so grows unpopular with a democracy like this. They misunderstood Robinson's idea, luckily for his popularity, and so turned all into commonplace. They allow their minds to dwell so completely on the logic that they do not notice what, as it were, swims upon it or juts up from its river-bed. That is how they combine religion with a journalism which accepts all the implications of materialism. A thought that stirs me in *Time* is that "only women and great artists love time, others sell it," but what is Blake's "naked beauty displayed," visible audible wisdom, to the shopkeeping logicians? How can they love time or anything but the day's end?

20

To-day Molly told me that Synge often spoke of his coming death, indeed constantly for a year past, and tried hard to finish *Deirdre.* Sometimes he would get very despondent, thinking he could not finish it, and then she would act it for him and he would write a little more, and then he would despond again, and so the acting would begin again.

My sister Lily says that the ship Lolly saw on the night of Synge's death was not like a real ship, but like the *Shadowy Waters* ship on the Abbey stage, a sort of allegorical thing. There was also a girl in a bright dress, but she seemed to vanish as the ship ran ashore; all about the girl, and indeed everything, was broken and confused until the bow touched the shore in bright sunlight.

21

I see that between *Time,* suggestion, and *Cross-roads,* logic, lies a difference of civilisation. The literature of suggestion belongs to a social order when life conquered by being itself and the most living was the most powerful, and not to a social order founded upon argument. Leisure, wealth, privilege were created to be a soil for the most living. The literature of logic, the most powerful and the most empty, conquering all in the service of one metallic premise, is for those who have forgotten everything but books and yet have only just learnt to read. They fill their minds with deductions, as they fill their empty houses, where there is nothing of the past, with machine-made furniture. I used to think that the French and Irish democracies follow, as John O'Leary used to say, a logical deduction to its end, no matter what suffering it brings, from a resemblance in the blood. I now believe that they do this because they have broken from the past, from the self-evident truths, from "naked beauty displayed." The English logicians may be as ignorant but they are timid.

Robinson should become a celebrated dramatist if this theatre lasts long enough. He does not argue like the imitators of Ibsen, though his expression of life is as logical, hence his grasp on active passion. Passion is logical when bent on action. In the drama of suggestion there must be sufficient loosening and slackening for meditation and the seemingly irrelevant, or else a Greek chorus, and neither is possible without rich leisurely minds in the audience, lovers of Father Time, men who understand Faust's last cry to the passing moment.

Florence Farr once said to me, "If we could say to ourselves, with sincerity, 'This passing moment is as good as any I shall ever know,' we would die upon the instant, or be united to God." Desire would have ceased, and logic the feet of desire.

22

April 5.

Walked home from Gurteen Dhas with D—— and walked through the brick-kilns of Egypt. He states everything in a slightly argumentative form and the soul is starved by the absence of self-evident truth. Good conversation unrolls itself like the spring or like the dawn; whereas effective argument, mere logical statement, founds itself on the set of facts or of experiences common to two or more. Each hides what is new or rich.

23

The element which in men of action corresponds to style in literature is the moral element. Books live almost entirely because of their style, and the men of action who inspire movements after they are dead are those whose hold upon impersonal emotion and law lifts them out of immediate circumstance. Mitchel wrote better prose than Davis, Mangan better poetry, D'Arcy Magee better popular verse, Fintan Lalor saw deeper into a political event, O'Connell had more power and Meagher more eloquence, but Davis alone has influenced generations of young men, though Mitchel's narrower and more faulty nature has now and again competed with him. Davis showed this moral element not merely in his verse—I doubt if that could have had great effect alone—but in his action, in his defence, for instance, of the rights of his political opponents of the Royal Irish Academy. His verses were but an illustration of principles shown in action. Men are dominated by self-conquest; thought that is a little obvious or platitudinous if merely written, becomes persuasive, immortal even, if held to amid the hurry of events. The self-conquest of the writer who is not a man of action is style.

Mitchel's influence comes mainly, though not altogether, from style, that also a form of power, an energy of life. It is curious that Mitchel's long martyred life, supported by style, has had less force than that of a man who died at thirty, was never in the hulks, did not write very well, and achieved no change of the law.

The act of appreciation of any great thing is an act of self-conquest. This is one reason why we distrust the serene moralist who has not approved his principles in some crisis. He would be troubled, broken even, if he had made that conquest. Yet the man who has proved himself in a crisis may be serene in words, for his battle was not in contemplation where words are combatants.

24

Last night my sister told me that this book of Synge's (his poems) was the only book they began to print on a Friday. They tried to avoid this but could not, and it is not at all well printed. Do all they could, it would not come right.

25

Molly Allgood has just told me of three pre-visions. Some years ago, when the Company were in England on that six weeks' tour, she, Synge and D—— were sitting in a tea-shop, she was looking at Synge, and suddenly the flesh seemed to fall from his face and she saw but a skull. She told him this and it gave him a great shock, and since then she had not allowed images to form before her eyes of themselves, as they often used to do. Synge was well at the time. Again last year, but before the operation and at a time when she had no fear, she dreamed that she saw him in a coffin being lowered into a grave, and a "strange sort of cross" was laid over the coffin. (The Company sent a cross of flowers to his funeral and it was laid upon the grave.) She told this also to Synge and he was troubled by it. Then some time after the operation she dreamed that she saw him in a boat. She was on the shore, and he waved his hand to her and the boat went away. She longed to go to him but could not.

26

Some weeks ago C—— wrote to me that it was a phase of M——'s madness to believe himself in heaven. All the great poets of other times were there, and he was helping to prepare for the reception of Swinburne. The angels were to stand in groups of three. And now I have just heard that Swinburne is dead.

27

Dined with Ricketts and Shannon. Ricketts spoke of the grief Synge's death gave him—the ending of all that work. We talked of the disordered and broken lives of modern men of genius and the so different lives of the Italian painters. He said in those days men of genius were cared for, but now the strain of life is too heavy, no one thinks of them till some misfortune comes—madness or death. He then spoke, as he often does, of the lack of any necessary place for the arts in modern life and said, "After all, the ceiling of the Sistine Chapel was the Pope's ceiling." Later he said in comment upon some irascible act of Hugh Lane's, "Everybody who is doing anything for the world is very disagreeable, the agreeable people are those for whom the world is doing something."

28

Our modern public arts, architecture, plays, large decorations, have too many different tastes to please. Some taste is sure to dislike and to speak its dislike everywhere, and then because of the silence of the rest—partly from apathy, partly from dislike of controversy, partly from the difficulty of defence, as compared with the ease of attack—there is general timidity. All creation requires one mind to make and one mind of enjoyment. The theatre can at rare moments create this one mind of enjoyment, and once created, it is like the mind of an individual in solitude, immeasurably bold—all is possible to it. The only building received with enthusiasm during my time has been the Catholic Cathedral of Westminster—religion or the politics of religion created that one mind.

29

I asked Molly if any words of hers made Synge write "I asked if I got sick and died" and she said, "He used often to joke about death with me and one day he said, 'Will you go to my funeral?' and I said, 'No, for I could not bear to see you dead and the others living.' "

30

Went to S——'s the other night—everybody either too tall or too short, crooked or lop-sided. One woman had an excited voice, an intellect without self-possession, and there was a man with a look of a wood-kern, who kept bringing the conversation back and back to Synge's wrong-doing in having made a girl in *The Playboy* admire a man who had hamstrung "mountain ewes." He saw nothing else to object to but that one thing. He declared that the English would not give Home Rule because they thought Ireland cruel, and no Irishman should write a sentence to make them go on thinking that. There arose before my mind an image of this man arguing about Ireland with an endless procession of second-rate men. At last I said, "When a country produces a man of genius he never is what it wants or believes it wants; he is always unlike its idea of itself. In the eighteenth century Scotland believed itself religious, moral and gloomy, and its national poet Burns came not to speak of these things but to speak of lust and drink and drunken gaiety. Ireland, since the Young Irelanders, has given itself up to apologetics. Every impression of life or impulse of imagination has been examined to see if it helped or hurt the glory of Ireland or the political claim of Ireland. A sincere impression of life became at last impossible, all was apologetics. There was no longer an impartial imagination, delighting in whatever is naturally exciting. Synge was the rushing up of the buried fire, an explosion of all that had been denied or refused, a furious impartiality, an indifferent turbulent sorrow. His work, like that of Burns, was to say all the people did not want to have said. He was able to do this because Nature had made him incapable of a political idea." The wood-kern made no answer, did not understand a word I said, perhaps; but for the rest of the evening he kept saying to this person or to that person that he objected to nothing but the passage about the "mountain ewes."

31

July 8.

I dreamed this thought two nights ago: "Why should we complain if men ill-treat our Muses, when all that they gave to Helen while she still lived was a song and a jest?"

32

September 20.

An idle man has no thought, a man's work thinks through him. On the other hand a woman gets her thought through the influence of a man. A man is to her what work is to a man. Man is a woman to his work and it begets his thoughts.

33

The old playwrights took old subjects, did not even arrange the subject in a new way. They were absorbed in expression, that is to say in what is most near and delicate. The new playwrights invent their subjects and dislike anything customary in the arrangement of the fable, but their expression is as common as the newspapers where they first learned to write.

34

October.

I saw *Hamlet* on Saturday night, except for the chief "Ophelia" scenes, and missed these (for I had to be in the Abbey) without regret. Their pathos, as they are played, has always left me cold. I came back for Hamlet at the graveside: there my delight always begins anew. I feel in *Hamlet,* as so often in Shakespeare, that I am in the presence of a soul lingering on the storm-beaten threshold of sanctity. Has not that threshold always been terrible, even crime-haunted? Surely Shakespeare, in those last seeming idle years, was no quiet country gentleman, enjoying, as men like Dowden think, the temporal reward of an unvalued toil. Perhaps he sought for wisdom in itself at last, and not in its passionate shadows. Maybe he had passed the threshold, and none the less for Jonson's drinking bout. Certainly one finds here and there in his work praise of country leisure sweetened by wisdom.

35

Am I going against nature in my constant attempt to fill my life with work? Is my mind as rich as in idle days? Is not perhaps the poet's labour a mere rejection? If he seek purity—the ridding of his life of all but poetry—will not inspiration come? Can one reach God by toil? He gives Himself to the pure in heart. He asks nothing but attention.

36

I have been looking at Venetian costumes of the sixteenth century as pictured in *The Mask*—all fantastic; bodily form hidden or disguised; the women with long bodices, the men in stuffed doublets. Life had become so learned and courtly that men and women dressed with no thought of bodily activity. If they still fought and hunted, their imagination was not with these things. Does not the same happen to our passions when we grow contemplative and so liberate them from use? They also become fantastic and create the strange lives of poets and artists.

37

December 15.

Deirdre of the Sorrows (first performances). I was anxious about this play and on Thursday both Lady Gregory and I felt the strain of our doubts and fears. Would it seem mere disjointed monotony? Would the second act be intelligible? The audience seemed to like it, and I was greatly moved by certain passages in the last act. I thought the quarrel at the graveside with its last phrase, "And isn't it a poor thing we should miss the safety of the grave, and we trampling its edge?" and Deirdre's cry to the quarrelling Kings, "Draw a little back with the squabbling of fools," as noble and profound drama as any man has written. On the first night the thought that it was Synge's reverie over death, his own death, made all poignant. "The filth of the grave," "death is a poor, untidy thing, though it's a queen that dies," and the like, brought him dying before me. I remembered his extreme gentleness in the last weeks, that air of being done with ambition and conflict. Last night the audience was small—under ten pounds—and less alive than the first night. No one spoke of the great passages. Someone thought the quarrel in the last act too harsh. Others picked out those rough peasant words that give salt to his speech, as "of course adding nothing to the dialogue, and very ugly." Others objected to the little things in the costuming of the play which were intended to echo these words, to vary the heroic convention with something homely or of the fields. Then as I watched the acting I saw that O'Donovan and Molly (Maire O'Neill) were as passionless as the rest. Molly had personal charm, pathos, distinction even, fancy, beauty, but never passion—never intensity; nothing out of a brooding mind. All was but observation, curiosity, desire to please. Her foot never touched the unchanging rock, the secret place beyond life; her talent showed like that of the others, social, modern, a faculty of comedy. Pathos she has, the nearest to tragedy the comedian can come, for that is conscious of our presence and would have our pity. Passion she has not, for that looks beyond mankind and asks no pity, not even of God. It realises, substantiates, attains, scorns, governs, and is most mighty when it passes from our sight.

38

December 16.

Last night Molly had so much improved that I thought she may have tragic power. The lack of power and of clarity which I still find amid great charm and distinction, comes more from lack of construction, through lack of reflection and experience, than from mere lack of emotion. There are passages where she attempts nothing, or where she allows herself little external comedy impulses, more, I now think, because they are habitual than because she could not bring emotion out of herself. The chief failure is towards the end. She does not show immediately after the death of Naisi enough sense of what has happened, enough normal despair to permit of a gradual development into the wild unearthly feeling of the last speeches, though these last speeches are exquisitely spoken. My unfavourable impression of Friday came in part from the audience, which was heavy and, I thought, bored. Yesterday the audience—the pit entirely full—was enthusiastic and moved, raising once again my hope for theatre and for the movement.

39

May 25.

At Stratford-on-Avon *The Playboy* shocked a good many people, because it was a self-improving, self-educating audience, and that means a perverted and commonplace audience. If you set out to educate yourself you are compelled to have an ideal, a model of what you would be; and if you are not a man of genius, your model will be commonplace and prevent the natural impulses of the mind, its natural reverence, desire, hope, admiration, always half unconscious, almost bodily. That is why a simple round of religious duties, things that escape the intellect, is often so much better than its substitute, self-improvement.

40

September 18,
S.S. "ZEELAND."

I noticed in the train, as I came to Queenstown, a silent, fairly well-dressed man, who struck me as vulgar. It was not his face, which was quite normal, but his movements. He moved from his head only. His arm and hand, let us say, moved in direct obedience to the head, had not the instinctive motion that comes from a feeling of weight, of the shape of an object to be touched or grasped. There were too many straight lines in gesture and in pose. The result was an impression of vulgar smartness, a defiance of what is profound and old and simple. I have noticed that beginners sometimes move this way on the stage. They, if told to pick up something, show by the movement of their body that their idea of doing it is more vivid than the doing of it. One gets an impression of thinness in the nature. I am watching Miss V—— to find out if her inanimate movements when on the stage come from lack of experience or if she has them in life. I watched her sinking into a chair the other day to see if her body felt the size and shape of the chair before she reached it. If her body does not so feel she will never be able to act, just as she will never have grace of movement in ordinary life. As I write I see through the cabin door a woman feeding a child with a spoon. She thinks of nothing but the child and every movement is full of expression. It would be beautiful acting. Upon the other hand her talk —she is talking to someone next her—in which she is not interested, is monotonous and thin in cadence. It is a mere purpose in the brain, made necessary by politeness.

41

October.

A good writer should be so simple that he has no faults, only sins.

The Bounty of Sweden

1925

1

Thirty years ago I visited Paris for the first time. The Cabbalist Macgregor Mathers said, "Write your impressions at once, for you will never see Paris clearly again." I can remember that I had pleased him by certain deductions from the way a woman at the other end of the café moved her hands over the dominoes. I might have seen that woman in London or in Dublin, but it would not have occurred to me to discover in her every kind of rapacity, the substance of the legendary harpy. "Is not style," as Synge once said to me, "born out of the shock of new material?"

I am about to write, as in a kind of diary, impressions of Stockholm which must get whatever value they have from excitement, from the presence before the eyes of what is strange, mobile and disconnected.

2

Early in November a journalist called to show me a printed paragraph saying that the Nobel Prize would probably be conferred upon Herr Mann, the distinguished novelist, or upon myself. I did not know that the Swedish Academy had ever heard my name; tried to escape an interview by talking of Rabindranath Tagore, of his gift to his School of the seven thousand pounds awarded him; almost succeeded in dismissing the whole Reuter paragraph from my memory. Herr Mann has many readers, is a famous novelist with his fixed place in the world, and, said I to myself, well fitted for such an honour; whereas I am but a writer of plays which are acted by players with a literary mind for a few evenings, and I have altered them so many times that I doubt the value of every passage. I am more confident of my lyrics, or of some few amongst them, but then I have got into the habit of recommending or commending myself to general company for anything rather than my gift of lyric writing, which concerns such a meagre troop.

Every now and then, when something has stirred my imagination, I begin talking to myself. I speak in my own person and dramatise myself, very much as I have seen a mad old woman do upon the Dublin quays, and sometimes detect myself speaking and moving as if I were still young, or walking perhaps like an old man with fumbling steps. Occasionally, I write out what I have said in verse, and generally for no better reason than because I remember that I have written no verse for a long time. I do not think of my soliloquies as having different literary qualities. They stir my interest, by their appropriateness to the men I imagine myself to be, or by their accurate description of some emotional circumstance, more than by any aesthetic value. When I begin to write I have no object but to find for them some natural speech, rhythm and syntax, and to set it out in some pattern, so seeming old that it may seem all men's speech, and though the labour is very great, I seem to have used no faculty peculiar to myself, certainly no special gift. I print the poem and never hear about it again, until I find the book years after with a page dog-eared by some young man, or marked by some young girl with a violet, and when I have seen that I am a little ashamed, as though somebody were to attribute to me a delicacy of feeling I should but do not possess. What came so easily at first, and amidst so much drama, and was written so laboriously at the last, cannot be counted among my possessions.

On the other hand, if I give a successful lecture, or write a vigorous, critical essay, there is immediate effect; I am confident that on some one point, which seems to me of great importance, I know more than other men, and I covet honour.

3

Then some eight days later, between ten and eleven at night, comes a telephone message from the *Irish Times* saying that the prize has indeed been conferred upon me; and some ten minutes after that comes a telegram from the Swedish Ambassador; then journalists come for interviews. At half past twelve my wife and I are alone, and search the cellar for a bottle of wine, but it is empty, and as a celebration is necessary we cook sausages. A couple of days pass and a letter from the Ambassador invites me to receive the prize at Stockholm, but a letter from the Swedish Academy offers to send medal, money, and diploma to Dublin.

I question booksellers in vain for some history of Sweden, or of Swedish literature. Even Gosse's *Studies in the Literature of Northern Europe* which I read twenty years ago is out of print, and among my own books there is nothing but the life of Swedenborg which contains photographs of Swedenborg's garden and garden-house, and of the Stockholm House of Nobles, built in Dutch style, and beautiful, with an ornament that never insists upon itself, and a dignity that has no pomp. It had housed in Swedenborg's day that Upper Chamber of the Swedish Parliament where he had voted and spoken upon finance, after the ennoblement of his family.

4

My wife and I leave Harwich for Esbjerg in Denmark, on the night of December 6, and find our alarms were needless, for the sea is still and the air warm. The Danish steamboat is about the size of the Dublin-Holyhead mailboat, but the cabins are panelled in pale birchwood, and when we sit down to supper, the table is covered by an astonishing variety of cold food, most of which we refuse because we do not recognise it, and some, such as eels in jelly, because we do. Our companions are commercial travellers and presently we are recognised, for somebody has a newspaper with my portrait, and a man, who has travelled in Ireland for an exporter of Danish agricultural machinery, talks to us at dinner. He was in Munster for the first part of our Civil War, and when the trains were stopped had found himself in great difficulties, and during parts of his journey had moved at breakneck speed, that his motor might escape capture by the Insurgents, but our Civil War was no part of his business, and had not stirred his imagination. He had, however, discovered a defect in Irish agriculture that was very much a part. Through lack of warm winter sheds and proper winter food for cattle, the Irish farmers had no winter butter, and so Ireland must import butter from his country. Though, as he said, against Danish interests, he had pointed this out to Irish farmers. "But you have a Government," they said, "which looks after these things," and this time he became really excited—"Put that idea out of your head," I told them. "It was we ourselves who looked after these things, our Government has nothing to do with it."

He asks why the Irish have so little self-reliance, and want the Government to do everything, and I say, "Were the Danes always self-reliant?" and after a moment's thought, he answers, "Not till the Bishop established his Schools, we owe everything to his High Schools." I know something of Bishop Grundtvig and his Schools, for I often hear A. E. or some other at Plunkett House tell how he educated Denmark, by making examinations almost nothing and the personality of the teacher almost everything, and rousing the imagination with Danish literature and history. "What our peasants need," he had said, "is not technical training, but mental."

As we draw near our journey's end, an elderly Swede comes to say "good-bye," and kisses my wife's hand, bending very low, and the moment he is out of earshot, the Danish commercial traveller says with a disgusted voice, "No Dane would do that. The Swedes are always imitating the French."

I see that he does not like Swedes, and I ask what he thinks of Norwegians. "Rough," he says, "and they want everything, they want Greenland now."

5

At Esbjerg I find a young man, a distinguished Danish poet sent by a Copenhagen newspaper, and he and I and my wife dine together. At Copenhagen journalists meet us at the railway station, and others at the hotel, and when I am asked about Ireland I answer always that if the British Empire becomes a voluntary Federation of Free Nations, all will be well, but if it remains as in the past, a domination of one, the Irish question is not settled. That done with, I can talk of the work of my generation in Ireland, the creation of a literature to express national character and feeling but with no deliberate political aim. A journalist who has lived in Finland says, "Finland has had to struggle with Russian influence to preserve its national culture." I ask many questions and one journalist says, "O—Denmark is well educated, and education can reach everybody, as education cannot in big nations like England and America," and he goes on to say that in Denmark "you may dine at some professor's house, and find that you are sitting next your housemaid, who is among his favourite pupils, and next morning she will be your housemaid again, and too well educated to presume, or step out of her place." Another, however, a very distinguished man, will have it that it is "all wrong, for people who should hardly know what a book is now read books, and even write them. The High Schools have made the intellect of Denmark sentimental." A little later on he says, "We may have a Socialist Government one of these days," and I begin to wonder what Denmark will make of that mechanical eighteenth-century dream; we know what half-medieval Russia has made of it. Another Dane speaks of the Danish Royal Family as "bourgeois and sporting, like the English"; but says, when I ask about the Royal Family of Sweden, "O—such educated and intelligent people." It is he, I think, who first tells me of Prince Eugene, friend and patron of Swedish artists, and himself an accomplished painter who has helped to decorate the Stockholm Town Hall, "beginning every day at nine o'clock, and working all day like the rest, and for two years," and how at the opening ceremony he had not stood among the Royal Family, "but among the artists and workmen," and that it was he who saw to it "that every artist was given freedom to create as he would." Another spoke much of Strindberg, and though he called him the "Shakespeare of Sweden," seemed to approve the Swedish Academy's refusal of recognition; "they could not endure his quarrels with his friends nor the book about his first wife."

A train-ferry brings us across some eighteen miles of sea, and so into Sweden, and while we are waiting for the train to start again, I see through a carriage window many faces, but it is only just as the train starts, when a Swedish interviewer says—for there are interviewers here also—"Did you not see all those people gazing at the Nobel Prize winner?" that I connect those faces with myself.

Away from the lights of the station it is too dark to see anything, but when the dawn breaks, we are passing through a forest.

6

At the Stockholm station a man introduces himself, and reminds me that I met him in Paris thirty years ago, and asks me to read a pamphlet which he has written in English upon Strindberg, and especially a chapter called "Strindberg and the Wolves." The pamphlet comes to the hotel a couple of hours later, and turns out to be an attack upon the Swedish Academy, and an ardent defence of Strindberg. That outrageous, powerful book about his first wife is excused on the ground that it was not written for publication, and was published by an accident. And somebody once met Strindberg in a museum, dressed up according to the taste of one or other of his wives, "with cuffs upon his pantaloons," by which the pamphlet meant, I imagine, that like "Mr. Prufrock" he wore "the bottoms of his trousers rolled." I had met its writer in the rooms of an American artist, who was of Strindberg's Paris circle, and it was probably there that I had heard for the first time of stage scenery that might decorate a stage, and suggest a scene while attempting nothing that an easel painting can do better. I am pleased to imagine that the news of it may have come from Strindberg, whom I seem to remember as big and silent. I have always felt a sympathy for that tortured self-torturing man who offered himself to his own soul as Buddha offered himself to the famished tiger. He and his circle were preoccupied with the deepest problems of mankind. He himself, at the time I speak of, was seeking with furnace and athanor for the philosopher's stone.

At my hotel, I find a letter from another of that circle, whom I remember as a fair girl like a willow, beginning with this sentence—"God's blessing be upon your wife and upon yourself through the many holy men and women of this land."

7

The diplomas and medals are to be given us by the King at five in the afternoon of December 10th.

The American Ambassador, who is to receive those for an American man of science, unable to be present, and half a dozen men of various nations sit upon the platform. In the body of the Hall every seat is full, and all there are in evening dress, and in the front row are the King, Princess Ingeborg, wife of the King's brother, Prince Wilhelm, Princess Margaretha, and I think another Royalty. The President of the Swedish Academy speaks in English, and I see from the way he stands, from his self-possession, and from his rhythmical utterance, that he is an experienced orator. I study the face of the old King, intelligent and friendly, like some country gentleman who can quote Horace and Catullus, and the face of the Princess Margaretha, full of subtle beauty, emotional and precise, and impassive with a still intensity suggesting that final consummate strength which rounds the spiral of a shell. One finds a similar beauty in wooden busts taken from Egyptian tombs of the Eighteenth Dynasty and not again till Gainsborough paints. Is it very ancient and very modern alone or did painters and sculptors cease to notice it until our day?

The Ambassador goes towards the King, descends from the platform by some five or six steps, which end a yard from the King's feet, and having received the diploma and medal, ascends those five or six steps walking backward. He does not go completely backward, but sideways, and seems to show great practice. Then there is music, and a man of science repeats the movement, imitating the Ambassador exactly and easily, for he is young and agile, and then more music, and two men of science go down the steps, side by side, for they have made discoveries that are related to one another, and the prize is divided between them. As it would be impossible for two men to go up backward, side by side, without much practice, one repeats the slanting movement, and the other turns his back on Royalty. Then the British Ambassador receives diploma and medal for two Canadians, but as he came from the body of the hall he has no steps to go up and down. Then more music and my turn comes. When the King has given me my diploma and medal and said, "I thank you for coming yourself," and I have bowed my thanks, I glance for a moment at the face of the Princess Margaretha, and move backward towards the stair. As I am about to step sideways like the others, I notice that the carpet is not nailed down, and this suddenly concentrates my attention upon the parallel lines made by the two edges of the carpet, and, as though I were hypnotised, I feel that I must move between them, and so straight up backward without any sidelong movement. It seems to me that I am a long time reaching the top, and as the cheering grows much louder when I get there, I must have roused the sympathy of the audience. All is over, and I am able to examine my medal, its charming, decorative, academic design, French in manner, a work of the 'nineties. It shows a young man listening to a Muse, who stands young and beautiful with a great lyre in her hand, and I think as I examine it, "I was good-looking once like that young man, but my unpractised verse was full of infirmity, my Muse old as it were; and now I am old and rheumatic, and nothing to look at, but my Muse is young. I am even persuaded that she is like those Angels in Swedenborg's vision, and moves perpetually 'towards the day-spring of her youth.'" At night there is a banquet, and when my turn comes, I speak of Swedenborg, Strindberg, and Ibsen. Then a very beautiful, stately woman introduces herself with this sentence, spoken slowly as though English were unfamiliar, "What is this new religion they are making up in Paris that is all about the dead?" I wonder who has told her that I know anything of psychical research, for it must be of that she speaks, and I tell her of my own studies. We are going to change the thought of the world, I say, to bring it back to all its old truths, but I dread the future. Think what the people have made of the political thought of the eighteenth century, and now we must offer them a new fanaticism. Then I stop ashamed, for I am talking habitual thoughts, and not adapting them to her ear, forgetting beauty in the pursuit of truth, and I wonder if age has made my mind rigid and heavy. I deliberately falter as though I could think of nothing more to say, that she may pass upon her smiling road.

8

Next day is the entrance of the new Crown Princess, and my wife and I watch it, now from the hotel window, now from the quayside. Stockholm is almost as much channelled by the sea as Venice; and with an architecture as impressive as that of Paris, or of London, it has the better even of Paris in situation. It seems to shelter itself under the walls of a great Palace, begun at the end of the seventeenth century. We come very slowly to realise that this building may deserve its great architectural reputation. The windows, the details of the ornaments, are in a style that has spread everywhere, and I cannot escape from memories of houses at Queen's Gate, and even, it may be, from that of the Ulster Bank at Sligo, which I have hardly seen since my childhood. Was it not indeed a glory and shame of that architecture that we have been able to combine its elements in all sorts of ways and for all sorts of purposes, as if they had come out of a child's box of wooden bricks? Among all these irrelevant associations, however, I discover at last a vast, dominating, unconfused outline, a masterful simplicity. The Palace is at the other side of the river, and away towards our left runs the river bordered by tall buildings, and above the roofs of the houses, towards our right, rises the tower of the new Town Hall, the glittering pole upon its top sustaining the three crowns of the Swedish Arms. Copenhagen is an anarchy of commercial streets, with fine buildings here and there, but here all seems premeditated and arranged.

Everywhere there are poles with flags, and at the moment when the Crown Prince and Princess leave the railway station for the Palace, the salvos of artillery begin. After each salvo there are echoes, and I feel a quickening of the pulse, an instinctive alarm. I remember firing in Dublin last winter, the sudden noise that drew like echoes from the streets. I have to remind myself that these cannon are fired out of gaiety and good-will. There are great crowds, and I get the impression of a family surrounded by loyalty and affection.

9

The next night there is a reception at the Palace, and the Nobel Prize winners are among the guests. We wait in a long gallery for our turn to enter the throne-room, and upon the black coats of the civilians, as upon the grey and silver of the Guards, lie the chains of the three Swedish Orders. Among the black-coated men are men of learning, men of letters, men of science, much of the intellect of Sweden. What model has made all this, one wonders: Goethe's Weimar, or Sweden's own eighteenth-century courts? There may be, must be, faults of commission or omission, but where else could a like assembly be gathered? I who have never seen a court, find myself before the evening is ended moved as if by some religious ceremony, though to a different end, for here it is Life herself that is praised. Presently we walk through lines of sentries, in the costume of Charles XII, the last of Sweden's great military Kings, and then bow as we pass rapidly before the tall seated figures of the Royal Family. They seem to be like stage royalties. Just such handsome men and women would have been chosen by a London manager staging, let us say, some dramatised version of *The Prisoner of Zenda*. One has a general impression of youthful distinction, even the tall, slight figure of the old King seems young. Then we pass from the throne-room into a vast hall hung with Gobelin tapestries, which seem in the distance to represent scenes like those in a Watteau or in a Fragonard. Their green colour by contrast turns the marble pillars above into a dusky silver. At the end of the hall musicians are sitting in a high marble gallery, and in the side galleries are women in white dresses, many very young and handsome. Others upon the level of the floor sit grouped together, making patches of white among the brilliant uniforms and the black coats. We are shepherded to our places, and the musicians play much Swedish music, which I cannot describe, for I know nothing of music. During our first long wait all kinds of pictures had passed before me in reverie and now my imagination renews its excitement. I had thought how we Irish had served famous men and famous families, and had been, so long as our nation had intellect enough to shape anything of itself, good lovers of women, but had never served any abstract cause, except the one, and that we personified by a woman, and I wondered if the service of woman could be so different from that of a court. I had thought how, before the emigration of our poor began, our gentlemen had gone all over Europe, offering their swords at every court, and that many had stood, just as I, but with an anxiety I could but imagine, for their future hung upon a frown or a smile. I had run through old family fables and histories, to find if any man of my blood had so stood, and had thought that there were men living, meant by nature for that vicissitude, who had served a woman through all folly, because they had found no court to serve. Then my memory had gone back twenty years to that summer when a friend read out to me at the end of each day's work Castiglione's commendations and descriptions of that court of Urbino, where youth for certain brief years imposed upon drowsy learning the discipline of its joy, and I remembered a cry of Bembo's made years after, "Would that I were a shepherd that I might look down daily upon Urbino." I had repeated to myself what I could remember of Ben Jonson's address to the court of his time, "Thou art a beautiful and brave spring and waterest all the noble plants of this Island. In thee the whole Kingdom dresseth itself and is ambitious to use thee as her glass. Beware then thou render men's figures truly and teach them no less to hate their deformities, than to love their forms. . . . Thy servant but not slave, Ben Jonson."

And now I begin to imagine some equivalent gathering to that about me, called together by the heads of some State where every democratic dream had been fulfilled, and where all men had started level and only merit, acknowledged by all the people, ruled. The majority so gathered, certainly all who had supreme authority, would have reached that age when an English novelist becomes eligible for the Order of Merit. Times of disturbance might indeed carry into power some man of comparative youth, of fifty or sixty years perhaps, but I think of normal times. Here and there one would notice sons and daughters, perhaps even the more dutiful grandsons and grand-daughters, but in the eyes of those, though not in their conversation, an acute observer might discover disquiet and a restless longing for the moment when they could slip away to some night-club compensating anarchy. In the conversation of old and young there would be much sarcasm, great numbers of those tales which we all tell to one another's disadvantage. For all men would display to others' envy the trophies won in their life of struggle.

Then suddenly my thought runs off to that old Gaelic poem made by the nuns of Iona. A Swedish or Danish ship had been cast upon the rocks, and all royalties on board had perished, but one baby. The nuns mothered the baby, and their cradle-song, famous for generations after, repeated over and over, praising in symbol every great man's child—every tested long-enduring stock—"Daughter of a Queen, grand-daughter of a Queen, great-grand-daughter of a Queen, great-great-grand-daughter of a Queen." Nature, always extravagant, scattering much to find a little, has found no means but hereditary honour to sustain the courage of those who stand waiting for the signal, cowed by the honour and authority of those who lie wearily at the goal. Perhaps, indeed, she created the family with no other object, and may even now mock in her secret way our new ideals—the equality of man, equality of rights—meditating some wholly different end. Certainly her old arrangements, in all pursuits that gain from youth's recurring sway, or from its training in earliest childhood, surpassed what begins to be a world of old men. The politic Tudor kings and the masterful descendants of Gustavus Vasa were as able as the American presidents, and better educated, and the artistic genius of old Japan continually renewed itself through dynasties of painters. The descendants of Kanoka made all that was greatest in the art of their country from the ninth to the eleventh century, and then it but passed to other dynasties, in whom, as Mr. Binyon says, "the flower of genius was being continually renewed and revived in the course of many generations." How serene their art, no exasperation, no academic tyranny, its tradition as naturally observed as the laws of a game or dance. Nor has our individualistic age wholly triumphed in Japan even yet, for it is a few years since a famous player published in his programme his genealogy, running back through famous players, to some player of the Middle Ages; and one day in the British Museum Print Room, I saw a Japanese at a great table judging Chinese and Japanese pictures. "He is one of the greatest living authorities," I was told, "the Mikado's hereditary connoisseur, the fourteenth of his family to hold the post." May it not have been possible that the use of the mask in acting, and the omission from painting of the cast shadow, by making observation and experience of life less important, and imagination and tradition more, made the arts transmittible and teachable? But my thoughts have carried me far away.

10

Near me stands a man who is moved also by the spectacle of the court, but to a Jacobin frenzy, Swede, Englishman, American, German, what does it matter, seeing that his frenzy is international. I had spoken to him earlier in the day and found him a friendly, even perhaps a cultivated man, and certainly not the kind of man who is deliberately rude; but now, he imagines that an attempt has been made to impose upon him. He speaks his thoughts aloud, silenced occasionally by the music, but persistent in the intervals. While waiting to enter the throne-room, he had been anxious to demonstrate that he was there by accident, drifting irresponsibly, no way implicated, as it were, and having accomplished this demonstration by singing a little catch "I'm here because I'm here," and commented abundantly upon all he saw: "The smaller the nation, the grander the uniform," "Well—they never got those decorations in war," and so on. He was certain that the breastplates of the sentries were made of tin, but added with a meditative voice, as though anxious to be fair, "The breastplates of the English Horse Guards are also made of tin."

As we came through the throne-room, I had heard him say, "One of the royalties smiled, they consider us as ridiculous," and I had commented, entangled in my dream, "We are ridiculous, we are the learned at whom the little boys laugh in the streets."

And now when, at a pause in the music, the Queen passes down the great hall, pages holding her train, he says in the same loud voice as before, "Well, a man has not to suffer that indignity," and then upbraids all forms of ceremony, and repeats an incident of his school life to demonstrate his distaste for Bishops.

As I leave the Palace, a man wearing orders stops for a moment to say, "I am the Head-master of a big school, I was the Prince's tutor, and I am his friend."

11

For the next two or three days we visit picture galleries, the gallery of the National Museum, that of Prince Eugene, that of Baron Thiel. At the National Museum pictures have been taken down and lean against the wall, that they may be sent to London for an exhibition of Swedish art. Someone, exaggerating the influence in London of the Nobel Prize winner, asks me to write something to get people to go and see it, and I half promise but feel that I have not the necessary knowledge. I know something of the French Impressionism that gave their painters their first impulse, but almost nothing of German or Austrian, and I have seen that of Sweden for the first time. At a first glance Impressionism seems everywhere the same, with differences of power but not of sight or mind, and one has to live with it and make many comparisons, I think, to write more than a few sentences. The great myth-makers and mask-makers, the men of aristocratic mind, Blake, Ingres in the "Perseus," Puvis de Chavannes, Rossetti before 1870, Watts when least a moralist, Gustave Moreau at all times, Calvert in the woodcuts, the Charles Ricketts of "The Danaides," and of the earlier illustrations of *The Sphinx*, have imitators, but create no universal language. Administrators of tradition, they seem to copy everything, but in reality copy nothing, and not one of them can be mistaken for another, but Impressionism's gift to the world was precisely that it gave, at a moment when all seemed sunk in convention, a method as adaptable as that box of architectural Renaissance bricks. It has suddenly taught us to see and feel, as everybody that wills can see and feel, all those things that are as wholesome as rain and sunlight, to take into our hearts with an almost mystical emotion whatsoever happens without forethought or premeditation. It is not, I think, any accident that their art has coincided everywhere with a new sympathy for crowds, for the poor and the unfortunate. Certainly it arrived in these Scandinavian countries just at the moment when an intellectual awaking of the whole people was beginning, for I always read, or am told, that whatever I inquire about began with the 'eighties, or was the outcome of some movement of that time.

When I try to define what separates Swedish Impressionism from French, I notice that it has a stronger feeling for particular places. Monet will paint a group of trees by a pond in every possible light, changing his canvas every twenty minutes, and only returning to a canvas when the next day's clock brings up the same light, but then it is precisely the light that interests him, and interests the buyers of those almost scientific studies. Nobody will buy because it is a pond under his window, or that he passed in his boyhood on his way to school. I noticed in some house where I lunched two pictures of the Stockholm river, painted in different lights by Eugene Janson, and in the National Museum yet another with a third effect of light, but much as the light pleased his imagination, one feels that he cared very much for the fact before him, that he was never able to forget for long that he painted a well-loved, familiar scene. I am constantly reminded of my brother who continually paints from memory the people and houses of the village where he lived as a child; but the people of Rosses will never care about his pictures, and these painters paint for all educated Stockholm. They have found an emotion held in common, and are no longer, like the rest of us, solitary spectators. I get the impression that their work rouses a more general interest than that of other painters, is less confined to small groups of connoisseurs; I notice in the booksellers' shops that there seems to be some little paper-covered pamphlet, full of illustrations, for every notable painter of the school, dead or living, and the people I meet ask constantly what I think of this painter or that other, or somebody will say, "This is the golden age of painting." When I myself try to recall what I have seen, I remember most clearly a picture of a white horse on the sea-shore, with its tints separated by little lines, that give it a general effect of mosaic, and certain portraits by Ernst Josephson, which prove that their painter was entirely preoccupied with the personality of the sitter, light, colour, design, all subordinate to that. An English portrait-painter is sometimes so preoccupied with the light that one feels he would have had equal pleasure in painting a bottle and an apple. But a preference after so brief a visit may be capricious, having some accidental origin.

12

On Thursday I give my official lecture to the Swedish Royal Academy. I have chosen "The Irish Theatre" for my subject, that I may commend all those workers, obscure or well-known, to whom I owe much of whatever fame in the world I may possess. If I had been a lyric poet only, if I had not become through this theatre the representative of a public movement, I doubt if the English committees would have placed my name upon that list from which the Swedish Academy selects its prize-winner. They would not have acknowledged a thought so irrelevant, but those dog-eared pages, those pressed violets, upon which the fame of a lyric poet depends at the last, might without it have found no strong voice. I have seen so much beautiful lyric poetry pass unnoticed for years, and indeed at this very moment a little book of exquisite verse lies upon my table, by an author who died a few years ago, whom I knew slightly, and whose work I ignored, for chance had shown me only that part of it for which I could not care.

On my way to the lecture hall I ask an Academician what kind of audience I will have, and he replies, "An audience of women, a fit audience for a poet"; but there are men as well as women. I had thought it would be difficult to speak to an audience in a language they had learnt at school, but it is exceedingly easy. All I say seems to be understood, and I am conscious of that sympathy which makes a speaker forget all but his own thoughts, and soliloquise aloud. I am speaking without notes and the image of old fellow-workers comes upon me as if they were present, above all of the embittered life and death of one, and of another's laborious, solitary age, and I say, "When your King gave me medal and diploma, two forms should have stood, one at either side of me, an old woman sinking into the infirmity of age and a young man's ghost. I think when Lady Gregory's name and John Synge's name are spoken by future generations, my name, if remembered, will come up in the talk, and that if my name is spoken first their names will come in their turn because of the years we worked together. I think that both had been well pleased to have stood beside me at the great reception at your Palace, for their work and mine has delighted in history and tradition." I think as I speak these words of how deep down we have gone, below all that is individual, modern and restless, seeking foundations for an Ireland that can only come into existence in a Europe that is still but a dream.

13

On Friday we visit the great Town Hall, which is the greatest work of Swedish art, a master-work of the Romantic movement. The Royal Palace had taken ninety years to build, and been the organising centre of the art of its time, and this new magnificence, its narrow windows opening out upon a formal garden, its tall tower rising from the quayside, has taken ten years. It, too, has been an organising centre, but for an art more imaginative and amazing. Here there is no important French influence, for all that has not come out of the necessities of site and material, no matter in what school the artist studied, carries the mind backward to Byzantium. I think of but two comparable buildings, the Pennsylvania terminus in New York, and the Catholic Cathedral at Westminster, but the Pennsylvania terminus, noble in austerity, is the work of a single mind, elaborating a suggestion from a Roman Bath, a mind that—supported by the American deference to authority—has been permitted to refuse everything not relevant to a single dominating idea. The starting hours of the trains are upon specially designed boards, of a colour that makes them harmonise with the general design, and all other advertisements are forbidden, even in the stations that the trains pass immediately after leaving or before entering the terminus. The mood of severity must be prolonged or prepared for. The Catholic Cathedral is of a greater magnificence in general design, but being planted in a country where public opinion rules and the subscribers to every fund expect to have their way, is half ruined by ignoble decoration, the most ignoble of all planned and paid for by my countrymen. The Town Hall of Stockholm, upon the other hand, is decorated by many artists, working in harmony with one another and with the design of the building as a whole, and yet all in seeming perfect freedom. In England and Ireland public opinion compels the employment of the worst artists, while here the authority of a Prince and the wisdom of a Socialist Minister of culture, and the approval of the most educated of all nations, have made possible the employment of the best. These myth-makers and mask-makers worked as if they belonged to one family, and the great walls where the roughened surface of the bricks, their carefully varied size and tint, take away all sense of mechanical finish; the mosaic-covered walls of the "Golden Room"; the paintings hung upon the walls of the committee-rooms; the fresco paintings upon the greater surfaces with their subjects from Swedish mythology; the wrought iron and the furniture, where all suggests history, and yet is full of invention; the statuary in marble and in bronze, now mythological in subject, now representations of great Swedes, modelled naked as if they had come down from some Roman heaven; all that suggestion of novelty and of an immeasurable past; all that multitude and unity, could hardly have been possible, had not love of Stockholm and belief in its future so filled men of different minds, classes, and occupations that they almost attained the supreme miracle, the dream that has haunted all religions, and loved one another. No work comparable in method or achievement has been accomplished since the Italian cities felt the excitement of the Renaissance, for in the midst of our individualistic anarchy, growing always, as it seemed, more violent, have arisen once more subordination, design, a sense of human need.

14

On Saturday I see at the Royal Theatre a performance of my *Cathleen ni Houlihan*. The old father and mother are excellent and each performance differs but little from an exceedingly good Abbey performance, except for certain details of scene, and for differences of interpretation, made necessary by the change of

audience. Lines spoken by Cathleen ni Houlihan just before she
leaves the cottage always move an Irish audience powerfully for
historical reasons, and so the actress begins at much the same
emotional level as those about her, and then works up to a climax
upon these lines. But here they could have no special appeal, so
she strikes a note of tragedy at once, and does not try for a strong
climax. The management had sent to the West of Ireland for
photographs of scenery, and the landscape, seen through the
open door, has an appropriateness and grandeur our poverty-
stricken Abbey has never attained. Upon the other hand the cottage and costume of the peasants suggest a richer peasantry than
ours. The management has, I think, been misled by that one-
hundred-pound dowry, for in Sweden, where the standard of
living is high, a farmer would probably have thought it more
necessary to feed his family and himself, and to look after his
daughter's education, than to save one hundred pounds for her
dowry. This affects the acting. The peasants are permitted to
wear a light buckle-shoe indoors, whereas they would in reality
have gone barefooted, or worn heavy working boots. Almost the
first thing a new actor at the Abbey has to learn is to walk as if
he wore those heavy boots, and this gives awkwardness and slowness to his movements. I do not point this out as an error in the
Swedish production, for a symbolic play like *Cathleen* should,
in most cases, copy whatever environment is most familiar to the
audience. It is followed by *She Stoops to Conquer,* and by comparison our Abbey performance of that play seems too slow.
Goldsmith's play is not in Sweden, I should think, the established
classic that it is with us, and so a Swedish producer is less rev-
erent. He discovers quickly that there are dull places and un-
realities, that it is technically inferior to Molière, and that we
may not discover this also, prefers a rattling pace.

15

Everybody has told us that we have not seen Stockholm at its
best because we have not seen it with the trees all white and the
streets deep in snow. When snow has fallen it has melted immediately, and there is central heating everywhere. While we

are packing for our journey a young American poet comes to our room, and introduces himself. "I was in the South of France," he says, "and I could not get a room warm enough to work in, and if I cannot get a warm room here I will go to Lapland."

The Irish Dramatic Movement

A LECTURE DELIVERED TO
THE ROYAL ACADEMY OF SWEDEN

Your Royal Highness, ladies and gentlemen, I have chosen as
my theme the Irish Dramatic Movement, because when I remember the great honour that you have conferred upon me, I
cannot forget many known and unknown persons. Perhaps the
English committees would never have sent you my name if I
had written no plays, no dramatic criticism, if my lyric poetry
had not a quality of speech practised upon the stage, perhaps
even—though this could be no portion of their deliberate
thought—if it were not in some degree the symbol of a movement. I wish to tell the Royal Academy of Sweden of the
labours, triumphs and troubles of my fellow-workers.

The modern literature of Ireland, and indeed all that stir of
thought which prepared for the Anglo-Irish war, began when
Parnell fell from power in 1891. A disillusioned and embittered Ireland turned from parliamentary politics; an event was
conceived; and the race began, as I think, to be troubled by
that event's long gestation. Dr. Hyde founded the Gaelic
League, which was for many years to substitute for political
argument a Gaelic grammar, and for political meetings village
gatherings, where songs were sung and stories told in the Gaelic
language. Meanwhile I had begun a movement in English, in
the language in which modern Ireland thinks and does its business; founded certain societies where clerks, working men, men
of all classes, could study the Irish poets, novelists and histo-
rians who had written in English, and as much of Gaelic literature as had been translated into English. But the great mass
of our people, accustomed to interminable political speeches,

read little, and so from the very start we felt that we must have a theatre of our own. The theatres of Dublin had nothing about them that we could call our own. They were empty buildings hired by the English travelling companies, and we wanted Irish plays and Irish players. When we thought of these plays we thought of everything that was romantic and poetical, because the nationalism we had called up—the nationalism every generation had called up in moments of discouragement—was romantic and poetical. It was not, however, until I met in 1896 Lady Gregory, a member of an old Galway family, who had spent her life between two Galway houses, the house where she was born, the house into which she married, that such a theatre became possible. All about her lived a peasantry who told stories in a form of English which has much of its syntax from Gaelic, much of its vocabulary from Tudor English, but it was very slowly that we discovered in that speech of theirs our most powerful dramatic instrument, not indeed until she herself began to write. Though my plays were written without dialect and in English blank verse, I think she was attracted to our movement because their subject matter differed but little from the subject-matter of the country stories. Her own house has been protected by her presence, but the house where she was born was burned down by incendiaries some few months ago, and there has been like disorder over the greater part of Ireland. A trumpery dispute about an acre of land can rouse our people to monstrous savagery, and if in their war with the English auxiliary police they were shown no mercy, they showed none: murder answered murder. Yet their ignorance and violence can remember the noblest beauty. I have in Galway a little old tower, and when I climb to the top of it I can see at no great distance a green field where stood once the thatched cottage of a famous country beauty, the mistress of a small local landed proprietor. I have spoken to old men and women who remembered her, though all are dead now, and they spoke of her as the old men upon the wall of Troy spoke of Helen, nor did man and woman differ in their praise. One old woman of whose youth the neighbours cherished a scandalous tale said of her, "I tremble all over when I think of her"; and there was another on the neighbouring mountain who said, "The sun and the moon never shone on anybody so handsome, and her skin was so white that it looked blue, and she had two little blushes on her cheeks." And there were men that told of the crowds that gathered to look at her upon a fair day, and of a man "who got his death swimming a river," that he might look at her. It was a song written by the Gaelic poet Raftery that brought her such great fame, and the cottages still sing it, though there are not so many to sing it as when I was young:—

> O star of light and O sun in harvest,
> O amber hair, O my share of the world,
> It is Mary Hynes, the calm and easy woman,
> Has beauty in her body and in her mind.

It seemed as if the ancient world lay all about us with its freedom of imagination, its delight in good stories, in man's force and woman's beauty, and that all we had to do was to make the town think as the country felt; yet we soon discovered that the town would only think town thoughts.

In the country you are alone with your own violence, your own ignorance and heaviness, and with the common tragedy of life, and if you have any artistic capacity you desire beautiful emotion; and, certain that the seasons will be the same always, care not how fantastic its expression.[1] In the town, where everybody crowds upon you, it is your neighbour not yourself that you hate, and if you are not to embitter his life and your own life, perhaps even if you are not to murder him in some kind of revolutionary frenzy, somebody must teach reality and justice. You will hate that teacher for a while, calling his books and plays ugly, misdirected, morbid, or something of that kind, but you must agree with him in the end. We were to find ourselves in a quarrel with public opinion that compelled us against our own will and the will of our

[1] See Note, p. 393.

players to become always more realistic, substituting dialect
for verse, common speech for dialect.

I had told Lady Gregory that I saw no likelihood of getting
money for a theatre and so must put away that hope, and she
promised to find the money among her friends. Her neighbour,
Mr. Edwin Martyn, paid for our first performances; and our
first players came from England; but presently we began our
real work with a company of Irish amateurs. Somebody had
asked me at a lecture, "Where will you get your actors?" and
I had said, "I will go into some crowded room, put the name
of everybody in it on a different piece of paper, put all those
pieces of paper into a hat and draw the first twelve." I have
often wondered at that prophecy, for though it was spoken
probably to confound and confuse a questioner it was very
nearly fulfilled. Our two best men actors were not indeed
chosen by chance, for one was a stage-struck solicitors' clerk and
the other a working man who had toured Ireland in a theatrical
company managed by a Negro. I doubt if he had learned much
in it, for its methods were rough and noisy, the Negro whiten-
ing his face when he played a white man, but, so strong is
stage convention, blackening it when he played a black man.
If a player had to open a letter on the stage I have no doubt
that he struck it with the flat of his hand, as I have seen players
do in my youth, a gesture that lost its meaning generations
ago when blotting paper was substituted for sand. We got our
women, however, from a little political society which described
its object as educating the children of the poor, or, according
to its enemies, teaching them a catechism that began with
this question, "What is the origin of evil?" and the answer,
"England."

And they came to us for patriotic reasons and acted from
precisely the same impulse that had made them teach, and
yet two of them proved players of genius, Miss Allgood and
Miss Maire O'Neill. They were sisters, one all simplicity, her
mind shaped by folksong and folk-story; the other sophisti-
cated, lyrical and subtle. I do not know what their thoughts
were as that strange new power awoke within them, but I

think they must have suffered from a bad conscience, a feeling that the patriotic impulse had gone, that they had given themselves up to vanity or ambition. Yet I think it was that first misunderstanding of themselves made their peculiar genius possible, for had they come to us with theatrical ambitions they would have imitated some well-known English player and sighed for well-known English plays. Nor would they have found their genius if we had not remained for a long time obscure like the bird within its shell, playing in little halls, generally in some shabby out-of-the-way street. We could experiment and wait, with nothing to fear but political misunderstanding. We had little money and at first needed little, twenty-five pounds given by Lady Gregory and twenty pounds by myself and a few pounds picked up here and there. And our theatrical organization was preposterous, players and authors all sitting together and settling by vote what play should be performed and who should play it. It took a series of disturbances, weeks of argument during which no performance could be given, before Lady Gregory and John Synge and I were put in control. And our relations with the public were even more disturbed. One play was violently attacked by the patriotic Press because it described a married peasant woman who had a lover, and when we published the old Aran folktale upon which it was founded the Press said the tale had reached Aran from some decadent author of pagan Rome. Presently Lady Gregory wrote her first comedy. My verse plays were not long enough to fill an evening and so she wrote a little play on a country love story in the dialect of her neighbourhood. A countryman returns from America with a hundred pounds and discovers his old sweetheart married to a bankrupt farmer. He plays cards with the farmer, and by cheating against himself gives him the hundred pounds. The company refused to perform it because they said to admit an emigrant's return with a hundred pounds would encourage emigration. We produced evidence of returned emigrants with much larger sums, but were told that only made the matter worse. Then after interminable argument had worn us all out Lady Gregory agreed to reduce the sum to twenty, and the actors gave way.

That little play was sentimental and conventional, but her next discovered her genius. She too had desired to serve, and that genius must have seemed miraculous to herself. She was in middle life, and had written nothing but a volume of political memoirs and had no interest in the theatre.

Nobody reading to-day her *Seven Short Plays* can understand why one of them, now an Irish classic, *The Rising of the Moon,* could not be performed for two years because of political hostility. A policeman discovers an escaped Fenian prisoner and lets him free, because the prisoner has aroused with some old songs the half-forgotten patriotism of his youth. The players would not perform it because they said it was an unpatriotic act to admit that a policeman was capable of patriotism. One well-known leader of the mob wrote to me, "How can the Dublin mob be expected to fight the police if it looks upon them as capable of patriotism?" When performed at last the play was received with enthusiasm, but only to get us into new trouble. The chief Unionist Dublin newspaper denounced us for slandering His Majesty's forces, and Dublin Castle denied to us a privilege which we had shared with the other Dublin theatres of buying, for stage purposes, the cast-off clothes of the police. Castle and Press alike knew that the police had frequently let off political prisoners, but "that only made the matter worse." Every political party had the same desire to substitute for life, which never does the same thing twice, a bundle of reliable principles and assertions.[1] Nor did religious orthodoxy like us any better than political; my *Countess Cathleen* was denounced by Cardinal Logue as an heretical play, and when I wrote that we would like to perform "foreign masterpieces" a Nationalist newspaper declared that "a foreign masterpiece is a very dangerous thing." The little halls where we performed could hold a couple of hundred people at the utmost and our audience was often not more than twenty or thirty, and we performed but two or three times a month, and during our periods of quarrelling not even that. But there was no lack of leading articles, we were from the first a recognized public danger. Two events brought us victory: a friend gave

[1] See Note, p. 394.

us a theatre, and we found a strange man of genius, John Synge. After a particularly angry leading article I had come in front of the curtain and appealed to the hundred people of the audience for their support. When I came down from the stage an old friend, Miss Horniman, from whom I had been expecting a contribution of twenty pounds, said, "I will find you a theatre." She found and altered for our purpose what is now the Abbey Theatre, Dublin, and gave us a small subsidy for a few years.

I had met John Synge in Paris in 1896. Somebody had said, "There is an Irishman living on the top floor of your hotel; I will introduce you." I was very poor, but he was much poorer. He belonged to a very old Irish family and, though a simple courteous man, remembered it and was haughty and lonely. With just enough to keep him from starvation and not always from half-starvation, he had wandered about Europe, travelling third-class or upon foot, playing his fiddle to poor men on the road or in their cottages. He was the man that we needed, because he was the only man I have ever known incapable of a political thought or of a humanitarian purpose. He could walk the roadside all day with some poor man without any desire to do him good or for any reason except that he liked him. He was to do for Ireland, though more by his influence on other dramatists than by his direct influence, what Robert Burns did for Scotland. When Scotland thought herself gloomy and religious, Providence restored her imaginative spontaneity by raising up Robert Burns to commend drink and the Devil. I did not, however, see what was to come when I advised John Synge to go to a wild island off the Galway coast and study its life because that life "had never been expressed in literature." He had learned Gaelic at College and I told him that, as I would have told it to any young man who had learned Gaelic and wanted to write. When he found that wild island he became happy for the first time, escaping, as he said, "from the nullity of the rich and the squalor of the poor." He had bad health, he could not stand the island hardship long, but he would go to and fro between there and Dublin.

Burns himself could not have more shocked a gathering of
Scots clergy than did he our players. Some of the women got
about him and begged him to write a play about the rebellion
of '98, and pointed out very truthfully that a play on such a
patriotic theme would be a great success. He returned at the
end of a fortnight with a scenario upon which he had toiled
in his laborious way. Two women take refuge in a cave, a
Protestant woman and a Catholic, and carry on an interminable
argument about the merits of their respective religions. The
Catholic woman denounces Henry VIII and Queen Elizabeth,
and the Protestant woman the Inquisition and the Pope. They
argue in low voices, because one is afraid of being ravished by
the rebels and the other by the loyal soldiers. But at last either
the Protestant or the Catholic says that she prefers any fate
to remaining any longer in such wicked company and climbs
out. The play was neither written nor performed, and neither
then nor at any later time could I discover whether Synge
understood the shock that he was giving. He certainly did not
foresee in any way the trouble that his greatest play brought
on us all.

When I had landed from a fishing yawl on the middle of
the island of Aran, a few months before my first meeting with
Synge, a little group of islanders, who had gathered to watch
a stranger's arrival, brought me to "the oldest man upon the
island." He spoke but two sentences, speaking them very
slowly: "If any gentleman has done a crime we'll hide him.
There was a gentleman that killed his father, and I had him
in my house six months till he got away to America." It was
a play founded on that old man's story Synge brought back
with him. A young man arrives at a little public-house and
tells the publican's daughter that he has murdered his father.
He so tells it that he has all her sympathy, and every time he
retells it, with new exaggerations and additions, he wins the
sympathy of somebody or other, for it is the countryman's
habit to be against the law. The countryman thinks the more
terrible the crime, the greater must the provocation have been.
The young man himself, under the excitement of his own
story, becomes gay, energetic and lucky. He prospers in love,

comes in first at the local races, and bankrupts the roulette tables afterwards. Then the father arrives with his head bandaged but very lively, and the people turn upon the impostor. To win back their esteem he takes up a spade to kill his father in earnest, but, horrified at the threat of what had sounded so well in the story, they bind him to hand over to the police. The father releases him and father and son walk off together, the son, still buoyed up by his imagination, announcing that he will be master henceforth. Picturesque, poetical, fantastical, a masterpiece of style and of music, the supreme work of our dialect theatre, his *Playboy* roused the populace to fury. We played it under police protection, seventy police in the theatre the last night, and five hundred, some newspaper said, keeping order in the streets outside. It is never played before any Irish audience for the first time without something or other being flung at the players. In New York a currant cake and a watch were flung, the owner of the watch claiming it at the stage door afterwards. The Dublin audience has, however, long since accepted the play. It has noticed, I think, that everyone upon the stage is somehow lovable and companionable, and that Synge has described, through an exaggerated symbolism, a reality which he loved precisely because he loved all reality. So far from being, as they had thought, a politician working in the interests of England, he was so little a politician that the world merely amused him and touched his pity. Yet when Synge died in 1909 opinion had hardly changed, we were playing to an almost empty theatre and were continually denounced. Our victory was won by those who had learned from him courage and sincerity but belonged to a different school. Synge's work, the work of Lady Gregory, my own *Cathleen ni Houlihan* and my *Hour-Glass* in its prose form, are characteristic of our first ambition. They bring the imagination and speech of the country, all that poetical tradition descended from the Middle Ages, to the people of the town. Those who learned from Synge had often little knowledge of the country and always little interest in its dialect. Their plays are frequently attacks upon obvious abuses, the bribery at the appointment of a dispensary Doctor, the attempts of some local politician to remain friends with all parties. Indeed the young Ministers and party politicians of the Free State have had, I think, some of their education from our plays. Then, too, there are many comedies which are not political satires though they are concerned with the life of the politics-ridden people of the town. Of these Mr. Lennox Robinson's are the best known; his *Whiteheaded Boy* has been played in England and America. Of late it has seemed as if this school were coming to an end, for the old plots are repeated with slight variations and the characterization grows mechanical. It is too soon yet to say what will come to us from the melodrama and tragedy of the last four years, but if we can pay our players and keep our theatre open something will come. We are burdened with debt, for we have come through war and civil war and audiences grow thin when there is firing in the streets. We have, however, survived so much that I believe in our luck, and think that I have a right to say my lecture ends in the middle or even, perhaps, at the beginning of the story. But certainly I have said enough to make you understand why, when I received from the hands of your King the great honour your Academy has conferred upon me, I felt that a young man's ghost should have stood upon one side of me and at the other a living woman sinking into the infirmity of age. Indeed I have seen little in this last week that would not have been memorable and exciting to Synge and to Lady Gregory, for Sweden has achieved more than we have hoped for our own country. I think most of all, perhaps, of that splendid spectacle of your Court, a family beloved and able that has gathered about it not the rank only but the intellect of its country. No like spectacle will in Ireland show its work of discipline and of taste, though it might satisfy a need of the race no institution created under the influence of English or American democracy can satisfy.

Notes

I. THE HERMETIC STUDENTS (page 124).

"The Hermetic Students" was founded by Macgregor Mathers, a Dr. Woodman and Dr. Wynn Westcott, the London Coroner. Notes and general instructions were given to Macgregor Mathers by a man whose name I am unable to discover, and of whom the only survivor from that time, Mrs. Macgregor Mathers, can tell me nothing except that he was probably introduced to her husband by Kenneth Mackensie, the reputed instructor in magic of Bulwer Lytton, that he lived in France, and was of Scottish descent, that he was associated with others of like studies, that he was known to her by a Latin motto, that he had super-normal powers. She adds, "I was an enthusiastic beginner and certainly greatly impressed." Upon this link with an unknown past, she says, and upon her husband's and her own clairvoyance, sought at hours and upon days chosen by the unknown man, the rituals and teachings of the Society were established. Dr. Wynn Westcott did receive certain letters which showed knowledge of or interest in the Society, but the writers did not, she considers, belong to nor were they among its founders, but were connected she believes with Continental Freemasonry. Dr. Wynn Westcott and Macgregor Mathers had, however, a bitter quarrel arising out of these things, and Dr. Wynn Westcott claimed an authority based upon the letters. The foundation of this society, which took place some forty years ago, remains almost as obscure as that of some ancient religion. I am sorry to have shed so little light upon a matter which has importance, because in several countries men who have come into possession of its rituals claim, without offering proof, authority from German or Austrian Rosicrucians. I add, however, that I am confident from internal evidence that the rituals, as I knew them, were in substance ancient though never so in language unless some ancient text was incorporated. There was a little that I thought obvious and melodramatic, and it was precisely in this little I am told that they resembled Masonic rituals, but much that I thought beautiful and profound. I do not know what I would think if I were to hear them now for the first time, for I cannot judge what moved me in my youth.

I give these few facts about the origin of "The Hermetic Students" with Mrs. Mathers' permission, but I have not submitted to her my account of her husband because I did not think it right to ask her either to condemn or to accept my statements. She was shocked at the account in the first edition, and apart from one or two errors of fact I have omitted nothing of it, though I have added new passages. Though he did not show me the truth, he did what he professed, and showed me a way to it, and I am grateful, but I think that I must describe notable faults of temper and of mind that fables may not grow. If I found myself a director of men's consciences, or becoming any kind of idealised figure in their minds, I would, or I fancy that I would, display or even exaggerate my frailties. All creation is from conflict, whether with our own mind or with that of others, and the historian who dreams of bloodless victory, wrongs the wounded veterans. My connection with the "Hermetic Students" ended amid quarrels caused by men, otherwise worthy, who claimed a Rosicrucian sanction for their own fantasies, and I add to prevent needless correspondence that I am not now a member of a Cabbalistic Society.

II. THE VISION OF AN ARCHER (see page 248 *sqq.*).

The description of the vision was not in the first edition of this book, and I add it now on the advice of a man learned in East Mediterranean Antiquities, met on a lecturing tour in England, who thought it important and promised annotation. I would like to give his name, or at any rate to write and ask if I might, but though I have spent several hours in the search I cannot find his letter, nor can I trace him at the house where I thought we met. He was no phantom, though a correspondent seems to think so, and I can only offer an apology for my seeming discourtesy. He sent me several pages of notes which I will comment upon and summarise.

(a) The Child and the Tree.

On a certain night in Devonshire, farmers and farm-labourers and their wives and children perform a ceremony at the finest apple-tree in the orchard. Punch is poured out at the roots and bread put among the branches, and a boy set among the branches "who is either the tree in boy-form, or the tree in bird-form," and the men fire blank charges at him. All dance round the tree singing some such rhyme as this:

> "Here's to thee, good apple-tree,
> To bear and blow apples enow," etc.

(*Transactions of the Devonshire Association*, 1867. Whitcombe, *"Bygone Days in Cornwall."*)

"This rhyme calls to mind its ancient prototype, the Hymn of the Kowetes found at Palaikastro in Crete. The Kowetes 'leap' the 'full jars and rich fruit crops.' Moreover, in a previous stanza is celebrated the baby made immortal for Rhea."

"This boy finds his analogue in Balder, 'who is shot to death that is life by means of a sprig or arrow of mistletoe.'"

In my vision the star is shot by an arrow from a bow, and in one of the child's dreams which I have described, God is shot with an arrow, while in another child's dream a star is shot with a gun. "Balder is the tree embodied. His name tells us that. Recent philology has said that the name means or is related to apple-tree, Abble, Apfal, etc. But that is not true enough. When the first decipherment of Cretan pictographs is published, it will be seen that his name goes back to the Cretan Apollo who in old Cretan belief was a tree-god." It is plain too that he is the "Child hidden in the scented Dikton near Mount Ida" (Phæn. 32 ff.) of Aratus' lines, and that part of his significance is solar. He was believed to be born and grow up in a year (Aratus. Calimichus, *Zeus*, 55 ff., etc.) and to die once more. Orpheus made much use of these facts (Lobeck, *Aglaophamas*, i. 552 ff.).

I had used Hebrew names connected with the symbolic tree, and the star at which the arrow was shot seems to have symbolised a Sephiroth attributed to the Sun, and my invocation had for its object the killing or overcoming in some way of a "solar influence."

(b) *The Woman who shot the Arrow.*

She was, it seems, the Mother-Goddess whose representative priestess shot the arrow at the child whose sacrificial death symbolised the death and resurrection of the Tree-spirit, or Apollo. She is pictured upon certain Cretan coins of the fifth century B.C. as a slightly draped, beautiful woman sitting in the heart of a branching tree. (G. F. Hill, *A Handbook of Greek and Roman Coins*, p. 163.) She goes back to the very earliest form of the religion of Crete, and is, it seems probable, the Tree as Mother killing the Tree as Son. But she is also Artemis, and there is a beautiful vase at Naples (Reinach, *Repertoire des vases peints Grecs* i. 379. 1) which shows her archaic image upon a tall pillar with a strung bow in her left hand and a *patera* in her right.

(c) *The Heart torn out.*

A Father of the Church, Firmicus Maternus, in his book, *On the Errors of the Profane Religions,* turns the Myth of the Child Slain and Reborn into a story of murder and adultery. The Cretan Jupiter "made an image of his son in gypsum and placed the boy's heart . . . in that part of the figure where the curve of the chest was to be seen." It had been kept by his sister Minerva and a Temple was made to contain the image. There were festivals and noisy processions that followed "a basket in which the sister had hidden the heart." "It may be conjectured, perhaps," writes my learned man, "that images were made with a chest cavity to contain the heart of the sacrificed."

(d) *The Star.*

The Star goes right back to the Cretan Mother-Goddess. The later Greek form of it was Asterios or Asterion. The latter, for example, is said to be Jupiter's son by Idaia (Pausanias ii. 31. 1). "This Star name did not mean in its primary use any particular

star. It appears to have meant the Starry Heavens. . . . Zeus-
Asterios is a late Gortynian (Cretan) collocation (Johannes
Malala, *Chronicum,* 5). In the earlier thought of Crete, her
deified kings bore the same name, Asterion or Asterios (*e.g.*
Bacchylides, frag. 47 and Diodorus iv. 60)."

(*e*) *The Centaur.*

There is a fragment of a very early Greek pot showing two
roughly drawn centaurs with long thin legs, one of the centaurs
touching with his hand a tree which has long leaves and what
seems to be a round fruit. Above the centaurs, but apparently
separate from the tree a bird perches on a twig. (Salzmann,
Necropole de Camires, Plate XXXIX.)

(*f*) *Sagitta.*

"About the third century B.C. we find Apollo is closely linked
with the constellation Sagitta." I find in a book upon Astrology
published this year: "Sagittarius. The symbol is an arrow shot
into the unknown. It is a sign of Initiation and Rebirth." (*A
Student's Textbook of Astrology,* by Vivian E. Robson, p. 178.)

Notes

(Page 380).—I was in my Galway house during the first months of civil war, the railway bridges blown up and the roads blocked with stones and trees. For the first week there were no newspapers, no reliable news, we did not know who had won nor who had lost, and even after newspapers came, one never knew what was happening on the other side of the hill or of the line of trees. Ford cars passed the house from time to time with coffins standing upon end between the seats, and sometimes at night we heard an explosion, and once by day saw the smoke made by the burning of a great neighbouring house. Men must have lived so through many tumultuous centuries. One felt an overmastering desire not to grow unhappy or embittered, not to lose all sense of the beauty of nature. A stare (our West of Ireland name for a starling) had built in a hole beside my window and I made these verses out of the feeling of the moment:—

> The bees build in the crevices
> Of loosening masonry, and there
> The mother birds bring grubs and flies.
> My wall is loosening; honey bees,
> Come build in the empty house of the stare.
>
> We are closed in, and the key is turned
> On our uncertainty; somewhere
> A man is killed, or a house is burned,
> Yet no clear fact to be discerned:
> Come build in the empty house of the stare.

That is only the beginning but it runs on in the same mood. Presently a strange thing happened. I began to smell honey in places where honey could not be, at the end of a stone passage or at some ·windy turn of the road, and it came always with certain thoughts. When I got back to Dublin I was with angry people who argued over everything or were eager to know the exact facts: in the midst of the mood that makes realistic drama.

(Page 383).—Josef Strzygowski in his *Origin of Christian Church Art* (a translation of a series of lectures delivered in Upsala in 1919) says that art "flourished less at courts than anywhere else in the world. For at the seat of power everything is subordinated to politics; the forces willing to accept this fact are always welcome; those which are not willing must either emigrate or remain aloof." The danger to art and literature comes to-day from the tyrannies and persuasions of revolutionary societies and from forms of political and religious propaganda. The persuasion has corrupted much modern English literature, and—during the twenty years that led up to national revolution—the tyranny wasted the greater part of the energy of Irish dramatists and poets. They had to remain perpetually on the watch to defend their creation, and the more natural the creation the more difficult the defence.

Index

woman, 47, 57, 70, 164, 201, 341, 353, 368
"Woman's beauty, like a frail white bird," quoted 243
Wordsworth, 43, 58, 158, 209, 318, 332
Wuthering Heights, 58

YEATS, JACK (BROTHER), 33, 44-45, 75, 89, 372
Yeats, John B. (father), 13, 14 ff., 33-34, 36-38, 40, 41, 42-43, 52, 53, 54, 56-57, 58, 59, 60, 66, 68, 75, 76, 78, 82, 89, 94, 104, 113, 137, 235, 292-293, 313, 327
Yeats, Rev. John (great-grandfather), 11, 13
Yeats, Lily (sister), 75, 89, 96, 334, 348

Yeats, Lolly (sister), 75, 89, 96, 334, 343, 348
Yeats, Mary (great-aunt), 11, 33
Yeats, Matthew (great-uncle), 11, 13, 34
Yeats, Robert (brother), 16
Yeats, Susan (mother), 16, 18, 19, 21, 25, 28, 38, 39-40, 75, 113, 319-320
Yeats, Rev. William B. (grandfather), 21, 22
Young Ireland, 63, 66-67, 133, 136, 151, 152, 199, 230, 320, 335, 352
youth, 71, 76-77, 79, 250, 322

ZOHAR, 175
Zolá, 271, 303